William Howitt

The History of Discovery in Australia, Tasmania, and New Zealand,

From the Earliest Date to the Present Day. Vol. 2

William Howitt

The History of Discovery in Australia, Tasmania, and New Zealand,
From the Earliest Date to the Present Day. Vol. 2

ISBN/EAN: 9783337268718

Printed in Europe, USA, Canada, Australia, Japan

Cover: Foto ©ninafisch / pixelio.de

More available books at **www.hansebooks.com**

THE

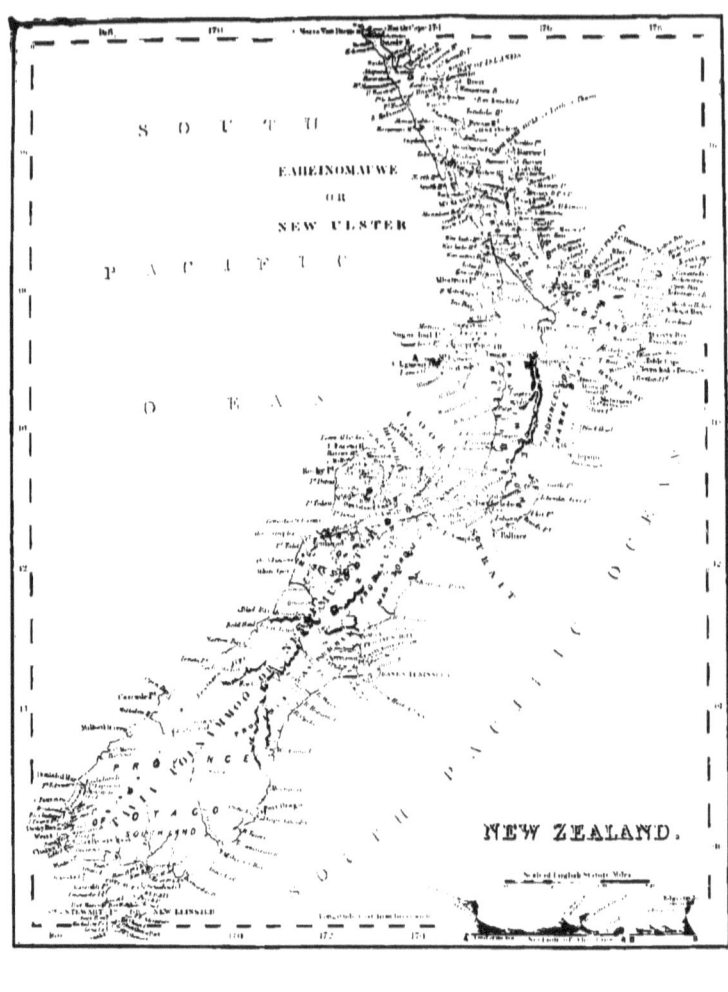

THE

HISTORY OF DISCOVERY

IN

AUSTRALIA, TASMANIA,

AND

NEW ZEALAND,

FROM THE EARLIEST DATE TO THE PRESENT DAY.

BY WILLIAM HOWITT,

AUTHOR OF "TWO YEARS IN VICTORIA," ETC., ETC.

With Maps of the Recent Explorations, from Official Sources.

IN TWO VOLUMES.
VOLUME II.

LONDON:
LONGMAN, GREEN, LONGMAN, ROBERTS, AND GREEN,
PATERNOSTER ROW.
MDCCCLXV.

BILLING,
PRINTER AND STEREOTYPER,
GUILDFORD, SURREY.

CONTENTS OF VOL. II.

CHAPTER I.

DR. LEICHHARDT'S EXPEDITION OVERLAND FROM MORETON BAY TO PORT ESSINGTON IN THE YEARS 1844 AND 1845.

Page

Proposition to send Sir Thomas Mitchell on an expedition across the continent. Dr. Leichhardt finally employed. Captain Sturt about to start from Adelaide for the same point. Dr. Leichhardt's antecedents. Rather scantily supplied with instruments. His party. At Brisbane. Abundant supplies offered. Their equipments. Messrs. Hodgson and Gilbert join the expedition. Start on the 1st of September. Cross the Darling Downs. Acacia scrubs. Leichhardt notes all facts of natural history. Trouble with the native guides. Dawson River. Calvert Plains. Pursued by hornets. Lakes and mountains. Expedition Range. Mount Nicholson. The Boyd. Sandstone Rocks. Creek of the Ruined Castles. Bigge's Mountain. Albinia Downs. Comet Creek and Comet Range. Startled natives from their dinner. Abundance of kangaroos. The Mackenzie. Wild beans which make good coffee. Mount Stewart. Honey plentiful. West Hill. A very mountainous region before them. Calvert's Peak, Gilbert's Downs, Lowe's, MacArthur's and Roper's Peaks. Leichhardt makes a reconnoissance northward. Mountainous region. Zamia Creek. Black ants and hornets. Alarmed black woman and infant. Coxon's Peak. Charley and Brown, the blacks, dismissed, but allowed to come back to the party. Intense heat. The Isaac's and Suttor. Fine valleys. Black man and woman mount into trees. The deaf black woman's fright at seeing Leichhardt on horseback. Water, water plants, and water fowl. Mount M'Connell. The Burdekin. Pelicans and black swans. Geological character of the rocks. Mount Graham. Gourds and calabash. Numerous fig trees. The figs full of ants. Luxuriant wild beans. Roby's and Porter's Ranges. Clarke River. Basaltic dykes and fossiliferous limestone. Only thirty miles from Halifax Bay. Hitherto a coast journey. Now strike more westward. The Perry. Fine country. Interesting descriptions of the routine of a day on the journey. Basaltic rocks, lava, lagoons. Mulberry trees. Dividing Range from 2000 to 3000 feet high. Granite, basalt, and lava. Obliged to diverge. Question of the blacks about the bullocks. Want of water. Separation Creek. A traveller's trials and pleasures. Blacks again fly, and leave their dinner. Fine rock crystal in a bag. New trees and plants. Daring kites. The Lynd. Kirchener's Range. Fig and cotton trees. Sandstone country. A sawfish found. Superior huts of the natives. The Mitchell River. The gum-tree ants. The crocodile. Palm trees appear. Natives numerous and hostile. Attempt to drive off the cattle. Murder of Mr. Gilbert. A nocturnal fight. Calvert and Roper wounded severely. The night intensely cold. Chase away the natives. Gilbert's funeral. In sight of the Gulf of Carpentaria. A wild plum found. Fine grassy country. Reach the salt water.

a 2

CONTENTS.

Lagoons, with white, blue, and pink lilies. A native suddenly appears in the camp. Native melons. The Gilbert River. Grevilleas, Barthenias, and Balfourias abound. Numerous natives. Kill abundance of ducks, spoonbills, and three emus. Cross the Plains of Promise. Pugnacious native boy. The Albert River. Carving of an emu's foot. Audacity of natives. The river Leichhardt. The Nicholson. Emu trap. Cross a succession of rivers to Tasman's River. Numerous kinds of animal life. Cycas palms. Fruit of the pandanus. Seven Emu River. The Robinson River. Zamia and Cycas palm groves. Desperate condition of their clothes. Moccasins of bullock hide. Tea and sugar gone. Pound seeds for a beverage. The white-barked tree of Tasman, figs, and sterculias. The MacArthur salt-water river. Soup of dry bullock hides. Blistering fruit. Cape Maria. Reduce their baggage. The Limmen River. Swamps, wild geese, ducks, alligators, and thickets of acacias. Native fish traps. The Wickham. Flat-topped sandstone rocks. The Four Archers. Their kangaroo dog died. Strike westward across the Arnheim Peninsula for Port Essington. The Roper River. Abandon more luggage and botanical specimens. A horse drowned. Cattle very much exhausted. Great swamps full of water fowl. Natives with English articles of dress. More speaking some English. East Alligator River. Rocks, hills, swamps, wild geese, and flying foxes. Shoot a buffalo. Port Essington. Return by sea to Sydney. Honours and rewards.

FRESH EXPEDITION IN 1847. Not heard of again. Traces of Leichhardt seen by Gregory and Walker. Lost probably in the great western desert. His supplies. Mr. Hovenden Hely sent in quest of Leichhardt. Journey fruitless. Blacks' report, Leichhardt murdered with all his party. Seventeen years passed without certain information of Leichhardt's fate. . 1

CHAPTER II.

THE EXPEDITION OF CAPTAIN STURT INTO CENTRAL AUSTRALIA IN THE YEARS 1844, 45, AND 46.

Reasons for the expedition.—Stuart's theory of an inland sea. His hope to clear this up. His party, and its equipments. Start August 18th, 1844. Reach Mr. Eyre's station at Moorundi, on the Murray. Captain Sturt restrained by his instructions from crossing to the North Sea. Mischiefs of stay-at-home wisdom. Leave Moorundi accompanied for some distance by Mr. Eyre. The River Rufus. Nadbuck and Toonda, black guides. Laidley's Ponds. The building rat. Quit the Darling. Mitchell, Sturt, Burke, and Wills all make journeys northwards from this point. Native remembrance of Sir Thomas Mitchell's castigation. Despatches from Adelaide by three natives. Their excessive fatigue. Talkativeness of Camboli. Mr. Poole reconnoitres a-head. Sturt moves to Cawndilla Lake. Measures a base line. Goes a-head to explore. Treachery of Topar, a native. The country destitute of water. Finds the Clianthus Damperi. A terrible hurricane. Break up camp, and advance. The Coonbaralba Range. Lewis's Hill. Stopped by rocks. Vast desert plains on each side of the ranges. Mr. Poole goes S.W. to seek Lake Torrens. Reached Lake Blanche. Mr. Flood precedes the main party to seek for water. Tremendous heat. Flood finds a little creek. They advance. See Mounts Lyell and Babbage from the hills. Curious hollow balls. Parties go out to seek for water. Abundance of emus and kangaroos. A visit from the natives. An excursion eastward. Burning plains. News of water northward. Drays falling to pieces with the heat. Dreadful travelling in the torrid heat. Two bullocks killed by it. Mount Arrowsmith, the magnetic hill. Plague of ants and flies. Camped in a pleasant glen by deep water in latitude 29° 40' 14" S., longitude 141° 30' 41". Detained there by drought for six

CONTENTS. v

Page

months. Their experiences there. Health of Messrs. Poole and Browne failing. Captain Sturt and others attacked by scurvy. The captain with a party rides forward to reconnoitre, carrying water-barrels. Reach within twenty or thirty miles of Cooper's Creek, but driven back. Two horses abandoned. Another attempt westward. Return to the camp. Discover a grassy valley which they call the Park. Effects of the heat on the ground and on their implements. Make an underground room. All the birds leave. A solitary native appears. A desert philosopher. Chain a line of thirty miles towards Lake Torrens. Rain and flood in the creek. Mr. Poole dies. A monument to him piled on Red Hill. Captain Sturt proceeds westward with a light party to Lake Blanche. Verifies Mr. Eyre's character of the country. Proceed N.W. The bare desert destroys all idea of an inland sea. A creek, with native huts and troughs for grinding seeds. The Stony Desert. Eyre's Creek. They return. Water hole with fish. Reach their camp, which they name Fort Grey. Captain Sturt entreats Mr. Browne to return to Adelaide on account of his health, but in vain. A last effort to penetrate northward. Endeavour to trace the extent of the Stony Desert eastward. Report as of a cannon in the desert. Dismal sandy regions. Salt Lake. The Stony Desert again, a gloomy, herbless, treeless region. Eleven days over this horrid desert. Exhausted condition of the horses. Reach Cooper's Creek, and name it. Sturt's account of this creek. The natives friendly. Signs of floods, and abundance of water fowl and fish. Leave behind a roan horse. Traced the creek eastward into hollow plains, bearing marks of periodical floods. Return to Fort Grey. Leave another horse. Bawley Plains. Intense heat again. Return journey to Adelaide. Results of this expedition, the explosion of an inland sea, and confirmation of desert, but westward. Exploration of the south-eastern sea coast of South Australia by Governor Grey in 1844 . 42

CHAPTER III.

EXPLORING EXPEDITIONS IN WESTERN AUSTRALIA—CONTINUED.

1. EXPEDITION OF MESSRS. LANDOR AND LEFROY IN SEARCH OF AN INLAND SEA, IN 1843. Journal published in Perth Inquirer. Leave York, January 9. Proceed to the Hotham River. Country level. Cross a large river. Byricring Lake. Lake Norring. Salt Lakes. Go down a fresh water lake. Discover a river named the Landor. Another named the Lefroy. See two Timor ponies. Return by a branch of the Hotham. General report of the country.
2. EXPEDITION OF MR. ROE, Surveyor-General of Western Australia, eastward of Perth, accompanied by Mr. H. GREGORY and others. Set out from York. Pass over heights to Cape Riche. The Jeeramungup. Good grazing country. Mount Madden and Mount Short. Poor country and salt lakes. Bremer Range. Mount Gordon. Fitzgerald Range. Barren country. Severe journey to the Russell Range: no grass, no water. Return by the shore to Cape Riche. Howick Hill, Mount Merivale, and Mount Hawes, named by them. The streamlet Gore and inlet Lort, Phillips's River, and Eyre's named by them. Found coal-beds at the junction of the Elwes and Jeeramungup. Between the Elwes and Cape Richie named Mount Bland, Gairdner River, and Gordon Inlet. In their homeward route by Bunbury, came on a sandal-wood-cutting station. Return to Perth.
3. EXPEDITION OF MESSRS. GREGORY INTO THE INTERIOR OF WESTERN AUSTRALIA. Start from Boyeen Spring, on Swan River, August 7th. Lake Brown. See ranges from N. to E.S.E. Eastward a discouraging country. Columns of red sand or dust. Took a N.W. course. Vast flats and bogs. Cross them by means of hurdles. Lake Moore. Salt, gypsum, and mud beds. Still on to September 3rd over wretched country. Strike the Arrow-

Smith River. Followed the river down to its mouth. Found beds of coal. Follow the coast homewards.

4. VOYAGE OF LIEUTENANT HELPMAN TO EXAMINE THE COAL OF THE ARROWSMITH. Examined the country from the Arrowsmith to the Hutt. Mistook the rivers as laid down by Captain Grey. The error rectified by Mr. Arrowsmith. Mr. Hillman's trip to Lake Moore.

5. SETTLERS' EXPEDITION NORTHWARD FROM PERTH UNDER A. C. GREGORY. Instructions for the tour from the Local Government. The object, to discover pasture lands. Joined by friends at Toodyay. At Arrowsmith Creek. Irwin Plains.—Large extent of good pasturage land found. Also on Champion Bay. The Murchison country poor. Freycinet Harbour. Country around wretched. Found lead ore at the Hutt. Some good land on the Bowes. Return to Perth.

6. VISIT OF GOVERNOR FITZGERALD TO THE MURCHISON. Sailed to Champion Bay. Find no coal, but lead in the Murchison. Attacked by natives. The Governor speared through the thigh. Shot one man. Mining commenced on the Murchison and Bowes 77

CHAPTER IV.

SIR THOMAS MITCHELL'S FOURTH EXPEDITION. DISCOVERY OF THE BARCOO.

Need of an overland route from New South Wales to the Gulf of Carpentaria. Two iron boats built. Expedition left Paramatta November the 7th, 1854. The party well selected and equipped. Blacks meet them on the Bogan to inquire their object. An old native resembling Socrates offers himself again. Traces of conflict between the natives and the squatters. Want of water. The Bogan dry. Attacked by ophthalmia. Encamp on a creek, and wait. Piper, the native guide, dismissed. On the 12th of April advance. Sudden coming down of waters in the Macquarie. A furious flood carrying trees along with it. Reach the Barwan. Messrs. Russell's exploration in 1841. Surprising changes. The white man now lord of the region. The Narran. The Balonne, a fine large river. The Calgoa. Sir Thomas now marks his camping places on trees. Lake Parachute. Advances with a light party. Lakes and lagoons. Lake Turaninga. Mount Toolumba. Name this district Fitzroy Downs. Natives. The Maranon and Amby. Curious embassage from the natives. Warned away by them. Mr. Kennedy, Sir Thomas's second in command, brings up the rear detachment. Sir Thomas again starts northwards. Distress for water. Water found through a dream. A sulphurous stream, the Salvator. The Claude, fertility of its banks. Abundance of fossil wood. Entered the tropics. The Belyando. Vast numbers of wild fowl and kangaroos. Menacing natives. Return to the Salvator. Beauty and fertility of the country. Remarkable meteor. The Claude. Encamp in a mountain gorge. The depôt fixed there. Sir Thomas sets out northwestward. The Nine. Discover the Barcoo. Sir Thomas's warm eulogium of the river and country around. Pronounced by him the finest river and district of Australia. Return homewards. See marks of squatters already on their track 92

CHAPTER V.

KENNEDY'S EXPLORATIONS OF THE BARCOO AND OF THE YORK PENINSULA, 1847.

Edward Kennedy sent to trace the Barcoo, and find a route to Carpentaria. Crossed the Barcoo at Sir Thomas Mitchell's lowest point on August the 13th. Found the river running a fresh course. The Thomson falling

CONTENTS. vii

Page

into the Barcoo. Traces the Barcoo down 100 miles. Then lightens his luggage, and advances downwards through a wretched country to latitude 26° 13' 9", longitude 142° 20'. A low, flat country. The river dividing into many channels. Convinced that it was identical with Cooper's Creek. Returns northwards. The natives had plundered his buried stores. Obliged by this to return home. Kennedy's journal edited by the Rev. W. B. Clarke.

KENNEDY'S EXPEDITION TO THE YORK PENINSULA. Proposed plan of a new expedition towards the Gulf. Provisions to be carried by ship to Albany. York Peninsula to be first examined, then the route towards Carpentaria. Kennedy and party land at Rockingham Bay in May, 1848. Compelled to diverge to the south-west by the mountains Abandon their carts and heavy stores. Leave eight men at Weymouth Bay. Kennedy and four men, including Jackey, the native guide, push on for Albany. One of the party wounded by a gun, which impeded them. Leave him and the other two whites, and Kennedy and Jackey proceed towards Albany alone. Attacked by natives near Albany. Kennedy killed. Jackey reaches Albany with his journal. Sufferings and deaths in the party at Weymouth Bay. Only two saved. Relief party from the "Ariel." The three other men sought for in vain. Ten out of the original thirteen of this expedition perished. Generous nature of Edward Kennedy 108

CHAPTER VI.

THE EXPEDITION OF MR. ROBERT AUSTIN, ASSISTANT SURVEYOR, INTO THE INTERIOR OF WESTERN AUSTRALIA, IN 1854.

Objects of the expedition. The party. Left Mombe Kine, on Swan River, in July. The samphire plains to Waddoming. The salt lake Cow-cowing. Thence a poor country to Mount Marshall. A miserable region of dead scrub to Mount Kenneth. Views from Mount Kenneth sterile and forbidding. Journey northward over this desert to August 20th. Their horses poisoned by a shrub. Fourteen died. Mount Magnet. Views all round still dismal. Miseries of tight boots. West Mount Magnet. Rude, rocky, and scrubby country. Natives refuse to eat a new kind of kangaroo. Believed it a demon. The Carved Cave Spring. Native art. Accident to Farmer by his own gun. Poison plants again. Farmer dies of lock-jaw. Bequeathes his property. Buried near a hill named Mount Farmer. Mount Charles. Views round into rocky and scrubby regions. Native cross, and springes for emus. Mounts Lake and Murchison. Murchison river. Advanced to within fifty miles of Shark's Bay. Driven back by wretched, waterless country. Mounts Narryer, Welcome, Grass, and Vinden. Sufferings on the retreat to the Geraldine Mines. Bury luggage. Native guide nearly dead. Generous offer of Captain Sanford, but unavailing. Return to Perth. Mr. Austin's estimate of the lands passed over. Mr. Phillip's Report 120

CHAPTER VII.

EXPEDITION FOR THE EXPLORATION OF NORTHERN AUSTRALIA IN 1855-6, UNDER THE COMMAND OF MR. A. C. GREGORY.

Mr. Uzzielli offers £10,000 for an expedition to explore the north of Australia. Offer of Mr. W. S. Lindsay, M.P. Undertaken by the Government. Outfit to be completed at Moreton Bay. The party. Sailed from Brisbane August 12th, 1855. Reached Port Patterson, Arnheim's Land, September 2nd. Run on a rock. Great damage to, and loss of horses. Land at

CONTENTS.

Point Pearce. Part of the expedition went by land to the higher part of the river. Two horses poisoned. Horses attacked by alligators on Fitzmaurice River. The party ascending the river struck on a rock. Great loss of stores and sheep. Out of 200 shipped, only twenty-six reached the camp alive. Rules laid down for the conduct of the party. Their good effect. Set out a small party southward. Exploration of the Victoria for 100 miles. Return to camp. Fresh exploration in January, 1856. Stupendous rocks on the river course. Basaltic country with deep gullies. The head waters of the Victoria. Dividing range. Wretched country. Retreat before the heat and drought. Mount Müller. Follow the Wickham to the Victoria. Serious injury to one of the party. Party formed to proceed towards Carpentaria. Start on 21st of June. Reach a creek of the Roper, July 12th. The Roper. Flat country. Creeks and lagoons. Marks of floods. The gigantic water-lily. Proceed S.E., leave basaltic country. Blacks try to surprise them. Two horses poisoned. Bad country. Limmen Bight. MacAdam range and MacArthur river. Sandstone hills. Cross the Robinson and Leichhardt rivers. Country better. Brimstone and basalt. Nicholson River. Poor Country. Beame's Brook a branch of the Albert. The Tom Tough not arrived. Determined to push on for the east course. Buried canisters to say this. September 3rd, continued their journey. Plains of Promise disappoint them. The Leichhardt. Attacked by the natives. The spring season, yet the country looked poor. Betwixt the Flinders and Gilbert saw good country. Gilbert nearly dry. Arrive at ranges 2500 feet high. Head waters of the Lynd. Basaltic country well grassed. Reach the Burdekin in October. Trees marked with an iron axe. Camp of Leichhardt. Rocks of various kinds. Trace the Burdekin to the "Suttor and Belyando." On the Comet noticed a camp of Leichhardt's. Arrival at Brisbane. The expedition completed in sixteen months. Objects accomplished by this expedition. The part of the expedition which went in the Tom Tough to Timor for supplies reaches Sydney by sea. Mr. Baines' boat-voyage of 650 miles. Remarks of Captain Sturt on Mr. Gregory's discoveries, and on the theory of the Australian interior.—Theory of Mr. Alfred Howitt. Diagram in illustration of it. Reports of Messrs. Elsey, Wilson, Flood, Baines, and Lieutenant Chimmo 133

CHAPTER VIII.

THE EXPEDITIONS OF JOHN M'DOUALL STUART, EXTENDING FROM ADELAIDE TO THE NORTH SEA, FROM 1858 TO 1862.

Mr. Stuart, draftsman of Captain Sturt's expedition, in 1844-5.—Aided in his attempts at discovery by Messrs. Finke and Chambers. In 1858 passed Lake Torrens for the north-west. Mr. Babbage at Yalticourie invites him to Coulthardt's funeral, and proposes to accompany him on his expedition. Mr. Stuart excuses himself. Bottle Hill. Bad country. Enquires after Wingillpin. Mr. Stuart's idea of Wingillpin. Mount Hamilton. Stony country. Mr. Stuart looking out for Cooper's Creek to the west. Supposes a creek near Mount Hamilton, to form the Glenelg of Captain Grey in Western Australia. Turns south, finding scrub and salt lagoons. Turned next N.W. till the 1st of August. Worthless country. Near Lake Gairdner. Proceeds towards Denial Bay. Dismal country about Mount Finke. Reach Gibson's Station, Streaky Bay. Return by Mount Arden.

STUART'S SECOND JOURNEY INTO THE VICINITY OF LAKE TORRENS. Assisted by Messrs. Finke and Chambers. Ascends the eastern side of Lake Torrens. Finniss's Springs. Mount Hamilton. Mount Hugh. Elizabeth Springs. Douglas Creek. Davenport Range. Other springs. The Hanson Range. Mounts Kingston and Younghusband. Good country. Barrow

CONTENTS.

and Freeling Springs. Neale Creek. Mount O'Halloran. No water.
Returns to Glen's Station, Termination Hill.
THIRD EXPEDITION. From the Spring of Hope to Mount Anna. Wild
grape at Parry's Springs. Thinks he saw Lake Torrens. December 20th
set his men to dig for gold. No gold. Returned to Chambers' Creek.
FOURTH EXPEDITION TOWARDS THE CENTRE OF THE CONTINENT. Advances beyond the Neale to new ground. Mount Ben and Head's Range.
Goes westward. Wretched scrub. West Neale. Enter extensive ranges.
Mounts Beddome, Daniel, Humphries, and the Twins. Gwyder and Finke
Creeks. Poor country. Extraordinary sandstone rock, which he names
Chambers' Pillar. Numerous hills named, ending in Mount Stuart.
This he named Central Mount Stuart, as the centre of Australia, and
planted a flag on it. Went west 150 miles, naming several hills, but found
all barren scrub. Again went northward till June 26th. Named various
hills and creeks as far as Mount Samuel. At Kekwick Pond says he met
with a native freemason. On June 26th at Attack Creek. The native
freemasons drive him back. Sufferings of the party. Mr. Stuart nearly
blind. Left a horse alive bogged in a creek. On returning found his bones.
Returned to Adelaide.
FIFTH EXPEDITION. Mr. Stuart's report of his progress in Adelaide. Fund
voted for another expedition. November 29th started from Adelaide.
His party and equipments. Squatting stations already near the 28th degree
of S. latitude. A little dog killed by the heat. Spitting native. Attack
Creek. Whittington Range. Morphett Creek. New plants and trees.
Finely grassed country. Mount Primrose. Carruther's and Hunter's
Creeks. Sturt's Plains. Ashburton Range. Vain attempt to go westward
toward the Victoria river. Curious baby's coffin. Difficult country. Newcastle Water. Mount Shillinglaw. Natives fire the grass. Howell's
Ponds. Return to Adelaide.
SIXTH EXPEDITION, IN WHICH THE NORTHERN COAST IS REACHED.—Offers
to proceed north again. News of Burke and Wills being found dead at
Cooper's Creek, after crossing the continent. October 21st, 1861, Stuart
starts again. Kicked by a horse. December 20th at Moolooloo. His party.
Two of these desert. Hottest season of the year. Natives hostile at Marchant's Springs, and Mount Hay. April 17, 1862, at their farthest point,
Howell's Springs. Difficulties from drought and dense scrub. Try right
and left. Push through. Frew's Water-Hole. King's Ponds. Return
to Howell's Ponds, defeated by the scrub. Once more advance. Auld's
and McGorrerey's Ponds. Better country. Daly Waters. New tree. Fine
grassy country. Blue Grass Swamp. The bean-tree again. Sickness from
eating gum. Purdie's Ponds. Strangways River. Hilly region. Tall
trees, and plenty of fish. Mount Müller. Reach the Roper. A horse
drowned. Natives firing the grass. Chambers' River. Stony hills. The
Waterhouse Creek. Mounts Helpman, Levi, and Watts. Chambers Range.
Fanny and Catherine Creeks. Basaltic country. Mount Stone. Eckwick's Springs. The Fan palm. The Adelaide River. Splendid view.
Palms and tropical plants. Through stony country. Mary Creek. William Creek. Priscilla Creek. Very tall grass. Helen Creek. The Adelaide again. The Daly Range. Reach the sea in Van Diemen's Gulf.
Plant a flag. Return homewards. Natives still fire the grass. Two
horses drowned in the Roper. Abandon luggage. Mr. Stuart seized with
scurvy. His eyes fail. August 27, a comet is visible. A remarkable
native mummy. Reach Attack Creek. Lose several horses through exhaustion. Stuart much worse. Make long halts. Men and horses failing
fast. Have to send ahead to look for water. Everywhere drought. Kill
now and then a horse for food. November 26, reach Jarvis's Station,
Mount Margaret. Stuart travels in a litter. Reach Adelaide, December
18th. General view of the advantages of these expeditions, and prospects
of this northern country. Dr. Hardman's edition of Stuart's Journal.

Question of telegraphic communication across the continent. Lease of 1000 square miles of land to Stuart. Grant of £2000 to Stuart, and different sums to other members of his party. Order in which the transit of the continent has been made by different explorers . . . 159

CHAPTER IX.

THE EXPLORING EXPEDITION OF VICTORIA IN 1860-1 UNDER THE COMMAND OF MESSRS. BURKE AND WILLS.

Offer of £1000 by Mr. Ambrose Kyte towards an expedition across the continent. £3400 subscribed by the public for this object; £6000 voted by the Victoria government: total, £12,400. Camels brought from India by Mr. Landells for the journey. Committee of Royal Society appointed managers of the expedition business. Robert O'Hara Burke selected as leader. His antecedents. Mr. Landells, manager of the camels. William John Wills, astronomer and surveyor. Names of the party.—Start August the 20th, 1860, in great eclât from Melbourne. Misgivings of Wills's father. Ferguson, the foreman, dismissed on the Murrumbidgee. Landells resigns. Prophecies the ruin of the expedition. Wills made second in command. His amiable character. Burke appoints Mr. Wright third in command. Unfitness of Wright. Leaves half of his expedition with Wright at Menindie. Advances to Cooper's Creek. Mr. Wright does not follow. Charged with looking out stations for squatters. Description of the country between Menindie and Cooper's Creek. Mr. Wills advances ninety miles direct northward from Cooper's Creek, but returns from want of water. Wills's description of the country about Cooper's Creek. News of Stuart having crossed the continent carried by Trooper Lyons to Menindie. Sent on by Wright, but returned without finding the way to Cooper's Creek. Wright sends back to Melbourne for more money. Mr. Wright not appearing at Cooper's Creek, Mr. Burke appoints Brahe to the command at Cooper's Creek, and sets out for the Gulf of Carpentaria with a small party. His haste. Threatens to throw the scientific instruments into a creek. Anxiety at Melbourne regarding the expedition. Efforts of Dr. Wills. An expedition sent in quest of Burke and Wills under Mr. Alfred W. Howitt 190

CHAPTER X.

EXPEDITION IN QUEST OF THAT OF MESSRS. BURKE AND WILLS, UNDER THE COMMAND OF MR. ALFRED WILLIAM HOWITT, 1861-2.

Previous bush experience of the leader.—Journey to Stuart's new country in South Australia. His report of that country. Appointed to search for gold in Gippsland. Success. Mr. Howitt met on his way to the Murray by Mr. Brahe with despatches stating that Burke and Wills left Cooper's Creek on the 16th of December, and nothing has since been heard of them. Dr. Becker, Messrs. Purcell and Stone dead. Great sensation in Melbourne. Wright's despatch. A too late visit of Wright and Brahe to Cooper's Creek. Their leaving it altogether.—Brahe's examination by the Exploration Committee. Mr. Howitt ordered to hasten north in quest of Burke and Wills. Mr. Walker ordered to proceed from Rockhampton to the Gulf of Carpentaria in quest of Burke and Wills. Captain Norman, with the Victoria steamer, ordered to the Gulf. The Firefly sent from Brisbane, with a party under Mr. Landsborough, to the Gulf, to proceed thence south for the same object. Mr. Howitt sets out, accompanied by Dr. Wheeler. Mr. Landells offer his services to conduct the camels.

These not accepted. Howitt and Wheeler left Melbourne July 4, 1861. August 13th arrived at Pomomaroo Creek, on the Darling. Menindie and its land-hunters. Dislike of the horses to the camels. At Poria Creek Mr. Howitt leaves Burke's track, and strikes N.W. to Cooper's Creek. Reaches the depôt. Finds the papers of Burke and Wills buried at Wills Fort, informing them of Burke and Wills having returned thither. Camel tracks. Find various articles. Find King amongst the natives, and learn the death of Burke and Wills. Find the remains of the explorers, with field-books and papers. Buried the remains.—Failure of an attempt to send word to Melbourne of the news by carrier pigeons. Presents made to the natives for their kindness to King. Return to the Darling. Mr. Howitt and Dr. Wheeler to Melbourne 212

CHAPTER XI.

THE JOURNEY OF BURKE AND WILLS TO THE GULF OF CARPENTARIA, AND RETURN TO COOPER'S CREEK.

Directed their course to Eyre's Creek.—The water in Cooper's Creek at 97·4 of Fahrenheit. Crossed the Stony Desert and found it not very bad. Spent Christmas Eve at a creek on the other side of the desert. On Christmas Day struck a creek, now called Burke's Creek. Alternate sand-ridges and grassy plains. King's and Wills's Creek. Australian spinach. Patton's Creek. Progress through good country, naming hills and creeks. River which Burke called the Cloncurry, a branch of the Flinders. Followed the Flinders to near the sea. A horse swamped in Billy Creek. Proceed on foot.—Here Wills's journal abruptly ceases.—On the 19th of February they are on their way homewards. Burke says they reached the sea, but not the open ocean. In great anxiety about their provisions holding out. Burke ill from eating snake. Lighten the loads of the camels. Kill a camel and a horse for food. Burke beats Gray for privately taking food. Gray cannot walk. His companions think him shamming. Gray dies. Sunday, April 21st, 1861. arrive at the depôt and find it deserted only seven hours before. Their consternation. Find some provisions, but are too weary to follow. Burke decides to make for Mount Hopeless. Leave memoranda of their return and present route at the depôt. Started for Mount Hopeless April 23rd. Received fish from the natives. Camel bogged and killed. Only one camel left. Kill that. Wills makes an excursion to find a better track. Treated to "nardoo," a seed, by the natives. Nardoo bread. Bury part of their provisions and return to the depôt. Rapidly sink on the nardoo food. Burke and King set out to find the natives. Too weak to carry anything. Burke dies. King returns and finds Wills dead. Joins the natives. Affecting notes in Wills's diary. Letter to his father in prospect of death. Hasty notes of Burke. King's life amongst the natives. Return of Howitt and party to Menindie. His opinion of the natives at Cooper's Creek . 239

CHAPTER XII.

THE EXPLORATION EXPEDITION OF MR. McKINLAY IN SEARCH OF BURKE AND WILLS IN 1861 AND 1862.

Order in which explorers have crossed Australia. McKinlay second as to the whole width. McKinlay summoned from Melbourne. Sets out at once. His party. Evidently well qualified for his office. Left Adelaide August the 16th, 1861. Baker's Station on Blanche Water. Squatting stations beyond Eyre's farthest point. Dry and stony country to Lake Hope. Mr. Elder and Mr. Stuckey. A pelican choked by a fish. Lakes Camel, Perigundi, and Buchanan. Straying of horses and camels. Hear from natives of white men at Cooper's Creek, and one of them dead.

Mr. McKinlay sets out for Cooper's Creek. Sees natives in European clothing. Further rumours of the white men. Lake Kadhi-baerri. Found a flattened pint pot. Abundance of grass and clover. Found a mutilated body in a grave. Story of a battle with white men. Fragments of a tin can, a nautical almanac, &c. Hear of iron-work of saddles, a pistol, &c. A native digs up some baked horse hair for stuffing saddles. Probably the grave was Gray's. The natives of Cooper's Creek are fired on. Probable cause of this. McKinlay and party imagine these natives to have killed and eaten Burke and his party. Name the water Lake Massacre. McKinlay sends despatches to Adelaide with news of his discovery. Laid up with the hot weather. Natives tell of a flood coming down Cooper's Creek. McKinlay rides there to see. No signs of flood. Trees marked by Howitt, indicating the graves of Burke and Wills. Saw a cobby horse. Deposited memorandum at Burke's grave of his visit, and intention to go northward. Moved on December the 20th. Dreadful journey to Lake McKinlay. A bullock killed by the heat. The black guide quits them. Lake Moolionboorrana. Heat awful. Lake Jeannie. Spent Christmas Day there. Natives making nardoo cakes. Lake Appam-barra. Naked country. Lake Hodgkinson. Natives' report, White fellows arrived at Lake Buchanan. A myth. Discovers various other lakes and creeks. Mount McDonnell. Abundance of wild-fowl. A peep at the Stony Desert. Four months nearly spent here. Start January the 6th, 1862. Compelled by intense heat and want of shelter to retreat to Lake Hodgkinson again. This lake soon dried up. Another ride to the Stony Desert.—Camp on Hayward's Creek till the 10th of February. Rain and thunder. The country now deep mud. Passed a camp of Burke's, and remains of his horse Billy. Surrounded by vast floods. Hamilton and Goyder's table-topped hills.—Passed the Stony Desert; still in the midst of floods. Escape Camp. Was Leichhardt caught in such a flood? The natives thereabout possess goat's hair. No goats probably ever there but Leichhardt's. Daly Ranges. Shepherd lost for six days. Name many creeks and ranges. Enter the tropical regions. Palms and grass up to the neck. Ant-hills like decaying columns. Natives firing the grass. New trees. Copper was found. Country looked auriferous. Marks of great floods. Mounts Elephant and McPherson. Jessie and Jeannie Creeks. Crossed the track of Burke and Wills on the Cloncurry. Struck the Leichhardt on the 9th of May. Its aspect. Many windings. Set their own baggage on fire. Stokes's Plains of Promise. Reached the tidal part of the river, but could not get at the sea for swamps and mangrove creeks. Collect salt for their journey. The grass too strong for sheep. Commence the route to Port Denison. Only two bullocks left, and no tea, sugar, or flour. Trees marked by Landsborough. Make boots for the sore-footed camels. Cross the Flinders and the Norman. Involved in ranges. Killed their last bullock. Mountains. Silk cotton growing. Wonderful view of rocky country. A terrible country. The River Gilbert. Losing horses from fatigue. Kill the last bullock. Several men very ill. Reached the Burdekin July the 5th.—Still killing horses for food, or leaving them behind. Only two pack horses and one camel left. Crossed the Burdekin on a raft amongst alligators. Killed their last camel. Reach the station of Harvey and Somers. Met there with Mr. Brahe. Returned by Rockhampton, Sydney, and Melbourne, to Adelaide . . . 254

CHAPTER XIII.

LANDSBOROUGH'S EXPEDITION FROM THE GULF OF CARPENTARIA IN QUEST OF BURKE AND WILLS, 1861.

Mr. Orkney sends his yacht, Sir Charles Hotham, to look out in the Gulf of Carpentaria for the lost explorers. Disabled on the voyage. The

CONTENTS.

Page

Government of Queensland send out Landsborough and party. The Firefly carrying the expedition stranded on Sir Charles Hardy's Island. Lose five horses. Assisted to the mouth of the Albert by the Victoria. Anchored in the Albert. Mr. Landsborough explores the Albert 120 miles. Driven back by natives and want of water. Finds Mr. Walker had been at the Albert, and gone back on the traces of Burke and Wills. Insists on going too. Sets out on the 10th of February, 1862. Sees tracks of Walker, but does not follow them. Ceases to speak of Burke and Wills, but strikes eastward in quest of good lands. Follows the Flinders 200 miles to the south-eastward. Crosses the Jardine Creek and Ranges. The Thomson. Follows it, and crosses the Barcoo and Warrego. At Williams's Station on that river hears of the death of Burke and Wills. Descends the Darling, and thence to Melbourne. Visits London. His skirmish with Mr Crawford about the growth of wool. Mr. Landsborough's real service is to have found a good track to the Gulf from Queensland, and good land for squatters. Comments of the *Melbourne Argus* on his tour. . . 284

CHAPTER XIV.

MR. FREDERICK WALKER'S EXPEDITION IN QUEST OF BURKE AND WILLS.

Mr. Walker celebrated in Queensland for explorations attended by blacks. His prompt attention to the calls on him to go in quest of the missing explorers. Started from Dutton's Station on the Dawson, September 7th, 1861. By the 16th reached the Nogoa. Went north to the Poma. Crossed the Ranges by his own, Walker's Pass. Began to mark trees where the new country commenced. Crossed at the Barcoo on the 27th. October 15th, found a tree marked by Gregory. Found two trees marked by Leichhardt. Went north-west for the Alice. Saw tracks of horses, which they thought Leichhardt's. Advanced over ranges to the Thomson. Saw other traces of Leichhardt. Remarks of Patrick, the native, on a vast view from Mount Macalister. Head waters of the Barkly. Camlaroy and Houghton Creeks. Mounts Gilbee and Castor and Pollux. Basaltic country on the Barkly, with good grazing land. Struck a tributary of the Flinders, the Norman. Numerous rivers and creek, chiefly dry. A fight with the natives. Their horses scarcely able to travel. Blacks say water all the way now. They must stick to the river. The junction of the Norman and Flinders. Traces of Burke and Wills. Second time traces of them on their return. Walker zealous to get supplies from the steamer, and follow these traces. Leaves of a memorandum book. Morning Inlet. Another fight with the natives. Other natives tell them of whites on the Albert River. Pushed over the box flats. Saw a tree marked V., and a broad arrow. Blacks try to cut them off from the Albert. See a tree marked "Dig," and find a paper in a bottle directing them to the Victoria. Arrived at the vessel in a storm of rain. The journey from Rockhampton thus made in three months and twelve days. Returns to track Burke and Wills. Lost them on the flooded flats of the Flinders. Burke's last camp. Believes Burke gone towards Queensland. Follows along the Norman. Recovers a horse. Jardine Creek. Mount Barry. Mounts Pylades and Orestes. Mount Picken. Numerous flooded creeks. Very mountainous region. On the Gilbert. Mounts Mica and Granite. The Cordilleras or dividing range. The Lynd. All boots worn out and horses lamed by the sharp slates. Enormous quartz reefs. Quartz Creek. The Yananno. The Clarke. The Burdekin and a large tributary. A very bad grass. Halt on account of the knocked-up horses. A light party goes on to seek provisions. A bad country. Reach the station of Messrs. Wood and Robinson. Reach Rockhampton June 4, having done the journey from the Gulf in five months and two weeks. Great promptness and merit of Mr. Walker. . 297

CHAPTER XV.

EXPEDITIONS OF DISCOVERY IN SOUTH AUSTRALIA IN 1856—57
—58, AND 59.

Page

Renewed spirit of discovery in South Australia. The causes. Mr. Babbage sent to examine the country, Tanunda and Angaston, etc. Collected 300 geologic specimens. Captain Cadell reports gold in Kangaroo Island. Tolmer's like report. Tolmer despatched to find it. Mr. Babbage sent to search for gold farther north. The Adelaide Philosophical Society recommends exploration N.W. Mr. Babbage discovers Blanche Water, etc. MR. BABBAGE'S THIRD TRIP, NOW IN QUEST OF LAND. Mr. Babbage's objects. His party and equipment. Set out in February, 1857. Difficulties from drought. Dromedaries recommended. Discovers the remains of Coulthard. Coulthard, Scott, and Brooks, land-hunters. Coulthard lost. Generous offer of Mr. Swinden for his discovery. Mr. Babbage finds his remains. Affecting account of his death. Babbage proceeds westward by Lake Gairdner and other salt lakes. Lakes Hart and Younghusband. Returns to Elizabeth Creek. Dissatisfaction in Adelaide at Mr. Babbage's progress. Mr. C. Gregory sent to assist him. Finds Mr. Babbage absent, sends back part of his horses and drays, and goes to seek him. Mr. Babbage's resentment. Major Warburton sent to supersede him. The Major finds Mr. Babbage gone north-west. Overtakes him, and turns him back. The Major returns himself, without further progress. Mr. Babbage's real services.
EXPEDITION OF MR. HACK FROM STREAKY BAY. ALSO OF MESSRS. MILLER AND DUTTON from the same point. Mr. Hack sent to examine the country north and east of Streaky Bay. His explorations amongst the salt lakes Indifferent country. Goes by the Gawler Ranges and Baxter's Range to the head of Spencer's Gulf. Messrs. Miller and Dutton proceed N.W. from Streaky Bay into the interior. Return for want of water. . . 311

CHAPTER XVI.

EXPLORING EXPEDITIONS IN SOUTH AUSTRALIA IN 1856—57
—58, AND 59, CONTINUED.

EXPEDITIONS OF MESSRS. GOYDER AND FREELING IN 1856-7-8. Mr. Goyder sent to examine the country about Blanche Water, and make a trigonometric survey of it. His marvellous report. Great sensation in Adelaide. The possessors of flocks and herds already on the way to this Goshen. Those of Victoria on the same march. Captain Freeling sent to ascertain the truth of these tidings. Finds all the results of mirage. His report. Close examination of Lake Torrens. Its old character restored. Mr. Swinden's discovery of available land west of Lake Torrens. MAJOR WARBURTON'S EXPEDITION TO LAKE GAIRDNER WITH THE HON. S. DAVENPORT. Proceed from Streaky Bay to the Gawler Ranges. Thence to Lake Gairdner. Theory of the country. Low estimate of it. Mr. Davenport's progress west. Major Warburton's examination of the lakes.
MR. PARRY'S SURVEYING EXPEDITION NEAR LAKE TORRENS. Reports all barren.
EXPEDITION OF GOVERNOR MCDONNELL TO LODDON SPRINGS. His voyage up the Darling in 1859. 328

CONTENTS. xv

CHAPTER XVII.
AUGUSTUS C. GREGORY'S EXPEDITION IN QUEST OF DR. LEICH-HARDT'S REMAINS.

A convict reports Leichhardt alive and in captivity in the interior. Mr. Hely's journey to ascertain the fact. Reports Leichhardt murdered by the natives. In 1858, the New South Wales Government sent out Mr. A. C. Gregory from Moreton Bay to seek for traces of Leichhardt. Traces of Leichhardt on the Barcoo near Mount Inniskillen eighty miles beyond Hely's farthest point. Proceeds to the Alice. A terrible country. Loses all traces of Leichhardt. Imagines him gone west. Traces down the Thomson. Return to the Barcoo. Follows down that river to ascertain its real course. Arrives at Cooper's Creek, thus identifying the two waters. Traces the course of Cooper's Creek by Strzelecki's Creek to Lake Torrens. Thus demonstrates the flow of this water from the Mountains of the east to Spencer's Gulf. Crosses Lake Torrens on solid bottom. Arrival in Adelaide. The fate of Leichhardt still a mystery. . . . 337

CHAPTER XVIII.
EXPEDITIONS IN WESTERN AUSTRALIA IN 1858 AND 1861.
BY MR. FRANK T. GREGORY.

EXPEDITIONS IN WESTERN AUSTRALIA, 1858.—Frank Gregory and party examine the country between the river Gascoyne and Mount Murchison. Proceed to the Geraldine Mines. Mount Nairn on the Murchison. Reach the Gascoyne. Country well grassed. Lockyer's Range. Lyons River. The Alma. Mount Augustus 3000 feet. Good country. Proceed S.S.E. Mounts Gould and Hale. Extensive tracts of good country. Return to the Nairn and Geraldine Mines. The natives numerous, and sometimes troublesome. New pigeons and new vegetables. Melons and sweet potatoes. Geologic character of the country. Babbage Island. New yam. EXPEDITION OF MR. F. T. GREGORY INTO THE INTERIOR OF DE WITT'S LAND, IN 1861. Land at Nickol Bay. Discover the Fortescue. The Hammersley Ranges. Mounts Augustus, Phillips, Samson. The Barlee Ranges. Neighbourhood of the Lyons. Second progress eastward. The Sherlock, Yule, and Oakover Rivers. Ranges in the interior. Great extents of pasturable land. The rivers Strelley, Shaw, and De Grey. Great sea-flats. Sufferings in the last journey. Character of the climate and country. Pearl oyster-beds. Natural productions. Return. . . 343

CHAPTER XIX.
EXPEDITION FOR BRINGING DOWN THE REMAINS OF BURKE AND WILLS.

Wonderful progress of Australia since this history commenced.—The expedition to bring down the remains of Burke and Wills sets out from Melbourne in December, 1861. The party and equipment. Vary the route from Menindie. Proceed more eastward. The country better. Mount Babbage. Boally and Bultilla Creeks. Intense heat and flies. Cadell's Range. Take the old route at Altolka. Rains and grass. Getting Camels over Wilkie's Creek. February the 27th, reach Wills's grave. Mr. Howitt starts to examine the route towards Mount Hopeless. Find McKinlay's mark at Burke's grave. A wilful guide. Return to camp. On March 5th, set out to reach Mount Hopeless. Strzelecki's creek. Gregory's camp.

CONTENTS.

Miserable country. Reach Blanche Water. Baker's Station. Blacks eating poisoned sugar. Barren cattle stations. Return by Lake Hope. Still very wretched country. Lake Hope. Idea that the waters from Cooper's Creek pass this way. McKinlay's guide. Reach the Depôt. Coming down of a great flood. Remove the remains of Wills out of its reach. Explore the country northwards. High rocks and red sand-hills. Bateman's Creek. Frightened natives. Other creeks. Natives say McKinlay's party detained by floods. Search for McKinlay's party. Teniel Ranges. Lake Lipsom. Kyejoran Creek. William's Creek. A funeral oration. Regain the Depôt. Hunt down a cow and calf. Catch Sturt's roan horse. Much frying of beef. Dishonest black guide. The flood still coming down. Arrival of Corporal Wanchope with despatches. Howitt returns with him to Blanche Water. Returns to the Depôt.—Orders to wait for arrival of Landsborough from the gulf, and to look out for McKinlay. Journey north-west across the Stony Desert. Appearance of the desert at the time. Very passable. Lake Short. Odd conduct of the guide. Tracks thought to be of McKinlay's party. Vain search for the party. Terrible country. Other horse tracks, supposed of land-hunters. Sampson's Range. Rumours of McKinlay. A camel lost. Another journey to Blanche Water for supplies. Angipena Police Station. Singular scenery. Wilpena Pound. Striking scenery of Jacob's Station. Constant war with the blacks. Try to kill Howitt's black boy. Bloodless affair with them. Their language imitated by the settlers in their converse with them. Evident fate of the aborigines. Seventeen years' residence of a sailor amongst them. His desire to mediate between the blacks and squatters. Opinion of Mr. Wentworth, that the whites are always the aggressors. Before setting out with the remains of Burke and Wills, Howitt buries supplies of food and clothing at the Depôt, should any exploring party arrive there. Journey down to Adelaide. An attempt made from Jacob's Station to open up a route eastward to the Darling. Found impracticable. Arrive at Adelaide. Dinner to McKinlay. Honours to the deceased at Adelaide. Arrival of the remains at Melbourne. Their reception by the committee. Lying in state. Meeting to receive the explorers. The funeral of Burke and Wills. Addresses of satisfaction presented to Howitt and his party, Captain Norman and Mr. Kyte, the originators of the expedition. Grants by government to the relatives of Mr. Wills, to the nurse of Burke, and others. 352

CHAPTER XX.

CONCLUSION OF DISCOVERY IN AUSTRALIA.

Introduction of steam on the Murray and other rivers by Captain Cadell, Mr. Randall, and others. Impulse given by the late expeditions across the continent. Squatters advancing on all the tracks of Gregory, Walker, and Landsborough on the east—on those of Stuart and McKinlay centrally. Advances into York Peninsula. Two towns to be built there. Other squatters on the Belyando, Burdekin, and Lynd. Advances on the track of Burke and Wills. In the Stony Desert itself. Of others on Lake Hope.—In Western Australia the same spread of flocks and herds into new regions. Nickol Bay. The De Grey region. Doubtful Bay. Camden Harbour. Applications for islands in Shark's Bay in Recherche Archipelago. Settlement in Dampier's Land. Further attempts to explore the country on the Australian Bight. New settlement on the Adelaide under Colonel Finniss. Conditions of sale of lands. Immediately bought up. News of Colonel Finniss at Adam's Bay. Hopes entertained from this settlement in the north-west.

FRESH EXPLORATIONS IN THE NORTH-EAST. Dalrymple's tour in the district of the Burdekin. Traces its course to the Rockingham Bay. Exploration of its mouth by Governor Bowen. Voyage of the Governor to Cape York to examine the site of a settlement. His admiration of the scenery along the coast. Advantages of the Great Barrier Reef. Progress of steam navigation on the east course. Sir Charles Nicholson recommends the exploration of New Guinea. Importance of that island to Australia. Mr. Scott traces the valley of the Burdekin from the Valley of Lagoons to the sea. A new port and town contemplated at Rockingham Bay, and direct road to the Lagoons. Amazing advance of settlement northwards. Discoveries of other kinds than geographical. Prospects of the great future. . 381

CHAPTER XXI.

INCIDENTS OF DISCOVERY AND SETTLEMENT IN NEW ZEALAND.

The survey of the coasts by Drury, D'Urville, and Stokes. Early explorers, Brunner, Monro, Mitchell, Dashwood, Thomson, Lieutenant-Governor Eyre. DISCOVERY in the Northern Island. Earliest explorers, traders, Pakeha-Maories, missionaries. Dr. Dieffenbach and Captain Symonds. Dieffenbach visits the islands in Cook's Straits. Examines the country north of Port Nicholson. Settlement of Wellington. Dieffenbach ascends Mount Egmont. Lands in the Bay of Islands, accompanied by Captain Bernard. Explores the north-east peninsula. Natives, missionaries, etc. Set out, accompanied by Captain Symonds and Lieutenant Best, for the interior. The Waipa river. A stupendous rata tree. The chief Te-Whero-Whero. The Waikato river. A volcanic country. Hot springs, sulphur jets, and boiling mud springs. The great central lake, Taupo. Forbidden to ascend the volcano Tongariro. Former ascent of it by Mr. Bidwell. The Warm Lake. The Valley of the Thames. Return to Auckland. Explorations and death of Captain Symonds. Explorations of Dr. Hochstetter, Messrs. Purchas and Heaphy. Dana's visit to the Bay of Islands. Hochstetter's journey to the Waipa, Waikato, and Tongariro, accompanied by Dr. Haast, Captain Drummond Hay, Bruno Hamel, and Herr Koch. They go over the same ground as Dr. Dieffenbach. The caves in the limestone district. The Mora Cave. Geologic results of this journey. Gold discoveries. German and French savans and naturalists, discoverers in New Zealand and Australia. Progress of botanical knowledge in New Zealand. Missionaries as openers-up of these islands. Collectors of Maori knowledge and poetry 398

CHAPTER XXII.

DISCOVERY OF THE INSULARITY OF THE SOUTH ISLAND.

Discovery of the insularity of the South Island by Stewart, a sealer. Settlement of the Middle Island in 1847. The River Owerrie already explored in 1840 by the Pelorus. Settlement of Otago by William Cargill, of Canterbury, by a Company projected by Gibbon Wakefield in 1850. Failure of the project. Surveys of Captain Stokes of the coasts of the Foveaux Strait. Discovery of the ports and rivers of the southern extremity of the Middle Island. Explores the New River. Explorations of Mr. Hamilton and Mr. Spencer. Journey from Jacob's River to Otago. Account of the South Island by Captain Stokes. Surveys of Mr. Tuckett. Discoveries of Brown, Duppa, and Thomson. Survey of M'Kerrow of the Lake District of Otago. 418

CHAPTER XXIII.

DISCOVERIES IN THE MIDDLE ISLAND CONTINUED.

Mr. Dobson's discovery of a route over the Canterbury Mountains to the west coast. Discoveries of Mr. Torlesse. Harper's expedition to the west coast. Mr. Dobson's attempt to find a way through the mountains to Nelson. Surveys of Mr. Rochfort on the mountains westward. Discoveries of Mr. Mackay.
Dr. HAAST'S EXPLORATIONS OF THE MOUNTAINS AND RIVERS OF THE MIDDLE ISLAND. Report of Dr. Haast's explorations in 1860. Proceeds from Nelson with a party to discover a route to the Buller on the west coast. Wairau Valley. Lake Howard. Passes discovered by Brunner, Heaphy, and Fox. Junction of the Tutaki and Buller. Ascend Mount Murchison. Cross the Buller and various rivers to the Grey. Ascend the Grey. Vast view from Mount Deception. Lakes Brunner and Hochstetter. Beds of coal on the Grey. Follow the coast north. Mounts Rochfort, William, and Frederick. Follow the coast to Cape Farewell, and sail to Nelson. Explorations of the Canterbury Mountains in 1861. Death, by drowning, of his companion, Dr. Sinclair. Continues these explorations in 1862. Sources of the Kowai. Ascends Mount Torlesse. Lakes Tekapo and Pukaki. The Great Tasman glacier and Moorhouse Range. Poetic beauty of the Southern Alps. In 1863 Dr. Haast pursued his explorations into the mountains of Otago. Dr. Drake reports good country between the Rivers Grey and Hokitika. Further explorations of Dr. Haast. Dr. Hector, in 1863, discovered the River Kaduku, the lake Kakapo, and a track to the central lake, Wakatipua. A direct highway across the island. Part of these discoveries made previously by Messrs. Caple, Alabaster, and others. Passes discovered by Mr. Rochfort and Mr. Clarke. These explorations small in extent, but arduous from the obstacles of high mountains, glaciers, and impetuous rivers. Mr. Rochfort's surveys. Mr. A. Dobson. 427

CHAPTER XXIV.

OPENING COMMUNICATION WITH THE WEST COAST.

Opening the way to the West Coast.—Arduous nature of the undertaking. The fatalities of 1863. The story of the loss of Mr. Whitcombe. LOSS OF MR. CHARLTON HOWITT AND PARTY. Life and Character of Mr. Charlton Howitt. Sojourn in Australia. Employed in Canterbury to seek for gold. Engaged in making a bridle-road over the mountains to the West Coast. Reputation for zeal and energy. Progress of the work. Wetness of the West Coast. Mode of subsistence in the mountains. Bird-catching. Mr. Herries' account of crossing the mountains. The grandeur of the mountain scenery. The charms of the forests of New Zealand. Enormous and curious trees. Mr. Howitt and two men drowned in Lake Brunner. The sufferings of James Hammett the survivor. Unavailing researches for the remains of the drowned. Subsequent drowning of Mr. Townsend in the Grey. Remarks on the climate of the West Coast. Concluding remarks. Probable extinction of the native race. Remarkable exemplification of native rights by a native. Persuasion of the Maories of their own fate. Appeal to our countrymen in New Zealand on their behalf 439

THE HISTORY OF DISCOVERY IN AUSTRALIA, TASMANIA AND NEW ZEALAND.

CHAPTER I.

DR. LEICHHARDT'S EXPEDITION OVERLAND FROM MORETON BAY TO PORT ESSINGTON IN THE YEARS 1844 AND 1845.

Proposition to send Sir Thomas Mitchell on an expedition across the continent.—Dr. Leichhardt finally employed.—Captain Sturt about to start from Adelaide for the same point.—Dr. Leichhardt's antecedents.—Rather scantily supplied with instruments.—His party.—At Brisbane.—Abundant supplies offered.—Their equipments.—Messrs. Hodgson and Gilbert join the expedition.—Start on the 1st of September.—Cross the Darling Downs.—Acacia scrubs.—Leichhardt notes all facts of natural history.—Trouble with the native guides.—Dawson River.—Calvert Plains.—Pursued by hornets.—Lakes and mountains.—Expedition Range.—Mount Nicholson.—The Boyd.—Sandstone rocks.—Creek of the Ruined Castles.—Bigge's Mountain.—Albinia Downs.—Comet Creek and Comet Range.—Startled natives from their dinner.—Abundance of kangaroos.—The Mackenzie.—Wild beans which make good coffee. Mount Stewart.—Honey plentiful.—West Hill.—A very mountainous region before them.—Calvert's Peak, Gilbert's Downs, Lowe's, MacArthur's, and Roper's Peaks.—Leichhardt makes a reconnoitrance northward.—Mountainous region.—Zamia Creek.—Black ants and hornets.—Alarmed black women and infant.—Coxen's Peak.—Charley and Brown, the blacks, dismissed, but allowed to come back to the party.—Intense heat.—The Isaac's and Suttor.—Fine valleys.—Black man and woman mount into trees.—The deaf black woman's fright at seeing Leichhardt on horseback.—Water, water plants, and water fowl.—Mount M'Connell.—The Burdekin.—Pelicans and black swans.—Geological character of the rocks.—Mount Graham.—Gourds and calabash.—Numerous fig trees.—The figs full of ants.—Luxuriant wild beans.—Roby's and Porter's Ranges.—Clarke River.—Basaltic dykes and fossiliferous limestone.—Only thirty miles from Halifax Bay.—Hitherto a coast journey.—Now strike more westward.—The Perry.—Fine country.—Interesting descriptions of the routine of a day on the journey.—Basaltic rocks, lava, lagoons.—Mulberry trees.—Dividing range from 2000 to 3000 feet high.—Granite,

A NEW EXPEDITION PROJECTED.

basalt, and lava.—Obliged to diverge.—Question of the blacks about the bullocks.—Want of water.—Separation Creek.—A traveller's trials and pleasures.—Blacks again fly, and leave their dinner.—Fine rock crystal in a bag.—New trees and plants.—Daring kites.—The Lynd.—Kirchener's Range.—Fig and cotton trees.—Sandstone country.—A sawfish found.—Superior huts of the natives.—The Mitchell River.—The gum-tree ants.—The crocodile.—Palm trees appear.—Natives numerous and hostile.—Attempt to drive off the cattle.—Murder of Mr. Gilbert.—A nocturnal fight.—Calvert and Roper wounded severely.—The night intensely cold.—Chase away the natives.—Gilbert's funeral.—In sight of the Gulf of Carpentaria.—A wild plum found.—Fine grassy country.—Reach the salt water.—Lagoons, with white, blue, and pink lilies.—A native suddenly appears in the camp.—Native melons.—The Gilbert River.—Grevilleas, Barthenias, and Balfourias abound.—Numerous natives.—Kill abundance of ducks, spoonbills, and three emus.—Cross the Plains of Promise.—Pugnacious native boy.—The Albert River.—Carving of an emu's foot.—Audacity of natives.—The river Leichhardt.—The Nicholson.—Emu trap.—Cross a succession of rivers to Tasman's River.—Numerous kinds of animal life.—Cycas palms.—Fruit of the pandanus.—Seven Emu River.—The Robinson River.—Zamia and Cycas palm groves. Desperate condition of their clothes.—Moccasins of bullock hide.—Tea and sugar gone.—Pound seeds for a beverage.—The white-barked tree of Tasman, figs, and sterculias.—The MacArthur salt-water river.—Soup of dry bullock hides.—Blistering fruit.—Cape Maria.—Reduce their baggage.—The Limmen River.—Swamps, wild geese, ducks, alligators, and thickets of acacias.—Native fish traps.—The Wickham.—Flat-topped sandstone rocks.—The Four Archers.—Their kangaroo dog died.—Strike westward across the Arnheim Peninsula for Port Essington.—The Roper River.—Abandon more luggage and botanical specimens.—A horse drowned.—Cattle very much exhausted.—Great swamps full of water fowl.—Natives with English articles of dress.—More speaking some English.—East Alligator River.—Rocks, hills, swamps, wild geese, and flying foxes.—Shoot a buffalo.—Port Essington.—Return by sea to Sydney.—Honours and rewards.

FRESH EXPEDITION IN 1847.—Not heard of again.—Traces of Leichhardt seen by Gregory and Walker.—Lost probably in the great western desert.—His supplies.—Mr. Hoveden Hely sent in quest of Leichhardt.—Journey fruitless.—Blacks' report, Leichhardt murdered with all his party.—Seventeen years passed without certain information of Leichhardt's fate.

VARIOUS expeditions of discovery had, as we have seen, been sent to the westward side of the Australian continent of late years, and much progress made in a knowledge of it. It was now the turn of Eastern Australia to make another advance, and to carry the same spirit of inquiry northward and westward beyond the regions into which Oxley, Cunningham, Sturt, and Mitchell had penetrated. Dr. Ludvig Leichhardt had been for two years engaged in explorations to the north of Moreton Bay, and, on returning to Sydney in the autumn of 1844, found the public and the colonial government proposing to send an expedition overland from Moreton Bay to Port Essington. Sir Thomas Mitchell was the person on whom the attention of the public was fixed to conduct this expedition. Considerable delay, however, had occurred in the course of correspondence with the Secretary of State for the Colonies on the subject, and it was now understood that Captain Sturt was about to start from Adelaide on an expedition towards the same point. The people of New South Wales were naturally anxious not to be forestalled in the honour of the projected progress through the continent, and at this moment Dr. Leichhardt offered himself as willing to head such a party as could be fitted out by public subscription, and to start immediately. His reputation for the necessary accomplishments and experience in bush travel at once secured the acceptance of his offer. It was an offer that was not likely to have many qualified competitors. The narratives of the gentleman just mentioned, as well as those of Grey and Eyre, had made the pre-eminent hazards and hardships of such an enterprise well known. "Many," says Dr. Leichhardt, "considered the very conception of such an undertaking as madness on my part, and the consequence of a blind enthusiasm, nourished either by a deep devotion to science, or an unreasonable craving for fame; while others did not feel justified in assisting a man who, they considered, was setting out with an intention of committing suicide."

In Sydney Leichhardt had been chiefly known as a lecturer on botany. In his previous enterprise he had associated with the natives as he advanced, and his medical skill, which he employed for their benefit, had given him great acceptance with them. Though born in Germany he was educated in Paris, but he had resided a long time amongst the English.

His past experience had given Leichhardt confidence of success; many generous friends were found to forward the object, and by the 13th of August, 1844, all was ready for the undertaking. The only instruments that he carried with him were a sextant and artificial horizon, a chronometer, a hand Kater's compass, a small thermometer, and Arrowsmith's map of the continent of New Holland. It is evident that by taking only one of each of these instruments he ran great risks of having an entire stop put to his scientific observations, but an expeditious preparation and lightness of carriage were the offsets to this danger.

His party was limited to six individuals on leaving Sydney, namely:—Mr. James Calvert; Mr. John Roper; John Murphy, a lad about 16 years old; William Phillips, a prisoner of the crown; and Harry Brown, a native of the Newcastle tribe, making with himself the six. They left Sydney on the 13th of August, for Moreton Bay, in the steamer "Sovereign," and arrived in Brisbane after an unusually tedious voyage of a week, causing much suffering to his horses from want of food and water.

At Brisbane Dr. Leichhardt was received with enthusiasm, and was overloaded with presents of all sorts of things that could be useful on such a journey. The principal population there belonging to the squatting interest, were well aware of the vast advantage to them of such expeditions, which lay open new regions for their occupation. Many of the supplies offered he was obliged to decline, because they would have overloaded his horses and bullocks. He had now of cattle sixteen head; of horses seventeen. Of provisions he had 1200 lbs. of flour; 200lbs. of sugar; 80lbs. of tea; 20lbs. of gelatine, and other articles of less consideration, but likely to add much to their comfort. They had 30lbs. of powder, and 8 bags of shot of different sizes, chiefly of No. 4 and No. 6. Every one had provided himself with two pair of strong trousers, three strong shirts, and two pair of shoes; and some of the party had ponchos, made of light, strong calico, saturated with oil, which proved very useful in keeping out the wet, but must have been very dangerous had they caught fire, as they would be all a-flame in an instant, and before they could be stripped over the head. They considered this a sufficient supply for seven months, in which time they calculated on completing the journey. Besides these they had a light spring cart to carry part of the stores, but they soon broke the shafts of it, and abandoned it. This was to be regretted, as Sir Thomas Mitchell had shown how well carts of a proper construction may be taken in very long journeys of this kind, and how greatly they relieve the labour of horses and bullocks in a hot climate like Australia, where the loads on the backs of cattle heat and exhaust them.

Numbers of young men at Brisbane were anxious to join the expedition, but Dr. Leichhardt resisted these importunities, except in the case of Mr. Pemberton Hodgson and Mr. Gilbert. The latter was a collector for Mr. Gould, the zoologist, and justly thought it a fine opportunity of coming in contact with new species of birds and quadrupeds. These gentlemen equipped themselves, and added two bullocks and four horses to the expedition. Besides these gentlemen Dr. Leichhardt took on from Brisbane Caleb, an American negro, and Charley, a native of the Bathurst tribe.

It was the end of September before they set out, and left the station of Messrs. Campbell and Stephens. They had a dray lent them to convey some of their heavy stores as far as Darling Downs, and in no part of their journey did they encounter more difficulties than in this portion of it. There had been heavy rains, which had flooded the brooks or creeks, as there named, and made the ground so soft that their loaded carriages and cattle sunk into it. Then the bullocks, unused to burdens, were unruly, and threw their loads and broke the packsaddles, which they had continually to repair and alter, so as to make them fit their particular beasts. They only made ten miles by a very long day's work on the first day. At night the bullocks, like sensible beasts, not liking this new business, endeavoured to wander back again, and had to be watched and hunted up. The horses being well hobbled, occasioned much less trouble. They passed the stations of Messrs. Hughes and Isaacs, and of Mr. Coxon, and on the 30th of September arrived at Jimba, the utmost limit to which the occupation by squatters extended.

They had now crossed the Darling Downs, for these last stations were on the western slopes of the Coast Range, established on creeks running thence to join the Condamine River. The Darling Downs are from 1800 to 2000 feet above the sea level, and the country, as they passed down from them, was covered with most luxuriant grass and herbage, and the trees such as will be frequently mentioned in this narrative, therefore I will give the account of them in Leichhardt's own words:—"Plants of the leguminosa and compositæ were by far the most prevalent; the colour of the former, generally a showy red, that of the latter, a bright yellow. Belts of open forest land, principally composed of the box-tree of the colonists, a species of eucalyptus, (in no respect resembling the box of Europe), separate the different plains; and the patches of scrub, consisting of several species of acacias, and of a variety of small trees appear to be the outposts of the extensive scrubs of the interior. There are particularly three species of acacias which bestow a peculiar character on these scrubs. The one is the myal, acacia pendula, first seen by Oxley on Liverpool Plains, and afterwards at the Barwan and Darling Downs, whose drooping foliage and rich yellow blossoms render it extremely elegant and ornamental. The second, the acacia of Coxon, resembles the myal, without its drooping character, its narrow, lanceolate phyllodia rather stiff, its yellowish branches erect. The third is the Bricklow acacia, which seems to be identical with the rosewood acacia of Moreton Bay. The latter, however, is a fine tree, fifty or sixty feet high, whereas the former is either a small tree or a scrub."—P. 3.

It may be as well here to observe that every page of Leichhardt's Journal abounds with the names, and often description of the plants and animals seen, so that it would be impossible to notice them all, except by devoting a space equal to his journal to them; and as the great object of this history is geographical discovery, I shall only notice such as are particularly remarkable, or are necessary to characterize the district where they appear.

Through such a country as already described, the party progressed till the 17th of October, when the two natives, Charley and Brown, became insolent and refractory, and Charley, threatening to shoot Mr. Gilbert, was dismissed, but allowed to return. They named a creek Hodgson's Creek, and saw a bird, which from the noise it made, they called the Glucking Bird, and which they met with on various parts of their route. On the 3rd of November they began to fear that their party was too large for their stores, and Mr. Hodgson and Caleb the negro returned. On the 6th of November they saw a small river in latitude 26° 3′ 44″, which they named Dawson River, and beyond it crossed fertile plains, which they called Calvert's Plains, showing here and there sand-stone ridges, covered with bastard box, and silver-leaved iron-bark trees. They saw kangaroos, emus, pigeons, ducks, and various other birds. On the 10th they came again upon the Dawson, now divided into a number of ana-branches, making a perfect maze in the valley, and Charley the black said he never saw such a "rum river in his life."

On the 14th they came, in travelling down the Dawson, on plains which, from the abundance of that plant, they named Vervain Plains. They shot occasionally an old man, or largest sized kangaroo, and were pursued by swarms of hornets, whose nests, suspended to branches, the cattle passing under with their loads, disturbed. They now, on some fine sheets of water, encountered the corypha palms, growing to the height of twenty-five or thirty feet, and beheld numbers of native companions—*Ardea antigone*, strutting along the banks, whilst ducks abounded on the lakes. They soon after crossed hills, which they named Gilbert's Ranges, from Mr. Gilbert, of the party. Between these and Lynd's Range, more to the south, they named a creek Palm-tree Creek, and a range of hills running north and south, and separating this creek from the Dawson, they named Middle Range. On reedy flats at the upper end of Palm-tree Creek, grew abundance of atriplex, or fat hen, and sowthistle, which they found, when young, as I and my sons also did in our bush life, made excellent greens, when boiled. They crossed also a creek, which they named Robinson's Creek, seeming to flow from the same quarter as Palm-tree Creek. On the left bank of Robinson's Creek, they saw a wide sheet of water, and beyond it, a range covered with dense scrub, which they named Murphy's Lake and Range. On the Condamine they had seen small orange trees in blossom, and on Robinson's Creek they found the same species of trees with fruit just setting.

They had now entered quite a mountainous country; the scenery beautiful, but the burr and spear-grass—*aristida*—greatly tormenting them. The lakes that they saw were partly covered by a yellow villarsia; there were black swans, and whistling ducks. In a camp of the natives here, they found several fine kangaroo nets, made of the bark of sterculia, one of which they took, leaving instead a brass-hilted sword, four fish-hooks, and a silk handkerchief. Amongst the variety of ants seen in that neighbourhood, the funnel-ant was the most curious. It sinks perpendicular holes into the earth, and keeps the mouth of them open by an elevated wall, sloping outwards, like a funnel. The presence of these ants indicates a rotten soil, into which horses and cattle sink beneath their fetlocks in dry weather, but in wet weather the soil is much firmer. Kangaroos and emus abounded.

On the 27th of November they ascended a range of hills, and travelled four or five miles along their level summit, which was covered with open forest, interspersed with thickets of acacias and casuarinas. From the extremity of the range they had a fine view of other hills with conspicuous peaks, cupolas, and walls of rock, extending from west by north to north-west. The most distant range was particularly striking and imposing. This Leichhardt called Expedition Range, and to a bell-shaped mountain, bearing north 68° west, he gave the name of Mount Nicholson, in honour of Dr., now Sir Charles Nicholson, who first introduced into the Legis-

THE CREEK OF THE RUINED CASTLES.

lative Council of New South Wales the subject of an overland expedition to Port Essington. To a sharp peak, N. 66° W., he gave the name of Aldis's Peak, after Mr. Aldis, of Sydney.

The next day, when in latitude 25° 19′ 19″, they came upon a river, which they named the Boyd, running in various channels from these hills in a S.W. direction, and which was afterwards discovered to fall into the Dawson. All these ranges were of sandstone, and impressions of calamites were visible in one of the gullies. From these gullies, densely filled by masses of cypress, pine, and scrub, they descended a space into a valley finely grassed, and adorned with corypha palms and casuarinas. This valley, surrounded by high sandstone rocks, fissured and broken like pillars and walls, and the high gates of ruined castles, reminded the Doctor of Germany, and he named the creek running through it, the Creek of the Ruined Castles. The whole system of these creeks and glens he thought admirably adapted for a cattle station. The Wonga-Wonga, and a variety of other pigeons, inhabit these glens.

On the 2nd of December, they followed down a creek, leading north-west, which they named Zamia Creek, from a magnificent Zamia of ten feet high and nine inches in diameter, bearing elongated cones, not yet ripe. A variety of plants and trees flourished in this glen; and a large mountain overlooking it, they named Bigge's mountain. On the 7th they encamped a few miles from Mount Aldis, where kangaroos abounded. Here the natives, who had been following them some time under cover of the scrub, managed to spear one of the horses in the shoulder. Mounts Nicholson and Aldis were found on nearer view to be of basaltic formation. They found two sorts of capparis in this district in fruit, which were eatable. To the N.W. by E., they saw ranges, which they named Christmas Ranges, hoping to reach them by Christmas.

In exploring these ranges and glens, they lost one of their fine kangaroo dogs, and some of the party very nearly lost themselves. Mr. Calvert and Brown were out all one night in the bush. In the scrub they found native lemons ripe, and of the amazing size of half an inch in diameter. These they made into a dish resembling gooseberry fool. On the 18th they killed a bullock and jerked the flesh; that is, dried it, cut into strips, in the sun, and melting the fat, rubbed their harness, saddles, &c. with it, to prevent the sun cracking them. They remained at this camp by some fine waters, which they called Brown's Lagoons, because Brown, the native, found them, and there spent their Christmas, having passed through a great myal forest, and seen a variety of birds and flowering plants. Their Christmas dinner consisted of suet pudding and stewed cockatoos. They must have been, as they expected, under Christmas Range, for on the 28th, they were at Albinia Downs, where they camped, and on the 30th at Comet Creek, under Comet Range. By this creek they found the remains of a hut, consisting of a ridge-pole and two forked stakes about six feet high, both having been cut with a sharp iron tomahawk, which led them to believe it the work of some runaway convict from Moreton Bay. Here, too, they suddenly came upon a camp of the natives, who fled crying, as it seemed to them, "white-fellow! white-fellow!" Brown said he saw a half-caste amongst them, which led Leichhardt to think that a white man was probably living with them. They found at their fires a capital dinner just ready, of roasted eggs, of brush turkey, roasted opossum, bandicoots and iguanas. In their dillis, or small baskets, were roots or tubers of an inch long, and half an inch thick, of an agreeable flavour, probably the murnong, or native yam. There were opossum cloaks, kangaroo nets, and dillis neatly worked of koorajong bark, with spears of Bricklow acacia lying about, which they left as they found them, with the exception of a single turkey egg, which they ate, and pronounced excellent.

From the last day of December, 1844, to January 12th, 1845, the party camped on the Comet Creek, and in its immediate neighbourhood at a branch creek. Here Dr. Leichhardt discovered a red passion-flower twining round the trunk of a gum-tree, a climbing capparis, and other plants. The valley was rich with verdure. They found portulac growing along the creek, which furnished an acceptable vegetable for their table. There were swarms of cockatoos greater than they had ever seen, vast numbers of ducks about the lagoons, and birds of various kinds and colours, flitting about after the insects. There were plenty of kangaroos, wallabies, brush turkeys, and bronze-winged pigeons. The natives, though in considerable numbers, did not molest them. In one of their exploratory excursions, they came upon a river into which the Comet Creek fell, and they called it the Mackenzie, after Sir Evan Mackenzie.

On the 12th of January they removed the camp to the Mackenzie, which at that season, though frequently from fifty to a hundred yards broad, formed only a chain of ponds or lakes, some of them of seven or eight miles long. The course of the river was towards the north-east, and has since been found to be a branch of the Fitzroy falling into Keppel Bay. The latitude of their camp was 23° 33' 38". A little to the north of the junction of Comet Creek with the Mackenzie, they crossed the line afterwards taken by the North Australian Expedition in 1856. In the dry and sandy parts of the river bed they found a bean with racemes of pink blossoms, running along the ground, or climbing round shrubs and trees. Its pods were from three to five inches long, and half an inch broad, containing from four to six seeds, very similar to a horse bean. This plant was afterwards found growing in the sandy beds, or along the bergs of almost all the broad rivers, and was always a welcome sight, for the seeds after roasting and pounding, afforded them a very agreeable substitute for coffee. Here finding the river running to the east, they began to fear the want of water as they proceeded north-west, and spite of all the game they had seen, not having procured sufficient meat, they killed a bullock and jerked its flesh. The natives appeared numerous, and they found them speaking a different idiom.

Taking Brown with him, the Doctor set out to explore the country northwards. They found some fine lagoons, and in latitude 23° 10', ascended a hill which they named Mount Stewart. Having advanced still farther to the north-west, among hills and dense scrubs, they turned back, but soon lost their way, and were four days wandering in the bush, in a state of all but utter starvation. The whole country over which they had travelled was of sandstone, with occasional outbreaks of basalt, and its attendant black, fertile soil. The plains and creeks abounded with fossil wood, charged with iron-ore and silica. On the 23rd, 24th, and 25th of January, 1845, they travelled forward over the country which the Doctor had just explored, and encamped at a place about twenty-five miles north-west from Mount Stewarts' Creek, and about thirty-four miles from the Mackenzie. Here Charley procured them abundance of honey from the hollow trees, which was extremely aromatic, from the quantity of marjoram growing there.

To the westward of their camp on the 25th of January, they saw a large hill which they called West Hill; and north and north-east they saw a very mountainous region. The country amongst the hills where they were abounded with creeks; the one on which they encamped they named Newman's Creek. In an excursion along the hills, they at length saw extensive plains open out towards the west. These plains were richly grassed. To the various peaks of this range the Doctor gave the names of Roper's Peak, after one of the party; to another Scott's Peak, to another Macarthur's Peak, to another Calvert's Peak, all after gentlemen of the colony. To the most remarkable he gave the names of Gilbert's Downs, after Mr. Gilbert of his party; and to one south-west of Macarthur's Peak, Lowe's Peak after Mr. Robert Lowe. There seemed, he observes, no end of isolated conical mountains, resembling the extinct volcanoes of Auvergne. But there was a dreadful want of water, which was a great drawback from the beauty of the scenery. If water were plentiful, the Doctor remarks, the downs of Peak Range would be inferior to no country in the world. On Roper's Peak they found a yellow hibiscus, a new species.

Mr. Gilbert made an expedition on horseback across the plains to the north-west, and found them rising in a succession of terraces till there appeared again in that direction other hills more imposing than Peak Range; but there was no water, except in one lagoon which abounded with ducks. The trees were variously marked by the natives, and one mark resembling an anchor or broad arrow, he imagined had been made, though it was with a stone tomahawk, by some shipwrecked sailor, or runaway convict from Moreton Bay, when it was a penal settlement. At this they calculated their longitude to be 148° 19', their latitude 22° 57', and that they were 175 miles from Keppel's Bay, and 100 miles from Broad Sound.

On the 2nd of February, Dr. Leichhardt took the two black-fellows with him, and rode northward to reconnoitre, and having passed Roper's and Scott's Peaks, they came to water in holes in the bed of a creek. Still advancing northward, they left the sandstone, and entered on a basaltic and fine country, with plenty of grass, though dried by the heat. They then came to a fine mountain, which they named Phillips' Mountain, and other peaks of Peak Range, which they named Fletcher's Awl, Lord's Table Range, and Campbell's Peak. On the 12th of February they came through a rocky, sandstone country, to a creek in a rich plain, which they named Hughes' Creek. Here they camped. The country around greatly resembled that of Zamia Creek. On the sandy ridges grew abundance of grass-trees, and there they first found the graceful drooping tea-tree, Melaleuca Leucodendron, which always after was found to be near water. An adjoining creek they named Tombstone Creek, from the upright isolated masses of sandstone, at the junction of the two creeks, thus worn by the waters.

Here they killed and feasted on two emus, and honey which Charley procured. A crow was shot and roasted, which they were astonished to find tender and excellent. They were, however, much tormented by black ants and hornets.

On the 13th of February they came upon the dry channel of a river, which promised to be of importance. It came from the north and north-west; large flooded gums and casuarinas grew at intervals along its banks, with fine, open timbered flats on each side, terminated at a distance by belts of scrub. They suddenly, near the river, came upon two black women digging roots, and another, perched on the top of a high flooded gum-tree, was chopping out an opossum or a bee's-nest. The poor women on seeing them set up the most piteous screams, and began swinging their sticks and beating the trees, as if they were wild beasts, and were thus to be frightened away. In spite of friendly signs, the two women on the ground ran off, and the one on the tree refused to come down. When, however, they shouted "Yarrai,"—water, she pointed down the river, and answered "Yarrai ya," which information they afterwards found correct. At the foot of the tree they found an infant, swathed in layers of tea-tree bark, and three or four large yams. Suddenly a great number of men, women and boys came running to the delivery of the screaming woman in the tree, but, on riding towards them, they turned and ran off into the scrub. Having encamped at a lagoon near the channel of the river, the natives camping somewhere near, they began to trace the river northwards towards its sources. They soon came to ranges on its left bank, which they named Coxon's Peak and Range, which were of sandstone, and fell off in terraces towards the east. The whole country to the coast appeared to be sandstone, and all in that direction was one immense sea of forest and scrub. Several streams appeared to fall into the Isaacs, as they named this river, or rather bed of a river, near this place. From Coxon's Range the exploring party returned to the river, where they killed and cured a bullock, and this time they made the discovery that the fat would dry just as well as the lean, and thus they added a great essential to their comfort, as the meat was far superior fried in a portion of fat, and on particular occasions they could indulge in fat-cakes, made of flour, and fried in their pan, a bush dainty to which I can add my approving testimony.

At this place the two black fellows, Charley and Brown, who had for some time showed symptoms of disaffection, came to such a pitch—Charley even striking Leichhardt in the face—that Leichhardt banished them from the camp, which soon brought them to their senses. They begged humbly to be taken back, which, after some hesitation, was accorded, and they were ever after the better for it. Here, too, they lost their little terrier dog from intense heat, and their remaining kangaroo dog was only saved by Mr. Gilbert carrying it on horseback during the terrible heat of the 21st of February. In following up the Isaacs they suffered still from scarcity of water; but on the 1st of March they arrived at some fine water-holes in the north branch of the Isaacs, and there they encamped, in latitude 21°42′, longitude 148°56′.

After tracing the Isaacs up to its source, about seventy miles, seeing abundance of wallabies in its rocky caves, they came to the head of another creek, which they called Suttor Creek, and going four or five miles down it found fine water-holes. The valley of the Isaacs, says Dr. Leichhardt, is a fine country, running between two ranges; perhaps one better adapted to pastoral pursuits is not to be found. There was a want of water, but that season was a remarkably dry one all over the colony. The country of the Suttor near the head was rocky, but became more open in descending. Casuarinas and Corypha palms adorned the feet of the ranges, both of the Isaacs and the Suttor, and the abundance of marjoram near the scrubs filled the air with a most exquisite odour. Mr. Roper made an excursion westward, and brought word of fine plains, with rich, black soil.

Travelling onward, they came to another watercourse running north, which appeared to be the main channel of the Suttor. Its bed was sandy and shallow, with occasional patches of reeds; on its left were scrubs, on its right well-grassed flats, with bastard box and ironbark. Coming suddenly on a native man and woman, they hastily mounted into two trees, and on whichever side the travellers went to speak to them they moved round to the other, and kept their faces averted, no doubt from fear of magic, or deeming these white men spirits. They found here a new species of datura, and a species of heliotrope extremely fragrant. The Mackenzie bean, and other papilionacious flowers were abundant. Natives were numerous; and for the first time since leaving Moreton Bay they came on primitive rock: there was a curiously close occurrence of flint with granite rock.

"Whilst riding on Easter Sunday with Charley along the banks of the Suttor," says Dr. Leichhardt, "I saw an old woman walking slowly and thoughtfully through the forest, supporting her slender, and apparently exhausted frame with one of the long sticks which the women use for digging roots. A child was running before her. Fearing that she would be too much alarmed if we came too suddenly upon her—as neither our voices in conversation, nor the footfall of our horses, attracted her attention—I cooèed gently. After repeating the call two or three times, she turned her head, and in sudden fright she lifted her arms, and began to beat the air, as if to take wing, then, seizing the child, and shrieking most piteously, she rapidly crossed the creek, and escaped to the opposite ridges. What could she think, but that we were some of those imaginary beings, with legends of which the wise men of her people frighten the children into obedience, and whose strange forms, and stranger doings, are the favourite topics of conversation amoungst the natives at night when seated round their fires?"

As they advanced they came on long reaches of water,

surrounded by polygonums, and overgrown with blue nymphæas, damasoniums, and utricularias, and inhabited by large flocks of ducks. Corypha palms grew in abundance. Sometimes the rocks were of sienite, containing hornblende and mica, and then changing to limestone, with flat tops. In latitude 20° 49′, a river as large as the Suttor itself joined it, coming from S.W. by W., and which changed the Suttor to the N.E. This they named Cape River. The trees about it were silver-leaved ironbark, rusty-gum, Moreton Bay ash, and water-box, but stunted. The flooded gum and drooping tea-tree were alone large enough for building. In latitude 20° 41′ 35″ the country improved, and was beautifully grassed, openly timbered, sometimes flat, sometimes ridgy, and the ridges covered with pebbles. Here they camped at the foot of a mountain, which they called Mount M'Connell, where the Suttor, sweeping round to the east, joined another river, the bed of which, at its junction, was a mile broad. In the channels considerable streams were flowing northeastward. There were about it pelicans, numbers of ducks, and black swans, being the most northern point at which they found the last. This river they named the Burdekin.

At this camp on the Burdekin they killed another bullock, and moved forward on the 2nd of April. They observed flood-marks which showed that the river was sometimes from fifteen to eighteen feet above its banks. They did not climb Mount M'Connell, but observed that it was composed of domite, and the subordinate hills showed sienite. In the bed of the river there was quite a collection of primitive rocks; there were pebbles of quartz, quartz-porphyry, felspathic-porphyry, sienite and hornblende. A very conspicuous hill, E.N.E. from the junction of the rivers, they named Mount Graham. They saw various cucurbitaceous fruits, which had been washed down by the floods, and amongst them a large calabash. The banks of the river were intersected by deep gullies and creeks. The forest vegetation was the same as that of the Suttor. They found numerous fig-trees, from fifty to sixty feet high, with a rich, shady foliage, and full of fruit of the size of a small apple, of agreeable flavour, but full of ants and small flies. The bed of the river was covered with the leguminous annual noticed at the Suttor, which grew so high and thick as nearly to conceal them when amongst it on horseback. High ranges rose to the north-east, north, and north-west. Those to the east they named the Robey Range. Still more to the north, in latitude 20° 14', they named the hills Porter's Ranges. Still farther northward the country became open and fine, and various creeks fell into the river as they advanced. In latitude 20° 8' 26", a range to the N.E. was named Thacker's Range. This hilly country continued to latitude 19° 12', where a river as large as the Burdekin itself fell into it from the west and south-west, which they named the Clarke, after the Sydney geologist, the Rev. W. B. Clarke.

Much fine country was found amongst the hills along the Burdekin, with a great variety of rock formation. In some places great dykes of basalt, in others fossiliferous limestone. They discovered a new fruit, about half-an-inch long, in taste like the fruit of the Loranthus, of which they eat a great quantity without injury. Some few miles before reaching the Clarke the river suddenly turned westward, and at this bend a considerable creek entered, which was named Bowen Creek. This was the nearest point on their journey to the east coast, and only about thirty miles from Halifax Bay. Any one consulting the map will observe, that though the proposed destination of the expedition was Port Essington, Leichhardt had, with a considerably tortuous course, held more nearly northward than westward. It was rather a coast journey than an interior one. No doubt the amount of good country which he found, and the number of new rivers led him on in a route so deviating from his proposed goal. It was all valuable discovery of fresh country, and, therefore, he could scarcely be said to be out of his way. It, however, greatly lengthened it. From this point he struck more westward, in direction for the eastern coast of the Gulf of Carpentaria.

Somewhat north of the junction of Clarke's River with the Burdekin, in latitude 19° 1′ 18″, they fell in with another river coming from the north, which they named the Perry. The country about the Perry, Leichhardt describes as a fine, well grassed one. Here they encamped and killed another bullock. At this place the Doctor gives us a description of their daily life in the bush, which is so complete a picture of such life, that I shall present it to the reader:—

"The routine of one of our days will serve as an example of all the rest. I usually rise when I hear the merry laugh of the laughing jackass—Dacelo gigantea—which, from its regularity, has not been inaptly named the settler's clock; a loud cooèe then rouses my companions; Brown to make tea, Mr. Calvert to season the stew with salt and marjoram, and myself and the others to wash, and to prepare our breakfast, which for the party consists of two pounds and a half of meat stewed over night; and to each a quart pot of tea. Mr. Calvert then gives to each his portion, and by the time this important duty is performed, Charley generally arrives with the horses, which are then prepared for their day's duty. After breakfast, Charley generally goes with John and Murphy to fetch the bullocks, which are generally brought in a little after seven o'clock, A.M. The work of loading follows, but this requires very little time now, our stock being much reduced; and, at about a quarter to eight o'clock, we move on, and continue travelling four hours, and, if possible, select a spot for our camp.

"The camp fixed, and the horses and bullocks unloaded, we have all our allotted duties. To make the fire falls to my share; Brown's duty is to fetch water for tea; and Mr. Calvert weighs out a pound and half of flour for a fat cake, which is enjoyed more than any other meal. The large tea-pot being empty, Mr. Calvert weighs out two pounds and a half of dry meat to be stewed for our late dinner; and during the afternoon every one follows his own pursuits, such as washing and mending clothes, repairing saddles, pack-saddles, and packs. My occupation is to write my log, and lay down my route, or make an excursion in the vicinity of the camp to botanize, etc., or ride out reconnoitring. My companions also write down their remarks, and wander about gathering seeds, or looking for curious pebbles. Mr. Gilbert takes his gun to shoot birds. A loud cooèe again unites us towards sunset round our table-cloth; and while enjoying our meal, the subject of the day's journey, the past, the present, and the future, by turns engage our attention, and furnish matter for conversation and remark, according to the respective humour of the parties. Many circumstances have conspired to make me strangely taciturn, and I am now scarcely pleased even with the chattering humour of my youngest companion, whose spirits instead of flagging, have become more buoyant and lively than ever. I consider it, however, my invariable duty to give every information I can, whenever my companions inquire, or show a desire to learn; and I am happy to find that they are desirous of making themselves familiar with the objects of nature by which they are surrounded, and of understanding their mutual relations. Mr. Roper is of a more silent disposition; Mr. Calvert likes to speak, and has a good stock of small talk, with which he often enlivens our dinners. He is in that respect an excellent companion, being full of jokes and stories, which, though old and sometimes quaint, are always pure, and serve the more to exhilarate the party. Mr. Gilbert has travelled much, and consequently has a rich store of *impressions de voyage*; his conversation is generally very pleasing, and instructive, in describing the characters of countries he has seen, and the manners and customs of the people he has known. He is well informed in Australian ornithology. As night approaches, we retire to our beds. The two blackfellows and myself spread out

THEY FIND A FINE PASTURAL COUNTRY. 21

each our own under the canopy of heaven, whilst Messrs. Roper, Calvert, Gilbert, Murphy, and Phillips, have their tents. Mr. Calvert entertains Roper with his conversation; John amuses Gilbert; Brown tunes up his corroborie songs, in which Charley, until their late quarrel, generally joined. Brown sings well, and his melodious, plaintive voice, lulls me to sleep, when otherwise I am not disposed. Mr. Phillips is rather singular in his habits, he erects his tent generally at a distance from the rest, under a shady tree, or in a green bower of shrubs, where he makes himself as comfortable as the place will allow, by spreading branches and grass under his couch, and covering his tent with them, to keep it shady and cool, and even planting lilies in blossom—Crinum—before his tent, to enjoy their sight during the short time of our stay. As the night advances, the blackfellow's songs die away; the chatting tongue of Murphy ceases, after having lulled Mr. Gilbert to sleep, and at last even Mr. Calvert is silent, as Roper's short answers become few and far between. The neighing of the tethered horses, the distant tinkling of the bell, or the occasional cry of night-birds, alone interrupt the silence of our camp. The fire which was bright as long as the corroborie songster kept it stirred, gradually gets dull, and smoulders slowly under the large pot, in which our meat is simmering; and the bright constellations of heaven pass unheeded over the heads of the dreaming wanderers of the wilderness, until the summons of the laughing jackass recalls them to the business of the day."—P. 233.

In following the Perry N.W.W., they came upon fields of basaltic lava, the rocks coming down close to the river. In the scrub they found a low Mulberry-tree, the fruit of which was good, but small. As they advanced, they arrived at extensive lagoons, in an extensive district of water, grass, mountains, plains, forest-land, and all the elements of a fine pastoral country. They saw a leguminous tree, which thence became common all over the north. At the termination of this stretch of country they came to a dividing range from two to three thousand feet high. The principal height they named Mount Lang, after Dr. Lang the Sydney historian. These ranges were chiefly of pegmatite, a species of granite, with outbursts of basalt and streams of lava, that had descended to their feet. Finding it impossible to cross these mountains, Dr. Leichhardt followed the feet of the hills for some distance southwards, to get round them, but in vain. He then directed his course northwards with the same intent. At this camp some natives came up, and seeing the bullocks, asked if they were not their gins, an idea furnished by the blackfellow's gins being really their beasts of burden. The travellers to show them the power of fire-arms, shot at a kite settling on one of the trees, but it not being hit, they laughed loudly at the poor fire-arm. Here the party had the misfortune to have the leg of a horse broken, and they therefore, killed it and dried its flesh for use, which they found very fair. Mr. Roper had nearly lost his life by another horse, which he absurdly caught by the tail to stop him, and received a severe kick in the chest in return. In this journey some of them were fifty hours without water, but on May 17th they came upon a creek, which they called Separation Creek, in regard to its geological position between granite and basaltic formations. North of this creek they found a passage through the hills, and having rounded them southward, came upon a river, to their satisfaction flowing N.W., which they named the Lynd. Whilst encamping on its banks, let us take another peep into the mind of the traveller and its workings on such a journey;—

"During the leisure moments of the day, or at the commencement of night, when seated at my fire, all my thoughts seemed rivetted to the progress and success of my journey, and to the new objects we had met with during the day. I had then to compel myself to think of absent friends and past times, and the thoughts that they supposed me dead, or unsuccessful in my enterprise, brought me back immediately to my favourite object. Much, indeed, the greater portion of my journey had been occupied in long reconnoitring rides; and he who is thus occupied is in a continual state of excitement, now buoyant with hope, as he urges on his horse towards some distant range, or blue mountain, or as he follows the favourable bend of a river; now all despairing and miserable, as he approaches the foot of the range without finding water, from which he could again start with renewed strength, or as the river turns in an unfavourable direction, and slips out of his course. Evening approaches; the sun has sunk below the horizon for some time, but still he strains his eye through the gloom for the dark verdure of a creek, or strives to follow the arrow flight of a pigeon, the flapping of whose wings had filled him with a sudden hope, from which he relapses again into a still greater sadness; with a sickened heart he drops his head to a broken and interrupted rest, whilst his horse is standing hobbled at his side, unwilling from excessive thirst to feed on the dry grass. How often have I found myself in these different states of the brightest hope and the deepest misery, riding along, thirsty, almost lifeless, and ready to drop from my saddle with fatigue; the poor horse tired like his rider, footsore, stumbling over every stone, running heedlessly against the trees, and wounding my knees! But, suddenly, the note of Grallina Australis, the call of cockatoos, or the croaking of frogs, is heard, and hopes are bright again; water is certainly at hand; the spur is applied to the flank of the tired beast, which already partakes in his rider's anticipations, and quickens his pace, and a lagoon, a creek, or a river is before him. The horse is soon unsaddled, hobbled, and well washed; a fire is made, the teapot is put to the fire, the meat is dressed, the enjoyment of the poor reconnoitrer is perfect, and a prayer of thankfulness to the Almighty God, who protects the wanderer on his journey, bursts from his grateful lips."—P. 266.

The course of the Lynd proved the most rocky and mountainous country they had ever travelled. The ranges formed the banks of the river itself, and frequently even entered its bed. Issuing from the granite and basaltic passes in latitude 17° 54′ 4″, they suddenly came on a camp of natives, who fled, and left their dinner of roasted bandicoot and yams. Their knives also left behind were formed of sharp flints bound to handles with human hair. A fine rock crystal was found in one of their bags. On this more open, but still rough, country they found various new trees and plants; a new Grevillea, with scarlet flowers; the native cotton trees, with bright yellow ones, and large capsules of silky cotton; the exocarpus latifolius, a very different shrub from the exocarpus cupressiformis, or native cherry, with fruit which was agreeable, as was its kernel.

Here they killed another bullock, but found plenty of work to defend the drying meat from the kites, *milvus isiurus* and the crows. Here they found all their salt used up, and had to imitate the natives, and do without it. On the 1st of June they camped upon the Lynd in latitude 17° 45′ 40″. Soon after they surprised some natives in their camp, who left their koolimans, water vessels, full of bee-bread, the tubers of a vine, the roots of a bean, and bitter potatoes—their supper. Here also they saw one of the venerated rock crystals. The koolimans were made of the inner layer of the bark of the stringy-bark tree. The whole extent of this mountainous country was of porphyry with crystals of quartz and felspar in a grey paste. On both sides of it the rocks were of granite and pegmatite with talc schist in the bed of the river. The Lynd ran north-west. On the 5th they arrived at a range which they named Kirchner's Range, where the river was half a mile wide, parts of the channel being scrub, in which they saw a species of myrtle. The sarcocephalus was the chief tree of the river, but the clustered fig of the Burdekin and the cotton were there.

On the 8th of June they came upon sandstone and a consequent change of vegetation. Various creeks fell into the river. Seeing that the natives steeped the flowers of the drooping tea-tree for drink on account of their honey, they did the same, and found it very agreeable. They were astonished to find on the banks of the river a saw-fish which, they imagined, confined itself exclusively to salt water. Another thing too surprised them, which were two-storied huts, or gunyahs of the natives, formed by a floor of stringy bark raised on four poles, and other bark bent over the floor so as at once to secure a defence from damp below and rain above. On the 16th, in latitude 17° 58′, they found the Lynd falling into another river, which they named the Mitchell after the explorer.

The bed of the Mitchell was very broad, sandy, and quite bare of vegetation, showing the frequent recurrence of floods. A small stream wandered through the sheet of sand, and sometimes expanded into large water holes. The bergs were covered with fine blood-wood trees, stringy-bark, and box. At a distance from the river the trees became scanty and scattered, and still farther, small plains extended, clothed but sparingly with a wiry grass. These plains were bounded by a forest of the acacia of Expedition Range. Running parallel with the river, were large and deep lagoons full of large and various fish, and covered with the broad leaves of the villarsia and nymphæa. Such was the scenery of the Mitchell, as first seen. Near here they had the misfortune to find their pony poisoned by eating some deleterious plant, or bitten by a serpent. It was swollen, bleeding from the mouth, and dead, when found. Here they killed another of their cattle. On the Lynd they had also, for the first time, become acquainted with the green ant, which lives in trees, and is such a nuisance to those who pass under. In the Mitchell they now, for the first time also, saw the crocodile. This was a proof that they were approaching the sea. They now began to see a change in the vegetation and the birds. They procured also from the natives a quantity of the nymphæa seeds, which they fried in fat, and found very agreeable and nutritive. They also began to see palm trees larger than the corypha, some forty and fifty feet high.

Dr. Leichhardt, now finding that the Mitchell would lead them too far towards the north, determined to cut across westward to the Gulf of Carpentaria. This he did in latitude 15° 52′ 38″. Having travelled a few miles, they encamped by a lagoon. The kites here were so daring that they hung on the trees over their heads, and whilst at dinner pounced down on their plates, and carried off their meat. One, not satisfied with imitating the harpies of Virgil, snatched a skinned specimen of a new species of honey-bird out of Mr. Gilbert's tin case. What was worse, they found the country swarming with natives, and these of a hostile disposition. They discovered a strong party of them driving off their bullocks, and another party prepared to spear them. The firing of a gun put them to flight, but they did not abandon their hostile intentions. The next day the party travelled about nine miles over a beautiful country of plains, forest lands, and chains of lagoons. They crossed a stream which they believed to be the Nassau; and at evening they encamped by a lagoon surrounded by a narrow belt of small tea trees. At night, under cover of these tea trees, the treacherous natives stole upon them, and, when the part had just retired to rest, attacked them with a shower of spears, which killed the naturalist, Mr. Gilbert. The scene is thus described by Leichhardt:—

"As the water occupied the lower part of this basin only, I deposited our luggage in the upper part. Mr. Roper and Mr. Calvert made their tent within the belt of trees, with its opening towards the heap of luggage, whilst Mr. Gilbert and Murphy constructed theirs amongst the little trees, with its entrance from the camp. Mr. Phillips's was, as usual, far from the others, and at the opposite side of the water. Our fire-place was made outside of the trees, on the banks. Brown had shot six whistling ducks and four teal, which gave us a good dinner, during which the principal topic of conversation was our probable distance from the sea coast, as it was here that we first found broken sea-shells at the fires of the natives. After dinner, Messrs. Roper and Calvert retired to their tent, and Mr. Gilbert, John, and Brown, were platting palm-leaves to make a hat, and I stood musing near their fire-place, looking at their work, and occasionally joining in their conversation. Mr. Gilbert was congratulating himself upon having succeeded in learning to plat; and when he had nearly completed a yard, he retired with John to their tent. It was about seven o'clock, and I stretched myself on the ground, as usual, at a little distance from the fire, and fell into a doze, from which I was suddenly roused by a loud noise, and a call for help from Calvert and Roper. Natives had suddenly attacked us. They had doubtless watched our movements during the forenoon, and marked the position of the different tents, and as soon as it was dark, sneaked upon us, and threw a shower of spears at the tents of Calvert, Roper, and Gilbert, and a few at that of Phillips, and also one or two towards the fire. Charley and Brown called for caps, which I hastened to find, and as soon as they were provided, they discharged their guns into the crowd of natives, who instantly fled, leaving Calvert and Roper pierced with several spears, and severely beaten by their waddies. Several of these spears were barbed, and could not be extracted without difficulty. I had to force one through the arm of Roper, to break off the barb, and to cut another out of the groin of Mr. Calvert. John Murphy had succeeded in getting out of the tent and concealing himself behind a tree, whence he fired at the natives, and severely wounded one of them before Brown had discharged his gun. Not seeing Mr. Gilbert, I asked for him, when Charley told me that our unfortunate companion was no more! He had come out of his tent with his gun, shot and powder, and handed them to him, when he instantly dropped down dead. Upon receiving this affecting intelligence, I hastened to the spot, and found Charley's account too true. He was lying on the ground at a little distance from our fire, and upon examining him, I soon found, to my sorrow, that every sign of life had disappeared. The body was, however, still warm, and I opened the veins of both arms, as well as the temporal artery, but in vain; the stream of life had stopped, and he was numbered with the dead.

"As soon as we recovered from the panic into which we were thrown by this fatal event, every precaution was taken to prevent another surprise. We watched through the night, and extinguished our fires, to conceal our individual position from the natives.

"A strong wind blew from the southward, which made the night distressingly cold; it seemed as if the wind blew through our bodies. Under all the circumstances that had happened, we passed an anxious night in a state of most painful suspense as to the fate of our still surviving companions. Mr. Roper had received two or three spear wounds in the scalp of his head; one spear had passed through his left arm, another into his cheek, below the jugal bone, and penetrated the orbit and injured the optic nerve, and another in his loins, besides a heavy blow on the left shoulder. Mr. Calvert had received several severe blows from a waddi; one on the nose, which had crushed the nasal bones; one on the elbow, and another on the back of his hand; besides which a barbed spear had entered his groin. Both suffered great pain, and were scarcely able to move. The spear that had terminated poor Gilbert's existence had entered the chest between the clavical and the neck, but made so small a wound, that for some time I was unable to detect it. From the direction of the wound, he had probably received the spear when stooping to leave his tent.

"The dawning of the morning, the 29th, was gladly welcomed, and I proceeded to examine and dress the wounds of my companions more carefully than I had been able to do in the darkness of the night. Very early, we heard the cooëes of the natives, who seemed wailing, as if one of their number was either killed or severely wounded; for we found stains of blood on their tracks. They disappeared, however, very soon, for on reconnoitring the place, I saw nothing of them. I interred the body of our ill-fated companion in the afternoon, and read the funeral service of the Church of England over him. A large fire was afterwards made over the grave, to prevent the natives detecting and disturbing the body. Our cattle and horses, fortunately, had not been molested."—P. 307.

Almost every Australian expedition of exploration seems as if it must have its victim, and thus fell poor Gilbert, a martyr to his zeal in his pursuit of knowledge of natural history. For fear of the return of the natives, and of their injuring or killing their cattle and horses, the party was compelled to proceed on their journey, notwithstanding the wounded condition of Calvert and Roper; but although the shaking of the horses on which they were mounted was extremely painful, their wounds healed well and rapidly, no doubt from the healthy state of their bodies from constant exercise and simple diet.

On the 1st of July they left this disastrous spot, and travelled on towards the gulf till the 5th, when they came in sight of it. Their journey was over plains abounding with emus and pandanus groves, with ant-hills built up like turretted pillars five feet high, in rows and clusters, presenting a strange appearance. They also found a middle-sized, shady tree, with a leaf like an elm, bearing a sort of oblong, yellow plum, with a rather rough stone. They called this tree the Nonda, from one resembling it in the Moreton Bay district. The natives and the emus fed largely on it, and the travellers found it very agreeable. On reaching a salt-water creek lined with mangrove trees, Brown speared a mullet, and they then came upon a fine salt-water river, whose banks were covered with an open, well grassed forest.

"The first sight of the salt water," says Leichhardt, "was hailed by all with feelings of indescribable pleasure, and by none more than by myself, although tinctured with regret in not having succeeded in bringing my whole party to the end of what I was sanguine enough to think the most difficult part of my journey.

We had now discovered a line of communication by land between the eastern coast of Australia and the Gulf of Carpentaria. We had travelled along never failing, and, for the most part, running waters, and over an excellent country, available, almost in its whole extent, for pastoral purposes." Having reached this first great point in their journey, they remained in camp the whole day, to rest the animals; and some of the men went to fish, hoping to catch enough to dry and carry with them, but were disappointed in the quantity.

They were now come upon that great region of plains on the south-eastern side of the Gulf of Carpentaria, which Captain Stokes thought so favourable for a settlement, and as a point of departure into the interior. From the 7th of July to the 9th they travelled over such plains till they reached Van Diemen River, which they found seventy or eighty yards broad, with steep banks, and a fine sandy bed, containing detached pools of water surrounded by polygonum. The country around was a fine, open, grassy, forest land, in which the apple-gum prevailed, and with many swampy, grassy lagoons, covered with white, blue and pink nymphæas. Acacias, mangrove-myrtle trees, and Grevilleas abounded on their way thither. Suddenly one evening, a native stood in the midst of their camp, as much surprised to see himself there as they were at the apparition. He had, no doubt, mistaken the fire for that of his own people. On discovering his error, he climbed up into a tree, whence it was in vain to persuade him to descend. He stood and birred and poohed, and spat at them, frantically shouting "Mareka! Mareka!" He then began to sing his most lamentable corroboric songs, and then cried like a child. As nothing could pacify him, as, on approaching him, he broke off branches and flung at them, they at length retired to a distance to allow him to descend, which he did in quick time, and disappeared. The next morning the whole tribe appeared at a distance, armed, and watching them depart, but not venturing to approach.

They passed much euphorbia on the plains, which the horses eat without damage, and also native melons, which were tolerable when peeled. The kites were as audacious here as before, and one pounced down and carried off out of the doctor's hand the fat gizzard of a bustard, which he was just going to grill. About thirteen miles more south, they crossed a small river, in a very beautiful and grassy country, which they named the Gilbert, after their lost companion. The camps of the natives were numerous, and various Grevilleas, bauhinias, Balfourias, box, and apple-gums abounded. They saw at the native camps, huts four or five feet high, and eight or ten feet in diameter; one of them was storied, as those at the Lynd. They were thatched with straw or tea-tree bark. On the 17th they reached the river Carron, which was rather a large creek, dry, but having parallel lagoons near it, covered with nymphæas, and made pleasant by forests of Grevillea and the beautiful drooping tea-tree. Charley occasionally shot an emu or a black ibis, but not sufficient to satisfy him, and he said it was a miserable country, nothing to shoot at, nothing to look at but box-trees and ant-hills. The Doctor, however, thought squatters would form a different opinion of it. As they advanced the game increased, and they killed above fifty ducks, spoonbills, etc., and three emus.

Crossing the Plains of Promise of Captain Stokes, they suddenly surprised a native camp, where the people all escaped except a little boy, who had been asleep. He was very much frightened, but defended himself manfully, throwing a stick at Leichhardt, and struggling stoutly when the Doctor caught hold of him to give him a present. His mother, seeing this, came down a hill to meet him, and joked him, and laughed at his adventure, perceiving that no harm was meant. On the 6th of August they had reached the river Albert, having seen evidence all the way of a numerous native population, and finding in one place the foot of an emu very well carved in the bark of a tree. In one case they had to discharge their pistols over the heads of the blacks, who came out against them armed. In some of their camps they found good supplies of convolvulus roots and terminalia gum. Here they killed another bullock. They had also crossed a river, which has since been named Leichhardt's River.

Emus and other game were plentiful on these plains. On the 20th of August they arrived at a small, but running river, in longitude 138° 55′, which they named the Nicholson, after an early patron of Dr. Leichhardt's, Dr. Nicholson of Bristol. On the 25th of August, on a lagoon they saw the contrivance, which they had noticed once before, of the natives to take emus. They had made a fence of dry sticks all round the lagoon, except at one place, and lying in wait for these birds when they came to drink, as soon as they entered the margin of the lagoon through the opening, they ran forward and entered after them. As these birds cannot fly, they were now in a complete trap, and easily killed.

Still journeying along the Gulf, they crossed successively a number of creeks and small rivers, Moonlight Creek, Smith's Creek, the Marlow, Turner's Creek, Wentworth's Creek, the Van Alphen of the Dutch navigators, Calvert's River, and on the 9th of September camped on Abel Tasman's River, in longitude 137° 23′. Here they came upon a rocky country, where they least expected it, and they encamped at a little creek running through a sandstone channel. Instead of the silence which had long prevailed at night, here a variety of sounds enlivened it. Frogs croaked amongst the reeds, crickets chirped, and owls hooted. They heard the cries of goat-suckers and the bleating of wallabies, that came down to drink, and were alarmed at the horses. Fish splashed in the water, and mosquitoes hummed. The banks of the river showed Cycas palms; the glucking bird was heard again. The pandanus fruit, fine-looking, was ripe, but took the skin off their mouths in eating it, and was only rendered mild by scraping off the pulp and boiling it.

In longitude 137° 5' they came to a river, which they called Seven Emu River, because they killed so many young emus there, and now travelled on through a succession of zamia and cycas groves, and scrubs of teatree and salicornia, to a river, which they called the Robinson. Here they observed in the camps of the natives that they first boiled the pandanus fruit, to obtain the sweet substance between its fibres, and then roasted it for the kernels. They were falling into a desperate condition as regarded shirts and other clothing, and had only preserved their shoes by wearing mocassins of bullock hide over the softer country. Mr. Gilbert's stock of clothes had been divided amongst them, and aided a little. Their tea was also exhausted, as their sugar had long been. They pounded and boiled the seeds of the sterculia for a beverage. The emus here they found so dry that they did not furnish oil enough to fry their own flesh. The leguminous iron-bark, the white-barked tree of Tasman, the fig-tree, and sterculia grew in the forest.

On the 21st of September they were stopped by the largest salt-water river which they had seen, and had to ascend it a great way before they could cross it. They named it Macarthur, after James and William Macarthur of Camden. They here discovered that the hide of bullocks made good soup, and henceforward this became a great resource to them, even pieces of hide that had long been dried and used to cover other things. They discovered here, too, that the fruit of the drooping grevillea had a great power of raising blisters, and also of rendering the skin where it touched black as nitrate of silver. The bean of the Mackenzie now furnished them their coffee: they were reduced to all kinds of experiments to live.

On October the 6th they saw an island out at sea, which they believed to be what was marked in Arrowsmith's map as Cape Maria. This was a place notable to the travellers from the sacrifice demanded. The diminished number of the pack-bullocks, and the exhausted condition of both them and the horses, compelled them to reduce their baggage. Dr. Leichhardt had to abandon his paper for drying plants, his specimens of woods, and a small collection of specimens of rocks made by Mr. Gilbert, as well as all the duplicates of the zoological specimens. Such a sacrifice could not be made without a lively regret.

Near this point they discovered a river, which from falling into the Limmen Bight, they called the Limmen Bight River. In the swamps near it they found the younger leaves of the bulrush tolerable eating. They were now again amongst wild geese and ducks, alligators, and thickets of acacia. In crossing the river they saw a long, funnel-shaped, fish-trap, made by the natives of the flexible stems of flagellaria. The latitude was now 15° 13′ (?) and longitude, 135° 30′. From the Limmen Bight River to one which they called the Wickham, they passed over stony ranges, and amongst lagoons, and through scrubby country, and saw southward four flat-topped cones of sand-stone, which they named The Four Archers, from four brothers of that name at Moreton Bay. The country abounded with wallabies and large kangaroos. After leaving the Wickham they lost their kangaroo dog, through fatigue and thirst, a great loss to them, as he had furnished their table on many an occasion.

They now struck westward across the great Arnhem peninsular, for Port Essington, and on October the 10th, they came upon a river flowing from the west towards the Bight, which they named after one of the party, the Roper. The country was still of the same character, the natives numerous. In passing this river, which lay deep between muddy banks, they had three of their horses drowned, and here, in fact, misfortunes began to come rapidly upon them with their cattle. This obliged the Doctor to abandon a great part of his botanical collections, as well as that of Mr. Gilbert. On the 23rd of October they named a creek Hodgson's Creek, and soon after the river Roper divided into two branches, the northern branch of which they named the Wilton.

Following the more eastward flowing branch they again had a horse drowned, by which their horses were reduced to nine. The country still continued rocky. Round the water holes grew a species of native tobacco. On the 27th they found themselves on fine grassy plains, but were nearly surprised again in their camp by hostile natives. They were able to shoot abundance of flying foxes. Their cattle were growing very much exhausted with the heat and rocky roads, but they were so urged by necessity they could give them very little rest. They were compelled soon to kill two other bullocks for food, and became more and more involved amongst rocks and gullies. They had but one bullock left, when, on the 24th of November, they reached the South Alligator River, about 60 miles from its mouth, and 140 miles from Port Essington. The bed of the river was densely fringed with pandanus; the hollows and flats were covered with groves of drooping tea-trees. Ridges of sand-stone and conglomerate approached the river in several places, and at their base were seen some fine reedy and rushy lagoons, teeming with wild fowl, and around them were black ibises, and white and black cockatoos. As they advanced they were impeded by great swamps, and the water pools swarmed with wild fowl.

On the 26th they fell in with natives, who had an English shawl and neckerchief, and an iron tomahawk, showing their vicinity to white people. They knew Pichenelumbo, Van Diemen's Gulf, and pointed northwest when the travellers asked for it. Amongst these swamps and lagoons, interspersed by rich grassy plains, they had plenty of fish and game, and they understood the use of fire-arms, and wanted Brown to go and shoot geese for them. On the 2nd of December they came upon natives speaking English, and were delighted to hear the words "Commandant!" "Come here!" "Very good!" "What's your name?" etc. They were a well-formed race, and very kind, giving them the rind of the rose-coloured euganea apple; the cabbage of the Seaforthia palm, and the nut-like swelling of the rhizoma of either a grass or sedge, the last being found excellent. One of these natives went as guide with them to the East Alligator, which they reached December 3rd.

The country still abounded with geese and flying foxes, of which the travellers procured numbers. Rocks and hills to the north and east drove them near to the coast. On the 9th of December they saw the track of a buffalo. Natives still flocked around them, from whom the travellers asked for "Allamur," the thick part of the sedge before mentioned. One of these natives, named Nyuall, contrasted the condition of these white people with those of Balanda, Port Essington:—"You no bread, no flour, no rice, no backi, you no good! Balanda plenty bread, plenty flour, plenty rice, plenty backi! Balanda very good!" On the 11th they managed to shoot a buffalo, which put them out of all danger of want of meat, and enabled them to take on their last bullock to Port Essington. These buffaloes had been introduced from Malay to Port Essington and Raffles Bay, and, straying into the forest, were, as the natives asserted, become numerous. Nothing further of moment occurred from this time to the 17th of December, when they arrived at Port Essington. The conclusion of this narrative may be given in their own words :—

"On the Vollir we came on a cart road, which wound round the foot of a high hill; and having passed the garden, with its fine cocoa-nut palms, the white houses, and a row of snug thatched cottages, burst suddenly upon us; the house of the commandant being to the right, and separated from the rest. We were most kindly received by Captain Macarthur, the commandant of Port Essington, and by the other officers, who with the greatest kindness and attention supplied us with everything that we wanted. I was, says Dr. Leichhardt, deeply affected in finding myself again in civilized society, and could scarcely speak, the words growing big with tears and emotion; and even now, when considering with what small means the Almighty had enabled me to perform such a long journey, my heart thrills in grateful acknowledgment of his infinite kindness."

After a month's stay at Port Essington, the party embarked in the schooner Heroine, Captain Mackenzie, and arrived in Sydney on the 29th of March, 1846, where they were naturally received with great exultation.

It had long been imagined that the whole expedition had perished. In 1845 Mr. Hodgson was sent out with a party, to endeavour to ascertain the truth of these rumours, but the reports of the different tribes, and other indications, convinced him that the expedition was safe, and he returned.

A public subscription was now raised to reward the successful adventurers, and £1500 was soon raised. To this the colonial government added £1000; and these sums were presented at a public meeting, at which the speaker of the assembly, Dr., now Sir Charles Nicholson, presided. Of these amounts Dr. Leichhardt received as his portion £1454. The two natives, Brown and Charley were not forgotten, they received about £100.

Leichhardt did not long remain at rest. In the beginning of the year 1847 he set out on an expedition, the object of which was to examine the country between Mitchell's last track and his own; but owing to a series of accidents and mischances which befel his party, he was obliged to return. Nothing daunted, however, by this failure, he showed himself ready to engage in a far more arduous enterprise. The object of the new expedition was to explore the interior of Australia; to discover the extent of Sturt's Desert, and the character of the western and north-western coast, so as to observe the gradual change in animal life from one side of the continent to the other. It is obvious from what Stuart, Gregory, M'Kinlay, Howitt, and others have since seen of this great western desert, that it was next to an impossibility to penetrate through it after a long and exhausting journey from the eastern coast. Instead of a Central, it has been shown to be a Western Desert, and at the spot where Mr. Walker, in 1862, came upon his trail, and saw trees marked with the letter L. namely, in latitude 22°, and longitude 145°, he was moving directly towards this terrible desert, yet was considerably to the east of Landsborough's tract from the Gulf of Carpentaria southward which skirted this desert, at least 250 miles east of M'Kinlay's tract, and 350 miles east of the tract of Burke and Wills, which still only passed partially through it. He had, therefore, little less than 2000 miles still between him and the western coast, and nearly the whole of it through this burning desert, which has still defied every effort to penetrate it in that direction, which has defied all the efforts of explorers from south to north, except those of Burke and Wills at the east of this line, and Stuart's, made by successive efforts from different points. No wonder then that he never reappeared, and that the fate of himself and all his party remains a mystery yet to be solved.

Dr. Leichhardt did not expect himself to complete this overland journey to Swan River in less that two years and a half. He set out in October of 1847 from Sydney for Moreton Bay. He proposed to make his way to the Barcoo, the Victoria River of Mitchell, or to follow his old route as far as Peak Range, before he struck off westward; as his course, however, depended on water, he thought it probable that he should be obliged to reach the Gulf of Carpentaria, and follow up some river to its source. This accomplished, he would endeavour to find the most practicable route to Swan River. By a letter received from him December 6, 1847, his party consisted of six whites and two blacks. The whites were himself, the Messrs. Hentig, Classen, a German, and relative of Leichhardt's, Donald Stuart, and Kelly. His stock consisted of fifty bullocks, twenty of which had been presented to him by J. P. Robinson, and thirty by the government; thirteen mules, twelve horses, and 270 goats. His provisions consisted of 800 pounds of flour, 120 pounds of tea, 100 pounds of salt. He had 250 pounds of shot, and forty pounds of powder. In the letter received from him February the 26th, 1848, he declared his intention of sailing down the Condamine, going to the lagoon, following Mitchell's outward track to the most northern bend of the Victoria, and then proceeding northward to some decided water of the gulf, and then to resume his original course westward. He expected to reach Swan River about the end of 1849 or the beginning of 1850.

But more than that time elapsed, and there were no tidings of him and his party. Fears were first excited for the safety of Leichhardt towards the close of 1850. Three years had nearly elapsed since his departure, and it was now called to mind that, though he had been successful in one expedition, he had failed in another, and Kennedy's fate was ominously mentioned. It was suggested that an expedition should be fitted out for the double purpose of making a journey to the Gulf of Carpentaria, and searching for the lost adventurer; but it was not till the month of January, 1852, that an expedition, under Mr. Hoveden Hely, was sent out for the latter purpose. It consisted of seven white men and three blacks, and was provided with sixteen horses and fifteen mules, and supplied with provisions for nine months. He proposed to proceed from the Darling Downs along the Dawson as far as Peak Range, where, in a spot known to himself, he hoped to find letters or other traces of Leichhardt. In this object he failed, and he wrote from the Balonne River in July to the Colonial Secretary, stating that in consequence of positive assurances by the natives of the murder of a party of white men on a creek ten days' journey from Mount Abundance, he had altered his route. Two blacks, one of whom professed to know all the circumstances of the murder, led him to an old camping place of Sir Thomas Mitchell's, and picked up sheep's bones and other remains as proofs of their story.

The account given by one of the blacks, then only about sixteen, was that he remembered the massacre taking place when he was young; that the cause of offence was the ill-usage of some black women by two blacks acting as guides to the party. They, the natives, followed the party several days, and speared the travellers while they were asleep; that only one shot was fired by the whites, which killed one black; and that the natives had driven off and killed all the horses and mules, but that some of the bullocks had escaped, and were still roaming the forest. In latitude 26° 4' S. Hely's party, on the river Maranoa, received further information from some gins, who told him that, at a place seven days' journey onwards, they would find the scene of the murder, and plenty of saddles and other accoutrements lying about. This story was repeated by other gins, but, on arriving at the place, they found no such indications of the white men, or saddles, and the like. An old woman there said that a big water had swept them away; but the party rightly concluded that had this been the case, various articles belonging to the explorers would still remain in the tribe. Ten miles farther they came on a camping place of Leichhardt's, where his mark was seen on a tree; he could not have been murdered, therefore, at the spot named by the blacks. The scene now again shifted onwards as much farther, and two blacks offered themselves as guides, but, when they were within four days' journey of the spot last named, the blacks absconded. This was in latitude about 25° 21' S. Since then Walker came upon Leichhardt's track considerably farther north in latitude 22° 30' S., between the Belyando and Thomson rivers.

After going on some distance farther, and provisions failing, Hely turned back, and on regaining the Balonne in fourteen days after the desertion of their interpreter, found him there, who excused himself by saying the natives were deceiving them, and would never have led them to the real place of massacre, as they would have been speared in revenge. Hely reached the Darling Downs on his return in four months from the time of his departure thence. The fate of Leichhardt was thus still left in mystery, for though Hely himself fully believed the stories of the blacks, the public did not give the same credit to it. Though all the blacks had kept to the same account, and some of them had accurately described the leading persons of the party, it was regarded as proving nothing but that they had really seen the travellers on their route. The story once invented would be propagated through the tribe, and in the same manner, but no relics of the lost adventurers ever turned up to support the story. For many years there were those in Australia who pertinaciously continued to believe the party alive. Still five, ten, seventeen years have passed over, and the most hopeful must now have ceased to hope. Since them other adventurers have fallen in those deserts of torrid sands, showing how soon the sultry sterility, the waterless and foodless wastes of the interior can pull down human life.

CHAPTER II.

THE EXPEDITION OF CAPTAIN STURT INTO CENTRAL AUSTRALIA IN THE YEARS 1844, 45, AND 46.

Reasons for the expedition.—Sturt's theory of an inland sea.—His hope to clear this up.—His party, and its equipments.—Start August 18, 1844.—Reach Mr. Eyre's station at Moorundi, on the Murray.—Captain Sturt restrained by his instructions from crossing to the North Sea.—Mischiefs of stay-at-home wisdom.—Leave Moorundi accompanied for some distance by Mr. Eyre.—The river Rufus.—Nadbuck and Toonda, black guides.—Laidley's Ponds.—The building rat.—Quit the Darling.—Mitchell, Sturt, Burke, and Wills all make journeys northwards from this point.—Native remembrance of Sir Thomas Mitchell's castigation.—Despatches from Adelaide by three natives.—Their excessive fatigue.—Talkativeness of Camboli.—Mr. Poole reconnoitres a-head.—Sturt moves to Cawndilla Lake.—Measures a base line.—Goes a-head to explore.—Treachery of Topar, a native.—The country destitute of water.—Finds the Clianthus Damperi.—A terrible hurricane.—Break up camp, and advance.—The Coonbaralba Range.—Lewis's Hill.—Stopped by rocks.—Vast desert plains on each side of the ranges.—Mr. Poole goes S.W. to seek Lake Torrens.—Reached Lake Blanche.—Mr. Flood precedes the main party to seek for water.—Tremendous heat.—Flood finds a little creek.—They advance.—See Mounts Lyell and Babbage from the hills.—Curious hollow balls.—Parties go out to seek for water.—Abundance of emus and kangaroos.—A visit from natives.—An excursion eastward.—Burning plains.—News of water northward.—Drays falling to pieces with the heat.—Dreadful travelling in the torrid heat.—Two bullocks killed by it. Mount Arrowsmith, the magnetic hill.—Plague of ants and flies.—Camped in a pleasant glen by deep water in latitude 29° 40′ 14″ S., longitude 141° 30′ 41″.—Detained there by draught for six months.—Their experiences there.—Health of Messrs. Poole and Browne failing.—Captain Sturt and others attacked by scurvy.—The captain with a party rides forward to reconnoitre, carrying water barrels.—Reach within twenty or thirty miles of Cooper's Creek, but driven back.—Two horses abandoned.—Another attempt westward.—Return to the camp.—Discover a grassy valley which they call the Park.—Effects of the heat on the ground and on their implements.—Make an underground room.—All the birds leave.—A solitary native appears.—A desert philosopher.—Chain a line of thirty miles towards Lake Torrens.—Rain and flood in the creek.—Mr. Poole dies.—A monument to him piled on Red Hill.—Captain Sturt proceeds westward with a light party to Lake Blanche.—Verifies Mr. Eyre's character of the country.—Proceed N.W.—The bare desert destroys all idea of an inland sea.—A creek, with native huts and troughs for grinding seeds.—The Stony Desert.—Eyre's Creek.—They return.—Water hole with fish.—Reach their camp, which they name Fort Grey.—Captain Sturt entreats Mr. Browne to return to Adelaide on account of his health, but in vain.—A last effort to penetrate northward.—Endeavour to trace the extent of the Stony Desert eastward.—Report as of a cannon in the desert.—Dismal sandy regions.—Salt Lake.—The Stony Desert again, a gloomy, herbless, treeless region.—Eleven days over this horrid desert.—Exhausted condition of the horses.—Reach Cooper's Creek, and name it.—Sturt's account of this creek.—The natives friendly.—Signs of floods, and abundance of water fowl and fish.—Leave behind a roan horse.—Traced the creek eastward into hollow plains, bearing marks of periodical floods.—Return to Fort Grey.—Leave another horse.—Bawley Plains.—Intense heat again.—Return journey to Adelaide.—Results of this expedition, the explosion of an inland sea, and confirmation of desert, but westward.—Exploration of the southeastern seaboard of South Australia by Governor Grey in 1844.

SIMULTANEOUSLY with the expedition of Leichhardt, two

others were in operation, that of Sir Thomas Mitchell in the north-east of the continent, in which he traced down a considerable river, to which, in an excess of loyalty, he gave the name of Victoria, there being already a Victoria on the western coast, and which eastern river is much better called by its aboriginal name, the Barcoo; and the expedition of Sturt to ascertain the nature of the interior of the continent. Mitchell's discovery lay south-east of Leichhardt's track, and was followed up by the unfortunate Kennedy, who found another river which he named the Thomson falling into it, and traced the united stream, or channel of a stream, S.S.W. into latitude 26° 13′ 9″, longitude 142° 20′, that is, into the immediate vicinity of Cooper's Creek, with which it is, no doubt, connected, Sturt's position of Cooper's Creek being latitude 27° 46′, longitude 141° 51′.

The reason for Captain Sturt again taking the field after sixteen years of quiet domestic life, are detailed by him in the opening of his account of this expedition. He had adopted an opinion that what is now the continent of Australia, had formerly been an archipelago of islands, and that the immense plains into which not only himself, but Oxley, Cunningham, and Mitchell had descended in proceeding towards the centre of the continent had been the sea-beds of the channels which had once separated the islands. All that Mitchell, Grey, and Eyre had done in their attempts to penetrate the burning and sandy deserts towards the interior, had only confirmed this idea. In an overland expedition which Captain Sturt had made in 1838, from Sydney, along the Murray to Adelaide, a journey which had also been made by Mr. Eyre and other gentlemen, Captain Sturt found that the channel of the Murray was one great fossil bed, and that the city of Adelaide stood on the same great fossil bed. It, therefore, appeared to him that a great ocean current had sometime set in from the north, and had swept southward, carrying the enormous mass of shells along with it, till being checked southward by some cause, probably by the accumulation of sand, this bed had been there deposited and covered with sand. Finally, he says :—" The information which I had collected as to the extent of the fossil bed, and my own past experience, led me to the following conclusions. That the continent of Australia has been subjected to great changes from subigneous agency, and that it had been bodily raised to its present level above the sea; that as far as we can judge, the north and north-east portions of the continent are higher than the southern or south-west portions of it; and that there has been consequently a current or rush of waters from the one point to the other, that this current was too divided in its progress into two branches by hills, or some other intervening obstacle, and that one branch of it, following the line of the Darling, discharged itself into the sea, through the opening between the western shore of Encounter Bay and Cape Bernouilli ; that the other taking a more westerly direction, escaped through the Great Australian Bight. From what I could judge, the desert I traversed is about the breadth of that remarkable line of coast, and I am inclined to think that the desert retains its breadth the whole way, or it comes gradually round to the south, thus forming a double curve, from the Gulf of Carpentaria, on the N.E. angle of the continent, to the Great Bight on the south-west coast."

For these reasons Captain Sturt imagined that the province of South Australia had been an island. He set out with the impression that he should probably find that in the centre of the continent, the sea-current cut off southward by accumulations of sand or by the elevation of the land by subterranean powers, yet remained as a great internal sea, probably surrounded by deserts of sand. This was the question which he proposed, if successful, to settle. He, therefore, addressed a letter to Lord Stanley, the present Lord Derby, tendering his services for the object. The scheme was supported by Sir Ralph Darling, under whose auspices he had performed his previous and most valuable expeditions, and this offer was accepted. Captain Sturt was now a resident at Adelaide, and Captain Grey, the explorer of the western coast, the Governor of South Australia. Under such circumstances, the expedition was likely to have all necessary advantages. On the 12th of August, 1844, the expedition was prepared to set out. It consisted of:—

Captain Sturt, *Leader.*
Mr. James Poole, *Assistant.*
„ John Harris Browne, *Surgeon.*
„ M'Dougall Stuart, *Draftsman.*
„ Louis Piesse, *Storekeeper.*
Daniel Brock, *Collector.*
George Davenport, } *Servants.*
Joseph Cowley,
Robert Flood, *Stockman.*
David Morgan, *attender on the horses.*
Hugh Foulkes,
John Jones,
—— Turpin, } *Bullock Drivers.*
William Lewis, *sailor.*
John Mack.
John Kirby, *with the sheep.*

Besides these, two natives, Camboli from near Lake Bonney on the Murray, and Nadbuck from another part of the Murray, attended them, one as far as his tribe on the Murray, the other to Williorara on the Darling. Nadbuck was an elderly man, but active, bustling, and very gallant to the ladies, as well as politic in his proceedings with the other natives. He was very useful, and grew very much attached to them while with them.

They had eleven horses, thirty bullocks, a boat and boat-carriage, one horse-dray, one spring-cart, three drays, two hundred sheep, four kangaroo dogs, two sheep dogs. The instruments sent out of England were but indifferent, and the tubes of the barometers were soon broken, which prevented them calculating accurately the altitude of hills. After sending the drays on before to Moorundi, Mr. Eyre's station on the Murray,

Captain Sturt breakfasted with a party of friends at Mr. Torrens', on the 15th, and then mounted his horse, and rode after his party. He had had his sheep shorn that they might travel more coolly; and he remarks, that during the time that he was in the hot regions, the wool ceased altogether to grow, as did their own hair and nails, a sufficient fact for those who profess to believe that sheep-stations may be extended into those regions. With this exception, the sheep bore the journey extremely well, and continued fat in the hottest desert, and most burnt-up deserts, but their flesh lost nearly all taste.

On the 18th of August, Captain Sturt arrived at Mr. Eyre's residence at Moorundi, on the banks of the Murray, where he and Mr. Gilles had purchased a government section of land of 4000 acres, and with which they would have a wide range of the waste pasture land for their cattle, some of the richest meadow land on the Murray. There Mr. Eyre was also district magistrate, and protector of the aborigines. On reaching the neighbourhood of Moorundi, they saw one of their horses, which had been taken wild from the bush on the Murray, and had escaped from the paddock at Adelaide, and was agreeably at home amongst the horses of the settlers at Moorundi. They caught him, and took him, and he was the first of three horses which they had to abandon in the desert.

In the instructions from Lord Stanley, or rather from Sir John Barrow, to whom the captain's proposed plans had been referred, Captain Sturt was restrained from prosecuting the whole of his intentions. Sir John in his wisdom, talked almost familiarly of a range of mountains running from N.E. to S.W., about latitude 28° or 29°. That this range must divide the waters, some running thence north, the others running south from this line of mountains. So Captain Sturt was on no account to attempt to cross this line and trace any river up to the north coast, but to confine himself to ascertaining the existence of this range, and the rivers running out of it southwards. By this stay-at-home wisdom, always the most confident, Sturt's farthest north instead of being as it turned out, nearly in latitude 24°, would have stopped about Cooper's Creek. It is needless to say that no such range of mountains existed; but what was worse, Sir John prescribed the very route for him direct north from Adelaide, from which Mr. Eyre had been so relentlessly driven back by the inhospitable and furnace-like desert. Fortunately Lord Stanley left the captain his choice of this route, or that by the Darling, and of course, he went by the Darling, as he had proposed; but he was "*absolutely prohibited*," from endeavouring to cross the continent, and that simply on the principle of *economy*. The great problem which all scientific men and accomplished travellers were most anxious to solve, that of the practicability of a passage across the continent from south to north, or *vice versâ*, was hence absolutely prohibited. In the captain's case, more imperative causes than any mortal commands limited his progress, or in a more favourable season he might have reached the north coast seventeen years earlier than it was done from this point, for he was at his farthest fast approaching a more travelable country.

On leaving Moorundi, Mr. Eyre, who, though he had been ambitious of conducting an expedition in this direction himself, had done everything to promote Captain Sturt's views, accompanied him and his party for some days along the Murray. We may pass over the well-known ground, and the grassy meadows of this track, to Lake Bonney, and to the 5th of September, where, amid luxuriant herbage, and fine woodland, they came upon a herd of fifty wild cattle, and shot a fine bull. On the 7th, they arrived at Camboli's tribe, where he left them. On arriving at the Rufus, the channel between the Lake Victoria and the Murray, they were at Nadbuck's home, where he remained awhile, but came after them again. At this place, some time before, the natives had attacked a party of overlanders under a Mr. Robinson, and had been fighting with it three days, when they were suddenly attacked in the rear by a party of police, who just came up in time to prevent the entire massacre of Mr. Robinson's party. The natives now showed the travellers a mound, under which thirty of their relatives lay, who were killed on that occasion; but they did not seem to harbour any resentment on that account. Here Mr. Eyre returned.

Captain Sturt now followed the ana-branch of the Darling northwards. Nadbuck rejoined the party, and they were also joined by another native of Williorara, named Toonda. Just before reaching the ana-branch of the Darling, Robert Flood, the stockman, had the accident to blow off the greater part of the fingers of his right hand in charging his gun, at full gallop after some wild cattle, and having foolishly put the cap on first; but Mr. Brown attended to him, and he did well. On the journey, Toonda was very indignant at their shooting a kangaroo, saying, "Kangaroo mine, sheep yours!" but soon after, coming for his share of a sheep killed, the captain said, "No! sheep mine; kangaroo yours!" which soon taught him a different creed. Progressing through the monotonous flats of the Darling, little worth recording occurred till they reached Laidley's Ponds. They managed to catch one of the rats first seen by Mitchell on the Darling, which build large conical heaps of small sticks in the bushes, five feet in diameter, and three feet high. In these they had several nests, and also a store-room under ground, from which habit they have been named *Mus conditor*. The natives gave the travellers a fearful account of the rocky hills and burnt up regions to the north, but not worse than proved to be true. The ground over which they were then travelling had been flooded, but was now cracked into great fissures of much depth, into which the cattle and the dray wheels fell, and made it difficult to proceed at all. The natives were numerous, but friendly.

Suddenly they came to a watercourse, into which the floods of the Darling were pouring with great violence, and this, they were informed, was the Williorara, or

Laidley's Ponds. No doubt they were called ponds, from forming only a chain of water-holes when the water was low; but now, after much rain, the Darling flowed furiously through this channel into two lakes, called Michandiche and Cawndilla, lying westward of the river. Here the Darling trended away to the N.E., and at this point, therefore, they were to leave it.

This is a remarkable spot, for on the left bank of the river, just opposite to where they were now encamped, Sir Thomas Mitchell had his camp in 1836, and from this place returned to the Murray. Here now was Captain Sturt, in 1844. In 1860, here stopped Burke and Wills, in their route for Carpentaria. Captain Sturt, in speaking of Sir Thomas Mitchell, does not fail to observe that the only bit of praise which Sir Thomas ever bestowed on him was for the correctness of his sketch of the junction of the Murray and Darling, which he himself says was so unlike that passing the place in 1838, he could scarcely recognise any likeness at all: that in fact, it was not the sketch which he made, for having lost that, he got a friend to make one from a verbal description, when he himself was blind, and could not do it. It was this Williorara tribe with which Sir Thomas had his famous skirmish near Lake Benanee, and they had by no means forgotten or forgiven it. Mr. Poole, who was short and stout, like Sir Thomas, and wore a blue foraging cap like him, was taken for him, and there was a danger of his being speared; but Captain Sturt assured them that he was quite another person, and Mr. Poole prudently laid aside his cap, and wore a straw hat, to weaken the resemblance, whilst there. Whilst here, Camboli arrived, with two other natives, from Lake Victoria, with letters and despatches from Adelaide. The three had travelled at such a rate to overtake them, that they were dreadfully fatigued, especially Camboli. His thighs and ankles, and the calves of his legs were much swollen, and he complained of severe pains in his back and loins; yet so great was his delight, that he could not keep himself still, but jumped about, and exclaimed, "Papung! I bring papung (papers) to Boocolo,"—meaning the Captain—"to Sacoback,"—meaning Doctor Browne; and "Mr. Poole, from Gobbernor,"—the Governor; "Hugomattin," Mr. Eyre; "Merrille," Mr. Scott, of Moorundi; and Bullockey Bob. "Papung! Gobbernor! Boocolo! Hugomattin!" Nothing could stop him. They were now, according to Sir Thomas Mitchell's date, in latitude 32° 25′ S., and longitude 142° 5′ E.

The character given by the natives, of the country to the northward, induced Captain Sturt to send on Mr. Poole with a reconnoitring party in that direction; but he returned with a report of rocky ranges, and next to no water. Here it was plain that their difficulties were to begin, and the Captain shifted the camp from Williorara to Cawndilla Lake, where there was more grass, and where he could make an exploration himself. On the 17th of October, they encamped at Cawndilla, but still on the Williorara, about half a mile from where it falls into the lake, and fortified themselves, so as not to be liable to any attack from the natives. Here they were visited by the Boocolo, or chief of the tribe; a friendly old man, of much superior bearing and habits to the natives generally. Indeed, the Captain says his manners were fit for a European drawing-room. At meal times, he delicately kept away from the table, never asked for anything, and, if offered something, received it with dignity, and ate it without displaying the greedy voracity which natives in general exhibit over their meals. If anything were stolen, he had only to be informed, and it was soon brought back.

The camp being fixed at Cawndilla on the 19th, Captain Sturt measured a base line of six miles, and then set out to make an examination of the country a-head himself. He took with him Mr. Browne, Flood, and Morgan. A young native, named Topar, had been recommended to Captain Sturt by Mr. Eyre, and he took him also with him, but soon found him most untrustworthy. They passed some miserable plains, almost wholly destitute of water, in a N.N.W. direction, and then more northward towards the range of hills which Mr. Poole had seen. On these plains they saw, flowering in all its beauty, the *Clianthus Damperi*, since generally called Sturt's Desert Pea. On the 24th they entered the hills, the basis of which was slaty, ferruginous rock, but along the ridges was a line of the finest hepatic iron-stone. From the presence of this stone, the compass deviated 37° from the north point, and they could not depend on the angles they took there. They had advanced about sixty miles, and now returned to the camp, but not before experiencing a hurricane, which tore off their hats and caps, and rent up bushes of atriplex, and sent them bounding along the plain like so many foot-balls.

On the 28th of October they broke up their camp to venture along the unpromising road they had just examined. Mr. Browne went first with two or three men and the light cart, to enlarge the few wells they had seen so that the cattle might drink out of them; and soon after the Captain and the rest of the expedition followed. They took a friendly leave of the old Boocolo, and on the 29th reached a well at a place called Curnpaga, and the next day came to a pool in the hills amongst rocks called Parnari, where they remained till the 5th of November in examining the country, and taking bearings from the loftiest points of the Coonbaralba Range. The weather was intensely hot, and men and cattle all suffered greatly. In fact, from this time, a year and five months, to which the journey extended, the story is one of the most intense and unremitting suffering.

On the 5th of November the Captain and Mr. Browne again set out to reconnoitre the route. They took with them a cart loaded with water. They went on winding their way amongst the hills towards the N.W. as well as they could, but by the 7th their tanks had leaked so much as to be useless, and they sent two men with the cart back to the camp, and went on with other two men. They named a hill which they ascended Lewis's Hill, the formation of which was a fine granite. From this hill they obtained a pretty clear notion of the sort of country into which they were advancing; rocky ranges, and outside of them immense and most sterile plains. They were soon completely stopped by the rocks, and compelled to find their way down into the plains. They were now in latitude 31° 32′ 17″ S. When down in the plains they could not follow the outlines of the hills, and then glance over the apparently boundless plains beyond them, without a conviction that these ranges once looked over the waters of an ocean, as they then looked over a sea of scrub. The direction of the hills was nearly north and south, and extending each way to a distance beyond the range of vision or telescope. From their latitude the party were then nearly half a degree to the south of Mount Lyell, and a degree to the south of Mount Serle. They continued this journey along the plains at the foot of the hills till the 20th, when they again ascended the hills. The weather had become rainy, and they now saw the plains flashing with waters. On this they determined to return to the camp and bring on the party thus far. They reached the camp on the 18th, and on the 20th Mr. Poole was sent off in a north-west direction to see if he could reach Lake Torrens, whilst the main party advanced to the spot which had been attained by the Captain and Mr. Browne. Mr. Browne now agreed to accompany Mr. Poole, and the Captain accompanied the main party onwards. On the 29th they encamped at the foot of the hills after having crossed them, and awaited at a well Messrs. Poole and Browne. These gentlemen reappeared at the camp on the 2nd of December. They had travelled N.N.W. till the 26th, that is, six days over these monotonous plains, under such intense heat that the pack-horses fell exhausted. That day they ascended a sand-hill, and saw Mount Serle due west at 50 miles distance. They then directed their course towards it, and on the 28th they saw a lake in a sandy bed, stretching north and south, which they had no doubt was Lake Torrens, but which in reality was Lake Blanche.

On the return of these gentlemen the Captain sent Flood forward in a northern direction, to ascertain what water was on the route, ordering him not to exceed sixty or seventy miles, but in the event of finding water within that distance to return immediately. The heat was now fearful, the thermometer seldom falling below 96°, and rising to 112° and 125° in the shade. The surface of the ground never cooled, and it was difficult to retain any stone in the hands that had been exposed to the sun; still there had been no hot wind. The horses that Messrs. Poole and Browne had had out had suffered a great deal, and the horses and cattle were now consuming daily from 1000 to 1100 gallons of water. They drank a fearful quantity, and what was to become of them should it fail anywhere on their journey under such heat?

Flood returned on the 7th. He had found a beautiful little creek, at the distance of forty miles, but none nearer. He brought the news that the Barrier Range, along the western side of which they were travelling, appeared to decline gradually northward, and as about to cease altogether. On the 9th the party moved on. Mounting the hills as they journeyed, the Captain saw Mount Lyell to the N.E. by N., distant fifty or sixty miles; and Mount Babbage just visible to the N.E. In crossing the stony plains to Flood's Creek they picked up a number of round balls of all sizes, from that of marbles to that of a cannon-ball. They were perfect spheres, and hollow, like shells, being formed of clay and sand, cemented by oxide of iron. Some of these were clustered like grape-shot, and some had rings round them like Saturn's ring: the plains were covered with them in places.

Though the heat was so intense, near the creek all looked green, and the grasses had not yet gone to seed. The animals were up to their knees in luxuriant vegetation. A native wheat, a beautiful oat, and a rye, as well as a variety of grasses, were found there. Whilst pausing here, the Captain sent out Messrs. Poole and Browne, with a fortnight's provisions, to hunt forwards to the N.E. for water; and Flood was sent along the feet of the hills on the same errand. Such was the caution with which Captain Sturt found it necessary to act in this broiling and arid country.

There was an abundance of emus and kangaroos: in every bush and tree there was a nest of some kind; and there were various vegetables, of which the natives are fond; yet they saw very few natives. One morning three women were seen, and taking Tampawang, a native going with the party, Captain Sturt rode to them. They endeavoured to get away, but the ground was very stony, and the horses soon overtook them. They were an old woman and two younger ones. The Captain explained to them when they became calm, for they were very much frightened, that he wanted the black fellows to come and see him, and taking the knife which hung from Tampawang's neck by a string, he showed them the use of it, and then putting the string over the old woman's head, patted her on the back, and allowed them to depart. To their surprise, in about an hour and a half afterwards they saw seven natives approaching the camp, with the slowness of a funeral procession. They kept their eyes on the ground, and appeared as if marching to execution. They were the poorest, most emaciated human beings they ever beheld. They were made to sit down under a tree, and a good breakfast and some presents were given them, when they stole away, and were never seen afterwards. They had, no doubt, received the command to visit the camp as from a superior being, and were much frightened. They were perfectly naked, were all circumcised, according to a very general custom amongst the natives of the interior, north and west, but had lost no front teeth.

During the absence of Messrs. Poole and Browne, Captain Sturt, taking Mr. Piesse, the store-keeper, Mr. Stuart and Flood, made an excursion eastward. After crossing the ranges they rode over plains for about sixty miles to another range of hills, the highest of which was Mount Lyell. They found some parts of the plain grassy, but without water, and passed several dry beds of lagoons. Farther on they rode for fifteen miles through a forest of pine and acacia scrub growing in fine sand. The farther they went the more barren the country became. Mount Babbage loomed large to the north-east, but they did not approach it, the whole region was so repulsive. The heat of the season was every day increasing, and on examining the drays on their return, they found the felloes all greatly shrunk, and the tires all loose, requiring well wedging up. The stock was all in good condition, the sheep really fat. The thermometer rose every day. in the shade to $114°$ or $118°$, in the sun to from $140°$ to $150°$.

On the 25th of December Flood returned, having found no water of a permanent character. The same day also returned Messrs. Poole and Browne. They had nearly reached the 28th parallel, and had discovered abundance of water, but the nearest occurrence of it was more than forty miles off. Beyond that to the 29th degree of latitude, they had found other creeks with water, and had climbed the hills and seen still a most barren and forbidding country. At their farthest point north, they travelled ten miles over hot, barren plains, covered with loose stones, where the horses lost their shoes, and compelled them to return.

On the 28th they left Flood's Creek, at half-past four o'clock in the afternoon, and travelling almost day and night, on the 30th, at three in the morning, reached the first water, having had a dreadful pull through heavy sand-ridges, which had killed two of their bullocks. Some of the men and drays did not arrive till the 3rd of January of the new year, and had been 36 hours without water. The bullocks every time they stopped, had pawed the ground to get to a cool bottom; and one of the men's shoe soles were burnt as with fire; the dogs had lost the skins from the soles of their feet, and one of them had died. The back of one man was badly blistered.

On the 3rd of January, 1845, Captain Sturt sent Mr. Stuart to the magnetic hill, Mount Arrowsmith, to verify Mr. Poole's bearing, in consequence of great deviation of the compass there; but Mr. Stuart found the same irregularity. From this time to the 27th of the month they made a desperate advance through a most desert country, what little water there was, fast drying up; and passing through ranges, where the flat-topped hills appeared to have been forced up from the surrounding plains by subterranean force, the surface of the hills being scattered with precisely the same stones, milky quartz, wood-opal, granite, and other rocks, as the plains below, whilst none of these species of rock occurred in the stratification of the ranges. They passed here and there a few huts of natives, and were dreadfully tormented by ants and flies. The glen at which they arrived on the 27th, was, for such a horrible desert, a delightful spot. A stream flowed through a little rocky gorge shaded by trees and cliffs. They pitched their tents on the margin of this creek, by a fine sheet of water, one of the deepest parts of the creek. Their position here was longitude 141° 30′ 41″ E., latitude 29° 40′ 14″ S. Mount Hopeless bore N.N.W. of them, 25 miles further north, the difference of longitude being 171 miles, and their distance from the eastern shores of what was then thought to be Lake Torrens, about 120. There was a small lagoon to the S.E. of them, and around it was a good deal of feed, besides numerous water-holes in the rocky gully. The creek was marked by a line of gum-trees, from the mouth of the glen to its junction with the main branch, in which, except in isolated spots, water was no longer to be found. The Red Hill, afterwards called Mount Poole, bore N.N.W. from them, distant 3½ miles; between them and it there were undulating plains, covered with stones or salsolaceous herbage, excepting in the hollows, where there was a little grass. Behind them were level stony plains, with small, sandy undulations, bounded by brush, over which the Black Hill, bearing S.S.E from the Red Hill was visible, distant 10 miles. To the eastward, the country was hilly. Westward, at a quarter of a mile, the low range through which Depôt Creek, as they named this creek, forces itself, shut out from their view the extensive plains on which it rises. This range extended longitudinally nearly north and south, but was nowhere more than a mile and a half in breadth. The geological formation of the range was slate, traversed by veins of quartz, its interstices being filled by magnesian limestone. Steep precipices, and broken rugged gullies alternated on either side of the creek, and in its bed there were large slabs of beautiful slate. The precipices showed the lateral formation with the rocks split into finest laminæ, terminating in sharp points. But neither on the ranges, nor on the plains behind the camp, was there any feed for the cattle, neither were the banks of the creek, or its neighbourhood, to be put in comparison with Flood's Creek in this respect, for around that there was an abundance as well as a variety of herbage. Pasture they afterwards found at some distance.

Such was the place where they were destined to remain locked up by the elements for six months. They pitched their tents on the 27th of January, 1845, and they were not struck again till the 17th of July following. The fact was, that all the waters before and behind them for vast distances were dried up, and so continued till that period. "It was not," says Sturt, "however, until after we had run down every creek in our neighbourhood, and had traversed the country in every direction, that the truth flashed across my mind, and it became evident to me, that we were locked up in the desolate and heated region into which we had penetrated, as effectually as if we had been wintered at the Pole. It was long, indeed, ere I could bring myself to believe that so great a misfortune had overtaken us, but so it was. Providence had, in its all-wise purposes, guided us to the only spot, in that wide-spread desert, where our wants could have been permanently supplied, but had there stayed our further progress into a region that almost appeared to be forbidden ground. The immediate effect, however, of an arrival at the Depôt, was to relieve my mind from anxiety as to the safety of the party. There was now no fear of our encountering difficulties, and perhaps perishing in want of that life-sustaining element, without which our efforts would have been unavailing."—Vol. i. p. 265.

It was not too soon that they reached this creek. The health of Messrs. Poole and Browne had been gradually failing for some time, as well as that of the men. A few days after their settling here, Mr. Browne had a dangerous illness; the men complained of what they thought was rheumatism, from sleeping on the ground, and Captain Sturt was similarly affected; but it was in reality a much worse ailment—the scurvy. But none of the party were idle. They examined the country round, and endeavoured to converse with the few miserable natives whom they met with, but their language was unknown to their black fellows. Messrs. Browne and Poole not being fit for the enterprise, the Captain took with him Mr. Stuart, and a fine active young fellow, Joseph Cowley. They were on horseback, and they took a one-horse cart with them loaded with water-barrels and provisions, and set out to proceed as far as they could north. In this journey they managed to reach the 28th parallel of latitude, in longitude 141° 18′ E. Another twenty or thirty miles would have brought them to Cooper's Creek, but they had already been compelled to leave behind two of their horses, and push on with one. Nothing but sand-hills, however, were seen ahead, and their water was growing short; they therefore turned back to an intermediate creek, where they left Mr. Stuart and Flood with the cart. From this point the captain made a ride of upwards of 60 miles to the westward, but found only the same sandy desert, burning under a sun at 157° of the thermometer; of 132° in the shade of a tree, the boiling point of water being 211°. On the 22nd of February they regained the camp. On this journey they had discovered one well-grassed valley, which they called the Park. The horse, Punch, which they had taken the whole way, never recovered the effects of its sufferings. Thus hemmed in by frightful, torrid deserts, they knew that even to the Darling they must proceed through a similar country for 250 miles.

On first settling at Depôt Creek, there were thousands of parrots, paroquets, pigeons, bitterns, cockatoos, and other birds. They seemed to collect there preparatory to migration, and they soon went off in a N.W. direction, small flights of ducks and pelicans, on the contrary, coming from that quarter. The captain, notwithstanding the intense heat, continued to make excursions in different directions, but finding everywhere the same drought. To the south all was dry, cutting off return: to the east they came on a salt lagoon, but dry. In the month of April they planted seeds in the bed of the creek, but the moment the young plants appeared above ground, the sun burnt them to cinders. The continued heat was such that the ground was hot to the depth of three or four feet. The mean temperature of December, January, and February had been 101°, 104°, and 101°, respectively in the shade. Under its effects every screw in their boxes had been drawn; and the horn handles of their instruments, as well as their combs, were split into fine laminæ. The lead dropped out of their pencils; their signal rockets were entirely spoiled; their hair, as well as the wool of the sheep ceased to grow, and their nails had become as brittle as glass. The flour had lost more than eight per cent of its original weight, and the other provisions in a still greater proportion. The bran in which the bacon had been packed was perfectly saturated, and weighed almost as heavy as the meat; and they were obliged to bury their wax candles. A bottle of citric acid in Mr. Brown's box became fluid, and escaping, burnt a quantity of his linen; and they found it difficult to write or draw, so rapidly did the fluid dry in the pens and brushes. "It was happy for us," says Captain Sturt, "that a cooler season set in, otherwise I do not think that many of us could much longer have survived. But although it might be said that the intense heat of summer had passed, there still were intervals of most oppressive weather."

To escape from the greatest heat, and to preserve some of their articles, they were obliged to have an underground room constructed, which proved of great service and comfort. Still, Messrs. Poole and Browne were growing every day worse in health from the scurvy, and the captain was little better. The men were not much affected, because they had stayed most of them in the camp, and lived on fresh mutton, while the officers had, in their excursions, used bacon. Once more the captain, with Mr. Browne and Flood, imagining, from heavy clouds having been seen in the direction of Mount Serle, that rain had fallen there, went off in that direction, and hoped that they might thus get forward in a north-west direction; but after riding two days, and finding all still dry and waterless, they returned to the camp. This was towards the end of April. Mr. Poole still grew worse, and Mr. Browne attended him most kindly and assiduously, though himself ill.

On the 11th of May, they had a visit from a solitary old native, who had come whence no one could imagine. He was reduced almost to a skeleton, and drank a great deal of water; then ate as much, says Captain Sturt, as would have served him for four-and-twenty dinners, and being furnished with a blanket, coiled himself up, and slept an immense time. This old man remained at the camp eating and drinking, and showing surprise at nothing. On seeing a sheep net, he thought it a fishing net, and said there were fish in the creek so large that they could not pass through the meshes. He gave them to understand that there was water N. and N.W. and N.E. On showing him the engravings of various fish, he recognised the Murray cod, the hippocampus, the chetodon, amongst sea fish, and the turtle. When he saw the pictures of snakes, he put his hand cautiously on them, and was astonished to feel only the paper. Though they now had had dew, and thunder, and a few drops of rain, he said there would be no rain yet. The old native quitted them on the 17th, first carefully burying the presents they had made him, and saying he should come again, which they believed from this circumstance, but they never saw any more of him.

As the captain now began to fear that the consumption of their provisions would prevent their advancing farther into the country on the return of rain, he determined to send a number of them home. The cattle had laid the ground bare for miles around the camp; the axe had made a broad gap in the gum trees along the creek; and the creek, which had been nine feet deep, had now shrunk to two feet, and from a broad sheet of water into a small line in the centre of the channel. Another month of drought, and they would be left without a drop of water in all that desert! May, June, and the beginning of July, and there was no change of weather. Captain Sturt proposed to endeavour to reach Lake Torrens, when the party to go home had been despatched; and Mr. Stuart and Mr. Piesse, with a party of chainers, chained a line of thirty miles in that direction. The shrunken wheels of the drays were wedged up, and preparations were then made for the departure of this section of the company. Mr. Poole, who was now greatly reduced, was to go with them in the spring cart, properly prepared for the purpose. Meantime, Mr. Poole became very restless; and at his request, he was removed from his tent into the underground room.

At length, on the 14th of July, after many appearances of rain and many disappointments, it came. Flood, who had been out looking after the horses, came and reported that, in the glen, he heard a roaring noise, and soon saw the waters pouring along, foaming and eddying amongst the rocks, and that he was sure there would be a flood; and in fact, in a few days, the creek was rushing onward full to the brim. No time was now lost in sending off the return party; and the captain proposed that, as Mr. Browne was himself very ill, he should return with Mr. Poole. Mr. Browne, though a surgeon by profession, was also a squatter, and had left his station and affairs at the request of the captain to accompany the expedition, where his services had been invaluable in many ways. But no arguments or entreaties could persuade him to leave the expedition under its critical circumstances: he declared, live or die, he should remain, and did remain.

Poor Mr. Poole did not proceed far, when, being raised to take some medicine, he suddenly said he thought he was dying, sunk back, and expired. This delayed the departure of the expedition. His body was brought back, and interred under a Grevillea, which stood close to the underground room. On this tree were cut his initials, above the grave, "J. P., 1845." One day shortly before his death, Mr. Poole had proposed that a pile of stones should be erected on the summit of each of the two neighbouring hills, to make them land marks. Accordingly, to employ the men, the captain had had a pyramid of stones erected, twenty-one feet broad at the base and twenty-one feet high, on the nearest, Red Hill. Little did they think, when doing this, that they were building Mr. Poole's monument; but so it proved, and the hill has since borne the name of Mount Poole. Almost every Australian expedition has demanded its victim, and Mr. Poole was the victim of the expedition into Sturt's Desert.

Immediately after the funeral of Mr. Poole, the camp was broken up, and the party set out north-west, it being the intention of Captain Sturt to see what sort of a country it was betwixt that place and Lake Torrens. The whole distance was chained by them, and found to be 131¾ miles—that is, to Lake Blanch; for what the captain always mistook for Torrens, was this more eastward lake. He found the country exactly of the same desert description, hills and hollows of a brick-red sand, with here and there a little water to be found. The bed of Lake Blanch was empty, and, like Torrens, of soft mud, which did not permit them to proceed far across it. Its bank was a high sand ridge. In one place they managed to dig out a number of jerboas, which they kept alive some time. At another, they came up with two natives who had dug out from 150 to 200 of these little animals, and roasted and ate them all the same evening by the white man's fire.

It must be remembered that Captain Sturt crossed this miserable district immediately after heavy rains, or he would not have found a single drop of water. At about sixty miles of this old camp, they made a new depôt at the grassy meadow, through which ran a clear stream, and which, from its resemblance to an English park, they called the Park. Here, having fixed the camp on a little sandy hill, with a broad view of the Park and a fine sheet of water in the pond, sheltered by gum trees, Captain Sturt ordered the men to form a stockade round the camp, and left it under care of Mr. Stuart, to reconnoitre the country to the north-west. They took all the horses but one with them, and provisions for fifteen weeks. Flood, Lewis, and Joseph accompanied him. They set out on the morning of the 14th of August, and for some time found the country of the same character, sandy and desert. Then they came to a number of creeks and grassy plains. The great flats resembled those of the Darling —gum trees and bauhinias marked the lines of the creeks. On the 22nd, in latitude $27° 38'$ S., longitude $140° 10'$ by account, they came upon a creek in which was a deep hole, where to their astonishment they caught a quantity of fish, wondering how they could possibly have got there. The country, however, soon got worse again, with beds of salt lagoons and saline plants.

In latitude $27° 4' 40''$ S., longitude $139° 10'$ E., they came upon a great plain, of a dark-purple hue, without vegetation, and its horizon like that of the ocean. This plain was covered by a continuous stratum of stones, which lay so thickly that they excluded vegetation. They were of various lengths, from one inch to six, all rounded by attrition and coated with oxide of iron, and evenly distributed. "In going over this stony waste, the horses left no track, and that of the carts was only visible at times. From the spot on which we stopped, no object of any kind broke the line of the horizon. We were as lonely as a ship at sea, and as a navigator seeking for land, only that we had the disadvantage of an unsteady compass, without any fixed point on which to steer. The fragments covering this singular feature were all of the same kind of rock, indurated or compact quartz, and appeared to me to have had originally the form of parallelograms, resembling both in shape and size the shivered fragments lying at the base of the northern ranges, to which I have already called attention."

At ten miles farther they descended into a belt of polygonum of two miles' breadth, and then entered on apparently boundless flats of naked earth like an enormous ploughed field, totally without vegetation; then again they came to the old sort of sand ridges succeeding each other like waves of the sea. All this country Captain Sturt regarded as once the bed of an ocean, the current of which ran towards Spencer's Gulf, but he no longer hoped to find an actual inland sea. Beyond these plains they came on some belts of scrub, and found a creek where were a few miserable natives, and, after many a day, once more saw and heard cockatoos, parrots, pigeons, calodera, crows, &c., in great numbers. By the creek were native huts with troughs and stones for grinding seeds, but no inhabitants. After this creek, and forest on its banks, came a plain cracked into deep gulfs, into which the horses' hind feet and the wheels of the cart continually fell. The horse which they had recaught at the Murray here dropped from fatigue, and the next morning, on being looked for, was gone to find his livelihood alone in the vast desert.

On the 21st of August they directed their course more northward in hopes of finding more water, or a better country, but in vain till the 4th of September, when they came upon a creek running from the N.W. To the 7th of the month they followed up this creek, when they lost it, having passed a salt lake on the way, and now coming to a salt-water creek. There the country was become so completely a desert of sand ridges, and looked the same as far as they could see, that they deemed it prudent to turn back. It was time. Mr. Browne was becoming very ill, their provisions were fast disappearing, and the horses were all but dead from fatigue and starvation. They were now 400 miles from the depôt. Spinifex and a pink-flowered mesembryanthemum were the only specimens of vegetation; the spinifex was close and matted, and the horses were obliged to lift their feet straight up to avoid its sharp points. Such was the aspect of the waste that even Mr. Browne, who had seen so much wretched desert, exclaimed, "Good Heavens! did ever man see such country?"

"Yet," says Captain Sturt, "I turned from it with a feeling of bitter disappointment. I was at that moment scarcely a degree from the tropic, and within 150 miles of the centre of the continent." As in a fit of desperation, he made another dash forward, but again was compelled to halt. The farthest point which he reached he calculated to be in latitude 24° 40′ S., in longitude 138° E., being 470 geographical miles to the north of Mount Arden, and about 350 from Mount Hopeless, or rather more than midway between the first of those hills and the Gulf of Carpentaria.

On the 8th of September, they finally turned, and commenced their journey homewards. On reaching the creek, which they had traced so far northwards, they encamped, and named it Eyre's Creek. Whence it came, or whither it went, however, they did not ascertain. On one of the flats they caught a dipus, a small, very pretty animal of a light grey colour, having a long tail, feathered at the end, feeding on insects, but ready to eat small birds, which it always devoured at night. It is one of the few Australian animals not marsupial. On reaching the creek where Flood's horse was lost, a native informed them that he had gone eastward, but they were too weary to seek after him, and, as he was a wandering brute, and not fond of company, they expected that he would find a living along the edge of the desert. Another native soon after also informed them that the great "cadli" (dog), for they had no name for a horse, had gone S.E. On reaching the water hole in the creek, where Mr. Browne had caught the fish, he caught another good dish. On crossing the first of the succession of creeks more southwards, they named it Strzelecki's Creek. Thence they had eighty-eight miles to travel without water, but they procured some by digging wells, and regained their camp at the Park on the 2nd of October, after an absence of seven weeks, during which they had ridden 800 miles. They now named this camp, because it had a stockade, Fort Grey, after Sir George Grey, the Governor of South Australia. They noticed a singularity of the E.S.E. and the N.E. winds in this part of the country. They expected them, from the kind of country they blew over, to have been warm, but, on the contrary, they were cold. On Eyre's Creek the weather was cool and agreeable, but now, in October, the heat was perceptibly increasing, and the thermometer ranged from 96° to 100°.

Whilst Captain Sturt was returning baffled from the north to Port Grey, he resolved still to make another effort to penetrate northward, but by a more easterly course. As Mr. Browne, however, was extremely out of health, he entreated him to take a part of the men and stores, and return to Adelaide, adding that his affairs as well as his health demanded his return; but nothing could induce Browne to leave his leader under these circumstances. As no rain had again fallen since that in July, he desired Mr. Browne, in case of danger of want of water on this creek, to fall back to that on the old depôt at Mount Poole. He then took with him Mr. Stuart, Morgan, and Mack, a ten weeks' supply of flour and tea, and all the horses but two, and on the morning of the 9th of October once more set out on his old track, intending to strike due north on reaching Strzelecki's Creek. By this route he trusted to test how far the Stony Desert stretched to the east. The captain here notes a circumstance which occurred during his late northern advance. Between Eyre's Creek and the Stony Desert both he and Mr. Browne heard at nine o'clock in the morning a report, apparently at the distance of half a mile westward, as of a great gun, and the same again the following morning, but farther off. He adds that in 1838 he heard a similar report on the Darling, but never could account for one or the other. This mystery, however, may be probably explained by what occurred to Kennedy on his first expedition to the Barcoo and Thomson Rivers in 1846. On the 24th of August, they observed a meteor rushing through the air with a red light and a wind that shook the tents. On the horizon it burst with the report of a cannon even at that distance. The report of such meteors, nearly at the same season of the year, was probably what Sturt heard. On the morning of the 13th, the fourth day of their journey, they came upon a splendid creek shaded by flooded gum-trees of a large size, and with abundance of grass about it. To the north-east, at about fifty miles distant, rose a high and broken chain of mountains, probably Stokes Ranges, and Sturt thought he would trace up this creek, believing it would lead him to these mountains, and probably out of the desert in which he had been so long. At this moment, however, heavy thunder rain fell, and thus opening his way to the north, he pushed on in that course. Through a desolate country, he pursued his way till the 16th, when they reached a salt lake, and saw a dismal sandy region again extending before them. The next day they entered extensive grassy plains, and found water; and on the 19th, again saw the Stony Desert lying dark below them. The sight of this gloomy, herbless, treeless region, occupying more than half the visible horizon, seemed to take their breath. From this time to the 24th, they continued to struggle through these frightful deserts, men and horses almost dead from want of water, the horses from want of grass too. In despair they then turned to the north-east, but with no better success till the 30th, the last day but one of October, when they struck a fine sheet of water, which stretched away to the south-east as far as they could see. This proved to be the creek since become so famous by the catastrophe of Burke and Wills—Cooper's Creek, thus named by its discoverer, Captain Sturt.

As this creek has through subsequent events become celebrated, I must give more particularly Captain Sturt's account of its vicinity. "The creek appeared, at the point where we first touched it, to be bounded by forest land, partly scrubby, and partly grassed. To the south there were flats, seemingly subject to floods, and lightly timbered; and beyond these were low sand hills. To the S.W. a high line of trees marked the course of a tributary from that quarter. To the north the country was exceedingly sandy and low, as well as the east; and the direction of the sand-ridges was only $5°$ to the west of north, so that from this point to our extreme west, they gradually alter their line $17°$, as in $138°$ longitude they ran $32°$ to the west of north. He now crossed this creek on an east course, and traversed sandy plains and low undulations, there being a tolerable quantity of grass on both. Going a little to the northward to a small conical sand-hill, from it darker hills were visible, somewhat more to the eastward. Directing his course towards these, and crossing the creek at four miles, he ascended a small, stony range towards the eastward, from which a flat-topped hill bore $24°$. The channel of the creek had been dry for several miles, but they then came to a large sheet of water bearing due east. From the top of the range the creek seemed to pass over extensive and bare plains, in many branches. Southward there were some stony hills, treeless and herbless, like those nearest to them. They observed now that the creek was leading them from the hills into low and desolate regions, almost as bad as those to the westward.

They now came upon natives—good-looking men, who had lost their two front teeth of the upper jaw. They swam like fish, and intimated by motions that they were acquainted with canoes. One of the natives, on the Captain asking by signs in what direction the creek ran, pointed to the south-east, and spread out his fingers, and then suddenly dropped them, to intimate that it had several channels, ending in one not far off. On asking if the creek ran into any large water, he said not. They saw plenty of fish in the creek, and thus this cleared up the mystery of the fish having got into O'Halloran's Creek, as the fall of the country was westward, and the neighbourhood of the creek exhibited signs of occasional great floods. They observed upon it pelicans, swans, ducks, cormorants, and sea-gulls, swimming on its waters, or perching on the rocks which rose out of it. They pursued the creek considerably to the north-east, where the country to the south and south-west was covered with brush, but to the north and east had immense grassy plains. In the space of four miles they encountered four different tribes, and saw at one time as many as 300 or 400 natives together. They were very friendly, and the finest race that Captain Sturt had met with.

Their horses were now greatly reduced by their labours, and the roan fairly knocked up; and they were obliged to leave him to wander at large along the sunny banks of the finest water-course they had seen. It will be found hereafter that this horse continued to live unmolested on the plains near the creek for seventeen years, and was captured by the party of my son, Mr. Alfred Howitt, when seeking for the expedition of Burke and Wills, and taken down to South Australia, where, no doubt, he was regarded with great interest.

Captain Sturt pursued the creek eastward, till it appeared to terminate in extensive hollow plains, where there were signs of a frequent and vast accumulation of waters. From this point they turned back, and regained their old camp at Fort Grey, on the 18th of November.

But on the journey they were forced to abandon the favourite horse, named Bawley, and leave him, as they expected he would die. The plains where this occurred have been named Bawley Plains. The heat that day was so great, that the thermometer had reached the degree of 127, the highest to which it was graduated, and burst the tube for want of room for further expansion; a circumstance which Captain Sturt believed no other traveller had had to record.

On reaching Grey's Fort, they found it deserted: what little water was left in the creek was become putrid, and they were left almost without any provisions. They had lost three of their horses on this last northern journey, and the Captain was now extremely ill; but they pushed on to Flood's Creek, where they found the party all pretty well, but the heat so intense, that they were seriously afraid that their retreat to the Darling was cut off. The heat was greater than in the preceding summer, the thermometer ranging between 110° and 123° every day. The wind blowing from N.E. to E.S.E. filled the air with impalpable red dust, giving the sun the most lurid and forbidding appearance. The ground was so heated, that their matches falling on it ignited; and having occasion to make a signal, they found the whole of their rockets in such a state that, on being lit, they exploded at once, without rising from the ground.

Having now followed the Captain and his party over the whole ground of their discovery, we may dismiss the story of their return briefly. It was under great difficulties that they made their homeward way. The Captain had lost the use of his limbs, and had to be lifted into and out of the cart as they travelled. Mr. Browne and Mr. Stuart were very ill too. As they approached the Darling, however, the temperature declined, and they enjoyed cool winds. They arrived at Cawndilla on the 28th of December, when they again had sultry weather, and where they spent the last days of the year 1845. On the 5th of January, 1846, Mr. Browne went on before them for Adelaide; and on the 15th, Captain Sturt arrived at Moorundi, the residence of Mr. Eyre, on the Murray. Mr. Eyre was absent, on a visit to England. On the 17th, the Captain again mounted his horse, the first time since November, and being met on the road by his friends, Mr. Charles Campbell, and Mr. A. Hardy, with a carriage, arrived in Adelaide at midnight of the 19th of January; and, crossing his threshold, lifted his wife from the floor, where she had fallen on hearing the carriage stop at the door.

Thus terminated an expedition of nearly a year and a half of a most arduous character, in which the idea of an inland sea was exploded, and that of a great central desert tending westward firmly established.

EXPLORATION OF THE SOUTH-EASTERN SEA-BOARD OF SOUTH AUSTRALIA BY GOVERNOR GREY IN 1844.

Captain Grey, the explorer of Western Australia, now Governor of South Australia, showed that the old spirit of bush travel was not extinct in him. The overland route, which had been opened from New South Wales and Port Phillip by Eyre, Hawdon, Bonney, and others, had proved for part of the way very difficult, and that part lay on the borders of South Australia. The country betwixt Adelaide and the River Glenelg was supposed to be of little value, and, therefore, not likely to soon possess a continued line of settlements between the two colonies. Captain Grey resolved to examine that district, and took with him Mr. Bonney, the commissioner of Crown Lands, who had been the first to find an overland track from Port Phillip for cattle.

It appears that Mr. Eyre, amongst his early adventures, had set out from Sydney to conduct cattle overland to Adelaide. He started on the 8th of November, 1837, from Sydney. He diverged to the south of the Murray, hoping to strike a more direct and practical path to Adelaide, but the country into which he had advanced proving sterile and destitute of water in the extreme, he was obliged, when about 200 miles from his destination, to retrace his steps to where he quitted the river. Owing to this detention, he did not reach Adelaide till the 13th of July, 1838. He had only six men on this expedition, and conducted 300 cattle and three drays through a wild journey of 1200 miles or more in safety. In the meantime, however, it appears that Messrs. Hawdon and Bonney, setting out from the Port Phillip district, had reached Adelaide before him. Mr. Eyre then set out again from New South Wales on the 5th of December, 1838, with 1000 sheep and 600 cattle, and arrived safely in Adelaide on the 23rd of February, 1839, having been less than three months on the road. On his first overland journey, he discovered the Lake Hindmarsh. By the spirited services of Messrs. Eyre, Hawdon, and Bonney, a great overland route from Port Phillip to Adelaide was opened up, but Governor Grey thought that a still more advantageous one might probably be found nearer the coast, and thus avoiding the great mallee scrubs nearer to the Murray.

Besides Mr. Bonney, Captain Grey took with him Mr. Burr, the deputy surveyor-general, a gentleman accustomed to the bush, and Mr. G. F. Angus, an artist. The account of the expedition is given by Mr. Burr. They set out from Adelaide on the 10th of April, and proceeded with drays and a number of sheep by Mount Barker, Lake Victoria, formerly Alexandrina, and Lake Albert, to the Coorong. They imagined this part of the country was unknown, but they soon met one party after another coming overland from Port Phillip with cattle and horses. They found the natives living in huts very superior to those commonly seen amongst them.

On the 20th, they encamped on the spot where M'Grath was murdered by the natives about two years before. On the Coorong, on the 23rd, they came to one of those singular appearances which have also been found on an Island in Bass's Straits. Mr. Burr thus describes this strange phenomenon:—"Amongst the sand hills between the Coorong and the sea, we saw several spots which are termed sand-patches. They are rather remarkable, for they have the appearance of shrubs composed of stone. On inspection, I found that these stone shrubs were invariably hollow, and in several cases, where I examined the inside of these tubes, the appearance was that of a cast taken from the stems or branches of a tree. This leads me to suppose the production of these sand-patches to take place thus. A shrubbery, similar to those at present seen on the sand hills, has, at some former period, been wholly, or in part, covered with drifting sand. The trees thus covered would naturally die; the dead wood absorbs the moisture, and forms a nucleus, around which the lime in the mass would accumulate, and cement the sand in the immediate neighbourhood. This would go on for a time, when a portion of the sand, which covered the shrubbery, being thus cemented, the remainder, which would still be loose, might by some peculiar eddy of the wind, caused by hills or dales formed in the mean time, be drifted to some other spot, leaving only the portions which had become consolidated, and which have now every appearance of petrified trees. At the same time, I believe that there are similar appearances, the origin of which is quite different."

In the whole of the way from the Albert to the Glenelg, they appear to have found a considerable amount of tea-tree swamp, and the country greatly improved as they approached the Glenelg. In latitude 36° 30′, they found the Coorong, which had run parallel to the sea from the sea-mouth of the Murray, now resolved itself into a series of lakes. Near this place, they came to the great red granite rock projecting into the sea, called by M. Baudin Cape Morard-de-Galles, lying four miles south of the Cape Bernouilli of Flinders. Here they met a third party of men coming over from Port Phillip, twelve in number, driving 550 head of cattle, 320 rams, the men being well mounted. They halted two days to visit Lacépède Bay. Thence they went on to Mount Benson, on the way to which they passed over a plain covered, as it appeared, with ship-biscuits. They were, in fact, cakes nearly circular of calcareous tufa, much resembling biscuits. From Mount Benson they had an extensive view of an undulating, grassy, and thickly-wooded country, and a good prospect of Guichen Bay. They had also a fine view of Cape Hawdon, so called after the discoverer, one of the first overland adventurers from Port Phillip to Adelaide. From this lake the overland route to Port Phillip struck off eastward.

From some ranges they had a view of Rivoli Bay and of several lakes in the intermediate space, as Lake Eliza and Lake George, which, being now first discovered, were named by the governor. On the 2nd of May, they crossed another biscuit plain near the sea, and on the 3rd, visited Rivoli Bay, where they fell in with some whaling vessels, the men of which rowed them over to an island covered with penguins. Proceeding from this point to visit Mounts Gambier and Schanck, they obtained views of the bay, of Capes Lannes and Martin, the Reefs, &c., as well as of fresh lakes, which the governor named Frome, after the surveyor-general, and Bonney, after the commissioner of Crown Lands. They had, turning north-west, views of Mounts Muirhead and Burr. At about twenty-eight miles on their way, they came to a singular chasm in the coral limestone of from 70 to 80 yards wide under perpendicular cliffs. This was filled with water to the depth of $103\frac{1}{2}$ feet. The governor named it the Devil's Punch-bowl. A mile further they arrived at another, and soon after at a third well of the same kind, near to Messrs. Arthur's Station. This last was 156 feet deep at the side. Several other wells of a like kind were found in the neighbourhood. They were also shown caverns in which were numerous bones of kangaroos, opossums, wombats, and wild dogs. On the summit of Mount Schanck, which reaches an elevation of 900 feet above the level of the sea, they found three distinct craters, the principal one 500 yards in diameter, the others 200 and 250 yards in diameter. The small craters are on the slope of the main one, all nearly circular, with no water in them, but covered with rich vegetation on the inner and outer slopes. From the summit there is a fine view over the country, on the south-east as far into Victoria as Cape Bridgewater.

From Mount Schanck to Mount Gambier, they found the country of the richest description and the scenery beautiful. Mount Gambier they found rather loftier than Mount Schanck, and of an oval form. This mount has also three craters, not lying in a triangle as those of Mount Schanck, but stretching in a line running E.S.E. The north-west one is the largest, and is divided by a ridge, running north and south, across it. One-third of the eastern portion of this crater forms a lake, very deep, and surrounded by perpendicular cliffs. It was covered with ducks. There were several lagoons in the western end. The central crater has no water in it; the third forms a large, deep lake. The party returned from Mount Gambier in a north-west direction to Mounts Burr and Muirhead. Mount Burr they found to be 1600 feet above the level of the sea.

On their return to Rivoli Bay, the governor and Mr. Gisborne went in a whaler's boat to Sherbert's Rock to shoot sea-lions, one of which they killed, and found in its stomach five pebbles, weighing altogether four and a half pounds. They were visited at their camp by two young natives, very merry fellows, who were allowed to sleep, or rather lie down, by a fire near the camp, and who, in the night, made off into the bush, and beyond recovery, with their knives, forks, spoons, a couple of towels, an axe, a sheep killed and hung in a tree, and the hats of two of the soldiers. On the way back they took compassion on an old native who had been ill, and was abandoned by his tribe, and nearly dead of hunger. They gave him food, and put him in a dray to convey him to Adelaide that he might not be liable to the same fate some other time. But no sooner was he pretty strong again, than he slipped away unobserved.

The governor's report of much of the country which they saw, especially as they approached the frontiers of Victoria, was that it was excellent, and in many places very beautiful. "From Rivoli Bay to Mount Schanck, and from thence round to Mount Gambier back to Rivoli Bay, we passed," he says, "for the most part, over a country of the richest description. The soil was a dark brown loam. The trees grew luxuriantly; the blackwood grows there to an enormous size; besides which, there are several trees quite different to those in the neighbourhood of Adelaide. We also saw several new birds."

CHAPTER III.

EXPLORING EXPEDITIONS IN WESTERN AUSTRALIA—CONTINUED.

1. EXPEDITION OF MESSRS. LANDOR AND LEFROY IN SEARCH OF AN INLAND SEA, IN 1843.—Journal published in Perth Inquirer.—Leave York, January 9.—Proceed to the Hotham River.—Country level.—Cross a large river.—Byriering Lake.—Lake Novring.—Salt Lakes.—Go down a fresh water lake.—Discover a river named the Landor.—Another named the Lefroy.—See two Timor ponies.—Return by a branch of the Hotham.—General report of the country.
2. EXPEDITION OF MR. ROE, Surveyor-General of Western Australia, eastward of Perth, accompanied by Mr. H. GREGORY and others.—Set out from York.—Pass over heights to Cape Riche.—The Jeeramungup.—Good grazing country.—Mount Madden and Mount Short.—Poor country and salt lakes.—Bremer Range.—Mount Gordon.—Fitzgerald Range.—Barren country.—Severe journey to the Russell Range: no grass, no water.—Return by the shore to Cape Riche.—Howick Hill, Mount Merivale, and Mount Hawes, named by them.—The streamlet Gore and inlet Lort, Phillips's River, and Eyre's named by them.—Found coalbeds at the junction of the Elwes and Jeeramungup.—Between the Elwes and Cape Richie named Mount Bland, Gairdner River, and Gordon Inlet.—In their homeward route by Bunbury, came on a sandal-wood-cutting station.—Return to Perth.
3. EXPEDITION OF MESSRS. GREGORY INTO THE INTERIOR OF WESTERN AUSTRALIA.—Start from Boycen Spring, on Swan River, August 7th.—Lake Brown.—See ranges from N. to E.S.E.—Eastward a discouraging country.—Columns of red sand, or dust.—Took a N.W. course.—Vast flats and bogs.—Cross them by means of hurdles.—Lake Moore.—Salt, gypsum, and mud beds.—Still on to September 3rd over wretched country.—Strike the Arrowsmith River.—Followed the river down to its mouth.—Found beds of coal.—Follow the coast homewards.
4. VOYAGE OF LIEUTENANT HELPMAN TO EXAMINE THE COAL OF THE ARROWSMITH.—Examined the country from the Arrowsmith to the Hutt.—Mistook the rivers as laid down by Captain Grey.—The error rectified by Mr. Arrowsmith.—Mr. Hillman's trip to Lake Moore.
5. SETTLERS' EXPEDITION NORTHWARD FROM PERTH UNDER A. C. GREGORY.—Instructions for the tour from the Local Government.—The object, to discover pasture lands.—Joined by friends at Toodyay.—At Arrowsmith Creek.—Irwin Plains.—Large extent of good pasturage land found.—Also on Champion Bay.—The Murchison country poor.—Freycinet Harbour.—Country around wretched.—Found lead ore at the Hutt.—Some good land on the Bowes.—Return to Perth.
6. VISIT OF GOVERNOR FITZGERALD TO THE MURCHISON.—Sailed to Champion Bay.—Find no coal, but lead in the Murchison.—Attacked by natives.—The Governor speared through the thigh.—Shot one man.—Mining commenced on the Murchison and Bowes.

EXPEDITION OF MESSRS. LANDOR AND LEFROY IN SEARCH OF AN INLAND SEA, IN 1843.

THE journal of these gentlemen was published as a

letter to the Perth Inquirer. It contains the following statements. They left York on the 9th of January with a pack-horse carrying flour, tea, and sugar for a month. They had two native guides, Konak and Quallet, who were ready at all times to carry game, or firewood, or do any little office required of them. They also took from York a native boy, to shoot kangaroos, and act as interpreter when the guides were unintelligible to them. Their whole journey out and back only occupied fourteen days, that is, from the 9th to 23rd. They proceeded by Nymbatilling to the Hotham River, and by Carbal to a mound spring, called by the natives Yungamening. The country was generally level, partly scrub, partly good grazing land. Beyond Yungamening they passed over some hills into another fertile valley. Beyond this, on the 14th, they crossed a large river, first flowing east, and then west, and were told by the natives that it was the Williams. The country about it was bad. The valleys were boggy, the hills covered with poison plants. Soon after, they reached a shallow lake, nowhere deeper than up to their knees, but the water fresh and excellent. The lake was about two miles by one and a half. This lake was called Byriering. It abounded with ducks. On the 15th they reached Novring, a salt lake, six miles by three. On the north and west the borders of the lake had good land; on the east and south very bad. From a hill they saw another lake, Quiliding, studded with islands, and the country east and south looking very flat and dreary.

The Lake Novring was their most westerly point. Their explorations began where Mr. Harris had ended. They then went east as far as Lake Barkiering, and still more east to Lake Quiliwhirring, quite salt. There, the valley of the lakes divided, running one part north-east, the other east by south. They proceeded due east over a hilly and bad country. Afterwards they went down into a valley, to a fresh-water lake, Goondering. On the 17th they reached Dambeling, the largest of the lakes, fifteen miles by seven or eight. It was like the others, shallow, with many low islands in varied and beautiful forms. The water was salt, the land on the north and east was good. They discovered a river running from the north into the lake, equal to the Mackie at York, and named it the Landor.

Being now prevented going further eastward by the desert country, they turned north and soon crossed a river at least twenty yards wide, its bed full of pools of fresh water, which appeared to have ceased to run within the last few days. It appeared to come from the eastern desert, and to fall into the Dambeling. They named it the Lefroy. Advancing five or six miles northward over good country, they came on a pool of fresh water named Jualing. Near Wardaming, another pool more N.W., they saw two Timor ponies, but could not catch them. They next crossed the north-east valley of the lakes, and returned by Yarlal and Warnup, to a branch of the Hotham, which they called the Cowit. On the 23rd they were again at Nymbatilling.

Their general report of the country they went over was bad, and that it was infested with poison. A great deal of the country seen on their return to the Cowit, had no water for sheep; all flocks must have wells dug, or tanks made. They could see no traces of the high granite ranges from which Mr. Harris supposed the Williams to come, and as they crossed neither that river nor the Hotham in returning, they felt that they must have headed them. The Lake Dambeling, they believed to be the large inland water talked of by the natives. Their experience confirmed the desert nature of the country farther eastward; and the most interesting feature of their discoveries was the River Lefroy, coming out of the desert, east. Its size and water-worn banks, in conjunction with the level nature of the country, seemed to imply that it either came from a great distance, or from a lake more inland and still larger than Dambeling.

In 1848, in consequence of the strong desire evinced by the public, and especially by that part of it engaged in pastoral pursuits, to ascertain what species of lands lay beyond the more familiar limits of the colony, the government, then under the rule of his Excellency, the Hon. Charles Fitz-Gerald, sent out two expeditions nearly simultaneously; one under the conduct of Mr. J. S. Roe, the Surveyor-General to the south-east of Perth, and the other under that of Mr. Augustus C. Gregory, the Assistant-Surveyor, northward of Perth. We proceed to narrate the events of the southern expedition first, and this from Mr. Roe's own report, as made to the Governor of Western Australia, and forwarded by him to the Imperial Colonial Office.

EXPEDITION OF MR. J. S. ROE, INTO THE COUNTRY SOUTH-EAST OF PERTH, AND EXTENDING EASTWARD TO THE BREMER AND FITZ-GERALD RANGES.

The number of men and horses employed in this expedition are not distinctly stated by Mr. Roe, but the persons of the party appear to have consisted of himself, Mr. H. Gregory, Mr. Ridley, and two private soldiers Lee and Burk. They had a considerable number of horses loaded with provisions, etc. They left York on the 14th of September, 1848, ascended the river Avon, and left Nal-Yaring, the upper sheep station of that district, following the compass directions of S. $\frac{1}{2}$ S. as intermediate between tracts of country previously traversed. From that point they soon entered on a poor and unpromising country, which led them to an elevated tract of sand plains, which furnishes the sources of the Rivers Avon, Williams, Arthur, Buchanan, and Beaufort. These heights they estimated to be from 1800 to 2000 feet above the sea-level. Descending from these sandy heights, they passed again through a poor country for fifty-five miles, and then came upon a branch of the Pallinup River, which they followed down as far as Pailyenup, near the N.E. extremity of Stirling

Range, and not far from Cape Riche, the latter part of the journey along the Pallinup valley being grassy, and affording plenty of water.

At the station of Mr. Cheyne, at Cape Riche, they met with hospitable entertainment, and there having left their heavier tents, and all other things that they could dispense with, they set forward on the 14th of October, in a north-east direction for the Bremer Ranges. Here, for the first time, we learn that the party consisted of six persons, and eleven horses, and that they took supplies for ninety days, and 300lbs. of corn for the horses. At Yunganup, on the Pallinup River, fifteen miles from Mr. Cheyne's station, in latitude 34° 24′ 6″ S., they made their first halt, and remained, amid excellent grass, till the 18th. Here they had various offers of natives as guides, but they had already one named Bob. They travelled through a generally good country till the 22nd, when they came upon a river with various branches, running through a good grassy country called Jeeramungup. This stream flowed to the sea near Middle Mount Barren. They calculated that there were 15,000 acres of excellent grazing land there, but they soon again entered on poor and scrubby country, with salt and brackish pools. On the 29th they reached a granite hill, which they named Mount Madden. Here they were fifty miles north of East Mount Barren, and beheld another hill thirteen miles S.E., which they named Mount Short. The rock formation was granite, and the country scrubby and poor, and almost destitute of water. Passing by several salt lakes, and being two days without fresh water, on the 3rd of November they reached the Bremer Range, and named its highest point Mount Gordon. The latitude of these hills was 32° 52′ 43″ S. All, however, was barren and inhospitable, and after pushing across sandy plains, and amongst salt lakes, samphire marshes and dense scrub, for thirty miles in a south-east direction, they reached other hills 1000 feet above the surrounding plains, which they named the Fitz-Gerald Ranges, and their different points Peak Charles, and Peak Eleanora.

This journey from these hills as far as the Russell Ranges reminds one of that of Mr. Eyre. They were now in part of that frightful region north of the Recherche Archipelago, in which he suffered such miseries, and they found it wholly answering to his description. Sultry, sandy deserts, without grass or water, but tantalizing them with the prospect of lakes, which always proved salt. On the 13th of November they reached a hill which they named Mount Ridley. Their horses were fast sinking from their want of food and water. After passing between two long salt lakes, on the 17th they encamped under a mass of rocks, which they named Mount Ney, after a favourite horse, which recovered a little under its shadow, and where they left him to rest. On the 23rd they reached the Russell Range, in a condition of great exhaustion, and found all a bare, naked mass of rock, 600 feet above the scrubby plain, but not a blade of grass, or the least appearance of fresh water anywhere. Fortunately, near the northern extremity of the range, they found grass and a watercourse, or they must have been lost, and there they remained four days to recruit. Not far to the north rose another hill, which Eyre had named Mount Ragged.

From these hills Point Malcolm, to the S.E., appeared about fifteen miles distant, with the broad ocean and the islands of the Recherche Archipelago. All eastward was one dreary, torrid, and forbidding desert. They had now travelled 1000 miles from Swan River, and felt it absolutely necessary to return. Indeed, after the description of this country by Eyre one wonders why they ventured into it at all. If they hoped on a more northern route than his to find a better country, they now learned that what the natives had told him of it was but too true.

In returning from the Russell Range to Cape Riche, Mr. Roe's track was very much the same as Mr. Eyre's, and it is not, therefore, to be expected that he could make any material geographical discovery; but he named some physical objects, yet unnamed, and made important discoveries of coal-fields. On the 28th of November they commenced their return: on the 2nd of December they reached a lofty and remarkable granite hill, which they named Howick Hill, after Lord Grey, then colonial secretary. At this point they were twenty-five miles south of the place at which they had left the horse Ney; they sent, and found him considerably recovered, and brought him to the camp. On the 7th they reached another high granite hill, fifteen miles N. from Cape-le-Grand, which they named Mount Merivale, and a similar hill, fifteen miles eastward, Mount Hawes. Near Red Island they named a river the Gore, and soon after an inlet the Lort, after Captain Lort Stokes, and the river falling into it, the Young. As they approached East Mount Barren, they came upon indications of coal, and on a river, which they named the Phillips, falling into an inlet which they named the Calham Inlet. In the banks of the Phillips were found cropping out coal shales, and farther on, near a range which they named Eyre's Range, these indications of coal became stronger. At their camp on the 20th of December, from which East Mount Barren bore S. 28° 45' W., and the north-east of Eyre's Range W. ½ S., Mr. Roe believed the main coal seam of the river would be found. The principal rock formation was sandstone, mingled with ironstone, quartz, and coarse conglomerates.

On the 26th they came upon the junction of the Elwes and Jecramungup rivers, falling into the Fitz-Gerald Inlet, and found considerable coal beds. Farther search disclosed still more extensive beds of coal. Into one of these beds they dug three feet, without any sign of change in it, and the coal on being tried burnt clearly and beautifully, without any snapping or flying, and leaving only a soft, white ash. Mr. Roe and his companions examined the course of the estuary down to the sea; saw along its course fresh evidences of coal, and ascertained that a conveyance of the coal to vessels in Doubtful Island Bay might readily be effected.

Between the Elwes and Cape Riche they pointed out and named a double-topped hill, Mount Bland, the Gairdner River, and Gordon Inlet. From their hospitable friends, Mr. and Mrs. Cheyne, they returned to Perth, by following up the Pallinup River, on whose banks they found a station for cutting sandal-wood, for exportation to China. They then crossed the Beaufort River, where they found squatters already removing their flocks and herds to convey them to the Fitz-Gerald River, and the grassy lands betwixt the Pallinup and the Elwes. Taking a W.N.W. course, they reached Bunbury on the coast, and thence pursued the line of the shore to Perth, where they arrived on the 2nd of February, 1849, after an absence of 149 days. They had traversed 1800 miles, and the great result of the expedition was the discovery of coal in two available situations.

EXPEDITION OF THE MESSRS. GREGORY INTO THE INTERIOR OF WESTERN AUSTRALIA, IN 1846.

The party on this expedition consisted of A. C., F. T., and H. C. Gregory. They had four horses, and seven weeks provisions. On the 7th of August they set out from Boyeen Spring, a farm of Mr. Yule's on the head-waters of Swan River, and proceeded through a swampy country to Lake Brown, where they were on the 12th. Near this lake were Eaglestone Hill, and other hills and lakes, chiefly dry. From this point they proceeded in a north-east direction over a tolerably level country to the 18th, when they ascended a hill of trap rock, of about 300 feet in elevation, and from this they saw other ranges of hills, extending from N. to E.S.E. The view of the country farther eastward was most discouraging. It was a level, sandy desert, without the least appearance of vegetation. To the west and north native fires were seen, but the extremely bad country to the E. and N., and the immense columns of red sand or dust, which the numerous whirlwinds raised to the height of from 200 to 500 feet, gave no encouragement to advance in that direction. They were now in latitude 30° 12′ 28″, longitude, by account, 119° 16′ 10″, and they now turned about and struck a north-westerly course. The country was generally of a scrubby and indifferent character, till August 25th, when they came upon a vast samphire flat, which was so boggy that they were obliged to get their horses over it by making hurdles of bushes bound with ropes and canvas saddle-bags. These they laid before the horses' feet for them to step upon, and so continually removed them as they advanced. The surface was covered by a hard crust of gypsum and salt, but this broke through, and without the hurdles the horses sunk up to the shoulders. Having crossed the swamp by this laborious means, and got upon a solid hill of granite, they found themselves on the eastern shore of an immense lake, since named Lake Moore. The great expanse of the lake did not, however, consist of deep water. It extended about ten miles to the east, twelve to the south, fifteen to the west, and eight to the north; but to the N.E. by E. it formed the visible horizon. Thus, it was more than twenty miles from north to south, and twenty-five from east to west, though it is represented in the Messrs. Gregory's map as much longer than broad. Shallow pools of water, a mile and upwards in extent, and low, wooded, and high rocky islands, were scattered over this vast expanse of salt, gypsum, and white mud.

After skirting this unattractive lake to its northern extremity, they held in a northern and north-western course, over a poor country of alternating hills of granite, acacia levels, forests of gum and cypress, and occasional patches of grassy country, till the 3rd of September, when they found themselves amid dry, salt lakes, and hills of trap. From the summit of a hill they could see the salt lakes and marshes still extending northward, and that all the hills within twenty miles appeared of the trap formation. They were now by account in latitude 28° 24' 20", longitude 116° 42' 2". Their horses had been twenty-four hours without water, and they saw no prospect of obtaining any by advancing farther; they therefore took a westerly course, to make the sources of the Hutt, or Arrowsmith river. Continuing in a south-westerly direction over a similar country, on the 8th of September they struck the upper part of the Arrowsmith river, and followed it down, believing it from its latitude, to be the river Irwin of Grey, from the fact of Sir George Grey having placed all the rivers that he passed too much south. Following down the Arrowsmith, not far from its mouth they discovered in its banks two seams of coal, one of five and the other of six feet in thickness. They found this coal burn well, and having made this valuable discovery, they returned homeward, keeping a line nearly parallel with the coast, at a distance of thirty or forty miles to the Moore river, which they reached on the 20th of September, and on the 22nd were again at Bolgart Spring, the station of Captain Scully, which they had passed on the day of their setting out, after an absence of 47 days, during which they had travelled 953 miles, tracing 3° of latitude, and nearly $4\frac{1}{2}$° of longitude.

VOYAGE OF LIEUTENANT HELPMAN TO EXAMINE THE COAL AT THE ARROWSMITH.

On the announcement of the discovery of coal, on what Mr. Gregory believed to be the Irwin of Grey, Lieutenant Helpman of the Champion was despatched, accompanied by some of the Gregorys, to examine and report on this coal bed. The Champion reached Champion Bay on the 6th of December, 1846, where horses and a cart were landed, and on proceeding to the place, they found the seam of coal running entirely across the bed of the river, and six feet thick, as the Gregorys had stated. They dug up two hundredweight of the coal, and conveyed it in the cart to the coast, where they put it on board. They found Port

Grey favourable for a coaling port; and they then set out to examine the country northward as far as the Hutt. In this trip they called the Irwin of Grey the Greenough, the Greenough they took for the Chapman. They also reversed the names of Mount Fairfax and the Wizard Hill, as given in Grey's narrative. In reference to these facts, Mr. Arrowsmith, in a note addressed to the Geographical Society, after the reading of Lieutenant Helpman's Report, on the 13th of December, 1847, explained the discrepancies by showing that "Captain Grey was shipwrecked in Gantheaume Bay in April, 1839—he and his party travelled thence by land to Perth, and he named every river which he crossed, and the description which he has given of each is so clear, that no difficulty exists in identifying the whole of them with the more recent account of Stokes, Roe, Helpman, and the Gregorys. The difficulties and privations which Captain Grey had to overcome, which may be seen by all who read his very interesting narrative, prevented his obtaining latitudes at the various rivers which he crossed, so that the map of his route, which was laid down by himself from Gantheaume Bay to Water Peak, is too long 14′ or 15′, and thence to Perth is too short by the same number of miles; all, however, that is required, is a simple correction of distances."

The consequence of this is, says Mr. Arrowsmith, that the names and positions of Mount Fairfax and Wizard Hill of Captain King, admit of no change. The names of Mount Fairfax, Wizard Hill, and Mount Hill, were misapplied by Captain Grey, who travelled over many hills of very similar appearance. Captain Stokes, and Lieutenant Helpman have, by sea and land, cleared up this discrepancy very satisfactorily. Captain Grey's names of the rivers admit of no change, as he was the discoverer of the whole of those that flow into the sea between the above latitudes, his distances only require correction.

During 1846, the same year that Messrs. Gregory made their tour into the interior of Western Australia,

Mr. Hillman also made an expedition to Lake Moore and back, by way of Moore River.

SETTLERS' EXPEDITION TO THE NORTHWARD FROM PERTH, UNDER MR. ASSISTANT SURVEYOR, A. C. GREGORY.

Whilst Mr. Roe and his party were exploring south-eastward from Perth, Mr. Augustus Gregory and another party were exploring northward from Perth. The object of both expeditions was the same, to discover new districts of good grazing or agricultural lands, and also to find coal. It was directed thus by instructions from Mr. R. R. Madden, the colonial secretary, to proceed to the Gascoigne river, which flows into Shark's Bay. They were directed to proceed north and north-east till ahead of Champion Bay, and then approach the Gascoigne from that point. They were directed to examine the course of the Gascoigne, and the nature of the bar at its mouth, to see whether it were practicable for boats. They were then to return south for about 40 miles, and examine a river there, seen but not named, by Captain Grey, and placed by him at Point Long. The discovery of new pasture lands was dwelt upon as of primary importance. "The chief object of this expedition," said the instructions from the colonial secretary, " is the examination of a new tract of unknown country for practical purposes, by practical men, that, in fact, the discovery of new land of an available kind for pasture, has become a thing to be desired, of paramount importance, and an object on the attainment of which the interests, and perhaps the fate of the colony depend."

In going out or returning as far south as the Irwin river, Mr. Gregory was to examine carefully the coal-beds which had been discovered there in 1846, by himself and brothers. He was directed to sink down to them, and examine their thickness, and to ascertain whether coal cropped out between these beds and the sea-shore, a distance of 30 or 40 miles, or more northward towards Shark's Bay, where Dr. von Sommer thought coal might again make its appearance.

With these important injunctions Mr. Gregory set out with Mr. C. F. Gregory and five horses on the 2nd of September, 1848, for Toodyay, where he arrived the next day, and was there joined by Messrs. Burges, J. Walcott, and A. Bedart, with six additional horses. On the 8th they were joined by Private W. King with the cart and provisions, and procuring another horse, they set forward from Welbing on the 9th with ten pack and two riding horses, the persons of the party being now six. On the 13th they were at Arrowsmith Creek, and on the following day entered the Irwin Plains. They calculated that on the Irwin were at least 100,000 acres of land well suited for agriculture, and around Champion Bay not less than 225,000 acres adapted to pasturage. This was a great object gained. They do not seem, so far as appears from their journal, to have made much examination of the coal beds. North of the Irwin, and as far as the Murchison River, the country was poor and scrubby. On the 25th of September they were at the Murchison, a broad channel of a river rather than a river, but with long shallow pools of brackish water, and marks of violent floods. It was bounded on all sides by sandy plains and dense scrubs. On the 1st of October they had reached to near the south point of Freycinet Harbour, having passed over a most miserable, sandy country, and there were compelled to turn back, finding that it would be the destruction of the whole party to attempt to force their way to the Gascoigne River.

On reaching the Murchison on their return on the 6th of October, they examined it down to the sea, and found the tide flowing about five miles up the channel, where it was stopped by rapids. The bar at the mouth appeared passable by whale boats in moderate weather. After this they traced the banks of the river upwards for sixty miles, finding the country one level dense scrub, and the gravel and sand brought down by the floods promising no better country farther eastward. The valley of the river was about five miles in width, dense with wattles and cypress. At the Hutt River, on the

16th, they picked up specimens of lead ore. On the 18th they entered the rich and grassy valley of the Bowes; the water, however, was brackish. They calculated that in this valley there was pasturage for 17,000 sheep on 100,000 acres. The existence of garnets, iron pyrites, and a mineral resembling plumbago, seemed to indicate the presence of metals. The remainder of their homeward route was through country too well known to need remark. They arrived at Perth on the 17th of November, having been absent ten weeks, and reached a distance north from Perth in a direct line of 350 miles, but having, as they calculated, traversed altogether 1500 miles.

VISIT OF GOVERNOR FITZGERALD TO THE MURCHISON.

In the month following Mr. Gregory's return, namely December the 1st, he again set out for the Murchison in company with the governor and Mr. Bland. They were attended by three soldiers, and the governor's servant. This time they proceeded by sea in the Champion for Champion Bay, where they landed on the 3rd. They immediately set forward north, and examined some black shale-like soil on the way, which had been supposed to indicate coal; but it proved to be only alluvial soil resting on sand. On the 6th they reached the Hutt River. The next day they camped on the left bank of the Murchison. The governor's object was to examine the veins of lead which had been discovered there. They encamped about 500 yards below the large lead vein, and traced it much farther than before, that is, 320 yards along the bed of the river. They saw, however, that steam power would be necessary to work it, on account of the water, and that, if the mouth of the Hutt River, thirty miles distant, did not admit the passage of boats, the ore would have to be carried to Champion Bay, distant 60 miles. In returning, as they were passing to the west of King's Table Hill, a party of natives surrounded them, and made an attack upon them. The governor, in self defence, shot one man, and was immediately himself thrust through the thigh with a spear. The party still managed to beat back the savages, but were followed by them seven miles towards their boats.

In consequence of what was seen in this journey, mining establishments were commenced both on the Murchison and on the Bowes. The rock in which the veins of lead appeared also contained garnets, and copper was afterwards discovered.

CHAPTER IV.

SIR THOMAS MITCHELL'S FOURTH EXPEDITION. DISCOVERY OF THE BARCOO.

Need of an overland route from New South Wales to the Gulf of Carpentaria.—
Two iron boats built.—Expedition left Paramatta November the 7th, 1854.—
The party well selected and equipped.—Blacks meet them on the Bogan to inquire their object.—An old native resembling Socrates offers himself again.—
Traces of conflict between the natives and the squatters.—Want of water.—
The Bogan dry.—Attacked by ophthalmia.—Encamp on a creek, and wait.—
Piper, the native guide, dismissed.—On the 12th of April advance.—Sudden coming down of waters in the Macquarie.—A furious flood carrying trees along with it.—Reach the Barwan.—Messrs. Russell's exploration in 1841.—Surprising changes.—The white man now lord of the region.—The Narran.—The Balonne, a fine large river.—The Culgoa.—Sir Thomas now marks his camping places on trees.—Lake Parachute.—Advances with a light party.—Lakes and lagoons.—Lake Turanimga.—Mount Toolumba.—Name this district Fitzroy Downs.—Natives.—The Maranoa and Amby.—Curious embassage from the natives.—Warned away by them.—Mr. Kennedy, Sir Thomas's second in command, brings up the rear detachment.—Sir Thomas again starts northwards.—
Distress for water.—Water found through a dream.—A sulphurous stream, the Salvator.—The Claude, fertility of its banks.—Abundance of fossil wood.—
Entered the tropics.—The Belyando.—Vast numbers of wild fowl and kangaroos.—Menacing natives.—Return to the Salvator.—Beauty and fertility of the country.—Remarkable meteor.—The Claude.—Encamp in a mountain gorge.—
The depôt fixed there.—Sir Thomas sets out north-westward.—The Nine.—
Discover the Barcoo.—Sir Thomas's warm eulogium of the river and country around.—Pronounced by him the finest river and district of Australia.—
Return homewards.—See marks of squatters already on their track.

Towards the end of the year 1845, an expedition was projected to discover a passage towards the nearest part of the Indian Ocean westward of Torres Straits. A trade in horses, required to mount the Indian cavalry, had commenced between India and New South Wales, and the dangerous navigation of the straits proving disadvantageous to this new branch of commerce, it was desired to establish an overland route from Sydney to the head of the Gulf of Carpentaria. It was still more desirable, or was thought so, to unite Australia by such a route with India, as India was already united to England by steam communication. In 1845 the Legislative Council of New South Wales voted £1000 towards the expense of such an expedition, and this vote, being referred to the home government by Sir George Gipps for its approval, received it in the course of the year; and the Legislative Council then increased the vote to £2000, and appointed the veteran explorer, Sir Thomas Mitchell, to head the expedition. The governor, who was himself an engineer, and a man of restless activity, appeared desirous to lay down the plan of the expedition himself, and thus, it was supposed, to claim in some degree the honour of it, but Mitchell was not a man to act so much on other persons' plans as on his own, and he succeeded in obtaining, not only the conduct of the expedition, but its projection.

Sir Thomas, according to his favourite ideas on this subject, had eight drays made of wood seasoned for the purpose, and two boats built this time, not of canvas, or even of wood, but of iron. The main body of the expedition left Paramatta on the 17th of November for Buree, where they were joined by the leader a month later. They consisted altogether of twenty-eight persons. With the exception of five, these were prisoners of the crown, in different stages of probation. The free men were Edward Kennedy, assistant surveyor, and second in command; W. Stephenson, surgeon and collector of objects of natural history; Peter M'Avoy, mounted vidette; Anthony Brown, tent-keeper; and William Baldock, keeper of the horses. The others were two mounted videttes, a store-keeper, eight bullock drivers, two carpenters, a blacksmith, a shoemaker, a barometer carrier, two chainmen, two keepers of the horses, a carter and a pioneer, a shepherd and a butcher, a sailmaker and a sailor. These men were selected from a large number of volunteers, including several free men. Two black guides, Piper, the former companion of Sir Thomas, and a man named Yuraniah, permanently attached themselves to the expedition at Buree. The appurtenances of the expedition consisted of the eight drays, drawn by eighty bullocks, the two boats, seventeen horses, and three light carts. The provisions were computed to last for a year, and included a flock of 250 sheep.

No man understood better than Sir Thomas how to arrange and supply an expedition of the kind. All sorts of men were thought of, and each was carefully selected for his particular duty. The barometer, having its especial carrier and carer for, was a most judicious arrangement. It was equally foreseeing to have, not only plenty of shoes, but a store of leather and a shoemaker to make it up. The flocks, the bullocks, the horses, the stores, all had experienced keepers. No better appointed exploratory expedition had ever set forth from the known parts of the continent to the unknown.

The route of the party first lay in the direction of that of 1835. Towards the end of the month they were met by a party of blacks from the Bogan, who had been sent forward by their tribe to ascertain the objects and route of the explorers. One of these blacks had been the guide of Sir Thomas's party in this quarter in 1835, and he now introduced himself, carrying a present of wild honey, and offered himself as formerly to be their conductor. He was observed to have a countenance greatly resembling that of Socrates.

On the 4th of January, 1846, the party had reached the last stations of the squatters, and they found abundant evidences that these stations had been advanced farther into the wilderness than the natives would permit them to remain. They had resisted the encroachments of the white man, and for a time successfully. Huts of stockmen burnt down, stock-yards in ruins, and roads again overgrown with grass, showed that the native had triumphantly thrown back the tide of white invasion. It would be only for a time. Fresh squatting companies would appear, armed and combined to drive before them the children of the desert, and once more to cover the fertile plains with their flocks and herds.

In 1841, the Messrs. Henry Stuart Russell, and Sydenham Russell and some of their friends, had made considerable explorations along the courses of the rivers

Condamine and Boyne, in the Bunya-Bunya country, and the neighbourhood of Wide Bay.

It was now midsummer of that hemisphere, and the party began to experience the usual suffering from the want of water in those regions. It was necessary before advancing with the whole party, to send forward scouts to discover water. Towards the end of the month, the bed of the Bogan was explored for three days, by an advanced party, but in vain, all was dry. The route, therefore, was changed. Amongst the effects of the heat, and glare of burning sand, the men began to suffer severely from ophthalmia, and the leader suffered as much as any. It was necessary to pause on many accounts, and this they were enabled to do on a creek with plenty of water, at a place called by the natives Cannonha. Not only did the ophthalmia threaten to compel Sir Thomas to return if he meant to save his sight, but the condition of the vehicles, shrunk and falling to pieces with the effects of the heat, made imperative a delay. They resolved, therefore, to remain on this creek for a fortnight. The tents were pitched amongst shady bushes, the blacksmith's forge was set up, workshops for the carpenters erected, and all were soon busy in repairing their waggons, whilst the cattle luxuriated on the abundant water in the creek, and fresh grass on its banks. Several articles were found at the bottom of a pond grown dry, such as kettles, a spade, a Roman balance, showing that they had been the property of the white man who had been repulsed from the place by the natives. An old woman, indeed, told the interpreter that three white men had been killed in the struggle which took place when this station had been destroyed.

Here it was found necessary to send back Piper, the guide of the former, and so far of this expedition. It was found that he had been endeavouring to persuade the two younger and more useful blacks to desert the party. He had allured them by a proposal to go in search of gins, and to prevent further mischief he was sent back to Bathurst in charge of a trooper.

On the 12th of February, the expedition again set forward, greatly recruited by this rest. In the evening of the next day they beheld a novel and very interesting sight—a flood in the channel of the Macquarie. It exactly resembled what had been witnessed by Sturt and his party on the creek, at their long encampment at Mount Poole. At first they heard a murmuring sound, as if of a distant waterfall, mingled with occasional cracks as if of breaking branches. The men hastened to the river bank, where the murmur soon increased into a loud rushing of waters, a louder cracking of timber, and anon, the flood came pouring into sight, rolling slowly but victoriously onwards, a foaming mass, tossing before it large trees, and snapping their trunks against the banks. The scene was beheld with equal wonder and delight, for independently of its novelty, it promised an abundance of that most necessary element in that climate. The progress of the flood, though powerful, was so slow that it was more than an hour before the sound of its leading billows ceased to be heard.

On the 28th the party reached the banks of the Barwan, or upper Darling. Great was the change which presented itself from that condition of things which had been there witnessed fifteen years before. Then it was the undisputed haunt of the savage; now flocks and herds were spread over the plains, and the civilization and even wealth of the white man was exhibited in the abodes of the settlers. Formerly, when exploring parties reached this place, they were obliged to fortify themselves against the attacks of the natives, but the whiteman now reigned here supreme. They crossed the river by a ford on a station occupied by Mr. Parnell, and encamped in latitude 30° 5′ 41″. On the 7th of March, they reached a river named the Narran, having, since leaving the Barwan, crossed a country never before trodden by the European.

Their encampment on the Narran was four hundred and forty-two feet above the level of the sea. As they advanced northwards from this point, they frequently found great want of water, and the bullocks were growing proportionably exhausted. Several of them died, and others strayed at night in search of water and better pasture, thus delaying the movements of the party. At the beginning of April, the party encamped on the banks of the Balonne, as fine a looking river as had been seen in Australia, the Murray excepted. A passage was effected by filling a shallow part of the stream with logs and earth, and the next day they encamped on the Calgoa, seven miles distant from the Balonne, and near there falling into that river. At this place, Sir Thomas began the system of marking a tree at each camping place, a practice partially carried out by Leichhardt, and a very useful one as furnishing indications to those who should reach those places afterwards, of their real position.

As the month advanced, they found the Balonne expanding into a magnificent stream, at one point being fully a hundred and twenty yards wide, and presenting a permanent sheet of water, which, for extent, was not to be surpassed by any other river in the colony. At the same time, the country along its course was of the most fertile character. A little later, a lake was seen containing several large islands, and this was named the Lake Parachute. At this point, Sir Thomas carried into effect a plan which he had been for some time meditating, namely, to go on with a lighter party, leaving the weaker animals and heavier stores in a suitable depôt, under a sufficient guard. Accordingly, on the 23rd, he set forward with eight men and two native boys, with twelve horses and three light carts, carrying with them provisions for ten weeks. His great object was to ascertain at what place the waters began to descend towards the Gulf of Carpentaria, a point of great importance for the main object of the expedition, a route to the Gulf, as a starting-place for India. Mr. Kennedy, who was left in charge of the heavier portion of the material of the expedition, was to follow in his track after a lapse of three weeks.

For several days their course lay amongst lakes and lagoons. There were many natives, but of a most peaceful and friendly nature. They walked into the midst of the camp totally unarmed, and surveyed the carts and tents with evident wonder. Their language sounded soft and agreeable. Very unlike savages in general, they exhibited no desire to plunder. A lake they called Turànimga; the river, the lagoon, and a neighbouring hill, Toolumbà. The weather was at this period extremely cold, and the thermometer at sunrise, stood at $19°$, yet, strange to say, the water was not frozen, and the native guides who slept in the open air, experienced no inconvenience. The district they named the Fitzroy Downs, after Sir Charles Fitzroy, the Governor. Here they met with that singular tree seen by Captain Grey on the north-west coast, the Gouty-stem Tree, which the reader will find described in the narrative of that expedition. On these downs they were visited by eight natives, a father and seven sons. These men were adorned with iron-ochre, and wore in their hair and beards, some feathers of the white cockatoo. They were of a merry disposition, and in their frequent laughter, showed rows of teeth of surpassing whiteness. Their language was not much understood, but their sonorous names for the hills and creeks were obtained from them, and were noted down.

On the 1st of May they struck a river falling into the Balonne, called by the natives the Culba, or Maranoa. Into this from the east fell a river named the Amby. About the 20th they encamped with plenty of water and grass on the banks of the Maranoa, and resolved to wait the arrival of Kennedy there. During the stay there, one day when Sir Thomas was absent on an exploring ride, two natives appeared before the camp, painted white, a martial demonstration, and carrying several spears and boomerangs. They were followed by two females, also carrying bundles of spears. The travellers turned out at this sight armed, and stood in rank in front of the tents, and one of the troopers beckoned the natives to retire. These pointed the way which the leader had gone, and motioned them to follow him. As the whites remained stationary, the natives became angry, and poised their spears, at a distance of ten or twelve paces. As the whites still stood firm, the natives now assumed attitudes of insult and contempt, at which the travellers, to intimidate them, fired a musket over their heads. At the report the natives sprang several feet into the air, and made a precipitate retreat, followed by the women.

They returned, however, soon after, and adopted another mode of getting rid of their unwelcome visitors —that of argument and reason. The travellers having again turned out armed as before, the chief speaker of the tribe advanced, and pointing to various landmarks and localities, which he indicated as boundaries, announced that this district belonged exclusively to his people. A female standing behind the orator, prompted him, and occasionally joined in his statement with great energy and fluency, pointing also in the various directions indicated by their discourse. They seemed to say:—
"These are our lands, bounded here by the mountains, there by the horizon. They are ours by right of possession and occupation, acquired by our ancestors ages ago; they are ours by every title nature confers, for without the animals and birds to which they give subsistence, and the fish which lives in their lakes and rivers, we could not subsist. Other tribes occupy all the lands lying beyond the limits of our possessions. If we pass those bounds we are met with war. The pangs of hunger will not save us from the rage of those on whose domain we intrude, nor their piteous condition preserve our women from bondage, and our children from slaughter. This necessity, not unkindness, compels us to require that you pass on, and cease to consume our rightful prey, and still worse, destroy or scare away that which you may not consume. You have provisions; you have

animals which bear your burdens; you have health and strength; you will elsewhere find territories to possess which will inflict no injury. By going you suffer no hardships; by staying, you become the cause of our ruin."

These harangues making no impression on the Europeans, the black chief proceeded to strike a spear into the ground, and having thus formed a landmark, he proposed by word and gesture, that on the one side the ground should be occupied by the whites, and on the other by the blacks. The arrangement was assented to, and the aborigines, seemingly satisfied, went their way. When Sir Thomas returned, he confirmed the treaty by ordering that the larger of the two reaches near the camp should be left exclusively to the aborigines; that no white man should visit its banks, and that the cattle should not be allowed to feed in its vicinity. Such an arrangement was not only due to ordinary justice, but was merited by the moderation of the demands made by the tribe, and by their bold and manly demeanour in urging their rights.

On the 1st of June Mr. Kennedy announced his approach by a shot. He brought up all his party and provisions in good order; and the very next day Sir Thomas prepared to start on another advance with a similar light party, the only additions to it being the surgeon, and two other men. The remainder again stayed under the command of Mr. Kennedy. The party thus again left for four months, as it was calculated, were to employ themselves in fencing a stockyard, and cultivating a garden. There was to be no intercourse with the natives.

On the 4th Sir Thomas set forward, conveying the stores and a boat in a dray, and the light carts drawn by horses. On the first day's journey a small tribe menaced the party, but a few shots fired into the air, and the sound of the bugle, awed them, and the travellers were allowed to encamp in peace. Towards the end of the month, the party were in great distress for water, but were rescued in an extraordinary manner. One of the men, Felix Maguire, dreamed that he found a pond, and rising, went directly to the spot indicated by the vision, and there found the much-needed fluid. Twice did the prevision of this man succour the party in a similar manner, and his tact in finding water was at all times greater than that of any of his companions.

On the 2nd of July the explorers came to a running stream, the water of which was clear and sparkling, but tasted strongly of sulphur. The native guide at once pronounced this to be the head of a stream which never dried up. They named the river the Salvator, and a lake into which it flowed, the Lake Salvator. An outlet appeared on the southern side of the lake, but its channel was now dry. Proceeding, they soon found water growing scarce, and determined to try another route, which proved most fortunate, for on the 11th they found themselves on the banks of a fine permanent stream, flowing from the west. They named this river the Claude, from the surpassing beauty of the waving lines of woods along its course. The land in its vicinity was of the most fertile character, but everywhere covered with fragments of fossil wood, silex, agate, and chalcedony. In some respects this beautiful country appeared to be a land of extremes. One day the explorers met with streams of limpid water, or large and beautiful lakes; on the next, they were lost amid a labyrinth of dry water-courses, and impassable gullies. In the morning they were encompassed by the remains of petrified trees; in the afternoon the air around was perfumed by the fragrance of a sweet-scented shrub.

Towards the end of the month the explorers, crossing the tropical line, entered the regions of the sun. The stream of the Claude still pursued its majestic course, flowing on to constitute the Belyando, which falls into the Suttor, as the Suttor into the Burdekin. Lagoons, covered with wild-fowl, were met with from time to time, and kangaroos in large numbers bounded over the plains. Towards the middle of August the party were at a point where the river, now forming a series of deep, broad reaches, brimful of pure water, was joined by a tributary from the south-west. The natives showed no friendly feeling. On occasions when Sir Thomas was absent with some of the party, a number of the natives were pretty sure to make their appearance at the camp, and showed a disposition to lay hands on any thing they could. On one occasion no fewer than seventeen made their appearance, armed with clubs, and made signs for the travellers to pack up and follow their leader. The heads of the party appeared to be an old man, and a gigantic fellow of less age. They began to seize on everything within their reach. The travellers restrained their pilfering, but treated them civilly, and asked them to sit down, hoping to obtain some information from them regarding the river which they called the Belyando. Soon, however, a violent altercation took place between the old chief and his colleague. The younger one rose, and approaching the tents, beckoned the rest to follow. It was plain that an assault for plunder was intended. But instantly the men in charge of the tents seized their arms, and formed into line in front of them. This movement, and the sight of their mysterious weapons, caused the natives to halt, and the dogs rushing forth furiously upon them, completed their discomfiture. They fled precipitately, followed by the united laughter of the whites, and the old chief's adherents.

Sir Thomas now resolved to discontinue the route northwards, seeing plainly that this river did not lead to the Gulf of Carpentaria. The elevation of the country had decreased, leaving no doubt that the division betwixt the eastern and western waters was to be sought for farther west. It was therefore determined to retrace the wheel tracks to the head of the Salvator, and thence to explore the country to the north-west. The journey had already produced important results. A line of communication had been established between the colony and an important river leading to the eastern coast; and by it was thrown open a country equal in pastoral resources to any hitherto discovered in Australia, and greater in extent than all the lands hitherto occupied by the colonists. On the 12th, therefore, the party turned their faces in a homeward direction. Foot-prints on the line of march showed that they had been followed for a considerable distance by numbers of the natives. The shepherd, with his small flock, strayed away about this time, and was lost during a day and a night. When found by one of the guides, he was in full march to the eastward, pursuing a course directly opposite to that in which the expedition was going. On the night of the 24th, a remarkable phenomenon was observed. A rushing wind from the west shook the tents, then a whirling mass of red light passed to the southward, accompanied by a low booming sound. When the meteor reached the horizon, a loud report, like that of a cannon, shook the air; and so great was the concussion, that the boat vibrated in its carriage for minutes. This event, as elsewhere observed, seems to explain the loud explosions twice heard by Sturt in the interior. On the 24th the party re-crossed the line of Capricorn, and camped at one of their old resting-places, having been exactly one month within the regions of tropical Australia. It was with feelings of regret that they left the land of glowing sunbeams, for to them it had been a region of pleasant hours, and of bright promise.

On the 1st of September, the camp was fixed on one of the downs, about ten miles from the Claude, and the next day they crossed that river. A few days later, they encamped in a mountain gorge, where it was intended the main part of the expedition should remain, whilst Sir Thomas made an excursion towards the north-west. Having completed his maps and written a despatch, on the 9th he set out, accompanied by three men, with a view of making a final effort to discover a river flowing into Carpentaria. Provisions for a month were borne on two pack-horses. Passing a small river, which received the name of the Nine, the party arrived, a few days later, on the banks of a stream, equal in every respect to any they had hitherto encountered. The trees which lined its banks were traceable to the horizon. Flocks of cockatoos filled the air with their deafening chorus; water-fowl were in large numbers floating on the ample flood, or flew up and down over the reaches: and columns of smoke, extending in various directions, told that this rich and beautiful spot of creation was not without inhabitants. The country on either side of the river they thought one of the finest regions hitherto seen in Australia. Swarms of bees, remarkable for their smallness, visited the innumerable flowers, and, notwithstanding that the gatherer was not larger than a gnat, the black guide cut out abundance of honey from the trunks of decayed trees; Nature providing for the sojourner on her wild domains a luxury which art could not improve.

"Et duræ quercus sudabant roscida mella."—Virgil, Æn. iv.

Sir Thomas thus describes his first view of this beautiful country:—

"On ascending the range early the next morning, I saw open downs and plains, with a line of river in the midst, the whole extending to the N.N.W., as far as the horizon. Following down the little stream from the valley in which I had passed the night, I soon reached the open country, and during ten successive days I pursued the course of that river, through the same sort of country each day, as far as my horse could carry me, and in the same direction again approaching the tropic of Capricorn. In some parts the river formed splendid reaches, as broad and important as the river Murray: in others, it spread into four or five branches, some of them several miles apart. But the whole country is better watered than any part of Australia I have seen, by numerous tributaries arising in the downs.

"The soil consists of rich clay, and the hollows give birth to numerous water-courses, in most of which water was abundant. I found at length that I might travel in any direction, and find water at hand, without having to seek the river, except when I wished to ascertain its general course, and observe its character. The grass consists of panicum, and several new sorts, one of which springs green from the old stem. The plains were verdant, indeed. The luxuriant pasturage surpassed in quality, as it did in extent, anything I had ever seen. The myall tree and salt-bush (acacia pendula and salsolæ), so essential to a good run, are also there. New birds and new plants marked out this as an essentially different region from any I had previously explored; and although I could not follow the river throughout its long course at that advanced season, I was convinced that its estuary was in the Gulf of Carpentaria,—at all events the country is open and well watered for a direct route thereto. That the river is the most important of Australia, increasing as it does, by successive tributaries, and not a mere product of distant ranges, admits of no dispute; and the downs and plains of Central Australia, through which it flows, seem sufficient to supply the whole world with animal food. The natives are few and inoffensive. I happened to surprise one tribe at the lagoon, who did not seem averse to such strangers being in the country: our number being small, they seemed inclined to follow us. I crossed the river at the lowest point I reached, in a great southerly bend, in longitude 144° 34′ E., latitude 24° 14′ S.; and from rising ground beyond the left bank, I could trace its downward course far to the northward. I saw no callitris (pine of the colonists) in all that country, but a range, showing sandstone cliffs, appeared to the southward, in longitude 145°, and latitude 24° 30′ S. The country to the northward of the river is, upon the whole, the best; yet, in riding ninety miles due east from where I crossed the southern bend, I found plenty of water, and excellent grass; and gravel there approaches the river, throwing it off to the northward. Ranges extending N.N.E. were occasionally visible from the country to the northward."

Sir Thomas bestowed on this river the name of Victoria, though it possessed a much more distinctive native name—the Barcoo, seeing that there was already a river Victoria on the western coast. The Barcoo was joined by another stream running from the N.E., which was called the Alice.

Having made this discovery, Sir Thomas turned now determinedly homeward. On the 6th of October, he and his attendants rejoined their companions at the camp near the sources of the Nine, and after a rest of four days, the homeward march was resumed. On the 18th, they regained Kennedy's camp, after an absence of four months and fifteen days. The party under Mr. Kennedy were all well; the cattle and sheep in good condition; a stockyard had been formed, and a storehouse built; a garden had been fenced in, and cultivated, and now contained melons, cucumbers, and other similar things. As regarded the natives, the people at the camp had only had one encounter with any of them. A woman very much advanced in years and her daughter were met by the commandant and one of the native guides. The young woman, at the approach of the strangers, sang a pleasing air; but the mother, who at first concealed herself amongst some reeds, rendered her naturally hideous person still more hideous by the rage with which she denounced the white men, as though she had a foresight of the decay of her race, which must follow the advent of the strangers.

Breaking up the encampment, which had been so long established that it began to present some of the appearances of a regular settlement, the entire party commenced, on the 22nd, their journey towards the colony, deviating slightly from their former track. As they advanced, the hoof marks of horses, pursuing the outward course of the expedition, proved that already the enterprising squatters had availed themselves of the new path in seeking territories, where flocks and herds, increasing in rapid ratio, would soon build up the fortunes of the lucky possessors. On the 21st of November, heavy rains set in, and the Balonne rising to a considerable height, and inundating the adjacent country, the explorers were detained by the waters for upwards of a fortnight. Resuming their journey on the 11th of December, they crossed the Gwydir. This river, as forming the boundary of a country which had been for a considerable time the seat of colonization, was considered the goal of the exploring journey, which had now occupied twelve months all but one day. Two days later, the leader set out for Sydney, and in a month the whole expedition had arrived in the metropolis.

Such was the last of the great exploring enterprises of Sir Thomas Mitchell. On the whole Sir Thomas must be ranked amongst the greatest of Australian explorers, and the discovery of the vast extent of fine country on the Nammoy, the Barwan, the Culgoa, the Balonne, the Maranoa, the Claude, the Belyando, and Barcoo rivers, was a most important service to the colony. He survived eight years to reap the fame and satisfaction of his successful enterprises in the opening up of the north-eastern portion of the continent. He finished his very useful career on the 5th of October, 1855, at his residence near Sydney. He had been on the staff of the Duke of Wellington in the Peninsular war, and received a silver medal and five clasps for his services on the field of battle. Besides his services in cutting roads through the Blue Mountains, in surveying and mapping various districts of the colony, and besides these his well known achievements as an explorer, Sir Thomas was equally devoted to literature and mechanics; was an accomplished classic and general scholar. He translated the Lusiad of Camoens, and though fond of art and poetry, he was equally practical, and, shortly before his death, he applied to the screw propeller the revolving principle of the boomerang of the Australian natives. His death resulted from bronchitis produced by exposure during a surveying expedition.

CHAPTER V.

KENNEDY'S EXPLORATIONS OF THE BARCOO AND OF THE YORK PENINSULA, 1847.

Edward Kennedy sent to trace the Barcoo, and find a route to Carpentaria.—Crossed the Barcoo at Sir Thomas Mitchell's lowest point on August the 13th.—Found the river running a fresh course.—The Thomson falling into the Barcoo.—Traces the Barcoo down 100 miles.—Then lightens his luggage, and advances downwards through a wretched country to latitude 26° 13′ 9″, longitude 142° 20′.—A low, flat country.—The river dividing into many channels.—Convinced that it was identical with Cooper's Creek.—Returns northwards.—The natives had plundered his buried stores.—Obliged by this to return home.—Kennedy's journal edited by the Rev. W. B. Clarke.

KENNEDY'S EXPEDITION TO THE YORK PENINSULA.—Proposed plan of a new expedition towards the Gulf.—Provisions to be carried by ship to Albany.—York Peninsula to be first examined, then the route towards Carpentaria.—Kennedy and party land at Rockingham Bay in May, 1848.—Compelled to diverge to the south-west by the mountains.—Abandon their carts and heavy stores.—Leave eight men at Weymouth Bay.—Kennedy and four men, including Jackey, the native guide, push on for Albany.—One of the party wounded by a gun, which impeded them.—Leave him and the other two whites, and Kennedy and Jackey proceed towards Albany alone.—Attacked by natives near Albany.—Kennedy killed.—Jackey reaches Albany with his journal.—Sufferings and deaths in the party at Weymouth Bay.—Only two saved.—Relief party from the "Ariel."—The three other men sought for in vain.—Ten out of the original thirteen of this expedition perished.—Generous nature of Edward Kennedy.

THE EXPLORATION OF THE BARCOO.

AFTER the laudatory, but at the same time just terms, in which Sir Thomas Mitchell had described Australia Felix, now the colony of Victoria, the eulogies which he had bestowed on the Barcoo river and the adjacent country, were certainly calculated to excite the intensest expectations in New South Wales. After all his explorations of Australian rivers, especially of the Lachlan and Darling, Sir Thomas was not cured of his belief that the great course of Australian waters must be north-west. Indeed, had the Barcoo continued the same course as in the portion which he saw, it would have fallen into the Flinders. The strong and truly surprising terms which Sir Thomas had bestowed upon this river and the adjacent country, naturally stimulated the government of New South Wales to have them further explored; and, unfortunately, the river neither proved "the most important of Australia," nor "the downs and plains through which it flowed, sufficient to supply the whole world with animal food." The river, soon after he quitted it, took a decided course to the S.S.W., and ran, not through the most fertile regions of Australia, but into flats resembling those of the Darling, and into the sterile deserts towards the centre of the continent.

Mr. Edward Kennedy, a young and experienced officer, whom we have seen accompanying Sir Thomas into the interior, was ordered on this service. Having reached the lowest point of the Barcoo attained by the Surveyor-General, on the 13th of August, he crossed over to its right bank, and for some time found it running through fine grassy plains on its north side, but on its southern one, bounded by a low sand-ridge, covered with the bricklow, or brigalow acacia. Some distance onward, he found the river divide into three channels, one only, the southernmost, continuing permanent. The course was generally S.S.W., again dividing into three channels, and several minor water-courses; the latitude 24° 52′ 55″, and longitude 144° 11′ 26″. The supply of water in the channel, and in lakes and lagoons formed by the river, had disappeared, and it was with difficulty that they obtained enough for their need. The course which the channel took, so opposite to that of the part seen by Mitchell, convinced Mr. Kennedy, that with his small stock of provisions, he could not reach the Gulf of Carpentaria, and trace the course of the river too. He wisely resolved, therefore, to determine the course of the river, of which Sir Thomas had raised such expectations. After having traced it down south-southwest for nearly 100 miles, he determined to proceed with a couple of men as far as latitude 26°, and then to return and follow the river upwards towards the north, and thus prolong the route thus far carried towards Carpentaria by Mitchell.

For this purpose he left his camp on the 20th of

August, and at twelve miles found several channels united, forming a fine reach, below which, the river took a turn towards the west-south-west, receiving the waters of rather a large creek from the eastward in latitude 25° 3′. In latitude 25° 7′, the river was again turned west and west by north, by a low range in its left bank, for nearly thirty miles, and in that course the reaches were from 80 to 120 yards wide; firm plains of poor white soil, extending on each side of the river. In latitude 25° 9′ 30″, longitude about 143° 16′, a considerable river was found coming from the north-east, and there joining the Barcoo, on which Kennedy conferred the name of the Thomson, in honour of Mr. E. Deas Thomson, the Colonial Secretary. On one of the fine reaches of the western course of the Barcoo, it measured 120 yards wide, and seemed to have great depth. Various rocks and small islets in its channel gave such a promise of a great river that Mr. Kennedy there returned to bring up his camp.

Having again reached his farthest point downwards, the ground in latitude 25° 24′ became so heavy, that Mr. Kennedy buried a considerable part of his provisions, to lighten the loads of the horses, retaining sufficient to carry them to Captain Sturt's farthest point on Cooper's Creek, to which point he was now convinced the river would lead them. He was soon compelled to leave more behind, for the horses now frequently sank up to their hocks in the fissures of the plains. Again they found a barren sandstone ridge driving the river westward, and causing its different channels to unite in another fine reach, in latitude 25° 51′. Soon after the river resumed its southerly course, spreading in countless channels over a surface bearing flood marks six and seven feet above its then level. Mr. Kennedy continued his pursuit of the river, the country becoming more barren, the channel more dry, to latitude 26° 13′ 9″ longitude 142° 20′. There the river in several channels trended due south, and the lowest point of the range which bounds that flat country to the eastward, bearing

25° east. This being the case, he felt satisfied that the Barcoo was identical with Cooper's Creek, that creek being abandoned by Sturt in latitude 27° 46', and longitude 141° 51'. This river proved another confirmation of the theory, that a vast extent of the dip of the Australian continent is from the N.E. to the S.W.

Mr. Kennedy now retraced his steps, and regained his encampment on the Barcoo, where he had buried the main portion of their stores, on the 16th of August. They had adopted Leichhardt's plan of making a fire over the place where they had buried their stores, that the natives might not see the freshly disturbed ground, and dig down to them. But they had already detected this stratagem, and when the men got down to the flour, they reported that the rats had been at it. A little further search showed that not rats but the natives had been at it. They had dug down to the stores, taken away the tarpauling and bags; emptied the flour and sugar into the hole again, covered them with a little straw, and filled up the hole carefully, and made a fire over it, as the travellers had done.

Mr. Kennedy not having been able to penetrate very far south, in following the river, had again intended to try to reach the Gulf of Carpentaria; but the loss of much of their provisions by this work of the natives, put an end to that project altogether. They now, therefore, pursued their homeward way, and were followed by numbers of natives, who displayed a disposition to attack them, and one indeed, threw his boomerang at Mr. Kennedy, and it was with difficulty they avoided a collision. The natives followed them for several days, when they fell back, having probably reached the boundary of their district, for other natives soon appeared, who behaved in a friendly manner. On the 7th of October they reached the spot where they had buried the carts, on account of the roughness of the route onwards, and were only just in time to save them, as the natives had been sounding the ground in two places. From this point their homeward journey was pursued by Mount Playfair, crossing the Warrego, and following down the Maranoa and Culgoa, to the Barwan, where they came upon a now well-tracked country, and soon after arrived safely in Sydney, where Mr. Kennedy, being appointed to a new expedition for the following year, 1848, namely, of the York Peninsula, was so much occupied in preparation, that he handed over his journal of this tour to the Rev. W. B. Clarke, the celebrated geologist, and one of the earliest announcers of gold in Australia, next to the convicts who found it in cutting the road through the Blue Mountains, in 1813.

KENNEDY'S EXPEDITION TO THE YORK PENINSULA.

Although the loss of provisions had prevented Kennedy proceeding to the Gulf of Carpentaria, the governor did not abandon the project, but connected it with another, the exploration of York Peninsula. It was imagined from the superior character of the country along nearly the whole extent of Eastern Australia, that this peninsula would prove a continuation of such country, which added to its situation, would make it the most desirable site of a new colony, on the highway from New South Wales to India and its world of islands. Kennedy's instructions were to proceed by sea to Rockingham Bay, and travel thence by land to Princess Charlotte's Bay, and Cape York. After communicating with a ship of war at Port Albany, and receiving a stock of provisions to be forwarded thither by the government four months after his departure, the explorer was to proceed along the east coast of the Gulf of Carpentaria to the Watre-Placts, for the purpose of ascertaining whether or not that was the estuary of Leichhardt's River Mitchell, and if so, to follow that river to its junction with the Lynd. Thence he was to strike off by a west south-westerly course, to the Flinders, for the purpose of ascertaining the source of that river; afterwards to connect his journey with Mitchell's discoveries in 1846, by the Belyando River, or some other convenient point, and thence return to Sydney.

The route was one of no trifling labour and hazard, but with his usual enthusiasm, Edward Kennedy prepared for it instantly. His party consisted of twelve men beside himself. They had twenty-seven horses, two hundred and fifty sheep, with a requisite amount of flour, tea, sugar, powder and shot. The arms of the party were eight carbines, four guns, one rifle, and thirteen brace of pistols. Leaving Sydney early in the year, they landed at Rockingham Bay on the 21st of May, 1848, and, on the 1st of June commenced their march northward for Cape York. But at their very outset, the country was so mountainous and rocky, some of the ranges rising 2000 feet, that they were compelled to proceed in a south-westward course, before they could advance northwards. They were even in this direction soon forced to abandon their carts, and the heaviest portion of their stores, so that on proceeding a few hundred miles farther, it became evident that their supplies would not hold out to Cape York, and it was concluded to leave eight men at Weymouth Bay, whilst Kennedy and the other four, including the native guide, Jacky, should push forward to Port Albany, and send round the schooner ordered thither with fresh supplies, or the long boat of the Rattlesnake, to bring them on. In steering for Princess Charlotte's Bay, they followed a stream upwards, a hundred miles or more from the east coast, crossed some sources of the Mitchell, and then went down another river, since called Kennedy's River, which falls into Princess Charlotte's Bay. From this point they were enabled to follow the coast line, the country being more open, to Weymouth Bay, and leaving the eight men there, Kennedy and his small troop started thence for Albany, on the 10th of November.

Misfortune still attended them. They had not proceeded many days when one of the party accidentally wounded himself with a gun; thus rendering the progress of the party much slower. Their provisions were rapidly consuming, and they were obliged to kill one of their horses, and dry its flesh to subsist upon it. Three weeks after leaving the rest of the party, the wounded man became too ill to proceed; Kennedy, therefore, resolved to leave him and the two other white men where they were, and hasten on to Albany, attended only by Jackey the native. He left instructions, that if the wounded man died, the other two were to follow on; if not, they were to wait till the assistance he proposed to send them should arrive. Thus the leader and the black travelled on till they came in sight of the sea, though yet at a considerable distance from Port Albany, and a bright hope of the termination of all their troubles cheered them on. But the hope was fallacious. They here came upon the haunts of a tribe of natives, who affected great friendliness, frequently rubbing their stomachs, and exclaiming "Pomad! pomad!" which means "peace! peace!" Kennedy made them some presents, which they received with apparent satisfaction, but Jackey bade his leader not to trust to them; they were too officious in their professions of good-will, and the event proved that he was not mistaken.

When the travellers resumed their journey after the interview, the blacks dogged their heels for three days, and eventually threw a shower of spears, one of which struck Mr. Kennedy in the back. Jackey fired, and killed one of the assailants, but these renewed the attack, sneaking behind the trees, and discharging their spears from time to time. Jackey cut out the spear which his master had received, and Mr. Kennedy then attempted to fire his gun, but it would not go off, the powder being wet; and he was soon further disabled by two other spear wounds, whilst Jackey was also wounded. The horses, having been also speared, rushed wildly into a swamp. Kennedy, growing weaker, now sat down at the instance of Jackey, while he went to collect the saddle-bags. When he returned, he found his master surrounded by the savages, who were stripping him of his watch and other articles about his person. The blacks, having satisfied at once their cruelty and cupidity, now went away, and Jackey carried his master into the scrub, to a place where he was more likely to be undisturbed, frequently asking, to use his own unaffectedly touching language, in describing the occurrence—" Are you well now?"

"I don't care for the spear-wound in my leg, Jackey," replied poor Kennedy; " but I suffer from those two other spear-wounds in my side and my back. I am bad inside." With bold, and not uncommendable candour, Jackey told his master, "that black-fellows always died when they were speared there;" meaning in the back. "I cannot breath," said Kennedy, growing worse. " Mr. Kennedy, are you going to leave me?" was the affecting response of his faithful follower. " Yes, my boy," said the dying man; " I am going to leave you. I am very bad, Jackey. You will take the books to the Captain, Jackey, but not the big ones: the Governor will give anything for them."

The guide now tied up the papers, whilst Kennedy, true to the last to his enterprise, asked for paper, to write. Having received pencil and paper, he attempted to put down some final notes in direction, but his strength utterly failing, he fell back. Jackey received him in his arms and supported him till he died; and then, having fulfilled his duty to his master, whilst living, turned round and paid him the tribute of his tears when dead. "I was crying a good while," he said, "until I got well; that was about an hour, and then I buried him. I dug up the ground with a tomahawk, and covered over the body with grass, a shirt and trowsers, and then with logs."

That evening Jackey left the fatal spot as it grew dark. The blacks threw spears at him, but by getting into a scrub, and walking half a mile in a creek, with his head only above water, he got away without further injury. He now travelled onwards towards Port Albany. For two days salt water was his only drink, and for the whole of the journey his best food was a few roots, and such snakes, lizards, and guanos, as he could catch. Sheer weakness on several occasions compelled him to rest for an entire day. After a lapse of thirteen days he arrived at Port Albany, and, following Kennedy's final instructions, proceeded to the place where the ship lay, and, having hailed the crew, was taken aboard.

In the meantime, the party of eight, left behind at Weymouth Bay, under the command of Mr. Carron, the naturalist of the expedition, were suffering deeply. Notwithstanding that their position appeared more favourable than that of those who had to face the perils of a journey through an untrodden forest and hostile tribes, their condition was deplorable. A few days after the departure of the leader, one of the men died, and very soon after, another. The principal food of the party was horse-flesh, and it soon became obvious, that whether from aversion, or from the insufficiency of nutriment, the men could not subsist on such diet. In four weeks, six of the party had died, and the survivors were so weak, that they were unable to bury the two who died last, but sunk the bodies in the creek, as a mode of sepulture requiring the least exertion. The camp had frequently been surrounded by a tribe of natives, numbering sixty or seventy men, who menaced the party, and, on one occasion, threw a shower of spears, which, however, did no injury; for on the whites discharging a volley of musketry, the assailants fled. When the party were reduced to two or three, humanity appeared to awake in the hearts of the natives, for they now became less troublesome, and even evinced kindness, by supplying to the starving whites small quantities of food.

On the 1st of December, the appearance of a schooner in the vicinity of the bay kindled the hopes of those who survived. They hoisted a flag and discharged rockets to attract notice, but the vessel passed, and left their position more gloomy than before. The two men who now remained, with difficulty procured by shooting, sufficient food on which to subsist, the blacks keeping them in constant terror, and their exhaustion rendering it a laborious work to move out of the tent.

Their deliverance, however, was at hand. One day, as the month advanced, a party of blacks approached, and one of them put into the hands of Carron a dirty piece of paper, which, on investigation, proved to be a note from Mr. Dobson, of the schooner "Ariel," the vessel which had been sent to Port Albany with provisions for the explorers. The crowd of blacks increased around the tent, and the whites feared lest they should fall victims to treachery just as their safety was about to be realised, when, to their great joy, Dobson himself appeared, accompanied by four others, including the faithful and determined Jackey. The two survivors were at once removed to the vessel, which was at anchor near the beach, three miles distant; one of them, owing to his complete exhaustion, being borne on the shoulders of the seamen: the blacks to the last displaying their savage disposition by wounding one of the ship's crew. In this they were true to the character of the natives of the north-east of Australia, Captain Cook, when laid up in Endeavour River, having found them the same.

The vessel had previously anchored near the place where Kennedy had left behind the three men; and a party was landed with a view of making an attempt, under the guidance of Jackey, to rescue them. The party penetrated into the woods till they were within a day's journey of the place, when the men halted. There they met with blacks, who had in their possession articles which Jackey pronounced to have belonged to the white men. As the provisions were failing, and as the safety of the vessel was at stake, the sailors, believing the men to have been murdered, refused to proceed any further, and the search was abandoned, and that the more readily, on account of the other eight men who were awaiting succour at Weymouth Bay. The vessel having accomplished its mission at Weymouth Bay, it was found impossible to persuade the sailors to renew the search for the other three, and Captain Dobson set sail for Sydney.

Early in March the schooner arrived in Sydney, carrying back three persons, as the sole survivors of the expedition. If all or any of the three left behind at the second encampment, by Kennedy in his chivalrous anxiety to procure succour for all, escaped starvation or the spears of the blacks, they were never again heard of amongst white men. Thus, in all probability, out of this party of thirteen, ten perished, including the leader, making the enterprise one of the most disastrous in the annals of Australian exploration.

Carron had kept a journal from the commencement of the expedition, and this, with the story of the aboriginal guide, formed a complete narrative of the progress and melancholy termination of the enterprise. A judicial investigation into the circumstances connected with the expedition was immediately instituted by the government; the two European survivors, and Jackey, being the principal witnesses. The whole of the evidence went to show that the conduct of the leader in no way detracted from the honours which he had previously won in this arduous field of enterprise. His surviving companions were unanimous in declaring that he had done all that was possible to save the party, and to alleviate the misfortunes of those under his care. He had given up his own horses for the use of the sick, and had taken a share in every privation, hardship, and danger, whilst he remained at the head of the party, and when it was evident that his efforts in this position would be unavailing, accompanied by the faithful black, he set out on a journey, which, under the circumstances, presented difficulties and dangers, which his devotion to his associates, and his fidelity to the duty imposed upon him, could alone have incited him to encounter. It was not poor Kennedy's fortune to succeed in the object of the expedition, but it was to his honour that he exerted every energy to accomplish it, and that he died bravely in the attempt. His name will for ever be connected with the York Peninsular, and probably years hence, when a populous colony exists there, a column of memorial will mark the spot where he fell.

CHAPTER VI.

THE EXPEDITION OF MR. ROBERT AUSTIN, ASSISTANT SURVEYOR, INTO THE INTERIOR OF WESTERN AUSTRALIA, IN 1854.

Objects of the expedition.—The party.—Left Mombe Kine, on Swan River, in July.—The samphire plains to Waddoming.--The salt lake Cow-cowing.—Thence a poor country to Mount Marshall.—A miserable region of dead scrub to Mount Kenneth.—Views from Mount Kenneth sterile and forbidding.—Journey northward over this desert to August 20th.—Their horses poisoned by a shrub.—Fourteen died.—Mount Magnet.—Views all round still dismal.—Miseries of tight boots.—West Mount Magnet.—Rude, rocky, and scrubby country.—Natives refuse to eat a new kind of kangaroo.—Believed it a demon.—The Carved Cave Spring.—Native art.—Accident to Farmer by his own gun.—Poison plants again.—Farmer dies of lock-jaw.—Bequeathes his property.—Buried near a hill named Mount Farmer.—Mount Charles.—Views round into rocky and scrubby regions.—Native cross, and springs for emus.—Mounts Lake and Murchison—Murchison river.—Advanced to within fifty miles of Shark's Bay.--Driven back by wretched, waterless country.—Mounts Narryer, Welcome, Grass, and Vinden.—Sufferings on the retreat to the Geraldine Mines.—Bury luggage.—Native guide nearly dead.—Generous offer of Captain Sanford, but unavailing.—Return to Perth.—Mr. Austin's estimate of the lands passed over.—Mr. Phillips' Report.

In 1854 the government of Western Australia sent out a further expedition, under the command of Assistant Surveyor, Mr. Robert Austin, to explore the interior towards the north and east of the colony. The objects of this expedition were stated to be to ascertain the geological structure, natural productions, water-parting, and general character of the interior of the colony to the north and east of the settled districts, and towards the Gascoyne river. A ship, under command of Mr. George Phillips, was despatched to await the arrival of the expedition at the mouth of the Gascoyne, to succour them with supplies, and convey them back to Perth.

The exploring party under the command of Mr. Austin, consisted of ten men, with twenty-seven horses, and 120 days' provisions. Mr. Woodward voluntarily accompanied them with Mr. Chidlow's team, escorted by two men, for whom he took forty days' rations, to

PASS THROUGH A MISERABLE REGION. 121

proceed as far as Cow-cowing, and thence to return with the leader's report to head-quarters. The expedition left Mombe Kine, on the sources of the Swan River, on the 10th of July. They proceeded north-east, crossing the tributary stream of the Mortlock, or Salt River, to Goolmalling, and on to the samphire plains and great salt lake of Cow-cowing, and thence to Waddoming, west of Lake Brown, having traversed very much the track of the Messrs. Gregory in 1846. There, however, they struck directly north, leaving the Gregory track to the right, and passed through a poor country, with much scrub and bare granite rocks, and with little water to Mount Marshall, where on the 11th of August, they dismissed Mr. Woodward and Chidlow's team, on their return with the dispatches. Thence they passed an arid, scrubby desert, where the bushes were all dead, and fell crashing before them, staking several of the horses. They were, however, stimulated to persevere through this miserable track, by the view of table-shaped and peaked hills, apparently fifty miles ahead. The highest table-land in this range they named Mount Kenneth, from Mr. Kenneth Brown, who first discovered it. They found grass and water at the feet of these hills, and halted two days to recruit the party. Mount Kenneth proved to be of sandstone formation, capped with ironstone, of about 180 feet above the level of the surrounding country, and 1401 feet above the level of the sea. The prospect from it on all sides was sterile, scrubby, and cheerless. To the north and east were sandstone ridges and stony plains; from north-west to west were hills of trap and greenstone, and the country undulating and scrubby. There were channels of streams, but all dry. They advanced north-east over this wretched country, amongst sandstone cliffs, quartz, and round scrubby hummocks of black, shining, iron-ore, with dry channels of streams, the beds of which were white and glistening. After fighting their way through dense scrubs of cypress and acacia, and totally without water, on the 20th of August, in latitude 28° 43′ 23″, longitude 118° 38′ E., as they were proceeding, suddenly their horses began to rear and spin round, and then kicking violently, fell. This was a sign that they had been eating of a poisonous shrub, a species of gastrilobium, which is the curse of some parts of Western Australia. They now observed this poison plant growing amongst the grass everywhere. They describe it as having a small, bright, orange-coloured pea-blossom, like bird's eyes. The leaves as opposite and spreading, two inches long, wedge-shaped, with a triangular apex, at the angles of which, and at the base of the leaf, are small thorns, and the breadth at the base of the apex is half an inch. The average height of the bushes is three feet, though many are much larger. Mr. Austin observes that this was the first instance that he had known of horses being seriously injured by this plant. That some years before Dr. Harris gave a large quantity of it to a pony without any prejudicial effect: and that he, therefore, was of opinion that the horses on this occasion were affected by it on account of their stomachs being empty and weak.

Whatever was the cause, the consequences on this occasion were most disastrous. All their horses except eleven were violently affected by the poison; and though they bled them, and gave them flour-gruel till they gained their strength again, as well as allowing them all the rest they could, fourteen of them died, and some of the others were left too weak to carry their loads. Wherever on their route they observed the poison bushes they were obliged to watch the horses day and night.

From this place, which they named Poison Rock, they endeavoured to penetrate more to the east, but found the country impracticable. They, therefore, proceeded northward, but over a tract not much better. Scrubby ranges, of ironstone or greenstone, and rocks of quartz, the earth wherever turned up looking white, like lime, alternating with samphire and salt-bush flats, and stony scrub, was the sort of country they had to pass, without water till the 24th of August, when they reached a wild, desolate, magnetic hill, which they named Mount Magnet.

This was in latitude 27° 58′ east, longitude 118° 37′. The views from it were of a most scrubby, rocky, and unpromising aspect.

Mr. Austin had only advanced to this point with a reconnoitring party, and he now hastened back, bringing his main party on to a flat where there was water and better feed, which he called Recruit Flat, and which they reached on the 5th of September. On their return to this flat, Mr. Austin and Narrayer, the native, found themselves waylaid by a savage, who rushed on Narrayer with his spear, and were compelled to fire at him with shot, on receiving some of which he decamped. On advancing from Recruit Flat, they found the country extremely stony, and a curious incident was observed on the journey. Mr. Frazer having on a pair of new boots, his friend Mr. Brown exchanged with him, allowing him the use of his old, easy ones; but Brown's feet soon becoming galled, too, with the new shoes, he pulled them off, and, putting on one of his old ones, allowed Frazer the other. Thus these two young men, each with one shoe, and the other foot wrapped up in cloths, hobbled on for sixteen miles over sharp rocks, and through high scrub, on a very hot day, without a single draft of water, and without a murmur.

They had now struck into a tract to the west of Mount Magnet, and on the 13th of September found themselves on some rocks of trap and quartz, mixed with hornblende schist, with brown mica slate above, overlooking a great salt lake, but dry. It extended north and east to the verge of the horizon. To the S.W. an extensive range of trap hills, similar to Mount Magnet, rose from the plains, covered with scrub, and stones around it. It was fifteen miles off, and they named it West Mount Magnet. The country all around was rude, rocky, stony and scrubby, abounding with purple, micacious, schist, and red conglomerate, resting on felspar grit cliffs. There were deep watercourses, but all dry.

Just before reaching this place an incident occurred,

which showed the peculiar superstition of the natives. Two female kangaroos, of the red kind, (*osphanter rufus*), were killed, which the native guide had never seen, and although they were particularly fat and tender, they could not be persuaded to taste of them. On being expostulated with on the folly of refusing to strengthen themselves, after much exhaustion, and when very hungry, with this delicate meat, Narrayer, says Mr. Austin, "became very much excited, and begged me not to propose such a thing to him; 'for,' said he, 'look at his head, truly it is that of a dog, with the ears of a cow. Saw you ever kangaroo so fat, or with meat that smelt so strange? No, sir, this creature is not natural, and it must be a *bwolyer* (magician or evil spirit). Glad I am to be the first of my tribe who has killed one of this odious race. But my father and mother never eat one, neither will I. Let the northern women eat it if they like, but I must become a great fool before I put any of this strange devil down my throat to give me the stomach ache."

The country which they traversed south-west of the Great Salt Lake, and betwixt that and West Mount Magnet, was of a most rough, stony, dry, and scrubby character, and they had infinite trouble in hunting up and recovering their horses, which strayed in search of water. At a spring in a cave, which they called the Carved Cave Spring, they found some specimens of native art. "This spring was in the sandy bed of a cave, under a felspar and quartz grit rock, and on the north side of this cave there were perfect representations of seven left hands of natives of the ordinary size, with one large right hand above, and to the left of them; five couples of red kangaroos' feet, and three emus' feet, of the natural size, having the appearance of impressions made by these hands and feet dipped in some acid fluid, which had corroded and discoloured the rock; and several rude imitations of the emus' and kangaroos' feet had been recently carved beneath them, by chipping the rock with a piece of hard stone, probably quartz, as I found a sharp fragment of that rock, suited for the purpose, in the cave."

The reader will recollect the account of the drawings in a cave near Prince Regent's River on the West Coast, discovered by Captain Grey, and others discovered by Allan Cunningham, and other explorers on islands and shores of the same coast, but of much superior execution and design. The natives of Australia seem particularly to select caves for their works of art. This cave was in latitude 27° 43′ 13″, east longitude 118°.

On September 21st, not far from this Carved Cave Spring, one of the party had an accident, which marked him for the victim of this expedition; for such expeditions seem as though they could not be exempt from the fatality of a victim. This was the poor youth Farmer. Mr. Austin had sent him to bring in a stray horse. Mr. Austin was out watching the flight of a native woman and child, whom they had observed approaching the spring, when he heard one double shot after another, announcing that something was wrong at the camp. Soon after he saw Mr. Guerin running towards him, who reported that Charles Farmer had shot himself. He found the poor lad stretched between the loads, under the shade of a horse-rug, the horse for which he had been sent standing by his side, and the natives, silent and sorrowful, were sitting at his feet. It was a saddening sight, they looked so wan and altered. Farmer's arm was shattered by a gun-shot wound received above the wrist, and extending along the muscles towards the elbow, where the charge of No. 4 shot had lodged, and had apparently injured the joint.

The accident, according to his own account, had occurred thus: while they were returning with the horse, Narrayer, on the 9th, shot a red kangaroo, and Farmer laid down his gun in a bush while he skinned and fastened the hind-quarters on the horse. This done, he laid hold of his gun by the muzzle to throw it over his shoulder, when the hammer caught in a branch, and discharged the contents of the left-hand barrel into his right arm. They had been travelling two days since this occurrence without any other water than the small quantity they were fortunately carrying at the time, and the natives had given Farmer the whole of it, though they themselves had been reduced to the utmost extremity by thirst, and the poor horse had been three days without water.

His arm was much swollen, and Mr. Austin washed it with tepid water, and put on a large poultice of linseed and oil to reduce the swelling. After it was dressed the poor fellow was very cheerful, and said he expected it would soon be well again, and marched quite strong to the spring. These favourable symptoms, however, did not continue.

They were now again amongst poison bushes, and had to watch the horses rigorously night and day, as some of them were determined in their efforts to get at them, and browze them. They were still travelling through a rocky, and bushy country, destitute of water. They saw at different times indications of gold, but had no water to wash for it, especially amongst some gravel and pipe-clay as they dug for a well, but uselessly. Their horses began to fail, and at length fell exhausted. At this juncture, Narrayer and Souper, the natives, saw two blacks, and tried to hail them, but they attacked them, according to their account, and obliged them to fire at them.

They had now reached a hill nearly parallel with the west end of the great salt lake, and poor Farmer showed signs of getting worse. This is Mr. Austin's account of his end. "I examined all the horses, made good their shoes, and dressed the backs of several, chiefly the withers, which our saddles began to press now the poor animals were thin. After this all hands were busily employed repairing boots, except Narrayer and Souper, whom I sent out to shoot a mess for Farmer, who at eight A.M. on this the 26th of September, complained of sore-throat, difficulty of swallowing, and pain across his stomach. His arm, however, looked much better, and several more shots came out. I gave him a dose of castor-oil at nine A.M. At noon, stiffness in the jaw alarmed the poor boy, and made him apprehensive that lock-jaw was coming on. This unfortunately was the case; but I told him that perhaps he had caught cold, and rubbed his throat with liniment. Towards evening he could scarcely open his mouth wide enough to admit the point of a spoon. I then bled him, taking a pint of very black blood from his left arm, and gave him ten grains of calomel. During the night he was in great agony, caused by violent pains in his stomach, which made him draw up his limbs in convulsive fits, on several occasions so bad that he carried away the tent that was over him. I put a large horse-blister on his stomach, but in his struggles it was rubbed off before it took effect; so, to give him immediate relief, I applied flannels, dipped in hot water. That, he said, eased him a little, but at dawn I saw that there were no hopes of his recovery, and spoke soothingly to him of his approaching dissolution. He then spoke calmly and sensibly to me about his affairs, and added, his sufferings were so great, that he was glad to hear that his death was, thank God, about to release him from them.

"Leaving him, for a moment, to the particular care of Messrs. Guerin and Buck, though all the party were anxious and ready during the night to do anything they could to alleviate his sufferings, I directed Mr. Whitfield, in company with Caunt and Souper, to proceed with a day and a half's rations, and explore the high hills ten miles N.W., for our next bivouac, and return the following afternoon. I also sent Mr. Brown with Narrayer, to find feed in the neighbourhood, if possible, better than the horses were in, as I feared, now this place was eaten off, they would soon begin eating poison.

"When I returned to Farmer's side, he told me he had four horses and some money; that he wished his brother Thomas to have the horses, and the money to be divided equally between his other brothers and sisters. I wrote a paper to this effect, and read each sentence to him as I wrote it, in the presence of the men, and he approved of what I had written. But whilst I was writing the concluding lines "in witness whereof I have signed my hand, etc.," he was seized with violent pains, and became insensible, or rather delirious, calling out for his brother Thomas, till he fainted away. He then lay apparently dead for a few minutes, then rallied, still delirious, and in great agony, for about twenty minutes, when he fainted again, and died at twenty-five minutes past two o'clock, on the afternoon of the 27th of September. As the poor boy could not sign his will, I obtained the signatures of those men to it, who were present when he made and approved of it. We then selected a nice spot for his grave on the summit of the hill, close to the camp, shaded by a beautiful drooping wattle-tree, but we reached the solid rock at two feet down, and were obliged to dig it lower down the hill, twenty yards from the left bank of the brook, eighty yards from the spring, and 1896 feet above the level of the sea, being the highest plains visited in S. latitude 27° 41′ 18″, E. longitude 117° 42′, where we buried him at sunset, sewed up in his blanket, with his saddle for a pillow, upon which we lowered him gently in a horse-rug. I read the beautiful service of our church for the burial of the dead, over him, after which we fired our guns, and retired in silence. I never saw men so strangely affected; not a tear was shed, but every man's voice was low and tremulous, and sounded hollow and unearthly all that night." After breakfast the next morning, they carried stones from the adjacent granite rocks, and placed them round and over poor Farmer's grave, with a slab at his head, on which, with a chisel and tomahawk, they carved "C. Farmer, 1854." They also named a neighbouring hill Mount Farmer.

Somewhat south of Mount Farmer rose a range to which they gave the name of Mount Charles. Mr. Austin then travelled on to Mount Farmer and ascended it as the highest point in the neighbourhood. The prospect thence for twenty miles round, was one of stony plains covered with scrub, and studded with trap rocks to the westward, and granite rocks from the E. to N.W. These were bounded on the N.E. by the western shore of the great salt lake, in which a distant blue peak loomed like a granite hill, apparently forty miles distant. The country between Mount Farmer and the camp, five miles W.N.W. presented a rocky thicket, covered with sharp quartz and ironstone round the foot of the hills, changing to brown gravel and sandy soil wooded with acacia.

From this time to the 10th of October, they proceeded N.W. over a rough and rocky country, with granite and sandstone cliffs, stony and dry, yet abounding with anourarungs, or rock kangaroos, which Mr. Austin suspected that Narrayer and Souper were afraid of shooting since Farmer's accident, from a superstitious feeling. The plains were frequently scattered with mica, hornblende and quartz. Narrayer and Souper returning from one of their excursions in quest of game, reported that they had seen four large stones laid in the form of a cross, round the base of a perpendicular stone, on a bare granite rock, as if to mark a boundary, and had seen traces of natives, and ambushes made by them to lay hold on the legs of emus and kangaroos, as they went to a spring for water. On the 4th they struck the dry channel of a river which they supposed to fall into the Murchison. They named it the Sanford after the Colonial Secretary. A little farther north-west they named a bare granite rock 240 feet above the plains, Mount Luke, after Mr. Luke Leake, of Perth. Crossing several dry beds of streams, probably tributaries of the Murchison, on the 8th they arrived at a high rugged range of green-stone trap lying on granite, the highest peak of which they named Mount Murchison. This mount was 400 feet above the level of the plain, and the hills altogether were scattered with stones of quartz. A little beyond they struck the Murchison River, but the farther they now advanced the more stony and impracticable the country became. Their horses had been three days without water, and were unable to proceed. The prospect a-head was still worse, they, therefore, beat a retreat to a spring twelve miles back, where they refreshed themselves and horses. By taking a more westward course, they again advanced northward till the 29th of October, when they were about fifty miles from Shark's Bay, and there the utter want of food and water compelled them to retreat. In their circuitous route from their farthest point on the 12th, they had named a hill to the north of their track, Mount Narrayer, and at different points Mount Welcome, Mount Grass, and Mount Vinden. At Mount Grass they picked up an old native, who acted as guide, though unwillingly for some days.

The sufferings of the party on their return to the Geraldine mines on the Murchison river were very great, from the failure of their supplies, the want of water, and the rocky nature of the country. They followed for the most part the course of the Murchison, but it was long before they found any fresh water in it. They were compelled to bury much of their baggage, to expedite their march, and the men began to be very desponding. Narrayer, the native, was quite done up, and was only recovered by Mr. Austin washing him with the brine in one of the holes in the river. On the 20th of November, however, they reached the mines in safety. On the 24th, Captain Sandford came in with a number of fine horses, and invited the party to Linton, offering to take Mr. Austin to Shark Bay in his cutter, and to enable him to push from the mouth of the Gascoyne to his last bivouac in the desert. This, however, proved impracticable, and the party returned to Perth, some by the schooner Daphne, and others overland. Mr. Austin, who took this latter course with Narrayer and Souper, arrived in Perth on the 27th of December.

In this expedition Mr. Austin extended the knowledge of the colony very much farther north than before; that is, taking Mr. A. C. Gregory's central point between the parallels of 29° and 28°, to nearly 26°, and including the Great Salt Marsh in the N.W. The least satisfactory discovery to the colony was that there was very little good or habitable country throughout all that space. Mr. Austin's general remarks on the results of the expedition are as follows :—

"Looking at the map of the country I have traversed, you will see—1st., that there are extensive marshes in 118° E. longitude, between 27° and 28° of S. latitude, flowing and trending N.W., and about 1400 feet above the level of the sea ; that the country between Toodyay, which is about 800 feet, and the base of Mount Farmer, on the N.W. side of these marshes, rises gradually to the height of 1896 feet above the level of the sea, and that this portion of the country is so inclined, that the water is shed over this area towards the S. and W., into Mr. Gregory's great lake, Moore, which is tributary to the lake Cow-cowing, flowing thence by the way of the Salt River and the Avon, to the ocean. 2nd. That there are four large rivers in 117° E., longitude (between 27° 20', and 26° 40' S. lat.), of a decidedly fresh character, coming from the N.E., and shedding into the Murchison, which itself flows from the same direction ; and that I appear to have struck near the N.W. extreme of its basin ; that large numbers of natives occasionally come down these streams at the latter end of our dry season ; and that red kangaroos, emus, and turkeys were numerous between these rivers, though the country on our route was very indifferent, and still worse to the westward, while everywhere else the country traversed was destitute of game, and afforded no traces of any number of natives, except at the eastern side of the cliff, near Farmer's Horse Camp."

From the geological character of the country, Mr. Austin infers that the country is a gold country : but if that be the case, it is of a description which must render the digging for gold most difficult. In such an inhospitable country, every means of existence must be conveyed for many hundred miles through the desert, and then, where is the water, necessary for gold washing? Mr. Austin, however, entertains the idea that farther eastward there must be a much more fertile country; but this yet remains a question. The great advantage of Mr. Austin's expedition has been to make the colony of Western Australia aware of the narrow limits of its good land in that direction.

Appended to Mr. Austin's report is one by Mr. George Phillips, giving some observations on the mouth of the river Gascoigne, in the north arm of Shark's Bay.

CHAPTER VII.

EXPEDITION FOR THE EXPLORATION OF NORTHERN AUSTRALIA IN 1855-6, UNDER THE COMMAND OF MR. A. C. GREGORY.

Mr. Uzzielli offers £10,000 for an expedition to explore the north of Australia.—Offer of Mr. W. S. Lindsay, M.P.—Undertaken by the Government.—Outfit to be completed at Moreton Bay.—The party.—Sailed from Brisbane August 12th, 1855.—Reached Port Patterson, Arnheim's Land, September 2nd.—Ran on a rock. — Great damage to, and loss of horses.—Land at Point Pearce.—Part of the expedition went by land to the higher part of the river.—Two horses poisoned.—Horses attacked by alligators on Fitzmaurice River.—The party ascending the river struck on a rock.—Great loss of stores and sheep. — Out of 200 shipped, only twenty-six reached the camp alive.—Rules laid down for the conduct of the party.—Their good effect.—Set out a small party southward.—Exploration of the Victoria for 100 miles.—Return to camp.—Fresh exploration in January, 1856.—Stupendous rocks on the river course.—Basaltic country with deep gullies.—The headwaters of the Victoria.—Dividing range.—Wretched country.—Retreat before the heat and drought.—Mount Müller.—Follow the Wickham to the Victoria. —Serious injury to one of the party.—Party formed to proceed towards Carpentaria.—Start on 21st of June.—Reach a creek of the Roper, July 12th.— The Roper.—Flat country.—Creeks and lagoons.—Marks of floods.—The gigantic water-lily.—Proceed S.E., leave basaltic country.—Blacks try to surprise them.—Two horses poisoned.—Bad country.—Limmen Bight.—MacAdam range and MacArthur river.—Sandstone hills.—Cross the Robinson and Leichhardt rivers.—Country better.—Brimstone and basalt.—Nicholson river.—Poor Country.—Beame's Brook a branch of the Albert.—The Tom Tough not arrived.—Determined to push on for the east course.—Buried canisters to say this.—September 3rd continued their journey.—Plains of Promise disappoint them.—The Leichhardt.—Attacked by the natives.—The spring season, yet the country looked poor.—Betwixt the Flinders and Gilbert saw good country.—Gilbert nearly dry.—Arrive at ranges 2500 feet high.— Head waters of the Lynd.—Basaltic country well grassed.—Reach the Burdekin in October.—Trees marked with an iron axe.—Camp of Leichhardt.— Rocks of various kinds.—Trace the Burdekin to the "Suttar and Rely-ando."— On the Comet noticed a camp of Leichhardt's.—Arrival at Brisbane.—The expedition completed in sixteen months.—Objects accomplished by this expedition.—The part of the expedition which went in the Tom Tough to Timor for supplies reaches Sydney by sea.—Mr. Baine's boat-voyage of 650 miles.— Remarks of Captain Sturt on Mr. Gregory's discoveries, and on the theory of the Australian interior.—Theory of Mr. Alfred Howitt.—Diagram in illustration of it.—Reports of Messrs. Elsey, Wilson, Flood, Baines, and Lieutenant Chimmo.

THE necessity for a more thorough exploration of the northern regions of Australia, after the various enterprises of the kind in its eastern, western, and southern portions, became eventually so strong, that Mr. W. S. Lindsay, M.P., offered to contribute towards this great object. Mr. Uzzielli also offered £10,000; and these noble acts seem to have shamed the Imperial Government into fitting action. The sacrifice on the part of Mr. Uzzielli was rendered unnecessary by the Government undertaking it. The experienced explorer, A. C. Gregory, was invited to take the command of the expedition, which was fitted out at Sydney, except so far as the horses and sheep were concerned, which were shipped at Moreton Bay. The objects of the expedition were clearly set forth in the instructions to the leader. The scene of exploration was to be the northern and north-western regions of Australia. The outfit was to be completed at Moreton Bay, and the men and material were to be conveyed to the Victoria river in a vessel, accompanied by a smaller one as a tender carrying stores. This smaller vessel was to remain, and bring them back. They were to ascend the Victoria, and to proceed in the first place southward, so as to reach that elevation whence the streams arose that ran into the interior, to lose themselves in desert sands, or to join an inland sea. It was hoped that extensive pastoral regions might be there discovered. Returning from this journey to the Victoria, they were then to endeavour to cross to the northern coast, and follow it to the Albert river, noting the quality of the land, its rivers, products, natives, etc., as they went along, and whether it afforded sufficient capabilities for a settlement. From that point, taking on board any further necessary supplies from the attendant vessel, they were to endeavour to find a good track to the northern settlement of New South Wales, on the east coast, by a more direct route than that which Leichhardt discovered.

On the 18th of July, 1855, Mr. Gregory, in the barque Monarch, attended by the schooner, Tom Tough, sailed from Sydney to Moreton Bay, where he found fifty horses and 200 sheep had been collected by Mr. H. Gregory. It was not till the 12th of August that they had taken on board their cattle, and set sail for Brisbane.

The staff of the expedition was as follows:—

NAMES OF THE STAFF.

1. Commander, . . . A. C. Gregory.
2. Assistant Commander, . H. C. Gregory.
3. Geologist, . . . J. S. Wilson.
4. Artist, ... T. Baines.
5. Surgeon and Naturalist, . J. R. Elsey.
6. Botanist, . . . F. Müller.
7. Collector and Preserver, . J. Flood.
8. Overseer, . . G. Phipps.
9. Second Overseer, . . C. Humphrey.
10. Farrier, . . . R. Bowman.
11. Harness Maker, . . C. Dean.
12. Stockman, . . . J. Melville.
13. . . . . W. Dawson.
14. . . . . W. Shewell.
15. . . . . W. Selby.
16. . . . . S. MacDonald.
17. . . . . H. Richards.
18. . . . . J. Fahey.

The provisions consisted of flour, salt pork, preserved beef, rice, peas, sugar, tea, coffee, preserved potatoes, sago, vinegar, lime juice, &c.; and were calculated to last eighteen months at full rations. On the 26th of August, they reached Port Albany in Torres Straits, where they were to trans-ship the hay from the schooner to the Monarch. On the 2nd of September they had reached Port Patterson, south of Clarence Strait, Arnhem's Land, when the Monarch ran on a rocky reef at the entrance of the harbour, where she received considerable injury in her bottom. This was the commencement of a series of disasters, which greatly crippled the strength and capabilities of the expedition. The vessel was not got off the reef for eight days, during which time she lay on her side, and the horses in consequence suffered severely. Two died, and the rest were so weakened that some had not strength to support them through the fatigue of landing when they reached Point Pearce, on the 18th of September. Several were lost in the landing, and the remainder were in such an exhausted state that they could scarcely travel to the water, three miles distant. The landing of the horses being completed, the Monarch was discharged on the 24th of September, and sailed thence to Singapore. The leader, Mr. H. Gregory, Dr. Müller, and seven men proceeded with the horses by land towards the upper part of the Victoria River; whilst Mr. Wilson and the rest of the party ascended the river in the schooner with the sheep, with orders to form a camp at the most eligible spot he could find, and there await the arrival of the horses.

The land party found the country from Point Pearce to the Macadam Range, consisting of grassy plains between the mangroves on the river and the sandy forest land, and low sandstone hills inland. Water abundant from various creeks and pools. The range itself was rocky and difficult; and before reaching the Fitzmaurice River, two horses were poisoned by some deadly herbs or shrubs, and in the river itself the other horses were attacked by alligators in the night, and three of them severely wounded. Above the influence of the tide, the Fitzmaurice proved a fine fresh-water stream, fifty yards wide. Beyond this, the hills became extremely rocky, and at length altogether stopped their way, except along the river bank. On the 20th of October they found Mr. Wilson's party encamped at a spring on the left bank of the Victoria, about seven miles above Sandy Island. Here they had to hear of fresh disasters. The Tom Tough had run on a rock in coming up the river, and afterwards grounded on a mud bank a few miles higher up, where it still remained. Both the vessel and cargo were seriously damaged, and it was feared that the vessel would become a total wreck. Mr. Wilson had still kept the sheep on board, and many had perished in consequence. In endeavouring now to land the sheep, eleven more were drowned by the sinking of the boat, so that out of 200 sheep brought from Moreton Bay, fifty only were alive on reaching the Victoria, and of these fifty, only twenty-six now reached the camp alive.

The schooner was at length got off the mud bank, and part of the cargo was landed, so as to lighten her and allow of the examination of her bottom, and a heavy frame was built inside of her and bolted to the sides, to cover the damages, and strengthen her sufficiently for further service on the expedition. Mr. Gregory then laid down his rules for the conduct of the party, and put the horses under the care of Mr. H. Gregory. Every person had a certain number of the horses to saddle, and were responsible for the packs and harness, all of which were numbered. By these regulations, every man knowing his duty, during the fourteen months which the journey occupied, all continued to go on in the camp like clockwork. They rose at four o'clock in the morning, an excellent plan in hot climates, so that they could perform their daily travel during the cooler parts of the day, and rest during the heat. In attempting to explore the course of the river upwards, in a boat formed of an India-rubber cloth stretched over a frame, it was soon found that the sun melted the india-rubber, and rocks on the bars destroyed the cloth. Sir Thomas Mitchell had before found how useless canvas boats were in Australian rivers.

On the 24th of November, Mr. Gregory set out to explore the country southward, accompanied by Dr. Müller and Messrs. H. Gregory and Wilson, and having seven of the best-conditioned horses, which notwithstanding were but weakly. They first attempted to ascend the creek a few miles above Captain Stokes' farthest in 1839, but there was not water enough in it. They found it an extension of the Beagle Valley, a fertile tract of land thirty miles long and from seven to ten broad. It was hemmed in by sandstone ranges of from 500 to 800 feet high, forming an elevated table land, and divided in the centre by the Fitzroy Ranges. They then followed the Victoria for twenty miles, the sandstone ranges gradually closing it in till it left only a rocky gorge half a mile wide and 600 feet deep, with perpendicular cliffs of sandstone, leaving only a passage close to the river, which formed deep reaches of water separated by rocky bars. Beyond these ranges they entered on a level plain, extending for twenty miles, and then followed a tributary creek S.W. for twenty-five miles through a grassy, thinly wooded country, till again reaching ranges of jasper rock, beyond which the sandstone table-land rose abruptly. By these they were compelled to return to the Victoria, and they followed it to latitude 16° 26', through a beautifully grassy country of sandstone, limestone, and basalt formations. There, the river divided into two branches, one coming from the south, the other from the west, for fifteen miles through grassy plains. There they ascended the table land, and saw no appearance of higher hills beyond; so having ascertained the character of the country for about a hundred miles, they returned to the camp. In their absence, Mr. Baines had discovered a small river westward falling into the Victoria, and on its banks a considerable quantity of grassy country.

On the 3rd of January, 1856, Mr. Gregory set out with a limited party to explore the south. As drays could not cross the steep sandstone ranges, they carried their provisions on their horses, which were now reduced to thirty-six, and these but weakly, though considerably improved since landing. The party on this occasion consisted of—

Commander	A. C. Gregory.
Assistant Commander	H. Gregory.
Artist and Storekeeper	T. Baines.
Botanist	F. Müller.
Collector	T. Flood.
Overseer	G. Phipps.
Farrier	R. Bowman.
Harness Maker	C. Dean.
Stockman	J. Fahey.

On the 13th of January they had reached the part of the river to which they had advanced in December, and found the country now beautifully grassed and thinly wooded with bauhinia and box trees. In latitude 16° 47' they made a fresh camp, and the leader went on with only Mr H. Gregory, Dr. Müller, and Charles Dean, taking only eleven horses and provisions for three months. Finding it impossible to follow the western bank of the Victoria, from the steepness of the rocks and the intense heat and humid air, they struck away S.E., through a fine grassy country, well watered by numerous creeks, though abounding with basaltic rocks and stones. About latitude 17°, they reached the bank of the main stream of the Victoria, coming nearly direct from the south, through basaltic valleys, deeply cut with lateral gullies. In latitude 18° 12', they reached the creeks constituting the head waters of the Victoria, and stood on the dividing range 1600 feet in elevation.

Descending the dividing range southward, they found a small creek, which soon lost itself in a grassy flat, beyond which all was dry and sandy, producing a low scrub of acacia, eucalyptus, and needle grass. Finding no possibility of proceeding southward, they followed a a creek W.S.W., which, however, led them through a country little better. On the 5th of March they had passed the limit to which the tropical rains of the N.W. extend, and the country south of 19° seemed only to be visited by occasional thunder-storms, producing green patches around wide stretches of desolation, in which no rain appeared to have fallen for twelve months. They there encountered the dry bed of a large salt lake, bearing evidences of occasional floods. But the waters which they had passed were now rapidly drying up, and having penetrated into this inhospitable region to nearly 21°, they felt it prudent to make their retreat. Parallel with the lake eastward, they named a hill Mount Wilson, and near 20° they saw and named another Mount Müller.

On the 28th of March they regained their nearest camp, and found the horses greatly improved by their pasture. Mr. Baines and his party had been annoyed by the blacks, who had made several attempts to burn their camp. Before retreating farther, Mr. Gregory from this camp made a trip eastward to the main course of the Victoria, through a well-grassed country, but almost wholly destitute of water. He then followed up a large creek from Roe Downs, and thence crossing to the Wickham, followed it down to its junction with the Victoria. At the camp on that river they found that one of the seamen had died, and others were disabled by the scurvy and dysentery. Henry Richards had also wounded his wrist by falling amongst some sharp reeds, which, though at first of apparently no consequence, led subsequently to the necessity for amputation. The Tom Tough had now been repaired, and fresh caulked, and the leader was anxious to commence his journey to Carpentaria.

The party organized for this overland journey consisted of the two Gregorys, Mr. Wilson, the geologist, Mr. Elsey, the surgeon and naturalist, with Dean, the harness-maker, Bowman, farrier, and Melville the stockman. They took provisions for six months. The rest of the party were to proceed in the Tom Tough to Timor for additional provisions, and then sail for the Albert, where the two parties were to rendezvous. Mr. Wilson afterwards declined to accompany the land party, and Dr. Müller took his place. On the 21st of June they commenced their important journey. They took advantage of the large creek falling into the Victoria in latitude 15° 38′, and which leads E.N.E. By this means they were in a direct course for the river Roper, and by reaching its most interior creeks they would be able to get to the northern coast without suffering so much from the arid desert which runs, as is supposed, from near Stuart's northern track into Arnhem Land. By the 28th of June they had reached the head of Victoria Creek, and found it running from an elevated and fine basaltic country, extending along the foot of a low, sandy table land. By the 12th of July they had reached a creek of the Roper in a level, sandy country, and followed it down to its junction with the river in latitude 14° 58′, longitude 133° 54′.

The country on the banks of the Roper was very flat, and had some tracks of basaltic, grassy land. To the north, hills of moderate elevation were seen. There was abundance of water in the Roper, running over rocky bars of limestone, and the limestone underlying the sandstone in the country, gave plenty of water under the surface, though it appeared parched to the eye. Near the junction of various creeks with the Roper they found the country flat, and covered with reeds and tall grass. They saw marks of inundations, and there, on some fine lagoons, saw, for the first time, the gigantic water-lily, Nelumbium.

On the 17th of July, in latitude 14° 52′, longitude 133° 42′, they quitted the banks of the river, and commenced their S.E. course. They soon left the basaltic country, and got upon hard sandstone. At night the blacks tried to surprise them, and were rebuffed with force. On the 21st they had two horses killed by eating some poisonous plant, as at Macadam Range. They now travelled through a broken, rocky country, with some patches of grass, but "the general character was extremely barren and worthless, stunted eucalypti, melaleuca scrub, acacia, bassinea, triodia, being the prevailing features of the vegetation." Of the Limmen Bight nothing was seen except some small creeks, none of which could extend more than a few miles to the southward of their route. Approaching the Macarthur, the arid nature of the country compelled them to draw near the coast, and even where they struck the little river, more than fifty miles from its mouth, the channel was dry and sandy, scarcely twenty yards wide. It bore, however, marks of floods. The country about it was very rugged, consisting of low sandstone hills, cut with deep ravines.

In latitude 16° 35′, longitude 136° 42′, they crossed the Robinson on the 8th of August. The channel was divided into two parts, each ten yards wide, and containing only a few pools of water. "The land near it was sandy and thinly grassed." On the 9th they crossed what they supposed to be Leichhardt's Seven Emu Creek, the country showing limestone and basalt, and of a better character, but still right and left the poor, sandy country was seen. Along the Nicholson River the country was equally poor, with alternate rocks and extensive plains. On the 30th of August they left the course of the Nicholson, and the same day, in longitude 139° 23', they came on the Beame's Brook of Leichhardt, a principal branch of the Albert. At the point of land betwixt this and another large creek was the spot appointed for Mr. Baines to leave letters, if the Tom Tough had arrived first. On approaching, they saw large letters cut on a tree, but, to their disappointment, they proved to be the record of the landing there of Lieutenant Chimmo of the Torch. The Tom Tough had not arrived.

A council being held to decide whether they should wait for the Tom Tough, or proceed at once across to the Burdekin and Moreton Bay, it was deemed most expedient to start at once overland. Their stock of provisions would not admit of much delay; the party in the Tom Tough, afresh provisioned at Timor, would be able to make the voyage without much difficulty, and the importance of opening a more direct track from Moreton Bay to the Albert than Leichhardt had done, had been urged in Mr. Gregory's instructions. They, therefore, resolved to push on, leaving information for Mr. Baines on his arrival at the Albert in sealed canisters, buried under marked trees.

On the 3rd of September they resumed their journey, steering S.E. across the Plains of Promise, "which," says Gregory, "disappointed my expectations, as they were very thinly clothed with inferior grass, and instead of the trees characteristic of a moist, tropical climate, which the engraver has, unfortunately, introduced into the sketches in Captain Stokes's work, stunted box-trees, and Chuncoa indicated an extremely arid country." Thirty-six miles from the Albert they came to a river about 100 yards wide, with large pools of fresh water, separated by dry, rocky bars. This river, which had been mistaken by Leichhardt, and had, therefore, caused an error of thirty miles in the longitude of many of his positions on the map of his route, they named the Leichhardt. In quitting their camp on this river in the morning, the blacks made a rush upon them, but they were repulsed, with the loss of their leader. On leaving the level, grassy plains, they entered low sandstone ridges, covered with scrub of melaleuca, terminalia, triodia, and a little grass. As far as longitude 14° 30' they passed some patches of good grass, but the country generally was sterile and worthless; a very different account from those of Captain Stokes and Landsborough, and yet this was the spring season.

The Flinders was reached on the 8th of September, in lat. 18° 9' long. 140° 50'; which was about a hundred yards wide, with shallow pools of water, separated by dry beds of rock and sand. It had the appearance of a stream which only drained a very limited extent of country. Its banks rose abruptly to the level of the grassy plain, which is about forty feet above the bed of the river. Betwixt the Flinders and the Gilbert, they found some good country near the coast, but more inland it became dry and destitute of watercourses. They were obliged to desist from an eastern course till they arrived at the Gilbert, in lat. 17° 15', long. 140° 45', on September 21st. To the south and east of their track, the country " was universally covered with melaleuca scrubs, small box and bloodwood trees, triodia and inferior grass."

On the Gilbert they shot one of their failing horses, and dried the meat, which they preferred to the salt pork, which had been carried through hot countries a thousand miles. The average course of the Gilbert was from the S.E., in which direction they traced it about 180 miles. The bed was remarkably broad and sandy, nearly destitute of water, several miles often intervening between the pools; the banks about twenty feet high, and the country so flat that no variation of level could be detected by the eye, though the aneroid showed a considerable elevation as they proceeded up the river.

Grassy plains and open bare flats of considerable extent existed along the course of the river; but the back country appeared to be very poor, wooded with small eucalyptus and melaleuca, needle grass, and a little common grass. Great quantities of mica, porphyry, slate, trap, and agates had been brought down by the stream, showing it to rise among primary rocks; but for the first eighty miles no hills were seen, but soon after they came to considerable ranges, the higher parts of which were wooded with ironbark and well grassed. These ranges, having sandstone summits, rose to 2500 feet. Having crossed these in latitude 18° 46', longitude 144° 1', they came on a creek which they deemed to be the head of the Lynd River. This was on the 11th of October. This and other large creeks had no water in them; then came some with scanty pools. Soon after, they came upon a basaltic plain of lava, ascending eastwards twenty-five miles, which they found to be the dividing range between the eastern and western waters, having an elevation of 2000 feet. This basaltic region was well grassed, and timbered with ironbark and box, except on the rough streams of lava, which rose thirty to forty feet, and well covered with scrub and trees.

Descending a small watercourse to the S.E., it soon enlarged into a sandy creek, and they entered again on the granitic country, and reached the bank of the Burdekin river, in latitude 18° 56', longitude 144° 57', on the 16th of October. The whole bed of the river, where they struck it, was about 100 yards wide, but nearly filled with melaleuca and casuarina trees, the water only forming a small stream ten yards wide. On the 17th of October, they observed some trees which had been marked with an iron axe, and found the bone of a bullock. As that was the camp of Leichhardt, of April 25, 1845, they attributed these appearances to his party. On the 30th they had reached the junction of the Burdekin with the Suttor, having passed through its mountains, and crossed much fine grassy country, timbered with ironbark, as well as some very poor country. After its confluence with the Suttor, the country much improved; and having permanent running water, it appeared well calculated for grazing stock. The rocks were various—granite, porphyry, trap, slate, and in other places sandstone and limestone.

Being anxious to connect the explorations of Leichhardt with those of Sir Thomas Mitchell, Mr. Gregory traced the course of the Suttor nearly south. Compared with the Burdekin, he found it an insignificant stream, the channel very irregular, and containing only pools of water. They ascertained that the Belyando and the Cape Rivers were not identical. They traced the Belyando up to latitude 22°, and having thus connected the routes of previous explorers, they left the river and steered southeast, through brigalow scrubs and open patches of ironbark, Moreton Bay ash, and bare forest, for sixty miles, crossing only two small creeks. On the 6th of November they saw Mount Narrien visible to the west, and Peak Range and the basaltic plains to the east. They then passed over a stretch of scrubby and dry country, though the soil of some downs which they crossed produced good grass. There seemed, however, no permanent water till they reached the Mackenzie, on the 15th of November. On the Comet River, on the 17th, they observed a marked tree, a number of the bones of goats, and the ashes of a fire, indicating the position of one of Leichhardt's camps. On the 21st, they reached the station of Messrs. Fitz and Connor on the Dawson River, the journey from the Victoria to that place having occupied five months and two days. Thence they pursued their journey to Brisbane, a distance of 400 miles through the Burnet district, experiencing the greatest kindness at the various stations, arriving there on the 16th of December; and "thus," says Mr. Gregory, "the explorations of the North Australian expedition terminated, after an absence of sixteen months without communication with the civilised world, and during which period we had travelled more than 2000 miles by sea and nearly 5000 by land. Perhaps," he adds, "no expedition has yet been undertaken in Australia, in which the elements of both success and failure have been so largely combined; for though the liberal manner in which the exploring party have been equipped and supported left nothing to be desired in this respect, yet the long voyage through a sea remarkable for its dangers and the extensive combinations necessary in the arrangements—a failure in any single point of which would have crippled or even annihilated the expedition—added to the ordinary liabilities attending exposure to the vicissitudes of a tropical climate, hostile natives, and desert country, present such an array of difficulties, that I feel our utmost endeavours could not have availed, had it not have been for the protection of that Providence without which we are powerless."

The North Australian expedition, though meeting with many disasters in the early part of its progress, yet was, on the whole, a very successful and useful undertaking. Though it could not penetrate far south of the Victoria River, it still showed the sort of country to be found there; and proceeding north-east, it connected the Victoria with the track of Stuart, an enterprise in which Stuart failed in two attempts. In passing through the country lying along the southern shore of the Gulf of Carpentaria, at the Albert, it gave a more temperate and less tempting account of the fertility of those regions than Stuart, and since then than Landsborough, an account, even from the inferences to be drawn from the journals of those explorers, apparently more reliable. Finally, it opened a more direct way between the Gulf and the north-eastern coast of Australia than Leichhardt had done, though not so direct as McKinlay has since effected. Both the experience of Gregory and McKinlay show that a great highway may some day be established, and that not far distant, from Queensland to the northern shores.

The members of the expedition who went by sea from the Victoria to the Gulf, proceeded first to Timor for further supplies. There the Tom Tough was found to be unseaworthy, and was discharged. Another schooner, called the Messenger, was chartered instead, to convey the party to the Gulf, and thence to Sydney. On the voyage, the Messenger encountering contrary winds, Mr. Baines thought he could reach the Albert in the longboat in less time, by sailing near the coast and amongst the islands. He started on this perilous voyage of 650 miles, but did not reach quite so soon as the Messenger. Both boat and schooner, however, got thither safely; and finding the land party gone, they turned about and proceeded down the west coast, and after putting in at King George's Sound, reached Sydney on the 1st of April, 1862.

Articles on the geological features of Northern Australia and on its capabilities for settlement will be found attached to Mr. Gregory's report, as well as some remarks of Captain Sturt on the theory of the formation of the interior of Australia and the consequent peculiarities of its rivers and other waters. The theory of an internal sea, of which Sturt was a great advocate, had been now for ever set at rest. The concluding remarks of Captain Sturt deserve quoting:—" I concluded and hoped that, in crossing Van Diemen's and Arnhem's Lands from the Victoria to the Albert River, Mr. Gregory would not only have found comparatively easy travelling, but that he might have discovered a stream, by which he could have again descended into the southern interior, and learnt more of its character.

" From the account he gives, however, of the country over which he passed, it is clearly one of the most barren description; so far, indeed, from finding a better tract at the base of the southern slopes, as I had hoped, he states that he was forced by its inhospitable character so far to the north as never to have seen them. He states, however, that at certain points he saw and ascended some rugged ranges to the south of this line of route, from which he could observe nothing but the sands of the desert for fifty miles in that direction.

" It is probable, therefore, that the winds have drifted

them against the face of the cliffs, along this face until, at length, they have risen to the level of the cliffs themselves, and thus absorb all the waters that might otherwise have found their way into the interior, which at once accounts for the difficulty Mr. Gregory experienced in penetrating south. His whole report, indeed, confirms the inhospitable character of that part of the interior, and would appear to confirm the fact that the desert has no defined margin to the north, but that it runs to the very summit of the table-land that intervenes between it and the coast.

"Taking the data with which Mr. Gregory has supplied me, together with my own experience, it would appear that the great desert cannot have a less breadth than 1000 to 1100 miles, or a length from east to west than 1200. A great portion of it, however, still remains to be explored, all that portion, indeed, lying between Mr. Gregory's position at the termination of Sturt's Creek and the great Australian Bight; whether it surrounds any better country remains to be proved. It would be difficult to determine from what point any attempt to survey it should be made, should such attempt be considered necessary; for I believe that the desert extends with unvarying sameness to the south coast, and that any anticipation of good from an exploration of it would end in disappointment. The only point of ingress that offers the slightest prospect of success is the River Glenelg of Captain Sir George Grey, which, if it be, as he seems to consider, second only to the Murray, might lead the explorer to a very different country from any that has yet been discovered in the south-western division of the continent. The changes of its physical structure, however, are so sudden and so unexpected that it would be unwise to hazard an opinion, as to what might, or might not be, the result of a further exploration of it. The altitude of its mountains and the magnitude of its rivers are so disproportioned to its size that it would be unreasonable to look for a country of corresponding value as in countries where such features exist upon a grander scale; and, although a country sufficiently fertile for occupation may yet be found in the unexplored regions of Australia, we cannot, I fear, hope that it will be of any great extent."

The want of great ranges of mountains under a climate so tropical is, unquestionably, the grand cause of the desert character of so much of Australia. The "magnitude of its rivers" depends on the magnitude of its mountains, and, instead of mountains, the interior of Australia abounds with depressions. Many parts of Africa and Asia have their deserts from similar causes, but neither of them, perhaps, so predominating in proportion to their extent.

On this question, as greatly affecting the future exploration and settling of the interior, the observations of one of the latest travellers in the interior may be here introduced with effect. Mr. Alfred Howitt says:—"As to the general drainage system of the continent, I think I have data upon which to found a somewhat new, but, I believe, correct view of it. In the first place, it may be laid down as a fundamental rule, that the tendency of every Australian river, or creek, is *to end in a lake*. The Murray, our largest river, does so, but in consequence of a constant supply of water from the high mountains in which it rises, it has sufficient power to force a passage for itself into the ocean. The same holds good of the rivers flowing southward from the Alps, and which form the Gippsland Lakes. It may be as well to remember here that the continent of Australia may be compared to an inverted saucer—the rim representing a line of coast ranges, more or less elevated, of greater or less width, and at a greater or less distance from the coast. This line of coast ranges is connected by chains of ranges, having a northerly direction, but varying from north to north-east. The Barrier Range and Flinders Range are examples. The former extends with breaks in a north and west direction into the tropics, and, I have no doubt, across to the north coast. The Flinders

Ranges, after abruptly ending at what was formerly called the Lake Torrens, bear north and west, and, I have no doubt, also cross the continent to the north-west coast.

"Returning to the rivers, we may now examine the tributaries of the Murray coming into that river on the north side. These, the Murrumbidgee and the Darling, with its tributaries, rise in the vast ranges of New South Wales and Queensland, and have a tendency to the south-west; and, as we proceed northwards, we find that they become more intermittent, and are liable to successive droughts and floods. These rivers, however, have sufficient water to have forced their way into the Murray.

"Following the eastern coast line northwards, we now meet with several smaller rivers, the Warrego, the Paroo, and Bulloo. The Warrego, after running south-west, turns to the south, and, I believe, joins the Darling during floods. The Paroo, following the same course, runs out on plain and dry lake, and, I believe, has not been known to join the Darling. The Bulloo, after dividing into Poria and Wilkie's Creeks, runs out on a bare expanse of clay, where it evaporates, Carriapundy being one of its receptacles. Next in succession to these, we have Cooper's Creek and its tributaries. This river, after forcing a passage through sandstone ranges, having a north-east and north-west direction, to about longitude 140° 30' E., reaches a very depressed portion of the continent, the lowest part of which is the so-called Lake Torrens' basin, and here assumes the character of which I have already spoken, as belonging to Australian rivers. It spreads out like the fingers of a hand, forming lakes, reforming into a number of creeks between the sand-hills, and, finally, ends to the southward in Lake Hope, to the northward in Lake Lipson.

"Northward from Cooper's Creek we find Wills' Creek, a river of a similar character, and subject to the same laws. Its flood-waters are separated from those of Cooper's Creek by Sturt's Stony Desert, which is a low, undulating spur from the range I have mentioned, as expanding N. and W. from the Barrier Range.

"Thus following round the Eastern Coast Range, we find the rivers running inland from them, have a general S.W. course, becoming more southerly as we approach the north-coast line. Starting now from that part of the Flinders Range which I have mentioned as running N. and W. across the continent, and somewhat on the line of Stuart's journeys, we find that the creeks have a S.E. direction. From this it is easy to see that there exists a chain of lakes from Lake Torrens in a north and west direction, until the creeks are met with coming from the northern coast range. Had these rivers and creeks had their sources in high mountains, such as those in which the Murray and its tributaries rise, there would have been a large tributary forming a junction with the Murray at the N.W. bend, instead of a chain of dry salt lakes, which now indicate the fall of the continent that way. The horse-shoe form of Lake Torrens is due to the creeks which radiate from the termination of Flinders Range, and end in a chain of dry salt lakes. Lake Eyre appears to be the great central receptacle for their water, and from which they evaporate.

"Judging from what we have already seen, I think we may not unfairly conclude that that portion of the continent lying next to the line of ranges from which the creeks rise, cut by Stuart's track, is similar in its formation to the Eastern portion. Namely, that the creeks run westerly until they meet those coming easterly from the coast ranges of Western Australia, and that they here form another chain of lakes of evaporation, extending in a N. and S. line. As there are no rivers entering the sea on the Great Australian Bight, I should conclude either that the rain-fall is considerably less in the western half of the continent, or that the lakes of evaporation are so extensive as to hold all the rains that fall on that half. In all probability both these causes may operate. Of one thing I feel tolerably certain, that there is a belt of country extending E. and W. across the interior of the continent, which is too far inland to be influenced by coast rain, and too far south to be certain of tropical rain-falls. Say within 27° and 31° S. latitude. I should look for a very dry country between S. of Western Australia and north of the Great Bight. This will have to be explored with camels. The following rude sketch may make clear my general idea :—"

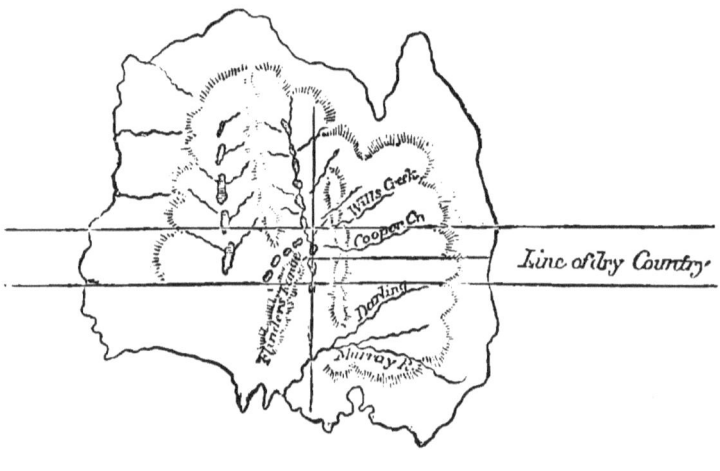

The scientific men attending this expedition have most of them published accounts of their parts and observations during its progress, which may be seen in the "Journal," and the "Proceedings" of the Geographical Society for the year 1858. The report of the surgeon, Mr. J. R. Elsey, is also appended to the account of the expedition. Mr. Elsey represents the climate of North Western Australia as, on the whole, healthy, but during the summer months, extremely hot. "As far," he says, "as our observations extended, there seems to be three seasons in North-West Australia; namely, the wet season, commencing about December, and lasting to February; the cool, or spring season, from March to July; and the dry, or hot season, from August to November. Our first arrival at the Victoria was in September. The whole country was parched, the vegetation dried up, and bush fires were frequent. The heat of the day was not followed by a cool night. Though the maximum was not excessive, rarely exceeding 114° Fahrenheit, the minimum was very high, seldom falling below 80° at any time; and I have known the thermometer, suspended in the air, to stand at 98° at sunrise. During these months there was hardly any dew. Lightning was constant to the E. and N.E., and was rarely absent for six months. This weather produced an enervating effect on us all, and caused the ailments mentioned—" namely, sickness and vomiting after eating, and affections of the eyes.

The effect of the excessive dryness, he says, was seen " in North Australia, in the absence of rich and luxuriant vegetation, the small and stunted growth of the trees, the rareness of ferns, mosses, and other cryptogamous plants. The scarcity of insect life was also remarkable."

Yet Mr. James S. Wilson, the geologist of the expedition, in his article on the "Physical Geography of North-West Australia," p. 137 of the Geographical Journal of 1858, says; "North-West Australia is in reality a grassy country. In no part of the world have I seen grass grow so luxuriantly; and Mr. H. Gregory observed to me, during a journey of ten days, when I accompanied him and his brother to the Upper Victoria, that he had seen more grass land than during all his life before." P. 141. He afterwards adds that the grasses are of great variety, from that fine grass capable of making sweet hay, to a species of wild oats growing on stony slopes and at the bare ranges, from three to six feet high. This Mr. McDouall Stuart has noticed lying when ripe on the ground, from a foot to eighteen inches deep, and clinging round the horses' feet as they travel, like masses of hay.

His opinion of the Plains of Promise in North Australia is not so favourable, agreeing very much with that of Lieutenant Chimmo, given hereafter. Yet even some parts of these, he says, are capable at one time of the year of producing much grass.

Dr. Ferdinand Müller, the chief botanist of the expedition, in his account, says, that "the climate of North Australia is a *dry Australian*, and not a *moist Indian climate*. Fevers do not, therefore, exist;" and that they escaped there such jungles and swamps as exhausted the strength of Kennedy's party. He is however of opinion, that the country cannot be settled without convict labour, to which the mind of the southern colonies is so decidedly opposed; and Lieutenant Chimmo expresses a like opinion.

Mr. James Flood, the assistant botanist, in his ascent of the Albert river, describes a great want of fresh water in the country; that two of the men, on the 14th of November, during the heat of the day, became quite delirious, but in the cool of the evening they became better. He and all the rest, though Mr. Elsey speaks of the "remarkable scarcity of insect life," describe the torment of the mosquitoes as incessant and intolerable. Mr. Flood also gives his opinion of the Plains of Promise. "I went to the Plains of Promise, which bear as barren an aspect as any country I had seen in North Australia. The soil is a light, sandy loam; the grass had been burnt off, so that a few crooked gum-trees were the most conspicuous of the flora. After taking a good view of the surrounding country, which gave no appearance of improvement in any direction, we returned to the boat, and pulled down to the junction." —Proceedings of the Royal Geographical Society of 1858, p. 379. At page 3 of the "Proceedings," of the same year, Mr. Baines, the artist of the expedition, gives a detailed, and very interesting account of his voyage to Coepang for provisions, and thence to the Albert, part of the way in an open boat, of which I have already spoken.

LIEUTENANT W. CHIMMO'S VOYAGE IN QUEST OF THE NORTH-AUSTRALIAN EXPEDITION.

Fears having been entertained for the safety of this expedition, at the request of the Secretary of State for the Colonies, the Admiralty sent out Lieutenant Chimmo in the Royal Charter, to proceed immediately to Sydney, and to take orders, if still found necessary, for a voyage in quest of the missing expedition. Lieutenant Chimmo, who had returned from Australia, where he had been engaged in the Torch steamer in surveying the coasts, set sail at two hours' notice, and reached Sydney on the 19th of April, 1856, but was detained there for two months, waiting instructions. By this unfortunate delay his voyage was rendered of no use to the expedition, but in the course of it he made some observations which well deserve record. He sailed in his old vessel, the Torch, and on the 17th of July he went in as close as he could to the coast about Albany Island and Cape York, that he might ascertain the character of a spot where he hoped ere long to see an establishment settled, so necessary to the succour of shipwrecked mariners in these dangerous waters. His opinion was most favourable to a settlement on Albany Island, from its elevated position, open to a healthy, brisk S.E. trade wind for half the year, and possessing smooth grassy slopes, and valleys with trees. Cape York appeared extremely barren, and surrounded partly by shoal-water bays.

The Torch visited Booby Island, but found no notice at the "Post Office" of Gregory's return to Sydney that way. Mr. Chimmo then proceeded to the Albert River, where, the bar not allowing the Torch to pass, on the 2nd of August he ascended the river in boats, and after a minute search of six days, came to the conclusion that neither Gregory's party nor the Tom Tough, the vessel in attendance on it, had arrived there. On reaching the source of the river, fifty miles from the ship, Lieutenant Chimmo and his officers went on shore and examined the country, in which they were much disappointed. Though early spring, all the grass had been burned off by the natives; the large gum and acacia trees, except those overhanging the river, wore quite an autumnal aspect; the land was furrowed and torn away by the deluge of rains during the N.W. monsoon; huge trees were torn up by the roots, depositing the finest of the soil in the river, and leaving on the surface a few flattened porphyritic stones, with quantities of small, perfectly round, ironstone particles. "In fine," he says, "I was not very favourably impressed with either the importance of the stream, or the richness of the country, though I saw it under the most favourable circumstances, the winter and S.E. trades. What must be the summer, during the north-west monsoon, the hot winds and changeable weather, I would hardly venture to say; the thermometer in the shade was max. 72°, min. 56°, in the sun 134·5°; the amount of ozone was 1 to 3."

They had an interview with the natives, who, though at first appearing hostile, soon became friendly. The description of the river and scenery by Lieutenant Chimmo resembles that of other visitors; for twelve miles the banks low and swampy, forty miles inland somewhat more inviting. He says the river abounds with snags, sand, mud-banks, embryo islets formed by sunken logs, etc., which are dangerously covered at high-water.

From the Albert they proceeded to Bountiful Island, and Sweer's Island, and visited the wells of Captain Stokes and Flinders. On Bountiful Island they found abundance of turtle, and deemed this island a good head-quarters for an exploring party. On the 26th of August they entered the river Victoria, after having carefully searched the north coasts between the Gulfs, especially Treachery Bay, where the expedition first landed, and where Captain Stokes was speared, and nearly lost his life. They ascended the Victoria for 100 miles to Gregory's abandoned camp, where they found notices that Mr. Gregory and part of the expedition had gone N.E. towards the Gulf, and the rest, with Mr. Baines, in Tom Tough to Coepang for provisions, and were then going to join Mr. Gregory on the Albert. Lieutenant Chimmo sailed immediately for Coepang, only to find that Mr. Baines had left for the Albert, so that he was on all points too late, through his forced delay at Sydney. His experience of the heat on the Victoria River at the end of August was much like that on the Albert. "The backs of all our books parched and curled in every shape and form. A box-wood rule on my table warped three eights of an inch in twenty-four. A box-wood thermometer, three-eights of an inch, warped one-tenth, threatening to break the glass tube."

As the north and north-west of Australia are now under process of settling, the experience of these different explorers deserve the careful attention of all who entertain the idea of trying their fortunes there.

CHAPTER VIII.

THE EXPEDITIONS OF JOHN M'DOUALL STUART, EXTENDING FROM ADELAIDE TO THE NORTH SEA, FROM 1858 TO 1862.

Mr. Stuart, draftsman of Captain Sturt's expedition, in 1844-5.—Aided in his attempts at discovery by Messrs. Finke and Chambers.—In 1858 passed Lake Torrens for the north-west.—Mr. Babbage at Yalticourie invites him to Coulthardt's funeral, and proposes to accompany him on his expedition.—Mr. Stuart excuses himself.—Bottle Hill.—Bad country.—Enquires after Wingillpin. —Mr. Stuart's idea of Wingillpin.—Mount Hamilton.—Stony country.—Mr. Stuart looking out for Cooper's Creek to the west.—Supposes a creek near Mount Hamilton, to form the Glenelg of Captain Grey in Western Australia.— Turns south, finding scrub and salt lagoons.—Turned next N.W., till the 1st of August.—Worthless country.—Near Lake Gairdner.—Proceeds towards Denial Bay.—Dismal country about Mount Finke.—Reach Gibson's Station, Streaky Bay.—Return by Mount Arden.
STUART'S SECOND JOURNEY INTO THE VICINITY OF LAKE TORRENS.—Assisted by Messrs. Finke and Chambers.—Ascends the eastern side of Lake Torrens.— Finniss's Springs.—Mount Hamilton.—Mount Hugh.—Elizabeth Springs.— Douglas Creek.—Davenport Range.—Other springs.—The Hanson Range.— Mounts Kingston and Younghusband.—Good country.—Barrow and Freeling Springs—Neale Creek.—Mount O'Halloran.—No water.—Returns to Glen's station, Termination Hill.
THIRD EXPEDITION.—From the Spring of Hope to Mount Anna.—Wild grape at Parry's Springs.—Thinks he saw Lake Torrens.—December 20th set his men to dig for gold.—No gold.—Returned to Chambers' Creek.
FOURTH EXPEDITION TOWARDS THE CENTRE OF THE CONTINENT.—Advances beyond the Neale to new ground.—Mount Ben and Head's Range.—Goes westward.—Wretched scrub.—West Neale.—Enter extensive ranges.—Mounts Beddome, Daniel, Humphries, and the Twins.—Gwyder and Finke Creeks.— Poor country.—Extraordinary sandstone rock, which he names Chamber's Pillar.—Numerous hills named, ending in Mount Stuart.—This he named Central Mount Stuart, as the centre of Australia, and planted a flag on it.— Went west 150 miles, naming several hills, but found all barren scrub.—Again went northward till June 26th.—Named various hills and creeks as far as Mount Samuel—At Kekwick Pond says he met with a native freemason.—On June 26th at Attack Creek.—The native freemasons drive him back.—Sufferings of the party.—Mr. Stuart nearly blind.—Left a horse alive bogged in a creek. —On returning found his bones.—Returned to Adelaide.
FIFTH EXPEDITION—Mr. Stuart's report of his progress in Adelaide.—Fund voted for another expedition.—November 29th started from Adelaide.—His party and equipments.—Squatting stations already near the 28th degree of S. latitude.—A little dog killed by the heat.—Spitting native.—Attack Creek.— Whittington Range.—Morphett Creek.—New plants and trees.—Finely grassed country.—Mount Primrose.—Carruther's and Hunter's Creeks.—Sturt's Plains. —Ashburton Range.—Vain attempt to go westward towards the Victoria river.—Curious baby's coffin.—Difficult country.—Newcastle Water.—Mount Shillinglaw.—Natives fire the grass.—Howell's Ponds.—Return to Adelaide.
SIXTH EXPEDITION, IN WHICH THE NORTHERN COAST IS REACHED.—Offers to

proceed north again.—News of Burke and Wills being found dead at Cooper's Creek, after crossing the continent.—October 21st, 1861, Stuart starts again — Kicked by a horse.—December 20th at Moolooloo.—His party.—Two of these desert.—Hottest season of the year.—Natives hostile at Marchant's Springs, and Mount Hay.—April 17, 1862, at their farthest point, Howell's Springs.—Difficulties from drought and dense scrub.—Try right and left.—Push through.—Frew's Water-Hole.—King's Ponds.—Return to Howell's Ponds, defeated by the scrub.—Once more advance.—Auld's and McGorrerey's Ponds.—Better country.—Daly Waters.—New tree.—Fine grassy country.—Blue Grass Swamp. —The bean-tree again.—Sickness from eating gum.—Purdie's Ponds.— Strangways River.—Hilly region.—Tall trees, and plenty of fish.—Mount Müller.—Reach the Roper.—A horse drowned.—Natives firing the grass.— Chamber's River.—Stony hills.—The Waterhouse Creek.—Mounts Helpman, Levi, and Watts.—Chambers Range.—Fanny and Catherine creeks.—Basaltic country.—Mount Stone.—Kekwick's Springs.—The Fan palm.—The Adelaide River.—Splendid view.—Palms and tropical plants.—Through stony country —Mary Creek.—William Creek.—Priscilla Creek.—Very tall grass.—Helen Creek.—The Adelaide again.—The Daly Range.—Reach the sea in Van Diemen's Gulf.—Plant a flag.—Return homewards.—Natives still fire the grass.—Two horses drowned in the Roper.—Abandon luggage.—Mr. Stuart seized with scurvy.—His eyes fail.—August 27, a comet is visible.—A remarkable native mummy.—Reach Attack Creek.—Lose several horses through exhaustion. —Stuart much worse.—Make long halts.—Men and horses failing fast.—Have to send ahead to look for water.—Everywhere drought.—Kill now and then a horse for food.—November 26, reach Jarvis's Station, Mount Margaret.—Stuart travels in a litter.—Reach Adelaide, December 18th.—General view of the advantages of these expeditions, and prospects of this northern country.—Dr. Hardman's edition of Stuart's Journal.—Question of telegraphic communication across the continent.—Lease of 1000 square miles of land to Stuart.—Grant of £2000 to Stuart, and different sums to other members of his party.—Order in which the transit of the continent has been made by different explorers.

THE reader will recognize in the present explorer the Mr. McDouall Stuart, who accompanied Captain Sturt in his expedition to the Stony Desert in 1844-5, as draftsman. This experience of exploring, though a very severe initiation, seems to have inspired Mr. Stuart with a passion for discovery, and in 1858 this passion was gratified by the generous aid of his friend, Mr. William Finke, who furnished the means necessary to make an exploration of the country on the west side of Lake Torrens. He started from Mount Eyre, at the southeast corner of the lake, and crossing its southern extremity somewhere about Sleep's Crossing, turned his face northwards. He was at Oratunga, the head station of Mr. John Chambers, on the 14th of May. Leaving there with only six horses, one white man, Foster, and a native. Mr. Barker accompanied him on this outset, and they arrived at Aroona the same evening. Stopping at different stations, on the 19th they were at Mr. Sleeps', who informed them that Mr. Campbell, who had been endeavouring to penetrate into the west, had returned for want of water. It was not till the 10th of June, that Mr. Stuart could be said to have made his actual start, which he did from Ootaina, still not far from Mount Eyre.

On the 13th of June he arrived at Beda, where he expected to find Mr. Babbage, who had been sent by the government to make a north-west course through the continent, but reached no farther than Chamber's Creek, a location which the reader will have to visit on these journeys repeatedly. He was informed that Mr. Babbage was still more northward at Pernatta, where, however, according to his journal, he looked in vain for him, but on the 16th heard from Mr. Babbage, at a place called Yalticourie, whence he sent to Mr. Stuart to say that he had found the remains of poor Coulthard, and requested Stuart to come and assist at his funeral, but he excused himself, and moved on to the Elizabeth Creek. Mr. Babbage sent him word that he would accompany him to the Elizabeth, but Mr. Stuart having waited for him *an hour*, started without him, evidently not very desirous of the company of rival explorers. It does not appear that he at this time saw Mr. Babbage at all.

On the 18th, he ascended Bottle Hill, and saw a pile of stones on its summit, and on the top a flat slab, inscribed with the names of Loudon and Burtt. The country seen from the hill, he describes of the very worst description. That on the Elizabeth Creek he found the same, and so as far as Andamoka, a permanent water-hole, towards the north-west of Lake Torrens, a country of stony plains and sand-hills with salt bush. No rain appeared to have fallen for a year on it. Over the lake he saw Mount North West, bearing 60° 30′, and Mount Deception 95°. More southward he observed Flinders Range. At Yarraout Gum Creek on the north-west point of Lake Torrens, Mr. Stuart inquired of his own black and of another native, for Wingillpin, and they both directed him north-west, the native of the place said it was "five sleeps off." Our traveller then remarks rather strangely, "Probably this Wingillpin Creek may be Cooper's Creek," Cooper's Creek lying at least 250 miles to the north-east of him. How could Mr. Stuart, who must have been actually on a part of Cooper's Creek himself with Sturt, imagine that it and Wingillpin could be the same?

On the 26th of June, near Mount Hamilton, he started on a westerly course, and along a country which he sometimes describes as grassy, but more frequently stony and sandy, and producing salt-bush, till the 10th of July, when he thought it would be a beautiful country in spring, yet if it continued so stony he should be compelled to leave it. What is most extraordinary, Mr. Stuart is still looking out for Cooper's Creek, nearly 6° of longitude west of its true situation. "My only hope of cutting Cooper's Creek is on the other side of the range. The plain we crossed to-day resembles those of the Cooper, also the grasses; if it be not there, it must run to the *north-west*, and form the Glenelg of Captain Grey!"—*Journal of* 1858, *July* 9th. Can Mr. Stuart really mean by the Glenelg of Captain Grey, the Glenelg in Western Australia? What Glenelg can he expect out north-west of his then position, where no one had yet penetrated for nearly 1000 miles?

From the 11th to the 15th of July, our traveller pursued a south-western course, following a creek, which he called Mulga Creek, from the Mulga, a kind of acacia, growing about it. He had to pass through stony ranges which lamed his horses. One night a black-and-tan dog was found barking at the horses, a very strange dog for a native dog, which are generally a dirty yellow. This dog barked too, whilst the true dingo generally howls like a wolf. Probably it was a dog belonging to the natives, though native dogs near stations will yaff as they pursue their game, as I have heard them, but this is rare. On the 15th, Mr. Stuart seeing only a desert and scrubby country all westward, struck off in a south-east direction till the 25th, when he had reached about seventy miles of his northward track on the west side of Lake Torrens, and a little past the 30th degree of S. latitude. The greater part of this track of country he represents as good pastoral country, but there does not appear any considerable creeks, and he describes a tolerably large portion of dense scrubby country. As he was there in winter and had rain, the apparent danger of that country is that in summer, it would be almost destitute of water. Day after day, he says "no creeks."

On the 25th he turned south, and journeyed through a reedy swamp, but all dry; then on over mulga scrub and sand-hills, and camped without water. On the 28th they changed the scrub and sand hills for salt lagoons. Finding no good in this direction, he then struck off north-west, and continued on that track till the 1st of August, over the same dry, sandy, and worthless country. From the 1st to the 4th of August they passed over a somewhat better country, and then fell in with salt lagoons, and immediately afterwards through granite ranges, no great distance beyond the north-western extremity of Lake Gairdner. On the 7th, he abruptly abandoned this course, and steered directly south for Denial Bay. He made one more effort to discover some good country from the top of Mount Finke, but saw only "a fearful country." "The prospect," he added, "is gloomy in the extreme, and is very disheartening to have sought a good country in vain." From this point to near Denial Bay, his progress was through a dismal desert resembling that through which Eyre had endeavoured to force his way along the southern coast westward. Their horses being exhausted by this waterless wilderness, and their own provisions failing, they made for Gibson's station on Streaky Bay. On the 22nd of August Stuart and Forster killed and fed on a crow, the first food for three days; the black had deserted them before. The next day they reached Gibson's station, and staid there to recruit till the 1st of September, when they held eastward to Mount Arden, at the head of Spencer Gulf, which they reached on the 11th of September, when they were in the settled district. Such was Stuart's first journey of exploration.

STUART'S SECOND JOURNEY INTO THE VICINITY OF LAKE TORRENS.

In the spring of 1859, Mr. Stuart set out on a second expedition. This time his friend James Chambers, as well as Mr. Finke contributed to the necessary supplies. He commences his journal at Mr. Glen's station on the 2nd of April, and this time took his way up the eastern side of Lake Torrens. He does not tell us the strength of his party, or his number of horses. We incidentally learn that he had men with him of the names of Herrgott and Müller, and that they crossed the tracks of Parry and Major Warburton, two travellers into the same regions, before they reached Decay Hill. Also, that Herrgott had found some ponds near those of St. Stephen, then dry, which could enable people to take cattle as far as Chambers Creek. On the 21st of April they reached Finniss's Springs, a little south of Lake Gregory, north of the Torrens. The country is too well known as a very dry one, to need particular remark here. On the 22nd they ascended Hermit Hill, and took a view of Lake Torrens. Between them and the lake, which was Eyre's farthest point in 1840, they saw the country very rough, containing springs which threw out soda and saltpetre; the lake itself was quite salt.

On the 27th they reached Chambers Creek, and on the 10th of May, Mount Hamilton, near which in the preceding year Stuart had struck off westward. This time he continued a more northerly course, and therefore, from to-day we accompany him on new ground, and which he had so frequently to retrace before he had accomplished his great enterprise, the crossing of the continent. Mount Hamilton had been visited by Major Warburton, who had piled a pyramid of stones on its top. On the hill are springs. The situation is latitude 29° 27′ 37″. Seven miles onward they ascended

Mount Hugh, on which also they found fine springs, and a few miles farther, they found other fine springs, which they named Elizabeth Springs. The country about was tolerable with grass and salt-bush. Having returned to Mount Hamilton to make some further survey of the country he again moved northward, and on the 24th of May, they were on the Douglas Creek. The country he pronounced not good, there was no water. He proceeded north, and struck the Davenport Range, and at five miles further a copious, but rather brackish spring, which he named the Spring of Hope. On the 2nd of June they reached other springs, which they called Hawkers' Springs, and on the 4th a creek which they named the Blyth. They soon after came on a range which they named The Hanson Range, and the highest point of it Mount Younghusband, and another isolated range to the north-west they named Mount Kingston. The country Stuart describes as excellent, and Mount Younghusband grassed to the top. Younghusband lies in latitude 28° 1' 32". On the 6th of June, they successively discovered and named the Barrow Springs, very plentiful ones; the Freeling Springs in a beautiful country; and a salt creek, which they named Peake Creek. In the ranges were seen quartz, ironstone, and slate, and Herrgott and Müller, who had been at the Victoria diggings, said they had seen no country so much resembling those diggings. The country looked as if covered with snow from the quantity of quartz.

Between this time and the 12th of June, they came upon a creek, which they called the Neale; and Stuart, still haunted by Cooper's Creek, says, "Can it be Cooper's Creek? the country very much resembles it." The map will show us that Cooper's Creek lies five geographical degrees, or 300 miles to the east of the Neale. Next came Mount O'Halloran, beyond which he advanced to latitude 27° 12' 30", and finding no water, though there was an abundance of grass, he determined to turn back, his horses being without shoes, and himself ill. He, therefore, retraced his journey, and again arrived at Glen's Station, near Termination Hill, on the 3rd of July. What he had seen on his journey only inspired Mr. Stuart with a desire to push further north, with a better equipped force, and he once more set out for his

THIRD EXPEDITION.

He commenced his journal at Chambers' Creek, on the 4th of November of the same year, 1859. In this journey he went over the same country, varying his route a little, and again reached the same vicinity, the Neale, whence, as before, he returned to Chambers' Creek, on the 21st of January, 1860, having reached the Neale on the 6th of that month. We may note the few new observations which this journey presents. From the Spring of Hope on the 15th of November, he went with a man to examine a hill out south-west. He found it composed of iron-stone, quartz, granite, etc., with an immense quantity of conglomerate of those substances, which appeared run together as in smelting works, with numerous courses of slate of different descriptions and colours. The country around was poor. He named the hill Mount Anna. Near Spring of Hope, he also named a creek, George Creek. At Mount Charles he built up a cone of stones, and there one of his men deserted, taking the mare on which he used to ride. At Fanny Springs where he staid some days, he laid down a base line of ten miles, and forty chains for his survey. They could there see the Neale; and they discovered several springs in the neighbourhood. There and at Parry's Springs they observed large quantities of the wild grape, both white and red, which were very good indeed, and which, if cultivated, they thought would make a nice fruit. At Primrose Springs, where the Neale runs into Lake Gregory, called by Stuart Lake Torrens, they also saw the wild grape in abundance. The Parry and Primrose Springs were both hot and cold.

On the 1st of December Stuart rode to south of east to visit Lake Torrens. Rode over sand-hills to the lake thirty-five miles. The Neale brackish. The next morning he ascended a sand-hill, and saw a small, dark, low line of land all round the horizon. "The line of blue water is very small. So ends Lake Torrens!" On the 4th, still more north, Mr. Stuart tells us that he thinks it was not Torrens, but a large lagoon that he had seen. At the mouth of the Douglas he thought he had found the Lake Torrens again, and on the 14th he is again as much puzzled as ever. "I am almost afraid that the next time I try the lake I shall not find the northern boundary of it. Where can all this water drain to? It is a mystery." As Mr. Stuart tells us that his eyes were so bad that he could scarcely see, I suppose that he really did see, at that period, nothing distinctly.

On the 20th of December he set his men at Fielding Spring to dig for gold; his own eyes were so bad he could not go himself. Up to the 27th they continued to dig, and found no gold, but great indications. "In fact, they found no gold whatever, but thought there might be some in the quartz reefs." Having advanced to the Hanson Ranges, our traveller found his stores rapidly waning, and his men, all but Kekwick—it does not appear how many he had—as bad as possible. He beat a retreat, as I have said, on January 6th, 1860. By the 21st of January he was at Chambers Creek, and by the 2nd of March he was again ready for a start on his

FOURTH EXPEDITION TOWARDS THE CENTRE OF THE CONTINENT.

This time we are informed that he had thirteen horses and two men. On the 22nd of March he had again reached the Neale, and advanced up it far enough to begin naming new objects, amongst which were two high peaks, Mount Ben and Head's Range. On the

24th he crossed the Neale, and struck away west to see what kind of country it was, and found it an apparently interminable scrub. On the 26th we find him on what he calls the West Neale, but have no intimation of how or where he found a West Neale. Then running north, through a mixture of good and bad country, we find him at a creek called by him the Frew, and soon after on another branch of it, in a country of scrub, mulga, and grass. On the 30th of March they crossed a creek, which they named the Ross, with wild oats, wheat, rye, and salt-bush growing on its banks. That evening they camped on another creek, which he named the Stephenson. They now entered on extensive ranges, consisting of gypsum, chalk, ironstone, quartz, and red sandstone. The chief of these hills they named Mounts Beddome, Daniel, Humphries, and the Twins. There were also the Goyder and Finke Creeks. The country improved, but still showed that poverty-index, the spinifex. On the 6th of April they saw before them a very extraordinary rock, which stood up in an isolated manner, at first presenting the appearance of a locomotive engine with its funnel. As they drew near, however, it stood forth a pillar of sandstone, based on a hill of upwards of a hundred feet high. The pillar itself was about a hundred and fifty feet high, and twenty feet by ten feet in diameter. It resembled some old cracked and time-worn tower of the middle ages, broken into two peaks at the summit. To this singular freak of nature Mr. Stuart gave the name of his friend and patron, James Chambers.

To the north and north-west showed remarkable hills, resembling ruined castles. They rose out of sand-hills. From Saturday, the 7th of April, till Sunday, the 22nd, they continued on a north-west course, chiefly through sandstone ranges, amongst which ran various creeks, but thick scrub tearing to pieces their clothes and saddle-bags, also prevailed. Amongst these creeks and ranges were the Hugh Gum Creek, and James's Range, the Waterhouse Range, the McDonald Range, Mount Hay,

Strangway Range, Brinkley Bluff, Mount Freeling, and, finally, Mount Stuart. Amongst these ranges Stuart says he saw the India-rubber tree, the cork-tree, and several new plants. They found a nut, which produced violent sickness. The country amongst the McDonald Ranges Stuart describes as a fine pastoral one.

Mount Stuart was a distinguished position to have attained. Mr. Stuart, in his journal, says:—"To-day I find from my observations of the sun, 111° 00′ 30″, that I am now camped in the centre of Australia. I have marked a tree, and planted the British flag there. There is a high mount about two miles and a half to the north-north-east. I wish it had been in the centre; but on it to-morrow I will raise a cone of stones, and plant the flag there, and name it Central Mount Stuart."

The position of Central Mount Stuart, by Mr. Stuart's own chart, appears to be latitude 22°, longitude 133½°. He describes it as high, or higher than Mount Serle, between Lakes Torrens and Blanche. It appeared nearly surrounded on all sides by broken ranges; where the view was open, it was over plains of gums, mulga, and spinifex. The range in which Mount Stuart stands he named John Range, after John Chambers, the brother of his great supporter, James Chambers.

From Mount Stuart he struck off in a north-west direction, after naming the large creek which flowed round Mount Stuart the Hanson. He went west because he did not like the arid, sandy appearance of the country to the north, and so long as he continued amid that group of ranges he found water. He named Mounts Denison, Leichhardt, Barkly, Turnbull, and the Arthur hills. Beyond Mount Barkley they found a scanty creek, which they named the Fisher. Beyond that all was gum scrub and spinifex plains, destitute of the slightest moisture, and having persevered for about 150 miles, he returned. On the way back he named Mount Rennie and Mount Peake, northward of Mounts Barkly and Leichhardt. Before he again reached Mount Stuart his men and himself were attacked with illness, he himself was suffering severely from scurvy, and the horses were in a woeful plight.

Still Mr. Stuart endeavoured to push on northwards, and he continued his way through a series of ranges, having between them at intervals scrubby or grassy plains, till the 26th of June. The hills he named on this course were Mounts Mann, Gwynne, Strzelecki, Morphett, the Forster Ranges, Crawford Range, Davenport Range, the Murchison and McDonald Ranges, Mount Samuel, Short Range, etc. The creeks and ponds amongst them were Bonney Creek, the McLaren, the Tennant, Bishop's, and Phillip's Creeks, Kekwick's Pond, and Hayward's Creek. As they advanced natives appeared more numerously, and at Kekwick's Ponds Mr. Stuart assures us that he saw and exchanged signs with native freemasons, an apparition, I imagine, rather startling, and still more unaccountable. Brother masons or not, on the 26th of June, at a creek fitly named Attack Creek, about thirty of them fell upon his party, consisting of only three individuals, with spears, waddies, and boomerangs, yelling and firing the grass, so that they were compelled to fire on them. With failing health and stores, and such ardent brother masons as these in the way, our travellers beat a hasty retreat; and in very hot weather, with a dread of finding the waters on their way dried up, and the natives following them, they made as active a retrograde march as possible. Mr. Stuart's eyes were nearly blind, his provisions in a regular decrease from plunder by his man Ben; Kekwick almost too ill to travel, the Finke and other creeks dried up on arriving at them. Under such circumstances they pursued their way back to Chambers' Creek, which they reached on September 1st, having been most hospitably entertained by Mr. Brodie at Hamilton Springs.

In the course of this journey, an accident occurred, which I wish I could omit, but humanity to animals, and especially to such an animal as the horse, performing his laborious and painful duty on an explorative march, demands the record of it. Near Kekwick Springs, on going outward on the 16th of March, the horse "Billy," in crossing a creek, was bogged, and could not be got out." Our traveller says:—" We tried for hours, but were unable to help him." Soon after he says :—" We tried again to get the horse on shore, but could not manage it; the more we tried to extricate him, the worse he gets. I have left him: I do not think he will survive the night."

Left him! and did not think he would survive the night! Did it not occur to Mr. Stuart that a single bullet would have put an end to his sufferings at once? that whether he survived the night, or for some nights and days, his death must have been one of the slow progress and tortures of starvation? In returning past Kekwick's Springs in the following August, occurs this entry :—" Proceeded to Kekwick's Springs to see if the horse we had left in the Peake had got out. We found his bones; he does not seem to have made a struggle since we left him, as he is in the same position. From the number of tracks, the natives must have visited him."

If there had been a chance for the horse getting out, the leaving might have been humane; but when the utmost efforts of the party had been exerted in vain to extricate him, what hope of him doing it himself? If it were doubtful whether he would live till morning, how *could* he have strength to free himself? It is altogether a painful passage.

FIFTH EXPEDITION.

In October of 1860, Mr. Stuart arrived in Adelaide from Chambers' Creek, and reported that he had at length not only reached the centre of the continent, and planted the British flag on Central Mount Stuart, but had penetrated 200 miles, or more, still farther north; that he had nearly reached the 18th degree of south latitude: the sensation was great. The sum of £2500 was voted by the colonial parliament to fit an expedition worthy of the country, the leader, and the object. Stuart, who never took long to recover from the dilapidations of an expedition, or to prepare for another, was again on the road from Adelaide northward on the 29th of November. On the 12th of December, he once more arrived at Chambers' Creek at the head of seven men and forty horses. At this familiar place, he remained till the 1st of January, 1861, killing and drying bullocks, changing defective or worn-out horses for better, and making various other preparations dictated by former experience. The veteran explorer was this time stimulated to his best exertions by the knowledge that, on the 20th of the preceding August, the best appointed expedition that ever left an Australian capital for the interior, had set out from Melbourne under Burke and Wills, with the very object which had so long inspired him, that of traversing the country to the northern sea.

Mr. Stuart this time left Chambers' Creek at the head of twelve men and fifty horses, save one, his stud having been augmented by the re-employment of some of his old stagers, and by others sent after him by his staunch friend, Mr. Finke. We are this time able to give the list of the party:—

John McDouall Stuart, Leader of the Expedition.
William Kekwick, Second in Command.
F. Thring, Third Officer.
— Ewart, Storekeeper.
— Sullivan, Shoeing-smith.
— Thompson, Saddler.
— Lawrence, — Masters, J. Woodforde.
— Wall, — E. C. Bayliffe, J. Thomas.

As we shall again have to follow the party over the ground traversed before as far as Hayward's Creek, between the 18th and 19th parallels of south latitude, we may pass over all that relates to the country, noting only a few of the incidents of travel. One of the first things which strikes us is the great distance to which squatting stations had already extended themself northwards, the farthest at this time appearing to be that of the Messrs. Levi, near Milne Springs, near Mount Younghusband, approaching the 28th degree of south latitude, at full 400 miles north-west of Adelaide. At this place Mr. Stuart was compelled to leave behind some of his horses which proved unfit for the journey, and to send two men back with them, reducing his party to ten individuals. At Milne Springs, January the 11th, the height of summer, a little dog, called Toby, was killed by the heat, though he was allowed to ride on one of the pack horses. At Mount Hugh, on the 6th of March, they encountered an old native who spit fiercely at them like a tribe on the Darling at Major Mitchell.

On the 25th of April, 1861, they had reached Attack Creek, near Hayward's Creek, whence they commenced their retreat on their last journey. Soon after they saw and named the Whittington Range, and camped in a creek in these hills, which they named Morphett Creek. In latitude 18° 35' 20", on a creek which they named Tomkinson Creek, the journal states:—"We found many new plants and flowers, also some trees, one of which grows to a considerable size, the largest being about a foot in diameter. The fruit is about the size and colour, and has the appearance, of plums; the bark is of a grey colour; the foliage oval, and of a dark green. Another is more of a bush, and has a very peculiar appearance; the seed-vessel is about the size of an orange, but more pointed. When ripe, it opens into four divisions, which look exactly like honey-comb inside, and in which the seeds are contained; they are about the size of a nut, the outside being very hard. The natives roast and eat them. The leaves resemble the mulberry, and are of a downy light green."

North of the Whittington Range, they came into country finely grassed, and to a hill, which they named Mount Primrose; the next day to a country just as poor, with spinifex and stony rises, but on which they crossed two creeks, Carruther's and Hunter's. On the banks of the Hunter, they noticed a new and beautiful tree, in some instances a foot in diameter, with drooping branches.

rough, grey bark, and dark green leaves shaped like a butterfly's wing. Still advancing, they crossed grassy plains which they named Sturt's Plains, climbed hills which they called the Ashburton Range, and which were composed of ironstone, granite, and a little quartz, but all very rough and broken. From a creek called Watson's Creek, Stuart determined to try a south-western course, not finding the northern one very practicable; but a single day over the waterless scrub, which presented itself as far as could be discerned from the top of a tree, quite satisfied our traveller that he could never reach the Victoria River by that route, as he had hoped. Still he made another attempt, and persevered till the 10th, when drought, spinifex, and dense scrub drove him back to make another effort towards the north.

Having regained Hawker Creek, in Ashburton Range, on the 12th, they observed in a tree a sort of miniature canoe, which was carved on the sides by some sharp instrument in small lines, on the top of it a number of pieces of bark, the whole bound together by a grass cord. They agreed that it was the finest piece of workmanship they had ever seen made by a native. It was found to contain the skull and bones of a child. From this date to the 12th of July, our traveller was vainly endeavouring to force his way through dense mallee scrubs, or waterless Sturt's Plains, sometimes west, sometimes east, sometimes north, but all in vain. During this time, he found and named a large sheet of water Newcastle Water, and a hill, which they called Mount Shillinglaw. Near Newcastle Water, on the 26th of May, the natives set fire to the grass, and endeavoured to surround Woodforde, who was alone duck shooting. He fired, and wounded one of them, which caused them to retire.

Having this time reached Howell's Ponds, in about 17° south latitude, Mr. Stuart again beat a retreat. On Loveday Creek, under Mount Hawker, they lost Masters for three days, which caused them much anxiety. On his recovery, on the 12th, they quitted Tomlinson Creek to return to Adelaide. On the 7th of September, they regained Chambers' Creek. On the 16th, Stuart left Moolooloo for Port Augusta, where he took the steamer for Adelaide, leaving the party to travel to Adelaide under the care of Kekwick.

SIXTH EXPEDITION, IN WHICH THE WESTERN COAST IS REACHED.

On the 23rd of September, Mr. Stuart made a public entry into Adelaide, where, notwithstanding the serious obstacle which he had found in the nature of the country north of the Ashburton Ranges, he professed himself ready to make another attempt to reach the north shores of the continent, and his offer was at once accepted by the government. In little more than a week after his return, the news reached Adelaide that the explorers, Burke and Wills, had been found dead at Cooper's Creek by Mr. Alfred Howitt, and that they had previously accomplished the long vainly attempted achievement of traversing the continent from shore to shore. This information, however, neither induced the South Australian Government to abandon the endeavour to effect the same object from Adelaide by Stuart's track, nor disheartened Stuart himself. With that rapidity of action which had before distinguished him, his preparations were made, and he was ready to start northwards again on the 21st of October, 1861. In accompanying the expedition a little way on the day of its departure, he was knocked down by a rearing horse, and in great danger of being killed. Notwithstanding this accident, he was able in five weeks to follow the expedition to Moolooloo, where a part of it waited for him. On Friday, December 20th, he reached Moolooloo, and Finniss's Springs on the 29th. His party was on this final occasion, as follows:—

John McDouall Stuart, Leader.
William Kekwick, Second Officer.
W. P. Auld, Assistant.

J. W. Waterhouse, Naturalist.
John M'Gorrerey, Shoeing Smith.
Stephen King.
John Billiott.
J. Woodforde.
James Frew.
Heath Nash.
— Jefferies.

Two of these soon quitted the expedition, refusing to obey orders; and Woodforde, who had been on the last journey, took the liberty of riding off with a horse, and sundry other things. They commenced their route in the very hottest season of the year; and by the time that they reached the Hugh, they had lost a great number of their horses. The natives, too, had begun to show themselves hostile at Marchant's Springs on the 17th of March, 1862, and were fired upon by one of the men. Again, at Mount Hay, they were menaced by them, and were again fired on with rifles. On the 17th of April, they had again reached their farthest point north at Howell's Ponds. There was fine grass about the ponds, but Sturt's Plains, and the whole country, except near ponds or creeks, as dry as ever, and the scrub seeming to defy advance every way.

On the 28th of April, Mr. Stuart tried a course east and south-east, but found only dense scrub, which tore their clothes and packs to pieces, and not a drop of water. A few slate-coloured cockatoos, and other birds, were all that spoke of life. Thus disappointed, he again made a determined push northward, and on the 1st of May, he discovered a fine deep water, which he called Frew's Water-hole. Persevering through the dense forest the next day, they discovered a chain of ponds, which they called King's Ponds; both of these being called after men of the party, in approbation of their conduct. The next day they failed to discover water; and, wearied of contending with the thick scrub, they returned to the camp at Howell's Ponds. So far, they had found it impossible to advance permanently beyond the farthest point of the last year's journey. The leader, therefore, determined to try once more a westward course, with the hope of reaching the Victoria. They started with a reconnoitering party on the 8th, but after persevering in that course for three days through thick scrub alternated with spinifex, they gave up the attempt as hopeless, and returned to Howell's Ponds. On this journey they met with one spring, which they called Nash Spring; but for the greatest part of the way they saw not a bird, nor heard the chirp of any to disturb the gloomy silence of the forest. Their so-called waterproof bags leaked hopelessly, and they lost one horse, besides seriously injuring others. They had now tried east and west, and if they were to break through the sturdy opposition of drought, scrub, and spinifex, it must be directly onwards. Accordingly, with most commendable resolution, they advanced to King's Ponds, and thence diligently sought for fresh waters. They succeeded, and named their discoveries Auld's and M'Gorrerey's Ponds. After two more days of distress from total want of water, they came into a grassy country, and on the 23rd of May, to fresh waters, which they called the Daly Waters. On the banks were fine gum-trees, and also a tree seen by Leichhardt, McKinley, Gregory, and others, in the northern district, having a long, straight barrel, dark, smooth bark, palmated leaves, and bunches of bright yellow flowers. The gum-trees were so thick, and the belts of lancewood so deceptive, that they thought it a fearful country to get lost in. There were pelicans and other water-birds about the Daly, which proved to be a creek. Pushing a-head again, on the 30th of May they came into an extensive swamp, splendidly grassed to the horses' knees, which they named Blue-grass Swamp. The ground, which in the wet season was evidently under water, was now so cracked, that the horses were continually plunging into the fissures, as they could not see them for the tall grass. They were now evidently getting into better country. The dip of the land was to the eastward, and the crimson-blossomed bean tree was there again.

On the 9th of June several of the party were seized with violent pains and severe sickness, from eating gum from a particular nut tree. Having brought up the party to the Blue-grass Swamp, at eleven miles onwards they came upon fresh ponds, which they named Purdie's Ponds. These ponds were nearly at the junction of latitude 16° and longitude 134°. The country was luxuriantly grassed. The next day they struck a creek, which continued to run northwards, and soon was evidently conducting them directly to the Roper. They named this the River Strangways, after the Chief Commissioner of Crown Lands. It soon entered by a gorge into a hilly region, and for the first time they saw the cabbage-tree growing on its banks, besides various new trees. The party was now brought up to this gorge, and the hills were then explored for a passage. This they found. The hills were rough and precipitous, variously of sandstone, iron-stone, and lime. On the 20th of June, they were encamped north of the gorge. The country around was sandy, but producing very tall trees, amongst them the stringy bark. The waters of the river were deep and clear, and they caught several kinds of fish, weighing, some of them, two pounds and a half. Some appeared a kind of perch; others, rock-cod, and others resembled gold-fish. On the banks of the river they found a large creeper with a yellow blossom, and bearing a large bean-pod.

As they advanced the river enlarged, and they began to feel that they should no longer suffer from want of water. From the time they left Mr. Levi's station, Mount Margaret, they had had only two or three slight showers of rain. At the first camp north of the gorge, they were in latitude 15° 15′ 23″. On the 25th of June they found their river Strangways falling into the Roper. Before reaching the Roper, they passed through rough stony hills, the highest of which they named Mount Müller, after Dr. Müller, the botanist, of Victoria. They now found that they were in the country through which Mr. Gregory had passed in 1856. The timber grew larger, the soil was rich, the grass up to the horses' sides. Numbers of cabbage trees grew about. On the 24th the grass was over their heads, so that the leader was lost in it, and only discovered by cooèeing for him. The natives were firing the grass in different directions, and the marks of their camp fires and heaps of mussel shells denoted their being numerous. They came upon the Roper in latitude 14° 5'. A number of natives on its banks set up wild cries, and fled at their approach.

After crossing the Roper, they lost a horse by his being set fast in the mud of the river banks. The water was excellent; the grass, though dry, was from two to five feet high; but the natives continued burning it, and putting their camp in constant danger. The leader pronounced the country as certainly the finest he had seen in Australia. On the 30th, they found themselves on a branch of the Roper, which they named the Chambers, after James Chambers, the leader's great patron, then deceased. The natives they now met with were friendly. Following up the river north-west, they came to extensive swamps, and found much difficulty from numerous creeks crossing their route, to advance. On the 2nd of July, they had got into some terribly rough stony hills. One of the men picked up a small live turtle. The rough hilly country continued some time, with fine grassy valleys amongst them, with melaleuca, gum trees, the bean tree, a climbing fern, and many new plants. On the 5th of July they saw a creek running S.W., and named it the Waterhouse, after the naturalist of the expedition. They suspected that it was one of the sources of the Adelaide River. The hills were of sandstone, ironstone, and some limestone. Latitude 140° 18' 30". They named, in this neighbourhood, Mounts Helpman, Levi, and Watts; and to the north-west, the Chambers Range. The waters were now all tending N.W., and they named the Fanny and the Katherine, after daughters of Mr. John Chambers.

On the 9th, they travelled over a basaltic country, splendidly grassed; ascended a hill, which they named Mount Stow, after which the basalt disappeared, and slate, limestone, and sandstone took its place. They then came upon copious springs, which they named Kekwick's Springs. In the stony hills beyond these springs they came to the top of a sandy table-land, thick with splendid stringy-barks, pines, and other trees and shrubs, amongst which, for the first time, they saw the fan-palm, some of them fifteen feet high, the bark on the stem marked similar to a pine-apple, the leaf resembling a lady's fan set on a long handle, and which soon after it is cut closes in the same manner. On the 10th, they caught sight of the Adelaide River. The scene was magnificent. The table land was suddenly broken, and tall cliffs, covered with fine trees, overlooked the broad valley of the river, which was hastening away N.W., through a rocky country. "The view," says Stuart, "was beautiful. Standing on the edge of the precipice, we could see underneath a deep river, thickly wooded, running on our course; then the picturesque, precipitous gorge in the table land; then the gorge in the distance; to the N.W. were ranges of hills."

They found the top course of the table land a layer of magnetic ironstone, which deflected the needle $20°$; underneath was a layer of red sandstone, very soft, and crumbling away with the action of the atmosphere. In the valley was an immense crop of grass, upwards of four feet high. There was abundance of cabbage-palms in the dry parts of the river bed, and many new plants and flowers. The cliffs seemed to be 250 or 300 feet high.

They now travelled north-westward, in the same direction as the river, over a rough country of ironstone and sharp rectangular flint-stone. Quartz-conglomerate imbedded in iron, and slates perpendicular in position, induced them to believe it a gold country. In latitude $13° 38' 2 4''$ they crossed a branch of the Adelaide, which they named the Mary, after Miss Mary Chambers. On the banks of this river, large clumps of bamboos, from fifty to sixty feet high and six inches diameter at the butt, were growing. A recent fire had raged down to the water's edge, destroying everything but the gum trees. They were compelled to shoe their horses here on the fore feet. They continued to cross a number of creeks, one of which they named William Creek, after the second son of John Chambers. The valleys between granite rises were very fertile, abounding with new trees and shrubs ; and thus it continued, the rock changing after a while to ironstone.

On the 18th of July they reached a creek, which they named Priscilla Creek, in latitude 12° 56′ 54″. Still their way lay over stony hills of ironstone, slate, and a hard white stone, and the valleys full of most luxuriant grass. Such were the quantities of the tall dry grass, that the horses collected it on their fore legs, and they were obliged occasionally to pull them in, in order to let the load drop off. After crossing a creek named Allen Creek, they came upon the Adelaide where it was about eighty yards wide, and so still that they could not perceive the current. The banks down to the water were twelve feet deep. They were lined with very tall stout bamboos, and the water deep and clear of snags or fallen timber. The hills on the opposite side, being the highest they had seen in this new country, they named them the Daly Range, after the Governor of South Australia, and the highest point, Mount Daly. A conspicuous hill, which they had passed at thirteen miles from the river, they named Mount Goyder, after the surveyor-general. Soon after they came into extensive marshes, in which grew a lily new to them, whence they named the marsh Lily Marsh. Still following the river, amongst marshes, palm groves, and rocks, they named one creek Anna Creek, and another Thring Creek, and another large marsh Freshwater Marsh. Here, in latitude 13° 22′ 30″, Stuart quitted the river, and struck a course due north, in order to make the sea coast. I shall now give the event in his own words :—" I have taken this course in order to make the sea coast, which I suppose to be distant about eight miles and a half, as soon as possible. By this I hope to avoid the marsh. I did not inform any of the party, except Thring and Auld, that I was so near to the sea, as I wished to give them a surprise on reaching it. Proceeded through a light soil, slightly elevated, with a little ironstone on the surface, the volcanic rock cropping out occasionally; also, some flats of black alluvial soil. The timber much smaller and more like scrub, showing that we are nearing the sea. At eight miles and a half, came upon a broad valley of black alluvial soil, covered with long grass; from this I can hear the wash of the sea. On the other side of the valley, which is rather more than a quarter of a mile wide, is growing a line of thick heavy bushes, very dense, showing that to be the boundary of the beach. Crossed the valley and entered the scrub, which was a complete network of vines. Stopped the horses to clear a way, while I advanced a few yards on to the beach, and was gratified and delighted to behold the water of the Indian Ocean, in Van Diemen's Gulf, before the party with the horses knew anything of its proximity. Thring, who rode in advance of me, called out, 'The sea!' which took them all by surprise, and they were so astonished that he had to repeat his call before they fully understood what was meant. Then, they immediately gave three long and hearty cheers. The beach is covered with a soft blue mud. It being ebb tide, I could see some distance; found it would be impossible to take the horses along it; I therefore kept them where I had halted them, and allowed half the party to come on to the beach and gratify themselves by a sight of the sea, while the other half remained to watch the horses until their return. I dipped my feet and washed my face and hands in the sea, as I promised the late Governor, Sir Richard McDonnell, I would do, if I reached it. The mud has nearly covered all the shells; we got a few, however. I could see no seaweed. There is a point of land some distance off, bearing 70°. After all the party had had some time on the beach, at which they were much pleased and gratified, they collected a few shells; I returned to the valley, where I had my initials (J. M. D. S.) cut on a large tree, as I did not intend to put up my flag until I arrived at the mouth of the Adelaide. Proceeded on a course of 302° along the valley; at one mile and a half coming upon a small creek, with running water, and the valley being covered with beautiful green grass, I have camped to give the horses the benefit of it. Thus have I, through the instrumentality of Divine Providence, been led to accomplish the great object of the expedition, and take the whole party safely as witnesses to the fact; and through one of the finest countries man could wish to inhabit—good to the coast, and with a stream of running water within half a mile of the sea. From Newcastle Water to the sea beach, the main body of the horses have been only one night without water, and then got at it within the next day. If this country is settled, it will be one of the finest colonies under the Crown, suitable for the growth of any and every thing. What a splendid country for producing cotton!"—McDouall Stuart's Explorations, 1861-62, pp. 56-7.

From the number of pathways from the water to the beach, across the valley, Stuart judged that the natives were very numerous, but they saw none, though they had passed numerous encampments. The cabbage and palm-trees grew plentifully during the whole day's journey. The creek near the beach they named Charles Creek, after the eldest son of John Chambers. Finding it not easy to get along the river to its mouth on account of the bogs on its banks, they then attempted to proceed along the sea-beach, but were stopped by similar obstacles. The leader, therefore, abandoned the design of reaching the mouth of the Adelaide, satisfied to have reached the Gulf of Van Diemen. He now resolved to erect the Union Jack on the shore, with his name sewn in the centre of it. "When this," he says, "was completed, the party gave three cheers, and Mr. Kekwick then addressed me, congratulating me on having completed this great and important undertaking, to which I replied. Mr. Waterhouse also spoke a few words on the same subject, and concluded with three cheers for the Queen, and three for the Prince of Wales. At one foot south from the foot of the tree is buried, about eight inches below the ground, an air-tight tin case, in which is a paper with the following notice:—

"'SOUTH AUSTRALIAN GREAT NORTHERN EXPLORING EXPEDITION.

"'The exploring party, under the command of John McDouall Stuart, arrived at this spot on the 25th day of July, 1862, having crossed the entire continent of Australia from the Southern Sea to the Indian Ocean, passing through the centre. They left the city of Adelaide on the 26th of October, 1861, and the most northern station of the colony on the 21st day of January, 1862. To commemorate this happy event, they have raised this flag bearing his name. All well. God save the Queen!'"

To this document was appended the signatures of all the party. As the bay had not been named, they named it Chambers Bay, in honour of Miss Chambers, who had presented the flag to the leader of the expedition. "At the same hour," says Stuart, "nine months after leaving Mr. Chambers' house in North Adelaide, was this flag planted on the north-west coast." On the bark of the tree on which the flag was placed was cut—"DIG ONE FOOT, S." They then bade adieu to the Indian Ocean, and returned to Charles Creek.

On Saturday, July the 26th, the party set out from Charles Creek on its return to Adelaide. We may note a few of the incidents of their travel homewards. In crossing the Mary, the banks of which were very boggy, they managed, by cutting large quantities of the long grass, and laying it on the sides of the bank, with a few logs and pickets driven into the bed, to prevent the current carrying the grass away. At Kekwick's Springs the natives evinced hostility by firing the grass round them to burn them out. The horses were growing very thin and weak, the natives leaving them but little food from continual burning of the grass. They had two drowned in the Roper river, and the others were so weak that they were compelled to leave a good deal of their loading, even clothes. The grass was so dried by the sun that it seemed to have no nourishment in it. On the 14th of August Mr. Stuart was taken ill, and from this time he appeared to get worse and worse through the whole journey. It turned out to be scurvy, and his eyes failed so much that he was quite blind after sunset. When the moon was out full he could only see her dimly, and as if painted on a piece of canvas. On the 27th of August, at Daly Waters, a comet was visible, but it was to him invisible. They found the streams and ponds on their way now fast drying up. Frew's Ponds were quite dry.

At North Newcastle Water, September 1st, amongst some natives who came to their camp, they had a most remarkable mimic, who imitated all the motions and proceedings of the strangers, and burlesqued them in a high degree. His peculiar and comical countenance and antics would have rivalled Liston in his best days, and they excited peals of laughter in his companions. His limbs were as lithe as those of any clown. Behind his back the other natives ridiculed him. Various of our explorers have encountered these native wits and mimics. On the 4th of September they found the Hawker, Watson, Powell, Gleeson, and finally, the Lawson, which had water as they went, now all dry. They obtained some at the Hunter, but none in the Burke, the Tomkinson, and very little anywhere till they reached Attack Creek, on the 13th. But again creek after creek was found, utterly dry; the horses were scarcely able to travel;

several they were forced to leave behind. Stuart himself was doubtful whether he should hold out through the journey. There did not appear to have been any rain in that part of the country for twelve months. On reaching the Bonney, on the 19th of September, men and horses appeared in the last stage of exhaustion, and, as there was water in it, they remained till the 26th, a week. There they also reduced their rations. The explorers' troubles were gathering fast upon them. When they found water, in spite of their scarcity of provisions, they were compelled to make a long halt, or all the horses would have perished. At the Taylor they remained from the 30th of September to the 18th of October, nearly three weeks. During this time men were sent on to see whether there was water anywhere ahead, as they dared not quit this creek. None was found nearer than the Anna Reservoir, except a very little by digging in the bed of the Stirling. The party seem to have greatly incommoded the natives by monopolising the water-hole in the Taylor, and they practised many arts to get them away. One of their sorcerers made a dreadful howling and incantation, and then they seem to have acted a corrobboree at night with lighted fires, and many violent gesticulations. Under cover of these antics they managed to get at the water-hole and satisfy themselves. After this they went off. All this time the leader of the expedition was suffering dreadfully from his illness, and was scarcely able to ride on moving forward on the 18th. On that day and the next they had a little rain, but on reaching the Hanson, on the 20th, there did not appear to have been any there—all was dry as ever.

In this miserable condition they managed, killing a horse now and then for food, to reach the Lindsay on the 14th of November, where Stuart exclaims—" Thanks be to God, I am once more within the boundary of South Australia! I little expected it a fortnight ago." On the 26th of November they reached Jarvis's Station, Mount Margaret, where they remained to recruit several days. On the 8th of December they reached Mr. Glen's Station, and the next day proceeded to Mount Stuart Station, where they met Mr. John Chambers, and found that there had been heavy rain in that vicinity. In company with Mr. Chambers, Mr. Stuart travelled on to Moolooloo, where his journal terminates. During part of the later journey he had been compelled to have a sort of litter constructed to travel in, not being able to bear horseback. On the 18th of December we find Stuart in Adelaide, reporting himself and his success in crossing the continent; and he terminates his journal with these remarks:—" In conclusion, I beg to say that I believe this country—*i. e.* from the Roper to the Adelaide, and thence to the shores of the Gulf—to be well adapted for the settlement of an European population, the climate being in every respect suitable, and the surrounding country of excellent quality, and of great extent. Timber, stingy-bark, iron-bark, gum, etc., with bamboo fifty to sixty feet high on the banks of the river, is abundant, and at convenient distances. The country is intersected by numerous springs and watercourses in every direction. In my journey across I was not fortunate in meeting with thunder-showers or heavy rains, but, with the exception of two nights, I was never without a sufficient supply of water. This will show the permanency of the different waters, and I see no difficulty in taking over a herd of horses at any time; and I may say that one of our party, Mr. Thring, is prepared to do so."

To these general remarks on the country northwards, and its facilities of access, Mr. Stuart adds a commendation of his party generally, for their satisfactory conduct, and for their kindly sympathy with him in his illness. That the country on the Gulf of Carpentaria and the Arafura Sea, will in awhile be colonized, and prove very valuable settlements, there can be no doubt. The information furnished by Flinders, Captain King, discoverer of the Alligator River, Captain Wickham, the discoverer by his officer, Mr. Fitzmaurice, of the

Adelaide, and Lieutenants Emery and Helpman, who sailed up it eighty miles, as well as by the later traversers of different parts of these northern regions, from the eastern shores of the Gulf of Carpentaria to the Adelaide, Leichhardt, Gregory, McKinlay, has satisfactorily determined that point. But in judging of the case of making the journey from the southern districts of Australia to the Adelaide, we cannot help remembering that Mr. Stuart did not accomplish that object till after five abortive efforts, and the loss of many horses, and with much human suffering, though, fortunately, at the cost of no lives. As to the permanency of the waters of which he speaks, we have but just closed the book of his own narrative in which, on his return homewards, we find him recording that three-fourths of all the waters in the interior were dried up, and that there did not appear to have been any rain there for a year. The caution which he was compelled to use in advancing without certainty of a supply of water within any possible distance, his long delay at the Taylor, and the great sufferings of himself, his men, and his cattle, stand in curious contrast to his assurances of the ease with which this great journey may be made.

Since writing this, I have seen Dr. Hardman's edition of Stuart's Journals, and I observe that he states in his preface that Mr. Stuart is anxious that a telegraphic line should be established along his route to the mouth of the Adelaide. He sees, indeed, "a few difficulties in the way," but these are merely as to finding timber at particular localities. The great and insuperable difficulties he entirely overlooks. Till there is a populous settlement on the Adelaide, or somewhere on the northern or north-western coast, and till the line can be protected along the whole course of the interior from the natives, the whole is a chimaera. A telegraphic line implies so many things not yet in existence, nor likely to be in existence for very many years, that, to say the least, Mr. Stuart will have abundant time to mature all his plans regarding it. That he has rendered a great service in opening up this line is a real merit, and it is satisfactory to find that the South Australian Government has liberally rewarded him for this service. Dr. Hardman, at page ix. of his preface, informs us that, on Mr. Stuart's return from his expedition to the west of Lake Torrens in 1858, the colonial government granted him a large track of land in the country discovered by him. The *South Australian* Register states the particulars of this grant:—" The Adelaide government in 1859 granted Mr. Stuart a lease of 1000 square miles of land in the country he discovered in the interior for seven years rent free; after which time he was to pay such a rental as should at that time be the usual one in that district." It was proposed to divide this into four runs of 250 square miles each, which Mr. Stuart was to be at liberty to underlet.

Again on his return from his successful expedition in 1862, the same government made him a grant of £2000; to Mr. Kekwick £500; to Messrs. Thring and Auld £200 each; and to Messrs. King, Belliatt, Frew, Nash, McGorrerey, and Waterhouse, £100 each. Since then the Royal Geographical Society of London has presented him with a gold medal and a gold watch.

The grant of the £2000 was originally made in favour of "the first colonist" who crossed the continent. It will be seen, in the opening of the chapter on McKinlay's expedition, that Leichhardt had done this in 1844—5 and Walker in 1861. But if it were objected that these two explorers only made an oblique journey, and not directly from south to north, or from east to west, or *vice versâ*, Burke and Wills accomplished this transit in February, 1861; McKinlay in March, 1862; Landsborough in June, 1862; and Stuart only in July, 1862. If it meant any Australian colonist, Stuart was the fourth only of those who had made the full transit. If it meant only a colonist of South Australia, McKinlay accomplished the enterprise on May the 18th of 1862, Stuart only on the 24th of July, 1862, or nearly two months after McKinlay. McKinlay, therefore, was, strictly speaking, the rightful recipient; but the government granted him an extra £1000, and, considering the repeated, arduous, and determined attempts of Stuart to force his way over the continent, morally, he was most justly entitled to the sum he received.

CHAPTER IX.

THE EXPLORING EXPEDITION OF VICTORIA IN 1860—1 UNDER THE COMMAND OF MESSRS. BURKE AND WILLS.

Offer of £1000 by Mr. Ambrose Kyte towards an expedition across the continent.—£3400 subscribed by the public for this object; £6000 voted by the Victoria government: total, £12,400.—Camels brought from India by Mr. Landells for the journey.—Committee of Royal Society appointed managers of the expedition business.—Robert O'Hara Burke selected as leader.—His antecedents.—Mr. Landells, manager of the camels.—William John Wills, astronomer and surveyor.—Names of the party.—Start August the 20th, 1860, in great eclât from Melbourne.—Misgivings of Wills's father.—Ferguson, the foreman, dismissed on the Murrumbidgee.—Landells resigns.—Prophecies the ruin of the expedition.—Wills made second in command.—His amiable character.—Burke appoints Mr. Wright third in command.—Unfitness of Wright.—Leaves half of his expedition with Wright at Menindie.—Advances to Cooper's Creek.—Mr. Wright does not follow.—Charged with looking out stations for squatters.—Description of the country between Menindie and Cooper's Creek.—Mr. Wills advances ninety miles direct northward from Cooper's Creek, but returns from want of water.—Will's description of the country about Cooper's Creek.—News of Stuart having crossed the continent carried by Trooper Lyons to Menindie.—Sent on by Wright, but returned without finding the way to Cooper's Creek.—Wright sends back to Melbourne for more money.—Mr. Wright not appearing at Cooper's Creek, Mr. Burke appoints Brahe to the command at Cooper's Creek, and sets out for the Gulf of Carpentaria with a small party.—His haste.—Threatens to throw the scientific instruments into a creek.—Anxiety at Melbourne regarding the expedition.—Efforts of Dr. Wills.—An expedition sent in quest of Burke and Wills under Mr. Alfred W. Howitt.

In the annals of Australian discovery it will have been observed that the colony of Victoria had taken little part, and won consequently few laurels. Whilst New South Wales had led the way by successive and successful expeditions, and Southern and Western Australia had followed bravely in the track, Victoria had lain wonderfully still, and seemed content to hear of the gradual unfolding of the wide regions of the common continent without a single desire to share in the glory and the sacrifice. The repeated tidings of the northern progress of Stuart from Adelaide appears at last to have roused the public mind of this colony to a resolve to enter the field of so noble a competition. This resolve was undoubtedly stimulated to more immediate action by the offer of £1000 for the purpose, made by a public-spirited colonist, who for some time withheld his name, but who has since become well known as Mr. Ambrose Kyte. Having once entertained the idea, the great gold colony put forth its strength, and the expedition projected by it has eclipsed all others in the magnificence of its outfit, and the mingled greatness and the disaster of its results. Their appointed explorers, Burke and Wills, accomplished the great task of traversing the entire continent from south to north, and perished in the attempt. They achieved this great journey, till then regarded with so much awe and doubt in five months, three weeks, and one day, having left Melbourne on the 20th of August, 1860, and reached the shores of Carpentaria on the 11th of February, 1861, out-stripping Stuart, who did not reach the north coast, near the mouth of the Adelaide, till the 24th of July, 1862, or nearly a year and a half afterwards. This first success, obtained at such a sacrifice, and amid so much suffering, suspense, and public excitement, was but the opening of a new era of exploration. The whole populated portion of Australia was roused to intense sympathy by the accomplishment of this grand enterprise. Numerous expeditions were sent forth in aid, and already McKinlay and Landsborough had traversed the continent, one from south to north, the other from north to south, winning each his goal a little before Stuart had reached the crown of his six enterprises. In this brave strife South Australia had again, in McKinlay, become a successful competitor. To these were added the effective expeditions of Walker and Howitt, showing that the mystery of the interior was now, in a great measure, dissipated, and that the transit of the continent, from shore to shore, must henceforth become a thing of comparative familiarity. Such were the grand results of the enterprise which we have now to detail—an enterprise baptised in suffering, effected at the cost of seven lives, and of a sum of money far beyond any precedent in Australian expeditions of discovery—but followed by results of which millions yet unborn will reap the benefits. It is still to be regretted that the loss of life might have been prevented by a little tact and management on the part of the leader, as eminently shown by the manner in which the expeditions under Stuart, McKinlay, Landsborough, Howitt, and Walker, were conducted; but that regret is, at least, softened by the splendid sequences of the sacrifice.

We learn from the despatch of Governor Sir Henry Barkly to the Duke of Newcastle, dated August the 21st, 1860, and published in the parliamentary report of this expedition, issued March the 28th, 1862, that, so far back as the 1st of September, 1858, a public meeting was held in Melbourne to promote this object, and a sum of £3400 having been collected by private subscription under the auspices of a committee of the Royal Society of Victoria, the government, which had already authorized Sir Henry Barkly to write to India for camels at a cost of £3000, then proposed to the legislature, on this year's estimates, a supplementary grant of £6000 towards the expenses of the expedition, which was readily voted, and placed at the disposal of the same committee. Total fund for the expedition £12,400.

Twenty-four camels from Peshawar of both the heavy and fleet species, were brought over from India by G. J. Landells, and put on shore at Melbourne in excellent health. This being effected, active measures were adopted to organise the exploring party. The committee of the Royal Society was now augmented by another committee, called the Exploration Fund Committee, and the united board now consisted of the following gentlemen :—The Hon. Sir William Stawell, Chief Justice of Victoria, chairman; The Hon. John Hodgson, M.L.C., vice-chairman; The Hon. Dr. Wilkie, treasurer; The Hon. Dr. Macadam, secretary; Dr. Embling; Mr. Surveyor-general Ligar; James Smith, Esq.; Professor M'Coy; Dr. M'Kenna; Professor Neumayer; Sizar Elliott, Esq.; Dr. Müller, government botanist; Dr. Iffla; Captain Cadell; Angus M'Millan, Esq.; A. Selwyn, Esq., government geologist; John Watson, Esq.; Rev. Mr.

Blensdale; Dr. Eades; Dr. Gilbee, deputy-surveyor; and — Hodgkinson, Esq.

The first and most important step was to appoint the commander. Mr. Augustus Gregory, the well-known explorer of Western Australia, but who had become Surveyor-general of Queensland, was the first applied to, but he declined, and recommended in his place Major Warburton, head of the Police, and well-known explorer of Adelaide, but this proposal was declined, on account of the major being an employé of South Australia, which was supposed to be naturally anxious that the desert country within its own boundaries should be first explored. Amongst the various candidates offering themselves for this arduous and very responsible post, was Robert O'Hara Burke. Of this gentleman we have the following account in the despatch of Sir Henry Barkly to the Duke of Newcastle, dated Nov. 20, 1861, to be found at p. 29 of the Parliamentary Report of this Expedition:— Robert O'Hara Burke, born in 1821, was the second son of James Hardiman Burke of St. Clerans, county Galway, an estate now possessed by the eldest son, Major Burke, late 88th Regiment. The youngest son, Lieutenant Burke, R. E., fell at the passage of the Danube in July, 1854, pierced by no less than 33 wounds. "Robert, like him, commenced his career as a cadet of the Woolwich Academy, but left at an early age to enter a regiment of Hungarian Hussars in the Austrian service. When this was disbanded in 1848, he obtained an appointment in the Irish Constabulary, which he in 1858 exchanged for the police force of this colony, of which he was at once made an inspector. On the news of the Crimean War, however, he hastened home on leave of absence, in hopes of getting a commission, but finding himself too late to share the glories of the campaign, returned to resume his duties here, in the discharge of which he rendered himself most popular at some of the chief gold-field towns." (Beechworth and Castlemaine.)

Mr. Burke received the appointment. He was just

forty years of age, and all accounts agree that he was, in the words of Dr. Wills, in the Memoir of his own son, " A brave and true man, covetous of honour, but careless of profit; one who would have sought reputation even in the cannon's mouth." Yet, with all the fine qualities of a genuine Irishman, courage for anything, an enthusiasm capable of carrying him through a thousand difficulties and dangers, and a disposition which attached those who served under him, at least in a majority of cases, Mr. Burke's appointment was certainly the grand and fundamental error of the committee, and the root of all the subsequent calamities attending the expedition. To bravery and impetuosity in a leader of such an enterprise, there required a spirit of careful calculation; a spirit of foresight; an administrative capacity, or in other words, a capacity for managing the details of the train of men and animals committed to his charge; and besides this, there required the seasoned constitution of a man accustomed to the climate and its bush-life. In all these qualities Mr. Burke appears to have been more or less deficient, and the consequence soon became apparent in his rushing forward on his way like another Prince Rupert, dropping behind him, from stage to stage, by fragments, the body of his band of men and animals, as well as of his supplies, till he dropped and died of inanition, with some of his ill-fated companions, in the very midst of his triumph. With all this, he accomplished the main object of his expedition, but at a cost of human life and suffering, which might have been avoided by the exercise of the higher duties of a leader; for it is quite clear, that notwithstanding the reproaches heaped on the managing committee, they had furnished him with men, camels, horses, and supplies, which, if kept together, would have enabled him to walk over the whole breadth of the continent and back, as in a summer's promenade. The whole of the facts of the expeditions of Stuart, Gregory, McKinlay, Landsborough, Walker, and Howitt, place this beyond a question; and this is rendered doubly apparent by the nature of the country over which they passed, as described in the journals of the travellers themselves.

The post of second in command, and especial manager of the camels, was conferred on Mr. G. J. Landells, who had so successfully brought these animals from India. The third in command, and the astronomical and meteorological officer of the expedition, was William John Wills, of whom Sir Henry Barkly gives us this short account, p. 30 of Parliamentary Report:—"William John Wills was born in 1834 at Totness, Devonshire, where his father practised medicine, and being destined for the same profession, entered at St. Bartholomew's, and distinguished himself, especially as student in chemistry. In 1852 the news of the gold discoveries induced him to try his fortune in this colony, and he settled at Ballarat, where he was subsequently joined by his family, and continued to assist his father for several years. His taste, however, had always been for astronomy and meteorology, and he passed all his leisure hours at the office of Mr. Taylor, the head of the Crown Lands Survey in that district, where he gave such proofs of ability, as to be put in charge of a field party. Here he soon attracted the notice of the Surveyor-general, Mr. Ligar, and on the establishment of a magnetic and meteorological observatory in Melbourne, under Professor Neumayer, he was attached specially to the staff, where he remained until selected for the post of observer and surveyor to the Exploring Expedition, with which his name will ever be indelibly associated. He, too, is not the first of his family to lay down his life for his country, his cousin, Lieutenant Le Visconte, Dr. Wills' sister's son, having accompanied Sir John Franklin in the Erebus, on the Arctic Expedition."

A more ample memoir of this very able and interesting young martyr to discovery will be found in his father's narrative of this expedition, published in 1863, under the title of "A Successful Exploration through the Interior of Australia, from Melbourne to the Gulf of Carpentaria." The letters of Mr. Wills to his family display not only great talents and a generous aspiration after useful distinction, but a moral tone and a sound sense that do him the highest honour. Had the years of Burke and Wills been reversed, and William John Wills been placed first in command, with Burke for his second, we may safely augur that a very different fate would have awaited the undertaking. Wills displayed all the qualities which, in maturer years, would have constituted a successful leader. Burke had already all those which would have made him an energetic and executive second, and the perfect harmony which existed betwixt these zealous but unfortunate explorers, would have undoubtedly led to the most happy results.

The whole expeditionary staff stands thus in the Memorandum of Agreement betwixt them and the Treasurer of the Exploration Committee, dated August 18, 1860:—

Robert O'Hara Burke, leader.
George James Landells, in charge of the camels, second in command.
William John Wills, as surveyor and astronomical observer, third in command.
Hermann Beckler, medical officer and botanist.
Ludwig Becker, artist, naturalist, and geologist.
Charles J. Ferguson, foreman.
Thomas F. M'Donagh, assistant.
William Paton.
Patrick Langan.
Owen Cowan.
William Brahe.
Robert Fletcher.
John King.
Henry Creher.
John Dickford.
And three natives of India in care of the camels.

However fitted for their posts in other respects, it was soon proved that the indispensable quality of seasoned bushmen had been wholly overlooked by the good natured leader, and several of them, accordingly succumbed to the heat of the climate and the hardships of the service, one of these hardships, as in several cases, being too much leisure and inaction.

On the 20th August, 1860, this splendid expedition set forth from Melbourne amid the collected mass of the population. Never before had camels formed a portion of an Australian expedition, and their appearance in the train, some carrying gentlemen of the expedition, others carrying loads and led by the Sepoys, excited deep interest. Altogether there were twenty-six, the account in the "Melbourne Herald," says twenty-seven camels, and twenty-eight horses. The staff of men was seventeen. Mr. Burke appeared at the head of the expedition, mounted on his pretty little grey. Before leaving the Royal Park, where the band of travellers assembled, the Mayor addressed them, wishing them "God Speed," and calling for three cheers for the different leaders and for the party itself. Mr. Burke briefly responded, and the impressive and picturesque procession moved on through Melbourne, accompanied by numbers of the leading inhabitants, both ladies and gentlemen, to some distance on horseback and in carriages. Little did the members of the expedition, little did the cheering spectators on that exciting day divine the strange neglects, the strange incautions, and the consequent disasters and deaths to which they were dismissing that splendid cavalcade of adventurers.

The progress of the expedition though slow, on account of the great amount of stores which they carried with them, was prosperous till they reached Balranald on the lower part of the Murrumbidgee, where they were on the 17th of September. There Burke was compelled to dismiss his foreman, Ferguson, for insubordination. Very soon after differences began to show themselves betwixt the leader and the second in command, Mr. Landells, on the way betwixt the Murray and the Darling. Mr. Wills in a letter to Professor Neumayer, dated Menindie on the latter river, October 16, relates the progress and crisis of this difference. So early as the 4th of October Landells complained to Wills that Mr. Burke interfered too much with his management of the camels, and that if he had his way, everything would go to the devil. At the station of Mr. M'Pherson, this gentleman complained that his shearers had got drunk on the rum which Mr. Landells carried for the camels, according to a practice he had learned in India. Mr. Burke, thereupon insisted on leaving the rum behind, and Mr. Landells declared that he would not go on without it. Further difference occurred betwixt the leader and Landells, regarding swimming the camels over the river. Both appear to have been very violent, and Landells resigned. His resignation was followed by that of Dr. Beckler, who assigned as a reason, that he did not like the manner in which Mr. Burke spoke to Mr. Landells, and that he did not consider the party safe without Mr. Landells to manage the camels. Dr. Beckler, however, subsequently withdrew his resignation. Mr. Landells returned to Melbourne full of violent complaints of the conduct of Mr. Burke; having declared before leaving Menindie, that Burke was a rash man; that he was frightened at his violence, and did not consider himself safe in the tent with him. He prophesied the ruin of the whole affair in his hands. Public opinion decided against Mr. Landells, and the committee expressed itself satisfied with the conduct of Burke, yet the readers of the narrative cannot avoid feeling that there was probably some ground in the impetuous Irish temper of Burke for these charges, and for the assertions which both these officers who had already resigned or been dismissed, and that of Wright afterwards, that Burke would ultimately ruin the party. It has been said, that he was suffering under the irritation of disappointed love, which made him moody, fitful, and, as expressed by the *Melbourne Argus*, " restless at nights, hasty in the day, and apparently undecided what course to pursue." Though the charges are all made by men dissatisfied with Burke, and whose conduct was not satisfactory to the public, yet it is worthy of note, that they all agreed in expressing a belief in the destruction of the expedition under him—a fact unhappily too fully verified. The words of Landells expressed the opinions of the others as well as of himself. "Not only is he ungentlemanly to his officers, and interfering with the best interests of the party—not only has he displayed such a want of judgment, candour, and decision, but he has also shown, in addition to these and many other shortcomings, such an entire absence of any and every quality which should characterize him as its leader, as has led to the conviction in my own mind *that under his leadership, the expedition will be attended by the most disastrous results.*"

These are ominous words, and when we find them not only echoed by others of the party, but literally fulfilled, however we may join in condemning these men for perilling the enterprise by their insubordination and desertion, we cannot avoid feeling that there was a certain ground in the mind and conduct of the leader for the charges.

These disorders, however, cast out by the departure of the complainants, were not likely in the same form to recur again, for Mr. Wills, who was now advanced to the second place in command, was of so sweet and conceding a temper, and had such a regard for his impetuous but generous leader, that he would never raise a voice of complaint or resistance. Indeed the strikingly prophetic remark of his father to Mr. Burke, on taking leave of him at Melbourne, prepares us for this almost culpable spirit of acquiescence in Mr. Wills. "On shaking hands with Mr. Burke, I said frankly, 'If it were in my power, I would even now prevent his going.' I then added, 'If he knew what I am about to say, he would not, I think, be well pleased; but if you ever happen to want my son's advice or opinion, you must ask it, for he will not offer it unasked. No matter what course you may adopt, he will follow without remonstrance or murmur."—Dr. Wills's Successful Expedition, p. 101.

Awfully significant words! With such an acquiescent second there could be no dissention, but there might be a peace leading to destruction—and we cannot avoid feeling how necessary to the spirit of Burke, naturally vehement, and certainly not endowed with great judgment, in moments when harassing cares distracted him and suffering depressed him—was a companion who would have urged steadfastly his better views, though never overstepping due subordination. Under this "fatal facility" of the excellent Wills, the daring and otherwise noble courage of Burke was destined to bring disaster on the associates of his enterprise. A lack of cool judgment was brought immediately into view by the mode in which he filled up the place of third in command, left vacant by the resignation of Landells, and the promotion of Wills. He appointed as third in command a Mr. Wright, whom he accidentally met with as the manager on a station called Kinchica, at which they halted. He was a stranger to him, yet that warm, impulsive nature of his led him to take a fancy to him, and to appoint him to this most important command—important and responsible in an eminent degree, because Mr. Wills, being necessarily occupied by the duties of manager, astronomer, and guide to the expedition, having to determine by observations their actual whereabouts, and to note and keep record of their proceedings and route, Mr. Burke, being destitute of the necessary scientific qualifications; on Mr. Wright must fall the main management of the camels and horses, and the superintendence of the men and stores—in a word, of the general economy of the expedition. It turned out, according to the official report, that Mr. Wright was as ignorant as he was unprincipled. It was discovered on his subsequent examination in Melbourne, that he could scarcely, if at all, write his own name: that, instead of devoting himself faithfully to his duties, he was actually engaged in looking out for stations for squatters, and in speculations of his own. This we have also in the speech of the Secretary of the Exploration

Committee, Dr. Macadam, at the meeting at St. George's Hall, Melbourne, January 21st, 1863, on the evening of the funeral of Burke and Wills:—" Wright had employed his time in serving the interests of the squatters, by going in search of land, instead of doing his duty to the man whose life was in his hands." Such was the man whom poor Burke unfortunately selected as third in command, and still more unfortunately almost immediately left behind him with nearly half the camels and horses, and the greater part of the stores. Mr. Wright was ordered to follow on to Cooper's Creek, where it was intended to establish a depôt immediately. How faithfully he obeyed this order may be seen at once from the dates. Mr. Burke set forward from Menindie for Cooper's Creek on the 19th of October, 1860; Mr. Wright, on the 26th of January, 1861, or after a delay of three months and seven days! But this was not all. He did not finally reach Cooper's Creek till the 10th or 12th of May, during which guilty delays, the unfortunate Burke and Wills had actually crossed the continent, and returned to Cooper's Creek, to perish for want of the supplies with which he had been entrusted! "To the misconduct of Wright," says the Report of the Melbourne Committee of Enquiry, "is mainly attributable the whole of the disasters of the expedition, with the exception of the death of Grey." But the death of Grey formed no exception, for had Wright followed up immediately to Cooper's Creek, Burke could have carried with him to Carpentaria a force and provisions, which would have made the journey perfectly easy.

Of the progress from Menindie on the Darling, situated in a locality where Mitchell and Sturt had previously encamped, to Cooper's Creek, we have a mere memorandum by Burke, of the route to Torowoto, lying about midway, to which is appended a list of the camps or halts on the route. In this memorandum, or despatch, addressed to the Secretary of the Exploration Committee, Burke announces his appointment of Mr. Wright, praises him highly; but adds,—" Under any circumstances it is desirable that we should soon be followed up." Mr. Wills furnishes the more complete journal of their route." From the Murray to the Darling, he describes the country as the most miserable that he had seen, abounding with much flats, and subject to yearly hurricanes of terrible violence, the effects of which they saw in the prostrated trees. He mentions a species of Pea, called the Darling Pea, on which, if horses feed exclusively, it occasions madness. The country about the Scrope and Daubeny Ranges he describes as better, but in many places destitute of permanent water. North of Naudtherungee Creek, as sandy and timbered with pines, acacias, and trees with which he was unacquainted, as the leopard-tree, so called on account of its spotted bark; in other respects it resembles a poplar. Quartz prevailed, and Mr. Wills deemed the district auriferous. About the Wonominta Ranges, which are high—two or three thousand feet above the sea—they found permanent water, though the natives said there was none in the hills. The plains from thence to Wannoggin they found intersected by creeks, which were sheltered by overhanging shrubs, tall marsh-mallows and salt-bushes, and abounding with ducks and water-hens. The land about Torowoto was swampy, but finely grassed, and better calculated for cattle pasture than for sheep. To this point they had fine weather, the temperature of the air ranging only from 65° to 75°.

From Torowoto to Cooper's Creek, we have some account of the journey in a despatch of Mr. Burke's, dated December 13th, being three days only before he left Cooper's Creek for Carpentaria. This despatch gives us the dates of their leaving Torowoto, and reaching Cooper's Creek, the more valuable, because Mr. Wills, in his journal, gives us accounts of the country, but rarely any dates at all. They left Torowoto on the 31st of October, and arrived at Cooper's Creek on the 11th of December, men, horses, and camels, all well. This despatch of Mr. Burke's, nevertheless, is very confused, for he says, that he arrived at Cooper's Creek on the

11th of December, and yet on the 11th of November, we find him "slowly travelling down the creek till the 20th of November," when he settled camp 63. Now camp 63, Wills expressly says, was on Cooper's Creek. See Parliamentary Report of Burke and Wills' Expedition, p. 13. They must, therefore, really have struck Cooper's Creek on the 11th of November, instead of the 11th of December.

At this camp 63 they remained till the 5th of December, when they were driven out by the rats, and moved on to camp 65. "From whence," says Burke, "I now write, and where I have permanently established the depôt," p. 8. "The feed," he adds, "on this (Cooper's) Creek is good, and the horses and camels have greatly improved in condition; but the flies, mosquitoes, and rats, which abound here, render it a very disagreeable summer residence." He informs the Committee that he has promoted Mr. Brahe to the rank of officer, and is about to leave him in charge of the depôt at Cooper's Creek with Patton, McDonagh, Dost Mohammed, six camels, and twelve horses; that no danger is to be apprehended from the natives, and that there was "nothing to prevent the party remaining there until their return, or until the provisions run short." He announced that he thought it advisable to ascertain a route between the Darling and Cooper's Creek more to the westward, on account of the state of the earthy plains on the route by which they had proceeded thither, and had left orders for the party with Wright, on arriving at Cooper's Creek, to endeavour to discover such a route. He informs the Committee that Mr. Wills had proceeded ninety miles direct northwards, but could not go further for want of water, and that he should try for Eyre's Creek north-westward.

Mr. Wills's Report from Torowoto to Cooper's Creek is of the character of the country. He describes this from Torowoto to Wright's Creek as traversed by several considerable creeks, but all likely to fail in a dry season, and the land itself as composed of low mud plains and clay flats, and pans subject to inundation; most of them void of vegetation of any kind, and others carrying only stunted salt-bushes, and coarse grasses struggling betwixt life and death. Bordering the flats are stony rises, well grassed and timbered. The more elevated plains are sandy, with healthy salt-bushes, and here and there some grass. On the hills were found quartz rock, forming rises in the schist ridges.

Wright's Creek, or the Balloo, they found a considerable creek, having deep water-holes, and its banks well lined with box timber, marsh-mallows, and wild spinach. The rest of the country was little better than that already described. On the 8th of November they left Wright's Creek, to cross the ranges to Cooper's Creek, and found the land adjoining these ranges well grassed, by places well timbered, yet sandy, and the watercourses dry. Amongst these they saw traces of drays, which they supposed to be De Rinsy's tracks. The first of their camps on Cooper's Creek was camp 57, and they followed the creek in a westerly and north-westerly direction from day to day to camp 65, the depôt. In some places the creek ran out and disappeared, in others it had deep water, and banks well timbered. It wound about very much amongst sand hills. In some places the feed was very good, though the grass was inclined to run coarse; the stony rises which ever and anon occurred, were bare and barren. The sand-hills, literally ridges of blown sand, were solid enough to walk on, and scarcely a plant growing on them, was unacceptable to the camels, except the spinifex. In the valleys were shallow clay-pans, in which the water from rains rapidly collects, and as rapidly evaporates. The chief herbage on the earthy flats is chrysanthemums, and marsh-mallows, which, though dry enough to powder, the cattle eat eagerly. These earthy flats are so cracked by the heat, that it is difficult and dangerous to travel over them, and in other places the ground is so boggy, that it is difficult to get the cattle to the banks of the creeks to drink. This state of the approaches to the creeks, Mr. Wills says, would entail heavy losses of cattle on settlers.

The ironstone pebbles mixed with the sandstone and quartz, on the stony rises, were found to possess considerable magnetic polarity. The dip of the country was south-west.

As Mr. Burke stated in his despatch, Mr. Wills, during their stay at Cooper's Creek, made a reconnoitring expedition northwards. In fact, Mr. Wills says, they made four attempts northwards, one with horses and the rest with camels. The country he describes as deplorably arid, birds very scarce, and native dogs numerous. On the last of these trips Wills, with McDonagh, and three camels penetrated about 80 miles, and would have gone further, as they saw a smoke at some fifteen miles distance in the N.N.E., but whilst Wills was making some observations, McDonagh, who had charge of the camels, probably fell asleep, for he let them escape, and the two travellers were compelled to walk back the 90 miles to Cooper's Creek, under a sun at 146°, where there was no shade, and with very little water, for they only found one creek on the whole way, and that on the first evening. Two of the lost camels are said to have been found afterwards near Adelaide.

All this time, namely, from the 19th of October, when Mr. Burke quitted Menindie for Cooper's Creek, to the 16th of December, nearly two months, Mr. Wright, who had with him eight men, ten camels, and thirteen horses, besides the great bulk of the stores, and who had been daily expected to arrive, had not appeared. There was one reason for Wright's delay, which was that he had accompanied Burke with two natives as far as Torowoto to show him the way, and had to return to Menindie to fetch up his portion of the party. Had Mr. Burke brought on the whole compact expedition to Cooper's Creek, his whole course would have been, as already observed, one of ease and comfort. But, having left half thus behind him, to take away its leader for 150 miles with him, making a journey of 300 thither and back, and creating a proportionate delay, was still more amazing. To add to this fatal delay, one of those *contretemps*, which Fortune always adds to the unfortunate, took place.

We have the facts in the Parliamentary Report, p. 3, and in Dr. Wills's Account, p. 135. While all this was passing, at the very moment when Mr. Burke left Menindie, news reached Melbourne of Mr. Stuart having returned from reaching nearly to 18° south latitude, and, as soon as definite information of the country which he had passed could be procured, the Exploration Committee despatched it to Mr. Burke. At Swan Hill Mr. Foster, superintendent of the police there, sent forward Lyons, a trooper, with the despatch after Burke's party. He arrived at Menindie just as Wright with his two natives returned from escorting Burke to Torowoto. Lyons refused to deliver the despatch to any one except Burke according to his special order. Here was a sufficient motive for Wright to break up his guilty lethargy, and start with bag and baggage after his leader, but, instead of this, he sent on McPherson, a saddler by trade, whom Burke had picked up on the journey as he had done Wright, with Lyons and Dick, a native, to overtake the leader, now having a start of eight days. With the usual luck attending the expedition. this embassage, including a native, could not follow the tracks of a party of nine men, sixteen camels, and fifteen horses. besides drays. They got completely lost, knocked their horses up, killed three of them, and were only saved from perishing altogether by Dr. Beckler and a party being sent in search of them. Mr. Wright, who was in no mood to stir before, now considered himself rivetted to the ground altogether for want of horses sufficient for the conveyance of his party. He, therefore, despatched Mr. Hodgkinson all the way back to Melbourne to solicit funds to purchase ten additional horses and one hundred and fifty sheep. Mr. Hodgkinson left Menindie for this journey of little less than 1000 miles, thither and back, on the 19th of December; so that three days after Burke left Cooper's Creek for Carpentaria, Mr. Wright was so far from appearing at Cooper's Creek, as Burke hoped, that he was just despatching a messenger for supplies to Melbourne, and about to wait at Menindie his return. What must the leader's feeling have been, could he have known this?

Mr. Hodgkinson displayed a very different degree of locomotion to his commander Wright, for he rode to Melbourne in eleven days, obtained an immediate order for £400 for the required purchases; started again on the 31st, without a day's delay, and arrived at Menindie again on the 9th of January, 1861. Still, Wright, this great " Fabius Cunctator" of the antipodes, though he never bought a sheep, remained another fortnight short of one day, that is, till the 24th of January, before he put himself in motion for Cooper's Creek. The reason which Wright afterwards assigned for not purchasing the sheep, was, that at that midsummer season all the grass was burnt up, with the striking facts either known to him, or which ought to have been known to an explorer, that not only Captain Sturt's flock, during his famous detention in the Stony Desert, when the heat stopped the growth of their wool, yet grew fat on the scorched-up grass, but that all explorers' sheep have flourished in the hottest and most grass consuming season. We shall soon find the consequence of the want of these sheep to the persons under his care.

Mr. Burke having committed the capital mistake of dividing his party and leaving half of it in the hands of an ignorant stranger, now perpetrated the more fatal one of again dividing his moiety, and plunging into the unknown wilderness with only two men besides Wills and himself, with six camels and one horse, and provisions for only three months, uncertain when Wright might arrive with the remainder of the party and stores, or whether, as it happened, he might never bring up these at all. From something which fell from him on the journey, it is probable that the fact of Mr. Stuart having made long stretches into the interior with a very small party, inspired him with the idea that he could do the same. But Stuart, however few in party, carried generally, ample provisions with him. Burke on the other hand, with yet 600 miles of utterly unknown country to traverse, 1200 thither and back, ignorant of what thwarting circumstances might detain him, set out with only such supplies as could last for the most rapid and prosperous transit; and with the certainty, which might have been expected to force itself on his mind, that should he ever accomplish the object of reaching the northern shores, he must rush back with a famine haunted impetuosity, which must be destructive to both men and animals. What occurred the public now know too well. With the finest and best supplied exploring expedition which ever issued from any colonial capital, we have, in the short space of eight months, the leaders of it perishing of starvation and excessive fatigue, after a transit, which, according to their own journals, presented no extraordinary obstacles whatever. The catastrophe was the direct consequence of the head of the expedition dropping and frittering away his resources as a dilapidated sack lets its contents slip through the bottom. The transit was made, the great enterprise was accomplished, as by a splendid piece of insanity. But though the crossing of the continent was accomplished, no scientific objects were effected. We have the evidence of Dr. Beckler, " that he kept back with him many of the scientific instruments entrusted to his charge, alleging that Mr. Burke, who was both unscientific, and impatient of the time lost in making and registering observations, threatened to throw them into the next creek." Dr. Wills's Narrative, p. 251. With such a leader, even the advantage of a zealous and accomplished scientific companion like Mr. Wills was lost, for besides the impatience of the go-ahead Burke, the insignificance of the means of carriage taken with them from Cooper's Creek, and the haste of their travel, prevented any solid observations and records. And all this time the forces and supplies so liberally provided by the public and the government, were lying inert and worse than useless at Cooper's Creek, at Menindie, and Bulloo, to the amount of nine men, thirteen camels, and twenty-three horses, besides abundant stores.

In the month of March, 1861, when the expedition had been on its way for seven months, yet no news of it had reached Melbourne since it left Torowoto in October, the public mind began to manifest anxiety on its account. A letter signed "Lockhart Moreton," in the Argus, put the plain question—"What has become of the expedition?" adding—"Surely the committee are not alive to the necessity of sending some one up? Burke has by this time crossed the continent, or is lost. What has become of Wright? What is he doing?"

These were very pertinent inquiries after such a lapse of time, and calculated to arouse the public solicitude. This, however, did not become excessive till another quarter of a year had passed. Dr. Wills, who was living at Ballarat, naturally in great suspense regarding the fate of his son, hastened to Melbourne in June, and endeavoured to stimulate the Exploration Committee to send out an expedition of search after the so long unheard-of travellers. The Exploration Committee, in their instructions to Mr. Burke (see Parliamentary Report, p. 72), had made it their very first injunction to him to form a depôt at Cooper's Creek, to "make arrangements for keeping open a communication in his rear to the Darling, if in his opinion advisable, and thence to Melbourne, so that he might be enabled to keep the committee informed of his movements, and receive in return such assistance in stores and advice as he might stand in need of. If he found a readier means of communication by way of Mount Serle and Adelaide, for writing to the committee, he was to avail himself of it." And almost their last injunction to him was to make full reports on any subject of interest, and forward them to Melbourne as often as practicable without retarding the progress of the expedition."

None of these measures had been adopted by Mr. Burke. He had taken none to keep open a communication in his rear with the Darling, and by that means with Melbourne; and had not Mr. Wright, loitering at Menindie, thought he wanted money, it does not appear that the Committee would have received a single despatch from Burke from the day of his crossing the Darling. When Mr. Wright was afterwards examined by the committee at Melbourne as to the cause of his not following up Mr. Burke to Cooper's Creek, he actually pleaded that he could not find the way; that beyond Bulloo, "the track of Burke turned suddenly to the west, and was not visible." Burke had, in fact, taken no pains to blaze trees along his route where the ground was too rocky to leave an impression, and hence Wright asserted that he did not reach Cooper's Creek because he could not find it. This does not say much for him as an able bushman, who would have struck circle after circle till he had cut across the leader's track; but it adds to the other proofs of Burke's neglect of "keeping open his rear." (See Progress Report of the Exploration Committee, adopted at a meeting of the Royal Society of Victoria, April 14, 1862.)

Much obloquy has been cast on the Committee for not inquiring after the progress and safety of the expedition earlier; but with the express commands thus laid on the leader to let them know of any matter of interest, to seek aid or advice from them if he required it, and after supplying him with such a force and such stores, these censures do not appear very reasonable. The Committee were familiar with the repeated progresses of Stuart into the same interior, and almost to the northern shores, with far inferior forces and equipments, from which he always returned. On the only occasion on which a messenger had come down for aid, it was promptly and generously granted. The confidence of the Committee, therefore, in the well-being of the expedition, appears perfectly natural.

The arrival of Dr. Wills in Melbourne, and his energetic appeals to the Committee, at once determined them to send out a party in search of the unheard-of expedition. A meeting was immediately called, namely, on the 18th of June, at which a resolution to that effect was passed unanimously, and this fact was announced the next day in the *Argus*. Various gentlemen were named to head this expedition. Dr. Wills offered to go himself, in the absence of any more youthful and, through bush seasoning, qualified person. The choice fell on my son, Alfred William Howitt, who had for some time been successfully engaged in exploring for the government the Gippsland mountains for gold, and who had previously had much experience both of bush life and of the business of exploration. We must now, therefore, for a while suspend the narrative of the original expedition, to follow that going in quest of it.

CHAPTER X.

EXPEDITION IN QUEST OF THAT OF MESSRS. BURKE AND WILLS, UNDER THE COMMAND OF MR. ALFRED WILLIAM HOWITT, 1861-2.

Previous bush experience of the leader.—Journey to Stuart's new country in South Australia.—His report of that country.—Appointed to search for gold in Gippsland.—Success.—Mr. Howitt met on his way to the Murray by Mr. Brahe with despatches stating that Burke and Wills left Cooper's Creek on the 16th of December, and nothing had since been heard of them.—Dr. Becker, Messrs. Purcell and Stone dead.—Great sensation in Melbourne.—Wright's despatch. —A too late visit of Wright and Brahe to Cooper's Creek.—Their leaving it altogether.—Brahe's examination by the Exploration Committee.—Mr. Howitt ordered to hasten north in quest of Burke and Wills.—Mr. Walker ordered to proceed from Rockhampton to the Gulf of Carpentaria in quest of Burke and Wills.—Captain Norman, with the Victoria steamer, ordered to the Gulf.— The Firefly sent from Brisbane, with a party under Mr. Landsborough, to the Gulf, to proceed thence south for the same object.—Mr. Howitt sets out, accompanied by Dr. Wheeler.—Mr. Landells offer his services to conduct the camels. —These not accepted.—Howitt and Wheeler left Melbourne July 4, 1861.— August 13th arrived at Pomonmaroo Creek, on the Darling.—Menindie and its land-hunters.—Dislike of the horses to the camels.—At Poria Creek Mr. Howitt leaves Burke's track, and strikes N.W. to Cooper's Creek.—Reaches the depôt. —Finds the papers of Burke and Wills buried at Wills Fort, informing them of Burke and Wills having returned thither.—Camel tracks.—Find various articles.—Find King amongst the natives, and learn the death of Burke and Wills.—Find the remains of the explorers, with fields-book and papers.—Buried the remains.—Failure of an attempt to send word to Melbourne of the news by carrier pigeons.—Presents made to the natives for their kindness to King. —Return to the Darling.—Mr. Howitt and Dr. Wheeler to Melbourne.

IN introducing the leader of the contingent exploration expedition, it may be as well to notice the preparatory steps by which he had become fitted for so reponsible a command. My son Alfred accompanied myself and his younger and only living brother, Herbert Charlton Howitt—who has since lost his life in New Zealand, whilst employed in making a road over the mountains from Christchurch to the western coast of the middle island. During my two years' travel through the colony of Victoria, and life in its forests and at its different diggings, my eldest son, Mr. Alfred Howitt, became familiar with bush life, and by the active management of the concerns of the party, acquired the tact and experience

MR. HOWITT'S PREVIOUS EXPERIENCE. 213

necessary for more extended duties. After my return in 1854, he was for several years engaged on different squatting stations, and in conveying flocks and herds to distant parts of the colony. In 1859, the accounts published by McDouall Stuart of the country discovered by him to the N.W. of Lake Torrens, induced a wealthy squatter of Victoria to engage my son to make a journey thither to ascertain whether it was really good grazing country, and whether cattle and sheep might be driven thither from Adelaide. Sailing for that port, Mr. Howitt there purchased a number of horses for riding and pack horses, and a light spring waggon also to carry part of the necessary supplies. His party consisted of four, one of them being Mr. Ligar, the son of the surveyor-general of Victoria. The general course of this journey was by the east side of Lake Torrens, thence N.W. to near Lake Gregory, and on in the same direction as far as the Davenport Range, where they were compelled to return by total want of water. Of the character of the country on this journey of at least 500 miles, we have already had the evidence of Sturt, Eyre, Warburton, and Parry. Mr. Howitt's experience of it was the same—that of a burning, arid, inhospitable desert, through which no cattle or sheep could travel without destruction to the majority of them, excepting in some exceptional and very rare season. Nor was the new country, as it is called, more auspicious when they arrived at it. His general impression of this region we may derive from one of his private letters. This is dated Wilpena, October 4, 1859 :—" You will find Wilpena on the map, about eighty-five miles south of Mount Serle. We are taking a day's rest for the horses, after coming over a hundred miles or more of country without a blade of grass. We travelled up to Mount Remarkable very comfortably, with plenty of grass, water, and fine weather; but the farther north we go the hotter it gets, and more barren the country is. They have scarcely had any rain here for three years, and there is scarcely any winter; it is one continual summer. This country and Victoria are as different as possible. The great features here are extensive plains, covered with salt bush, and with grass after rain. These plains run between hills varying from 100 to 2000 feet high, and quite destitute of timber. Indeed, the only timber found here grows on the banks of the watercourses, and a few he or she-oaks on the hills. The lower ranges are most like sheep downs; the higher ones are masses of rock, torn into all kinds of jagged peaks and precipices, and generally of a reddish hue, but seen in the distance, of a deep indigo. The country is intensely stony, being, so to say, 'metalled,' and the roads are naturally splendid. It is very hot and dry, and I should fancy must be very like the interior of South Africa, only that there are no animals to be seen excepting kangaroos and kangaroo rats. Large flocks of emus stalk about the barren plains like some enchanted creatures in the "Arabian Nights." The air is so clear that the distances are difficult to estimate. Altogether, it is a very wild, strange country. Places that we have passed through, among huge, towering masses of mountains, give an impression of vastness and perfect desolation and solitude that I never experienced in the timbered ranges of Victoria. This interior part of the country is not to be compared with Victoria, and I have but small hope of the new country: it gets worse as we proceed. The run we are now on is very large, extending sixty miles in one direction, but only carries a comparatively small herd of cattle.

From a station at Mount Serle, October the 10th, he writes:—"When we left Wilpena, we had the worst part of our journey before us. Since then we have been travelling among wild, rocky mountains, the road in places winding down gorges with precipices on each side, and pines and mallee scrub growing on the spurs. Sometimes we went for miles along the dry beds of rivers full of boulders, and shingle, and gum-trees, then over saltbush plains with distinct mountain defiles stretching for miles, each side the exact counterpart of the other; yet some of the places we passed through were wonderfully strange and picturesque. Imagine the difficulty of getting feed for our horses, and water for us and them in such a country! Frequently we have to dismount, and all put to our strength in pushing the wagon over rocks, only thankful, when it is done, that it is not knocked to pieces. The temperature was very mild in the earlier part of the journey. On September the 2nd, 49°, noon 55°, evening 56°, and so on; but as the summer advanced, it advanced to 90° and 110°. As far as Mount Remarkable, as observed, the country was passable, well watered, and the stations good; beyond, the country grew desert, and the squatters appeared to partake in general of the inhospitality of the country. The notices in the journal are continually, 'a miserable country,' 'a miserable place.' In some places clouds of grasshoppers flew up before the horses with a sound like a smart shower on dry leaves; in others, flocks of emus were seen in full career to avoid them; and again they came to wide burnt-up plains, here and there divided by dried-up creeks, and hemmed in by ranges of barren hills; then still more miserable country, than the imagination can conceive—dry, sandy covered with stones, without a sign of grass, or a drop of water; then a squatting station—a collection of huts standing in a sandy desolation; near it a large flock of ewes and lambs, looking about for something to eat—starvation written all over them. Your road you could trace for miles before you by tall whirlwinds of yellow dust stalking along after each other like the Genii let out of the bottle by the fisherman in the 'Arabian Nights Tales.' And this, it must be remembered, was the spring of the Australian year.

"Some of the squatters gave a melancholy account of their flocks. They had had great losses, and it was difficult to see how they were to get through the heat of the summer, the ground then being absolutely bare. The cattle looked miserable, not one of them all in tolerable condition. As they advanced northwards, they found high ranges with reefs of slate standing like fortifications, the slates jutting up edgeways. Some of these reefs and rocky gullies about Mount Serle were especially formidable. Such continues the description of the country, sand, stones, rocks, dry creeks, and high rocky ranges, alternating on by Fortress Hill, Mount Clive, the Frome River, Shamrock Pool, Dry Lake, Mount Delusion, Mount Attraction, to Hermit Hill and Finniss Springs, a little south of Lake Gregory. About some of these springs, which are numerous, were evidences of volcanic action—blocks of stone melted and glazed like clinkers, heaps of cinders that clinked with a metallic sound as you rode over them, and, in the centre of the lake, a ragged depression in the ground as of a former crater. Fragments of quartz, flint, ironstone, covered the country around, and numerous fragments of clear quartz crystal, looking like broken glass, whilst I found it almost impossible to discover a single crystal which was entire. In this dry lake, which was near the springs, stood up six or eight large mounds, green with rushes, and surrounded by crystalized soda.

"On one occasion, after a long day's ride through intense heat, and not a drop of water to be seen, we came to a singular fountain. It consisted of a pool of water, clear as crystal, in which stood up a number of tall columns of earth covered with grass and rushes, out of the summit of each of which gushed springs of water, which ran down their sides, and filled the pool. On fire with thirst, both we and the horses rushed forward to drink, when we found the water so intensely charged with soda that it was impossible to swallow it. Numbers of these springs abound between Hermit Hill and Mount Attraction, probably not less than fifty, with mounds ten feet high, which, if opened, would give a great supply of water; but the country between them and Mount Attraction is perfectly worthless, and would not feed a bandicoot, and it is the same beyond them.

"Salt Creek, west of Hermit Hill, Tuesday, October the 25th; thermometer 72°, 90°, 83°. The country between the springs, where we camped last night, and the springs under Hermit Hill, was a shade better, but, in fact, relapsing into a desert. I firmly believe a good season here is only a mirage. Finniss's Springs, however, are well worth seeing. They surround Hermit Hill on three sides. The hill itself is an ancient volcano, the crater being plainly visible, and the depression all round, formed by its upheaval, is now the watercourse in which lie the springs. How many there are, it would be difficult to tell, but their reed beds, and rushes, and pools of water are visible, as far as one can see, between the stony banks of the watercourse. Outside of these are scrubby sand-hills, or dry watercourses, and stony table-lands. When Major Warburton saw these springs after a wet season, when vegetation here would be extraordinary, I admit that he must have been surprised, as they are different from anything I have heard of; but now, when the country round is seen in its true colours, and when 'the beds of reeds, ten feet in height, and almost impenetrable, are sadly dwindled down, as are the sheets of water,' it produces rather a feeling of regret that such splendid springs as these, even now are, should be thrown away in such a worthless country."

From Hermit Hill to Strangway Springs, the country was of the same character—very different to that which a wet season had given to it in the eyes of Major Warburton. There were sandy, burning deserts, dry watercourses, with tall stalks of mallows dried to brittle wands, salt springs, so intensely salt that the water seemed to take the skin from their mouths, when tasting it; soda springs, the water of which effervesced with tartaric acid, plains covered with stones, and bare, broken, flat-topped hills. The heat grew oppressive. At Hermit Hill, October the 27th, the thermometer stood, morning, noon, afternoon, and night, 63°, 125°, 86°. At Mount Hamilton, October the 29th, 78°, 127°, 101°, 92°. At Strangways, October the 30th, 66°, 142°, 128°, 110°. Such a country did not invite the flocks and herds of Victorian squatters. Mr. Howitt's report extinguished all thoughts of such an enterprise.

Yet our travellers still advanced as far as the Davenport Ranges, Mount Margaret, Warburton's farthest, considerably north of 29° south latitude, and near 136° east longitude. They would have gone much further but for the failure of their provisions. A squatter, whose station lies far up the country, having been in Melbourne before their setting out, assured them that he could furnish them with ample provisions for the further prosecution of their route north-west; but, on reaching his station, they found this not only an empty boast, but he was by no means hospitably inclined. From this disappointment, they were compelled to return, when about thirty miles to the north of what Stuart had laid down as a well grassed country. They were, however, anxious to reach the mysterious Wingillpin of the blacks, that land of lakes, wild fowl, stringy-bark ranges, and black-fellows, according to native accounts, and from which, they supposed, they were not more than 200 miles distant.

After reaching Adelaide on their return, the travellers rode overland to Melbourne, having made a journey of 2000 miles by land, and 500 by water. The whole of the party behaved admirably.

In the following year, 1860, the Melbourne Government sent out two parties to explore for gold in Gippsland. Mr. Nicholson, who was one of the first who explored Gippsland, being a companion of the first discoverers of that territory, McAllister and McMillan, and who had had nine years experience as a practical miner, was placed at the head of one party, Alfred Howitt at the head of the other. At the same time two other small parties were sent out under Messrs. M'Crae and M'Donnell, into districts nearer to Melbourne. The recommendations of Mr. Howitt to this post of prospector, to use the diggers' phrase, were his recent successfully executed journey into the torrid deserts north of Lake Torrens, and his practical knowledge of gold mining. During his bush campaign with me I had recommended an examination of the creeks beyond the Ovens diggings, and Alfred and a working digger were despatched to prospect these creeks. They soon returned with the news of plenty of gold in the Upper Yackadanda and Nine-Mile Creeks, above the junction of these creeks, and we speedily proceeded thither, and settled ourselves on the Upper Yackadanda, within half-a-mile of Nine-Mile-Creek, and thus were discovered the Nine-Mile-Creek Diggings, which have continued prolific diggings ever since. When we made our progress thither the country was trackless forest, and we were compelled to cut asunder fallen trees, or remove them with levers to make a way for our cart, so thickly did they in places encumber the ground. In a few weeks 5000 persons had followed us. In a few months before we came away there were upwards of 10,000.

Mr. Nicholson appears to have commenced his operations in Gippsland, on the creeks of the river Tambo, near Bruthen, and to have pursued them along the spurs of the mountains in the lower country, finding traces of gold in various places. Mr. Howitt turned his attention to the river Mitchell and its tributaries, following them up into the mountains themselves. These are a part of the great chain of the Snowy Mountains, or Warragong chain, running from New South Wales to within twenty miles of Melbourne, and terminating in the Dandenong Hills. At the sources of these rivers they reached the height of more than 5000 feet, Mount Tamborita being 5380 feet. The appointment being made in the middle of May, we find Mr. Howitt, with thirteen men and ten horses, early in June, already far up amongst the mountains, near two conspicuous ones, Bald Hill and Notch Hill, about 3000 feet in height. He had taken the most eastern branch of the Mitchell, the Wentworth. The gold was but scarce on this branch, thin and flakey, but the scenery was splendid. It was, however, midwinter, and the frost during the nights very severe. The leaves on the evergreen trees tinkled as if made of tin, and water froze in a bucket only five feet from their fire. Already they had to send down ninety miles for their provisions. In a journey of inspection, accompanied by one of the men, Mr. Howitt traced up the western branch of the Wentworth, and followed a spur of the Mount Steve Range over the Birregun, 4500 feet high, to the Dargo, near where that river divided into the Little Dargo and the Upper Dargo, which ran north-east, and then north-west into snowy plains, 5000 feet high, crowned by Mount Smythe. On the Upper Dargo, near a mountain which they named Mount Pyke, they came upon the traces of diggers having been already at work. Part of the river bank was sluiced, and the sluice-boxes and old tools were there. All these lay in solid ice; it was clear that the works had only been abandoned for the winter. Farther up they found other sluice-boxes, tools, cuttings, and a bark hut. There they also procured a good specimen of gold. In the course of July, ascending the Dargo still further, amid mists and snows, and intense cold, he found a log-hut, and other mining works, which appeared to have been in operation of two years during the summer. In August, accompanied by M. D. F. Jones, the special correspondent of the *Argus*, Mr. Howitt completed the inspection of the Upper Dargo, finding gold enough to enable men to make ten shillings per day. They also ascended into the Snowy Plains, where the snow was two feet deep, and continued their researches to Bingo Mungee, on the road to Omeo, and near to Livingstone. They obtained extensive and splendid views of Castle-Hill, Mount Wellington, the snowy mountains at the head of the Dargo, Mount Birregun, Mounts Pyke, Steve, and several mountains beyond Omeo.

At Bingo Mungee, on the Cobbungrah Creek, they found a hut, and in it two young men, who had been amongst the first workers on the Dargo. They reported the average returns of gold had been from £3 to £4 per week per man, and occasionally as high as £9; but that they had suffered much damage from floods carrying away their apparatus.

In October they were tracing up the western branch of the Mitchell to where it branches into the Crooked, the Wongungarra, and the Wonangatta Rivers, lying each one more westward than the other, and the most westerly, Wonangatta River, terminating in Snowy Plains, 5000 feet in elevation. On these rivers they found almost everywhere gold that would yield 10s. to 12s. per day per man; in six dishes, two feet from the surface, they obtained 20s. worth of gold; and in one day three men got about £7 10s. worth of nuggetty gold. It was quite clear that good and extensive gold fields existed in these mountains. On the Dargo, forty miles of river would produce paying gold. Besides this, in the valleys amongst these mountains lay considerable quantities of good pasturage lands. They might require the sheep and cattle to descend lower in winter, but in summer they would be fine alpine feeding grounds, and seemed well adapted to Alpacas. As the summer advanced the birds which had gone down to the lower country returned, and the forests were loud with the quaint notes of the leatherheads and wattlebirds. As for the scenery, in the opinion both of Mr. Howitt and of the celebrated French landscape painter, De Guerard, who made a journey thither in consequence of the accounts of the country in the *Argus*, it is the most truly sublime and grandly beautiful of any in Australia. The snow-covered mountains rising, some of them to 6000 feet, the deep defiles through which the rivers rush impetuously, the dark, misty gorges opening in different directions, with the dim outlines of mountains and plains beyond, especially on the Wangungarra, Wanongatta, and Moroka rivers, produced in De Guerard, who had seen Italy and the Alps, the intensest delight. When Mr. Howitt observed to him, "This will take you six months to paint," he exclaimed—"Six months!—six years!"

In forcing a way along some of these defiles along the course of the rivers they were obliged to use fire, especially on the Warrangarra, before its dividing into the Wonguugarra and Wonangatta. In a letter on this subject is this passage :—" It will take six months to prospect this river (Warrangarra) properly, as we have to cut our way as we go. Sometimes through scrub, sometimes along the face of the hill-sides. To-morrow we commence a fresh piece of road, in the first mile of which we shall have to form a horse-track under some tremendous precipices, building the detached blocks of slate into a path about two feet wide, for the horses to walk along; and some of these blocks of stone will require our whole party of thirteen to move and lever. You may imagine what it is to make such a track. After this we have two miles of level travelling, over flats and grassy spurs, or rather what were grassy spurs, as I have set fire to all before me for three miles. The flats are a jungle of brambles, fern, reeds, scrub, and grass ten feet in height, and you may imagine what a grand sight it was when all this immense mass of combustibles was roaring in sheets of flame thirty feet in height. One lucifer match does more to clear a road than all of us could do in a week. We are leaving a track of fire and smoke as we go, and I daresay that the latter is visible down in the low country. I mean to burn all that will take fire, and shall leave a track that will open this country effectually; as it is, I have no doubt that our bridle track will be visible by places for a century to come, though it were never used after us."

By such energetic means, the leader sharing in every labour and hardship with his men, their horses going up and down for 100 miles or more for supplies, and with a little flock of sheep grazing near them for fresh mutton, these mountain regions were effectually opened up. The special correspondent of the *Argus*, in that journal of June 20, 1860, expresses his astonishment at the indomitable energy and perseverance of the leader, and the admirable conduct of the men. In approaching the Dargo he says he found a cleared track of upwards of forty miles.

In November the Crooked River was found so auriferous, that the men were impatient for their discharge, to commence gold-digging. Accordingly, they all resigned in one day, and the leader sent a despatch to Melbourne to announce this result. The gold field thus established has continued to be worked unceasingly, and now has, according to a report, January 28, 1864, by Mr. Howitt, as gold warden of Omeo, a population of 1200 or 1300 souls, and profitable workings on most of the rivers, with capabilities from quartz reefs and river deluvium to a far greater extent.

The Rev. W. B. Clarke, of Sydney, who discovered gold in New South Wales in 1841, and who has contributed so much to the progress of gold discovery both in Australia and Van Diemen's Land, stated long since that in a geological point of view he considered the Lake Omeo district as the great centre of all the Australian gold fields, and that in or near this richer fields would yet be found than any yet known.

The energy, tact, and successful zeal evidenced in the expedition to the north-west of South Australia, and in the opening up of these gold mountains, marked Mr. Alfred Howitt out as the fitting man for the search after the unheard-of Burke and Wills expedition. He lost not a moment in setting out. On proceeding towards the Murray, where he proposed to dry beef for the expedition, and there collect the necessary horses and vehicles, he met Brahe on the Loddon, coming down with despatches from Mr. Wright. The news which Mr. Brahe brought was of so important a nature, that he immediately telegraphed to the Secretary of the Exploration Committee in Melbourne from Sandhurst:—" Sandhurst, 29th June. I met Mr. Brahe at the Loddon with despatches, and received the following message: 'Mr. Wright has reached Menindie with eight men, having being joined by Mr. Burke's depôt party from Cooper's Creek. Messrs. Becker, Purcell, Stone, and Patton died on the journey. Mr. Burke left Cooper's Creek on the 16th of December. Nothing has been heard of him since that date. He was accompanied by Messrs. Wills,

Gray, and King. The natives proved hostile, and the country for 150 miles was waterless. Two camels and three horses died, and one was lost. (Signed) W. Wright. I shall be in town with Mr. Brahe to-morrow morning." (Signed) A. W. Howitt, Leader of Contingent Party. The Hon. John Macadam, M.D.

The telegram, as may be supposed, excited a deep sensation. A special meeting of the Royal Society was called for the afternoon of the next day—Sunday—by which time Mr. Howitt and Mr. Brahe would have arrived. At this meeting the despatches and other documents brought down by Mr. Brahe, were produced and read. The first was a long despatch from Mr. Wright, in which he detailed what had occurred to his party since his last despatch announcing his moving forward from Menindie to Cooper's Creek. The despatch was very confused, but showed that Mr. Wright had delayed at Menindie till all the water was dried up on the road, (October 19th). He then made attempts to proceed, but only got to Bulloo with his party. There Dr. Becker died as well as Messrs. Purcell and Stone, from scurvy and exhaustion. Dr. Becker who was at once an artist and a botanist, a German by birth, was greatly regretted for his amiable qualities, but he had not had the bush seasoning necessary for such a life. Wright was in the act of retreating to the Darling when Mr. Brahe arrived from Cooper's Creek on the 18th of April. He had with him Patton, then in a dying state, McDonagh and Botan, with twelve horses and six camels, very much infested with scab.

As Mr. Wright had in his own party, including himself, six persons, and was now joined by Brahe, with himself and three others, his total of men was ten, but of these, four died, so that after the junction of Brahe, six men, including himself, he had sixteen camels and five-and-twenty horses. He soon lost three of the diseased camels, but he had yet thirteen. Yet with six men, thirteen camels, and twenty-five horses, he began his retreat towards the Darling, on the 1st of May, after a pause of three days. Much as Mr. Brahe has been blamed for leaving Cooper's Creek till he had some knowledge of the fate of Burke and Wills, Wright had no thought of his having come away too soon, or of the necessity with all his force of making a push into the interior to endeavour to come upon some trace of them. He retreated as far as Koorliatto, when some idea of the necessity of making a little effort to learn something of the lost party came across him, and he rode back with Brahe to Cooper's Creek, leaving his party at Koorliatto during this ride. "He was desirous," he says, "of ascertaining whether Mr. Burke had returned, as the provisions left there by Mr. Brahe had been discovered by the natives;" "I found," he adds, "no signs of Mr. Burke's return or of the cache of stores having been disturbed, and returned to Koorliatto on the 12th of May." Parliamentary Report, Burke and Wills, p. 7.

We now know from Wills's Diary, see Parliamentary Report, p. 58, that Wright when he thus returned to Cooper's Creek, ostensibly to examine the cache, never examined it at all, as he would have found that the cache had been just then visited, and the provisions and Brahe's note taken out; and the "Field Books," and other journals of Burke and Wills, containing the account of their journey to Carpentaria and back, deposited there instead, with a note by Burke himself, dated April 22nd, in which he stated, that Gray being dead, he, Wills, and King had arrived at the depôt the night before, and were "greatly disappointed at finding the party there gone on that very day. That they were then gone towards Mount Hopeless, but in a very exhausted condition."—Parliamentary Report, p. 35. This also stood in the Journal of Burke and Wills, which at the very time Mr. Wright professed to examine the condition of the cache, were lying in it.—Parliamentary Report, pp. 59 and 60.

Such was the manner in which Wright discharged his duty. Mr. Brahe had indeed quitted Cooper's Creek, fearing the holding out of his provisions, and the death of his party, after remaining there more than four months, but when Wright returned with Brahe thither in the beginning of May, had he opened the cache, as was his plain duty, and as he ostensibly went back to do, the whole mischief would still have been averted; he could have put himself on the track of the three unhappy men towards Mount Hopeless, and must have rescued them. Surely never did such a series of fatalities attend any other expedition; surely never was the fate of devoted public men intrusted to such a man as Mr. Wright. Wright, instead of returning to Melbourne with the expedition, had gone off to Adelaide. Mr. Wright stated in his despatch, that if he were wanted, he might be telegraphed for. His despatch and notes from Burke and Wills, as well as the journal of Wills from Torowoto Swamp to Cooper's Creek, of which we have already copied the main events, informed the committee that Burke, Wills, Gray and King, had left Cooper's Creek for Carpentaria on the 16th of December, 1860, with six camels, one horse, and twelve weeks provisions. They had now been gone not three months but six, and the necessity of the promptest measures, if not already too late, was imminent. Mr. Brahe was stringently questioned by the Committee, why he left Cooper's Creek at all. In a verbal reply, and afterwards in a written diary put in, Mr. Brahe stated that Mr. Burke ordered him to follow him towards Carpentaria, should Mr. Wright, as he expected, soon arrive at Cooper's Creek, but Mr. Wright never came. Mr. Burke also ordered him, in case Mr. Wright did not relieve him, to remain at Cooper's Creek three months or longer, if provisions would allow him; that he remained eighteen weeks, and was compelled to leave on account of the dying condition of Patton, and the illness of himself and the other men with scurvy, and still more because his provisions were getting so low that he feared they would not suffice to carry him to the Darling. That he left in the cache at the creek, 50lbs. of flour, 50lbs. of oatmeal, 50lbs. of sugar, and 30lbs of rice. That he took with him, for

himself and three men, 150lbs. of flour, a bag and a
half of sugar, a bag of rice, and four pounds of tea.
Mr. Burke expressed his firm determination to return to
Cooper's Creek, but that if he could not reach Cooper's
Creek, without being obliged to return another way, he
would not go on to Carpentaria. Mr. Brahe, therefore,
concluded that he was set fast somewhere in the interior
for want of water.

Various plans for the discovery and relief of Burke's
party were discussed by the Committee, but the public
was impatient to see the contingent party under Mr.
Howitt on its way. The *Melbourne Herald* of July 1st,
1861, said, "The prompt measures taken by the Exploration Committee to dispatch aid to Mr. Burke's party
will give general satisfaction! It is just the course that
ought to be taken. Mr. Howitt is unquestionably the
very man for this work. He will carry with him the
entire confidence of the public, and their heartiest wishes
for the successful issue of his enterprise. But the Committee must give him *carte blanche* as to mere details."
This was done, and Mr. Howitt, explaining his plans of
action to the especial meeting of the Royal Society, held
on the 30th of June, it was decided that his party should
consist of twelve men, including two natives, a doctor,
and an assistant surgeon. Mr. Hugh Glass generously
offered to provision the party from his stores on the
Darling at cost price. Mr. Howitt was to take five
months' rations from Menindie, and by employing such
of the camels and horses as had returned with Brahe
and Wright and were fit for the service, he was to make
up the number of seven camels and thirty-seven horses.
On the 4th of July he left Melbourne, taking with him
Mr. Brahe, who was well acquainted with the route to
Cooper's Creek, having travelled it thither and back,
and in whose integrity, notwithstanding the blame cast
on him for leaving the creek, Mr. Howitt had perfect
faith—a faith justified by the subsequent experience.
Having entered the new leader on his journey, we may
now return a moment, to notice the other measures in-

stituted by the Exploration Committee for the relief of Burke and Wills.

At a meeting of this Committee after the resolution was taken to send Mr. Howitt direct to Cooper's Creek, Mr. Morris, formerly a member of the Legislative Assembly of New South Wales, stated that a Mr. Lee had been exploring the north-east part of Australia with a party of seven blacks and one white, and had discovered tracks, which he believed to be Leichhardt's, as well as several of Leichhardt's cattle, on the Barcoo. This gentleman Mr. Morris recommended the Committee to send out from Rockhampton, in Queensland, in quest of Burke and Wills, as a first-rate bushman, and one always friendly with the blacks. Afterwards it was concluded to send on that route Mr. Walker, also strongly recommended by Mr. Morris, as an able bushman, and also one possessing great influence over the natives. It was next resolved to send the steam sloop Victoria, under command of Captain Norman, to the Gulf of Carpentaria, to look out for Mr. Burke and his companions, and if found, to bring them off. Besides this, Mr. Orkney dispatched his small steam-yacht, the Hotham, under command of Captain Wyse, to the gulf, for the same purpose, and at his own expense. It was still further agreed, in conjunction with the government of Queensland, to send an exploring party from Brisbane by sea in the Firefly to the river Albert, in the Gulf of Carpentaria, to co-operate with Captain Norman, of the Firefly. This party was to be commanded by Mr. Landsborough, and was to proceed southward from the Albert in quest of Burke, if he had not turned up on the gulf coast. The progress and results of these various expeditions, as well as that sent out simultaneously from South Australia, under Mr. McKinlay for the same object, we shall notice hereafter. We now follow the party of Mr. Howitt, direct from Melbourne, in the very footsteps of Burke himself.

Before leaving Melbourne, Dr. Wheeler was appointed the medical man of the expedition. A memorial from Mr. Landells to His Excellency the Governor was read, in which Mr. Landells, no doubt strengthened in his opinion of the indispensability of his command of the camels by the reported ill condition of these animals, and the mysterious disappearance of Messrs. Burke and Wills, represented that it was he who, " by the assistance of the camels, could thoroughly overcome the difficulties Mr. Howitt's party would have to encounter;" and that without them, "and himself included," he clearly inferred " Mr. Howitt's expedition was almost hopeless." *Argus*, July 5th, 1861. Both the Governor, the Committee, and the new leader, however, ventured to dispense with Mr. Landell's services, and, as it will be seen, the camels, with one exception, and that already diseased, and every other creature, man and beast, returned in health and safety.

Leaving Melbourne on the 4th of July, we find Mr. Howitt and five of his party at Sandhurst on the next day, and leaving the same day for Swan Hill, on the Murray. The five fellow travellers were Brahe, H. M. Sampson, W. H. Calcott, W. F. Wheeler, the surgeon who had been at one time attached to Stuart's exploration party, and Weston Phillips, one of Howitt's exploring party in Gippsland, a man of trust, ability, and reliability. On the 13th of August, we find by his despatches, Howitt at Pamomaroo Creek, on the Darling, where he had not only arranged and equipped his party, but was about to start thence the next day for Cooper's Creek. His animals were in fair condition, his men all well, and in high spirits. He had been favoured by plenty of rain, and in a private letter he describes the Pamomaroo lake as abounding with all sorts of waterfowls, ducks, cranes, spoon-bills, and the like. Menindie, the township, seven miles off, as having an inn, a store, and a lock-up, a place *sui generis*, and one which you might imagine a frontier village, or fort, in one of Captain Mayne Reid's books. A place essentially belonging to exploring, and where parties fit out for trips in search of country for stations, and the whole conversation being of who is out and who is in; what country they have seen, what country they have taken up, new waters discovered, and new tracks made, and, especially, what parties have "had brushes with the niggers," etc., etc., etc. The conduct of explorers they found dissected in a very critical manner by this bearded conclave who assembled at the inn. The people about had a thorough veteran bushman look,—beards, pipes, boots, and cabbage-tree hats being the fashionable costume; and one of the great employments being to criticise the provisions offered at the store for explorers, as dried beef, which was talked about, tasted, and smelt, with the air of connoisseurs. From Menindie to Poria Creek, a little beyond latitude 29°, and upwards of 200 miles from Menindie, Mr. Howitt sums up the journey in his despatch of October the 10th, on his return journey, in the following words:—"I may state regarding my diary, that I have only transcribed that portion subsequent to our reaching this place on our outward journey, as up to that time we had followed the expedition track, and nothing of interest had occurred. It may suffice for me to state, that leaving Menindie, we had travelled without meeting with any particular hindrances, finding splendid feed all the way, and sufficient water for our use, with the exception of three nights, when our horses were without."

One of their greatest troubles arose from the excessive aversion of the horses to the camels, and their becoming restless, and endeavouring to break away even when they perceived the print of their feet in the sand. The classical reader will be reminded of the antiquity of this antipathy, and of the stratagem of Cyrus, to whom this fact was known, and who, by placing camels in front of his army, caused the horses of the cavalry of Crœsus to wheel round, and throw the Lydian army into confusion, thereby causing their defeat.—See Herodotus, Clio. lxxx. Gibbon tells us that the natural antipathy of the horse to the camel is affirmed by the ancients, but that it is disproved by daily experience, and derided by the best judges, the Orientalists. The ancients knew much better than Gibbon the truth of what they wrote, and here is a curious proof of it. In the east, or elsewhere, horses become gradually reconciled to camels, but still they have an original antipathy to them. Here, indeed, were oriental camels introduced in a new country, and the horses at once vindicated the ancients.

From Poria Creek Mr. Howitt, instead of following the wide circuit which Mr. Burke had made first north-east and then westerly, made a nearly direct north-western course to Cooper's Creek, a course which Mr. Burke had desired Wright to endeavour to discover during his absence on his passage to Carpentaria, which that gentleman appears to have treated with the same neglect as the other orders of his leader. The relief party reached Poria Creek on the 1st of September, and travelled to Cooper's Creek in a week, reaching it on the 8th. In rather less than a fortnight he reached the Depôt, Fort Wills, namely on the 13th of the same month. The country over which he passed was poor and dry. Poria Creek appeared to be a permanent water, but beyond there was next to no water till they came on Cooper's Creek. In a flooded clay flat they observed the clover-like plant from which the natives obtain the nardoo seed, on which they subsist so much. They noticed also some trees new to them. The gum-trees were a new species. On the 4th they crossed Stokes' Ranges, a stony table-land, almost devoid of vegetation, and the rough, rocky ground, tried the feet of the camels and horses greatly. A hill overlooking the country towards Cooper's Creek was covered with large masses of a white crystalline stone, grouped in irregular columns, and ringing when struck, with a metallic sound. It is the same stone which is universally strewn over the country, and of this, a coarse sandstone and conglomerate, the ranges are mostly found. On the 6th they saw a few natives, and came on Brahe's down track, and on softer ground, so that the horses and camels pushed on cheerfully; they soon also found water. Rain came, and they had plenty. On Cooper's Creek they found the sandhills of an orange colour, covered with the pink flowers and light green vegetation of the chrysanthemum, producing a singular effect. On the 9th they travelled over the earthy plains described by Wills, all cracked with deep fissures, forming a network of channels, and everywhere standing up the dry stalks of marsh-mallows, and flowering plants close together, and as high as the horses' backs. On the 10th and 11th they came to reaches of water, but the plains sandy and parched up. The leader writes in his journal, "It is long since I have seen such a barren, miserable place as this part of Cooper's Creek."

On the 13th they reached the Depôt, Fort Wills, and found the papers buried in the cache, which must have informed them that Burke and Wills had been there on their return from Carpentaria. They found fish, water-fowl, and turtle plentiful, but the country far as they could see, destitute of vegetation, and very stony. But now the interest became very painful. They came on camel tracks, which puzzled Brahe, as different to those he had left there. "The next morning," the leader's diary states :—" I went ahead with Sandy to try and pick up Burke's track. At the lower end of a large water-hole I found where one or two horses had been feeding for some months. The tracks ran in all directions to and from the water, and were as recent as a week. At the same place I found the handle of a clasp-knife." The horse-track only a week old was that of a horse of Captain Sturt's, which had been running wild here seventeen years, and which was caught on Mr. Howitt's subsequent journey hither. The diary continues :— "From here struck out south for a short distance from the creek, and found a distinct camel's track, and droppings on a native path; the footprint was about four months old, and going east. I then set the black boy to follow the creek, and struck across some sandy country in a bend on the north side. No tracks there; and coming on a native path leading my way, I followed it as the most likely place to see any signs. In about four miles this led me to the lower end of a very large reach of water, and on the opposite side were numbers of native wurleys. I crossed at a neck of sand, and at a little distance again came on a track of a camel going up the creek. At the same time I found a native who began to gesticulate in a very excited manner, and to point down the creek, bawling out "Gow, gow!" as loud as he could. When I went towards him he ran away, and I found it impossible to get him to come to me; I therefore turned back to follow the camel track, and to look after my party, as I had not seen anything of them for some miles. The track was visible in sandy places, and was evidently the same I had seen for the last two days. I also found horse-tracks in places, but very old. Crossing the creek, I cut our track, and rode after the party. In doing so, I came upon three pounds of tobacco, which had lain where I saw it for some time. This, together with the knife-handle, the fresh horse-tracks, and the camel track going eastward, puzzled me exceedingly, and led me into a hundred conjectures. At the lower end of the large reach of water before mentioned, I met Frank and Sandy looking for me, with the intelligence that King, the only survivor of Burke's party, had been found. A little further on I came on the party halted, and immediately went across to the blacks' wurleys, where I found King sitting in a hut which the natives had made for him. He presented a melancholy appearance, wasted as a shadow, and hardly to be distinguished as a civilized being but by the remnants of clothes upon him. He seemed exceedingly weak, and I found it occasionally difficult to follow what he said. The natives were all gathered round, seated on the ground, looking with a most gratified and delighted expression. I camped where the party had halted, on a high bank close to the water, and shall probably remain here ten days to recruit King before returning."

The next day the party began shoeing their horses, preparatory to their return. King already looked better. On the following day, September 18th, this is the entry in

Mr. Howitt's diary:—" Left camp this morning with Messrs. Brahe, Welch, Wheeler, and King, to perform a melancholy duty, which had weighed on my mind ever since we have camped here, and which I only put off until King should be well enough to accompany us. We proceeded down the creek for seven miles, crossing a branch running to the southward, and followed a native track leading to that part of the creek where Mr. Burke, Mr. Wills, and King camped after their unsuccessful attempt to reach Mount Hopeless, and the northern settlements of South Australia, and where poor Wills died. We found the two gunyahs pretty much as King had described them, situated on a sandbank between two waterholes, and about a mile from the flat where they procured the nardoo seed, on which they managed to exist so long. Poor Wills' remains were found lying in the wurley in which he died, and where King, after his return from seeking for the natives, had buried him with sand and rushes. We carefully collected the remains, and interred them where they lay; and not having a prayer-book, I read Chap. xv. of 1 Corinthians, that we might at least feel a melancholy satisfaction in having shown the last respect to his remains. We heaped sand over the grave, and laid branches upon it, that the natives might understand by their own tokens not to disturb the last repose of a fellow being. I cut the following inscription on a stone close by, to mark the spot:—"

```
W. J. WILLS,
XLV. YDS.
W.N.W.
A. H.
```

The field-books, a note-book belonging to Mr. Burke, various small articles lying about, of no great value in themselves, but now invested with an interest from the circumstances connected with them, and some of the nardoo seed on which they had subsisted, with the small wooden trough in which it had been cleansed, I have now in my possession. We returned home with saddened feelings; but I must confess that I felt a sense of relief that this painful ordeal had been gone through. King was very tired when we returned, and I must most unwillingly defer my visit to the spot where Mr. Burke's remains are lying, until he is better able to bear the fatigue."—Parliamentary Report, p. 40.

In setting out on this journey, a gentlemen in Melbourne had presented Mr. Howitt with a number of carrier-pigeons, in the hope that they might be able to bring news from the expedition. These had been carefully carried on a horse, their cages being padded to prevent the friction of their feathers. Nevertheless, in so long, and frequently rough a journey, their tails had been rubbed down by friction, and their balance destroyed. It was now attempted to supply this defect, by inserting the tail feathers of crested wild pigeons into the stumps of the carriers, fastening the splices with wax, and thus to see whether they would make their way home. They were given the space of a tent to exercise their wings in, and it was found they could fly very well. The next morning therefore, the pigeons were turned up, each with a message fastened to its legs. On throwing them up they commenced wheeling round the camp, but soon separated, one being chased by one of the large kites which were always hovering about the creek. After flying round in various directions with great speed, they gradually drew across the creek, where they were lost sight of; the fourth, after making a large circle, perched on a tree about a mile off. After breakfast he was found under a bush, with a kite watching him, and the feathers of one of the other pigeons not far off, which had been killed. Two were seen no more; the one recaptured was turned up again in the afternoon, but he only flew into a gum-tree in the camp, and remained there. The experiment was a failure. Probably the instinct of these birds does not operate beyond a certain space of time; and was lost for the occasion after a two months removal from home. Probably their long confinement had rendered them unfit for immediate flight to any great distance; and it is very doubtful, had all conditions in themselves been favourable, whether they could for a thousand miles have escaped the legion of kites and eagle-hawks which infest the Australian forests. At all events, the hope of their being able to carry to Melbourne this sad but important news was at an end.

On the 21st of September, the entry in Mr. Howitt's diary, is as follows:—" Finding it would not be prudent for King to go out for two or three days, I could no longer defer making a search for the spot where Mr. Burke died; and with such directions as King could give, I went up the creek this morning with Messrs. Brahe, Welsh, Wheeler, and Aitkin. We searched the creek upwards for eight miles, and at length, strange to say, found the remains of Mr. Burke lying among tall plants under a clump of box-trees, within 200 yards of our last camp, and not thirty paces from our track. It was still more extraordinary that three or four of the party, and the two black boys had been close to the spot, without noticing it. The bones were entire, with the exception of the hands and feet, and the body had been removed from the spot where it first lay, and where the natives had placed branches over it, to about five paces. I found the revolver which Mr. Burke held in his hand when he expired, partly covered with leaves and earth, and coroded with rust. It was loaded and capped. We dug a grave close to the spot, and interred the remains wrapped in a union-jack—the most fitting covering in which the bones of a brave but unfortunate man could take their last rest. On a box-tree, at the head of the grave, the following inscription is cut:—

```
R. O'H. B.
21 | 9 | 61.
A. H.
```

Previous to setting out homewards, the object of this sad expedition being now completed, Mr. Howitt visited the camp of the natives who had been so kind to Burke and Wills, and still more so to King, who owed his life to them. These he assembled, and distributed to every one of them something, knives, tomahawks, neck-laces, looking-glasses, combs, flour, which they called the "white fellow's nardoo," articles of clothing, and other things, to their evident and great delight. They made it understood that they knew these things were given them for having fed King, and they struck up an impromptu corroboree in sign of their joy and thanks. "I feel confident," says Mr. Howitt in his diary, "that we have left the best impression behind us, and that the 'white-fellows,' as they have already learned to call us, will be looked on henceforth as friends, and that, in case of emergency, any one will receive the kindest treatment at their hands."—Parliamentary Report, p. 43-4.

On the 25th of September, they turned their faces homewards, but with the deepest regret that their instructions, unlike those of McKinlay, from his government at Adelaide, forbade them to continue the work of exploration. "This morning," says the leader in his diary, "I turned my face homewards. The object of our mission being fulfilled, I had to do so, but I return with a great regret at not being able to go on. We take back five months rations from this date, at the scale we have been using them, and which has proved sufficient. The party are in the best of health, the horses in fine order, and the camels none the worse for their journey, and decidedly in better health than when they left the Darling. On the edge of a country so well worth exploring, in a tolerably good season, and with the means I now have at my disposal, I feel how much might be done."—Parliamentary Report, p. 43.

In his letter, Howitt expresses still more strongly his chagrin at being compelled by his instructions to forgo so tempting an opportunity to extend discovery. He felt that with his expedition all compact, in training, health, and order, he could have walked to the gulf as on a summer excursion, and the journals of Burke and Wills, McKinlay, Landsborough, and Walker, confirm entirely this opinion. We must now, however, trace from the notes and journals found near the remains of the deceased travellers, their passage to the gulf, and their tragic return to this spot; one of the most sad and moving stories which the annals of discovery contain. It is curious that within a few days of the discovery of the remains of the lost wanderers on this occasion, a report reached Melbourne from Adelaide, through a letter from James Howe a Police Trooper, up the country, brought down by a black, that white men were living on a lake on a raft, which from the locality, appeared to be Cooper's Creek; that they were nearly naked, and supported themselves by fishing. The truth wrapped in fable.

CHAPTER XI.

THE JOURNEY OF BURKE AND WILLS TO THE GULF OF CARPENTARIA, AND RETURN TO COOPER'S CREEK.

Directed their course to Eyre's Creek.—The water in Cooper's Creek at 97·4 of Fahrenheit.—Crossed the Stony Desert and found it not very bad.—Spent Christmas Eve at a creek on the other side of the desert.—On Christmas Day struck a creek, now called Burke's Creek.—Alternate sand-ridges and grassy plains—King's and Wills's Creek.—Australian spinach.—Patton's Creek.—Progress through good country, naming hills and creeks.—River which Burke called the Cloncurry, a branch of the Flinders.—Followed the Flinders to near the sea.—A horse swamped in Billy Creek.—Proceed on foot.—Here Wills's journal abruptly ceases.—On the 19th of February they are on their way homewards.—Burke says they reached the sea, but not the open ocean.—In great anxiety about their provisions holding out.—Burke ill from eating snake.—Lighten the loads of the camels.—Kill a camel and a horse for food.—Burke beats Gray for privately taking food.—Gray cannot walk.—His companions think him shamming.—Gray dies.—Sunday, April 21st, 1861, arrive at the depôt and find it deserted only seven hours before.—Their consternation.—Find some provisions, but are too weary to follow.—Burke decides to make for Mount Hopeless.—Leave memoranda of their return and present route at the depôt. Started for Mount Hopeless April 23rd.—Received fish from the natives.—Camel bogged and killed.—Only one camel left.—Kill that.—Wills makes an excursion to find a better track.—Treated to "nardoo," a seed, by the natives.—Nardoo bread.—Bury part of their provisions and return to the depôt.—Rapidly sink on the nardoo food.—Burke and King set out to find the natives.—Too weak to carry anything.—Burke dies.—King returns and finds Wills dead.—Joins the natives.—Affecting notes in Wills's diary.—Letter to his father in prospect of death.—Hasty notes of Burke.—King's life amongst the natives.—Return of Howitt and party to Menindie.—His opinion of the natives at Cooper's Creek.

We have already seen that Messrs. Burke and Wills, with Gray and King, having six camels and one horse, and provisions for three months, set out on the 16th of December, 1860, to endeavour to reach the Gulf of Carpentaria. We now follow them in this journey by the aid of Wills's so-called field-books, constituting in fact his diary. The loose, cursory notes of Burke, also entered in a memorandum book, and both found near their remains at Cooper's Creek, will be afterwards adverted to. They followed the creek down till the 19th, the scenery improving as they went. The water of the creek was generally at the temperature of 97·4, and when they had cooled some in water bags till it appeared delightfully cool, they were annoyed to find it still 78°. On the 19th they left what appeared to be the end of the creek, and steered N.W. for Eyre's Creek. They found the country well grassed, and the scenery very pleasant, abounding with various birds, red-breasted cockatoos, pigeons, crows, &c. They met some natives on the 20th, who gave them fish. From the 22nd to the 24th they were crossing Sturt's Stony Desert, but they did not find it at all bad travelling over. The stony ground and the sand ridges were bare of grass, but the rest of the country was not destitute of grass, and in fact, Mr. Wills remarks, " Many a sheep run is worse grazing than there was there."

They spent a day at a fine creek on the skirts of the desert, running from east to west, in order to celebrate Christmas, or rather Christmas Eve, for they left the creek at half-past four A.M. on Christmas Day. This creek was a splendid sheet of water, more than a mile long, and averaging nearly three chains broad, but only two or three feet deep. They were wonderfully more favoured than Sturt at the same place, and Wills accordingly remarks :—" This was doubly pleasant, as we had never in our most sanguine moments anticipated finding such a delighful oasis in the desert. Our camp was really an agreeable place, for we had all the advantages of food and water attending a position on a large creek or river, and were at the same time free of the annoyance of the numberless ants, flies, mosquitoes, that are invariably met with amongst timber or heavy scrub." On Christmas Day, they struck a large creek running N.N.W., and this they followed till the 30th, by which time it had trended considerably to the N.E. Though they gave no name to this creek, it has received that of Burke's Creek. The country around it was an alternation of sand ridges and grassy plains. They now quitted the creek, and struck off directly north, travelling over plains of a clayey nature, in some places bearing the marks of floods, in others sandy, and with masses of box forests. In many places there was abundance of grass, and they crossed and camped on creeks which, though not named by them at the time, both Burke and Wills refer to afterwards as King's and Wills' Creeks. On the latter, which is situated near the tropic of Cancer, they encountered a severe hurricane; but the country beyond it was of the most luxuriant description, abounding with timber, grass, and various vegetables, amongst them the Australian spinach, or Portulaca oleracea, so welcome to all these travellers. "As we proceeded," says Wills, "the country improved at every step. Flocks of pigeons rose and flew to the eastward, and fresh plants met our view at every rise: everything was green and luxuriant. The horse licked his lips, and tried all he could to break his nose-strings to get at the feed, which was equal in quantity and superior in variety to any that I have seen in Australia, excepting, perhaps, in soils of volcanic origin."

On the 11th of January, 1861, they crossed another fine creek, which they called Pattens. Till the 19th, they continued passing over splendidly grassed flats, and by hills which they named Mounts Standish, Murray, and Forbes, on the latter of which ran creeks which they called Foster's and Green's. This is in or near latitude 21°. Soon after this they came upon a creek, which they named Turner's Creek, apparently rising from Mount Collis, and then on a creek or river running N.E., to which they give no name in their diaries, but which, in the headings of the diary, is named the Cloncurry. On January 27th, we find them on the banks of this creek, or of the Flinders River, it is by no means clear which, nor do they name the river at all; but there were palm trees on its banks, which were earthy and perpendicular, and plenty of vegetation on the borders of it. In the dry bed of this Golah, one of the camels, was left, as they could not get him along. On the 3rd of February, Burke and Wills set out on foot to endeavour to reach the sea. They were soon obliged to leave the camels, and take on only the horse to carry their provisions; but

he, too, was swamped in the Billy Creek, where it falls into the river, and only extricated with difficulty. They struggled on through boggy woods all day, and the next morning left the horse at the camping place, and went on without him to endeavour to reach the sea. They saw some blacks on the way, who fled in amazement. This part of Wills' journal ends without further remark, and we only learn from it that, the day previous, they came to a marsh flooded at times by the sea-water; and in crossing the marsh, to a sea channel through which the sea-water flowed. The journal is not renewed till the 19th of February, on their way homewards. In Burke's notes, the latest entry on their way north is January 20, but he says, on March 28th, "At the conclusion of the report, it would be as well to say that we reached the sea, but we could not obtain a view of the open ocean, although we made every endeavour to do so."
—(Parl. Report, p. 59.)

Nothing can be more scanty and desultory than the few notes of Burke. He says, January 13, 1861 :—"As I find it impossible to keep a regular diary, I shall jot down my ideas when I have an opportunity and put the dates." As they were provisioned for only twelve weeks, and had now consumed nearly seven out of the twelve, they had already the fear of famine before their eyes, and were hurrying along without being able to take the necessary observations to ascertain their position in the country, or to find really on what river they were, which they do not appear to have known. The excellent qualifications of Wills for such notices were thus necessarily sacrificed to the stern necessity of speed. This pressure of fear of famine always before their eyes must have increased rapidly on their return, and led to the catastrophe of the destruction of the horse and camels, and consequently of their own through hunger, excessive fatigue, and anxiety. It became a race for life, insuring by its rigour the peril of death. The notices of Wills, on the return, are brief but most painful. They had a great deal of rain, which made the ground boggy, and thus impeded their career. On the 2nd of March they picked up Golah, the camel they had left behind; but on the 6th, they were again compelled to leave him altogether. On the 5th, the day before, Burke became very ill, from eating part of a large snake which they cooked. On the 20th, they began to lighten the loads of the camels by leaving 60lbs. weight of things behind. Rain fell in torrents, and compelled them to keep to the ridges to avoid being bogged. On the 25th, Gray was found eating skilligolee behind a tree. He complained that he was suffering from dysentery, and therefore had taken a little flour. For this, Burke gave him a severe thrashing. On the 30th of March, they killed the camel Boocha. On the 10th of April, they killed the horse Billy. "On the 8th of April," it is entered in Wills' diary, "halted fifteen minutes to send back for Grey, who *gammoned* he could not walk." On the 17th, he died! "He had not spoken a word distinctly since his first attack, which was just as we were about to start." These are most painful records in this sad history, and the treatment which the cruelty of their circumstances led such truly humane men as Burke and Wills to extend to Gray in the last miserable condition of his existence, must have come sharply home to them in their own immediate and most sorrowful circumstances recorded in this concluding paragraph of this portion of the diary :—

"Sunday, 21st of April, 1861. Arrived at the depôt this evening, just in time to find it deserted. A note left in the plant by Brahe communicates the pleasing information that they have started to-day for the Darling, their camels and horses all well, and in good condition; we and our camels being just done up, and scarcely able to reach the depôt, have very little chance of overtaking them. Brahe has fortunately left us ample provisions to take us to the bounds of civilization, namely :—flour, 50lb.; rice, 20lb.; oatmeal, 60lb.; sugar, 60lb.; and dried meat, 15lb. These provisions, together with a few house-nails, and some castaway odds and ends, constitute all the articles left, and place us in

16—2

a very awkward position in regard to clothing. Our disappointment at finding the depôt deserted may be easily imagined; returning in an exhausted state, after four months of the severest travelling and privation, our legs almost paralysed, so that each of us found it a most trying task only to walk a few yards. Such a leg-bound feeling I never before experienced, and hope I never shall again. The exertion to get up a slight piece of rising, even without any load, induces an indescribable sensation of pain and helplessness, and the general lassitude makes one unfit for anything. *Poor Gray must have suffered very much, many times when we thought him shamming.* It is most fortunate for us that these symptoms which early affected him did not come on us until we were reduced to an exclusively animal diet of such an inferior description as a worn-out and exhausted horse. We were not long in getting out the grub that Brahe had left, and we made a good supper off some oatmeal porridge and sugar. This, together with the excitement of finding ourselves in such a peculiar, and almost unexpected position, had a wonderful effect in removing the stiffness from our legs. Whether it is possible that the vegetables have so affected me, I know not, but both Mr. B. and I remarked a most decided relief, and a strength in the legs greater than we had had for several days. I am inclined to think that but for the abundance of portulac that we obtained on our journey we should scarcely have returned to Cooper's Creek at all."

Here, then, were the travellers, after a desperate run to Carpentaria, and a more desperate plunge back again, having destroyed or left behind all their camels but two, and their horses, and worn down by violent and continuous exertion, arrived at the hoped-for goal of relief, and found it deserted only seven hours previously. It was a most cruel disappointment. But yet the case was not altogether so desperate. They found in the cache what Wills terms "ample provisions to take us to the bounds of civilization." True, they might not hope to overtake Brahe before they reached the Darling, but they might find the stationary Wright somewhere on the way. At all events, by taking a few days rest and refreshment they might have travelled moderately on, and by care could have reached Menindie. This was the worst which they had to fear; but as it was, there was a chance for them on that known route which they did not expect. Even then, Brahe and Wright were approaching the depôt, and, by a short delay, they would have been found at the depôt. But here, again, Burke's ill-fortune and defective judgment turned the scale to their ruin. Contrary to the opinion of Wills and King, as reported by King, "Mr. Burke resolved to endeavour to reach a station of South Australia by Mount Hopeless. Mr. Wills was not inclined to follow this plan, but wished to go down our old track, *but at last gave in to Mr. Burke's wishes:* I also wished to go down our old track."—Parl. Report, p. 32. Thus the sound judgment, but gentle and conceding mind of Wills, was overborne by the more impulsive and less calculating Burke, and the last fatal turn was given to the great catastrophe!

King says they stayed four or five days to recruit before they set out on this ill-omened journey; but he is clearly wrong—they only stayed one day, as is shown by Wills's diary. They arrived at the depôt on the evening of Sunday, April 21, and started on Tuesday morning, April 23. They only remained over Monday. At the moment of their arrival at the depôt Brahe was only fourteen miles distant. But the evil star of Burke led him to seek a South Australian station, through a most torrid and frightful desert. Before leaving on this route Burke wrote and enclosed in the cache, along with Mr. Wills's journals, and his own notes, the following affecting memorandum :—

" Depôt No. 2, Cooper's Creek, Camp 65.

"The return party from Carpentaria, consisting of myself, Wills and King, (Gray dead), arrived here last night, and found that the depôt party had only started on the same day. We proceed on to-morrow slowly down the creek towards Adelaide by Mount Hopeless, and shall endeavour to follow Gregory's track: but we are very weak. The two camels are done up, and we shall not be able to travel faster than four or five miles a day. Gray died on the road from exhaustion and fatigue. The provisions left here will, I think, restore our strength. We have discovered a practicable route to Carpentaria, the chief position of which lies in the 140° of east longitude. There is some good country between this and the Stony Desert. From thence to the tropic the land is dry and stony. Between the tropic and Carpentaria a considerable portion is rangy, but it is well-watered and richly grassed.

"We reached the shores of Carpentaria on the 11th of February, 1861. Greatly disappointed at finding the party here gone.

"R. O'HARA BURKE, Leader.
"22nd April, 1861.

"P. S. The camels cannot travel, and we cannot walk, or we should follow the other party. We shall move very slowly down the creek."—Parliamentary Report, p. 35.

The reader cannot avoid being struck by the singularity of this P.S. That the camels could not travel, and they could not walk, are given as reasons why they did not go down their old and known track, and yet they were going to walk, and to make the camels travel, but only in an opposite and unknown direction! Mr. Burke, however, was under the impression that the station at Mount Hopeless was only some 150 miles distant. Mr. Wills's diary records this most mournful and doomed of journeys.

They left, as stated, on the 23rd of April. For several days following down the creek, their strength, and that of the camels, seemed to improve. The blacks were very friendly, and repeatedly supplied them with fish. The weather was agreeable. But on the 28th, Linda, one of their two camels, got bogged, and they were obliged to shoot him, and dry as much of his flesh as they could carry. On the 2nd of May, they followed down a branch of the creek leading S.S.W., till it broke into a number of sandy channels, and lost themselves in the earthy soil of a box forest. They had then to retrace their steps, when their last camel failed, and Mr. Wills went off by himself in a westerly direction, to examine the country, but found it equally hopeless. On the 6th, they moved back still farther up the creek, in great depression of spirits, and Mr. Wills writes:—"The present state of things is not calculated to raise our spirits much. The rations are rapidly diminishing; our clothing, especially our boots, are all going to pieces, and we have not the materials for repairing them properly. The camel is completely done up, and can scarcely get along, although he has the best of feed, and is resting half his time. I suppose this will end in our living like blacks for a few months."

They were obliged to kill the last camel, and whilst Burke and King cured the flesh, Wills again made an excursion, to endeavour to hit on a track towards Mount Hopeless. He was received and hospitably entertained by the blacks, but was obliged to return to his companions. They now began to enquire of the blacks after the nardoo seed, imagining it the produce of a tree; and received from the natives some of their dried narcotic herbs, which they chew, called pitchery. They soon found the nardoo seed in abundance, on a flat, and congratulated themselves in the idea that on this they could subsist in the wilderness, if all other food failed; a hope in which they were doomed to a great disappointment. Such was their life till the 15th of May, visiting the blacks, and collecting nardoo seed. The blacks suddenly disappeared, and they went in quest of them in vain. On the 15th, once more, they prepared to strike a course for Mount Hopeless, but having no beast of burden, they were compelled to bury all their provisions that they could not carry. They were again disappointed, and seemed to have lived in this state of wretched uncertainty till the 24th, when they heard an explosion, as of a gun, no doubt that of a meteor, as experienced by Sturt. On the 27th, they returned to the depôt at Cooper's Creek, having, according to Governor Barkly, in his despatch of November 20th, 1861, "reached within fifty miles of Mount Hopeless, which would have appeared above the horizon, had they continued their route for even another day. Thus they were repeatedly within a hair's breadth of being saved, but never to be saved. When they arrived at Cooper's Creek from Carpentaria, it appears that Brahe was at that moment camped only fourteen miles off!" On reaching the depôt this time, they employed themselves in collecting and pounding nardoo, and endeavouring to live upon it; but found that it did not digest, except with King, and Burke and Wills began rapidly to sink. They were reduced to live entirely on nardoo, which gave them no nourishment, and exhausted their little strength in pounding, cleaning, and baking it.

On the 20th of June, poor Wills says he cannot understand the nardoo at all; that it certainly would not agree with him in any form. He sponged himself all over at noon, but found no benefit from it. Burke felt himself getting very weak in the legs. The next day, Wills says he himself is weaker than ever, and can scarcely crawl out of the mia-mia—the hut. "Unless relief comes in some form or other, I cannot possibly last more than a fortnight." And he then uttered some natural expressions of chagrin at being left in such a situation by the party which should have been up to receive them. On the 22nd, he says he is too weak to get on his feet. The next day, that all hands were at home, he too weak to move, King holding out well, Burke finding himself weaker every day. The next day, King himself complained that he could no longer do the work of collecting and preparing the nardoo. They must seek out the blacks, or perish. This is the last day that Wills dates his diary correctly; he is evidently become unsteady in his mind. According to what he sets down as the 24th of June, but in fact the 26th, Burke and King set off to seek for the blacks, leaving poor Wills some nardoo, and wood and water, to serve till their return. They showed much reluctance to leave him thus, but the poor fellow told them it was his and their *only chance*, and they went.

In King's narrative, he says, they left nardoo, wood, and water for eight days. Burke was still very unwilling to leave him thus, but Wills repeated it was their only chance. He then gave Burke a letter and his watch, for his father, and they buried the remainder of the fieldbooks near the gunyah; and Wills told King that, should he survive Burke, he must give the watch and letter to his father. Thus these companions in travel and distress, parted, not to meet again in this world. Burke appeared almost too weak to walk, and on the second day broke down altogether, first throwing away all that he carried. King also threw away everything but his gun, some powder and shot, and matches. King got him to the water-side, where they camped; shot a crow, prepared some nardoo, and thus made what he calls " a good evening meal." But Burke was fast sinking; said he felt convinced he had not many hours to live; gave King his watch, which belonged to the Committee, and his pocket-book, in which he wrote some notes, to give to Sir William Stawell, and said;—" I hope you will remain with me till I am quite dead; it is comfort to know that some one is by; but when I am dying, it is my wish that you should place the pistol in my right hand, and that you leave me unburied, as I lie." " That night he spoke very little, and the following morning I found him speechless, or nearly so, and about eight o'clock he expired."

Well might King say that he now felt " very lonely," but he proceeded in quest of the natives, and two days after found, not them, but a deserted camp, with a bag of nardoo sufficient to last him a fortnight. Two more days he remained to recover his strength, and then returned to Mr. Wills. Thus he must have been absent seven days, and arriving found Wills so long dead, that he had been visited, and stripped of some of his clothes by the natives. Poor Wills had, no doubt, made his solitary end some days before. His diary contains only two more notices, the last of which was made the day before they left him, and a most remarkable and affecting specimen it is of patient equanimity in the near prospect of such a deserted and isolated death :—" Friday, the 29th of June; clear, cold night, slight breeze from the east, day beautifully warm and pleasant. Mr. Burke suffers greatly from the cold, and is getting extremely weak. He and King start to-morrow up the creek to look for the blacks; it is the only chance we have of being saved from starvation. I am weaker than ever, although I have a good appetite, and relish the nardoo much; but it seems to give me no nutriment, and the birds here are so shy as not to be got at. Even if we got a good supply of fish, I doubt whether we could do much work on them and nardoo alone. Nothing now but the greatest good luck can save any of us; and, as for myself, I may live four or five days if the weather continues warm. My pulse is at forty-eight and very weak, and my legs and arms are nearly skin and bone. I can only look out, like Mr. Macawber, ' for something to turn up.' Starvation on nardoo is by no means very unpleasant, but for the weakness one feels, and the utter inability to move one's self; for, as far as appetite is concerned, it gives the greatest satisfaction. Certainly fat and sugar would be more to one's taste; in fact, these seem to one the great stand-by for one in this extraordinary continent; not that I mean to depreciate the farinaceous food, but the want of sugar and fat in all substances obtainable here is so great that they become almost valueless to us, as articles of food, without the addition of something else."

His last letter to his father displays the same wonder-

ful calmness under the circumstances. It commences:—
"My Dear Father, These are probably the last lines you will ever get from me. We are on the point of starvation, not so much from want of food, but from the want of nutriment in what we get." And it concludes:—"I think to live about four or five days. My spirits are excellent." Wonderful equanimity!

The last hasty notes of Burke, jotted down in his pocket book, almost in the moment of death, betray a little stronger resentment, but an equally heroic resignation:—

"I hope we shall be done justice to. We have fulfilled our task, but we have been aband——. We have not been followed up as we expected, and the depôt party abandoned their post.
"R. O'HARA BURKE.
"Cooper's Creek, June the 26th."

"King has behaved nobly. I hope that he will be properly cared for. He comes up the creek in accordance with my request.
"R. O'HARA BURKE.
"Cooper's Creek, June the 28th."

"King has behaved nobly. He has stayed with me to the last, and placed the pistol in my hand, leaving me lying on the surface, as I wished.
"R. O'H. BURKE.
"Cooper's Creek, June the 28th."

The story of King is soon told. The latest date of Burke's notes is June the 28th. They had then left Wills to his solitary death. King did not return to Wills for seven days. Thus from the time that King saw both his leaders dead, probably the 5th of July, to the time when he was discovered by Mr. Howitt's party, the 15th of September, he had been about two months and ten days alone in the wilderness. He says he remained by himself some days before going to the blacks. Thus he had still lived with the natives upwards of two months, and though they had desired to be quit of him at first, yet they had become reconciled to his company, especially as he cured the sore arm of one of the women, and occasionally shot them a crow or a hawk. On the whole, they behaved very kindly to him.

Mr. Howitt's estimate of the natives in that quarter is much more favourable as to their abilities than is the general one, but is like every other traveller's as to their thievish propensities, which they possess in common with all savages. We may take one scene with the natives near Cooper's Creek from his journal:—

"Where we camped happened to be not more than a couple of hundred yards from a large native camp, situated in a branch channel, and completely hidden by dense timber and scrub. When we arrived, all the men excepting three old fellows were away, and only the lubras and piccaninnies were at home, in a terrible fright at so many white-fellows squatting down close to them. They began to pack up their things for a flight; but an amicable understanding being brought about, and some of the men returning, we were soon the best of friends. I distributed the few remaining presents, and they gave in return some chewed pitchery and nardoo balls. One old greybeard had been as far as Wonominta Creek, and could repeat the names of the various waters between here and that place, *via* Bulla; but I found him impenetrable on any other road. There were about twenty men, all well made and well fed, and several were old patriarchs, and some of them apparently old rascals, too. They were far more inclined to be troublesome and importunate than our friends lower down, particularly one tall young fellow, rubbed all over with red earth, who pestered me for a tomahawk. One of them had had his arm broken above the wrist, and roughly bandaged up with rags and grass cord; the doctor set it properly, and it was remarkable to see the perfect composure with which the black-fellow bore the operation. In assisting, I had to use my clasp-knife to cut bark splints, and laying it down beside me, it, of course, vanished, and I saw no more of it; but strange to say, in the same place shortly afterwards, one of the knives was found which I had given the black-fellows, which, I suppose, they had exchanged for mine, on the principle of the old saying, that 'exchange is no robbery.' After a while, the natives began to draw in too close to our camp, talking a good deal about our 'portos,' or bundles, so that we had to draw a line as a boundary, a hint they took at once, and all squatted down beyond it. At dusk I fired off two rockets, to their unbounded surprise, but they were not so alarmed as I expected, probably from feeling that we were kindly disposed towards them. I believe that the sight of us smoking, and seeing the smoke coming out of our mouths, alarmed them much more, as some made signs to put the pipe away, and others got up and walked off, looking behind them. At dark they retired to their camp."

Mr. Howitt returned safely to Menindie, on the Darling, with his party all in health, and without the loss of a man, a horse, or a camel. Thence he despatched Mr. Brahe with the news of the discovery of the remains of the lost leaders, accompanied by King, the sole survivor. They left Pamomoroo Creek on the 11th of November, 1861, and reached Melbourne on the 28th of November. This closes the narrative of the expedition of exploration under Messrs. Burke and Wills, and of the expedition under Mr. Alfred Howitt in search of that party. We shall have to notice briefly the second expedition of Howitt to fetch down the bodies of the deceased leaders, in as much as it included some further exploration westward; but we now have to trace the journeys of Messrs. McKinlay, Landsborough, and Walker, sent out simultaneously on the same errand of search for the lost leaders.

CHAPTER XII.

THE EXPLORATION EXPEDITION OF MR. M'KINLAY IN SEARCH OF BURKE AND WILLS IN 1861 AND 1862.

Order in which explorers have crossed Australia.—McKinlay second as to the whole width.—McKinlay summoned from Melbourne.—Sets out at once.—His party.—Evidently well qualified for his office.—Left Adelaide August the 16th, 1861.—Baker's Station on Blanche Water.—Squatting stations beyond Eyre's farthest point.—Dry and stony country to Lake Hope.—Mr. Elder and Mr. Stucky.—A pelican choked by a fish.—Lakes Camel, Perigundi, and Buchanan.—Straying of horses and camels.—Hear from natives of white men at Cooper's Creek, and one of them dead.—Mr. McKinlay sets out for Cooper's Creek.—Sees natives in European clothing.—Further rumours of the white men.—Lake Kadhi-baerri.—Found a flattened pint pot.—Abundance of grass and clover.—Found a mutilated body in a grave.—Story of a battle with white men.—Fragments of a tin can, a nautical almanac, &c.—Hear of ironwork of saddles, a pistol, &c.—A native digs up some baked horse hair for stuffing saddles.—Probably the grave was Gray's.—The natives of Coopers' Creek are fired on.—Probable cause of this.—McKinlay and party imagine these natives to have killed and eaten Burke and his party.—Name the water Lake Massacre.—McKinlay sends despatches to Adelaide with news of his discovery.—Laid up with the hot weather.—Natives tell of a flood coming down Cooper's Creek.—McKinlay rides there to see.—No signs of flood.—Trees noticed by Howitt, indicating the graves of Burke and Wills.—Saw a cobby horse.—Deposited memorandum at Burke's grave of his visit, and intention to go northward.—Moved on December the 20th.—Dreadful journey to Lake McKinlay.—A bullock killed by the heat.—The black guide quits them. —Lake Moolionboorrana.—Heat awful.—Lake Jeanie.—Spent Christmas Day there.—Natives making nardoo cakes.—Lake Appam-barra.—Naked country.—Lake Hodgkinson.—Natives' report, white fellows arrived at Lake Buchanan.—A myth.—Discovers various other lakes and creeks.—Mount McDonnell.—Abundance of wild-fowl.—A peep at the Stony Desert.—Four months nearly spent here.—Start January the 6th, 1862.—Compelled by intense heat and want of shelter to retreat to Lake Hodgkinson again.—This lake soon dried up.—Another ride to the Stony Desert.—Camp on Hayward's Creek till the 10th of February.—Rain and thunder.—The country now deep mud.—Passed a camp of Burke's, and remains of his horse Billy.—Surrounded by vast floods. —Hamilton and Goyder's table-topped hills.—Passed the Stony Desert; still in the midst of floods.—Escape Camp.—Was Leichhardt caught in such a flood? —The natives thereabout possess goat's hair.—No goats probably ever there but Leichhardt's.—Daly Ranges.—Shepherd lost for six days.—Name many creeks and ranges.—Enter the tropical regions.—Palms and grass up to the neck.—Ant-hills like decaying columns.—Natives firing the grass.—New trees. —Copper was found.—Country looked auriferous.—Marks of great floods.-- Mounts Elephant and McPherson.—Jessie and Jeannie Creeks.—Crossed the track of Burke and Wills on the Cloncurry.—Struck the Leichhardt on the 9th of May.—Its aspect.—Many windings.—Set their own baggage on fire.—Stokes's Plains of Promise.—Reached the tidal part of the river, but could not get at the sea for swamps and mangrove creeks.—Collect salt for their journey.—The grass too strong for sheep.—Commence the route to Port Denison.—Only two bullocks left, and no tea, sugar, or flour.—Trees marked by Landsborough.—Make boots for the sore-footed camels.—Cross the Flinders and the Norman.—Involved in ranges.—Killed their last bullock.—Mountains.—Silk cotton growing.—Wonderful view of rocky country.—A terrible country.—The River Gilbert.—Losing horses from fatigue.—Kill the last bullock.—Several men very ill.—Reached the Burdekin July the 5th.—Still killing horses for food, or leaving them behind.—Only two pack horses and one camel left.—Crossed the Burdekin on a raft amongst alligators.—Killed their last camel.—Reach the station of Harvey and Somers.—Met there with Mr. Brahe.—Returned by Rockhampton, Sydney, and Melbourne, to Adelaide.

The impression which the long period which had brought no tidings from Burke's expedition across the continent had produced, was general throughout the colonies, and whilst Victoria was preparing to send a party in quest of the missing one, Queensland in the east, and New South Wales in the south were doing the same. Walker with his blacks set out stoutly from Rockhampton, and McKinlay did the same from Adelaide. From McKinlay's report addressed to his own government, and printed by order of the House of Assembly, 9th of October, 1862, and from Westgarth's account, including extracts from the journals of McKinlay, and of Davis, one of the party, we have a very full and clear narrative of this expedition, which although too late to discover the wreck of the Burke expedition, was successful in making its way across the continent, and having the honour of being the second in time which had performed this great passage, as would appear from the following dates.

Partial Transits.

1. Leichhardt's Journey from Moreton Bay to Port Essington, in 1844-5.
2. Walker's ditto from Rockhampton, in Queensland, to the Gulf Carpentaria, which he reached December 7, 1861.

Entire Transits.

1. Burke and Wills reached the mouth of the Flinders, Feb. 11, 1861.
2. McKinlay reached the mouth of the Albert from Adelaide, May 18, 1862.
3. Landsborough reached the Darling from the Gulf of Carpentaria, June 1, 1862.

4. Stuart reached the coast near the river Adelaide, from Adelaide, July 24, 1862.

It appears that Mr. John McKinlay was in Melbourne at the time that the South Australian government proposed to him by electric telegraph the leadership of the Burke Relief Expedition, for which the necessary funds had been voted by the assembly. He at once accepted this responsible post, and Mr. Davis states that within three weeks of the parliamentary vote he was already on his way, and at Kapunda, fifty miles north of Adelaide. The expedition was equipped for crossing the whole way to the Gulf of Carpentaria, if necessary, to which point the Victoria steamer had been despatched by the Melbourne Government to look out for Burke's party, or to send a detachment thence in quest of it. The persons of the party of McKinlay are nowhere distinctly stated, either by McKinlay himself, Davis, or Westgarth, but we incidentally pick up the names of Mr. Hodgkinson, as second in command, Ned Palmer in charge of the cart, Kirby in charge of the sheep, Middleton, Bell, Davis, Wylde, Poole, and Maitland, ten in all. They had four camels, twenty-four horses, twelve bullocks, and a hundred sheep. They struck away in an almost direct northern course, which they maintained with little deviation to the 26th degree of S. latitude, where they began a more easterly track, gradually returning westward till they struck the river Leichhardt, near the 17th degree of latitude, and 140th degree of longitude, and finally reached the Albert near the gulf coast, May 18, 1862.

McKinlay seems to have been extremely well qualified for the command of such an expedition. He was a practical bushman, acclimated and accustomed to the fatigue of long journeys on horseback in the open forests and torrid plains of Australia. Mature years had given him steadiness of purpose, and the necessary caution and calculation for such a command. Whilst kind and communicative with those under him, he appears at all times to have maintained a firm authority, and to have been familiar with the habits and requirements of the animals which they had with them, so that his progress was satisfactory and successful. His great defect seems to have been that of taking next to no observations necessary to determine his exact position at the different stages of his journey, so that you are often at a loss to know where he is, and in consequence, the places named by him are probably not very accurately placed in any of the maps since published. Even in the track of his course published by Westgarth, we look in vain for the names of the majority of the spots, creeks, rivers, and hills named by him in his journal. He committed also the great error of giving the same name to different lakes and creeks on his route. Though he passed the well-known Lake Blanche or Blanch-Water, east and north of Lake Torrens, he names another water still farther on, Lake Blanche, and gives to two creeks the name of Brown, at no great distance from each other, the only difference in the names being that one terminates with the letter e, and the other without it. He seems also to have named two William's creeks, or William's Creek and William Creek. With these geographical drawbacks, McKinlay shows himself an effective, energetic, and discreet conductor of the expedition.

He started from Adelaide with the camels, etc. on the 16th of August, 1861, some of his party with the horses, cart, etc. being already on the way before him. He says nothing particular occurred till they reached Mr. Baker's station, on Blanche Water, and were preparing to cross it. To those who have read the difficulties which Mr. Eyre encountered on this route in 1840, from excessive drought which forced him back, it will be a surprise not only to find Mr. McKinlay dismissing this progress of about five weeks without an observation, but still more, that there was a squatting station now established beyond Mr. Eyre's farthest reach, upwards of 400 miles north of Adelaide. To Kapunda, fifty miles north of Adelaide, they had gone by railway, such was the difference betwixt 1840 and 1861.

Mr. Davis in his journal, up to the crossing of Lake Blanche, gives us some details, but they are chiefly of stopping and jollifying at the different stations, showing how these have gradually invaded the regions described as so aridly and frightfully sterile by Eyre, in 1840. On the 28th of September they had crossed Blanche-Water, or Lake Torrens, as McKinlay terms it, though that lake lies a full degree south of this. They saw no water anywhere in crossing, and came to the conclusion that Lakes Torrens and Blanche are merely lakes in times of floods, the waters descending thither from the low country about Cooper's Creek, and by Strzelecki's Creek, and so on into Spencer Gulf. From Blanche-Water to Pando, or Lake Hope, they proceeded over a very dry and stony country, where the cattle suffered much from want of water. They were accompanied on this journey of fifty miles by their friends Mr. Elder and Mr. Stuckey, the latter of whom had already explored the way as far as Lake Hope. From this point to Sturt's Stony Desert, they found themselves in a country poor and sterile, but abounding with lakes and creeks, in the immediate neighbourhood of which there was grass, and in the lakes abundance of fish; and, accordingly, natives too abounded. Here they stayed ten days to refresh the animals. They also sent back a party to bring up stores left at Blanche-Water, and as the country was now soft, they took off the shoes of the horses. Whilst at Lake Hope, they found a pelican just choked by attempting to swallow a perch about a foot long, the tail of the fish hanging out of its mouth. During the progress hither they had much trouble through the straying of horses and camels, as well as with native guides, who now and then decamped. They successfully travelled on to a whole series of lakes, the chief of which were lakes Camel, Perigundi, and Buchanan. At Lake Camel some natives told them that some white men were in the interior of the east, and that one of them " sit down " at

Cooper's Creek, and die. Having left his party at Kierie Creek, camped on a water, which they named Wantula Depôt, Mr. McKinlay, on Friday the 18th of October, set out for Cooper's Creek, accompanied by Mr. Hodgkinson, Middleton, and a native of the country called Bulingani, four camels, and store of provisions. In about nine miles they arrived at a fine lake, Cudyecudyena, which they named Lake Buchanan, full six miles long, and surrounded by fine timber, and abundance of grass and clover. McKinlay sent back Hodgkinson to order the party to go on to this fine water, and soon after camped on a large creek, where the natives, fishing, had caught four different sorts of fish; the catfish of the Murray, the nombre of the Darling, a brown perch, and a small cod. The next day they passed another lake, called Canna Catta-jandide, about nine miles long, and in the evening reached yet another little lake, nearly circular, and about a mile and a half in diameter, with plenty of clover and some grass.

Here the natives informed them that the white people had removed to a place called Undaganie. They saw about 150 natives in different camps, and various articles of European clothing amongst them, a plain proof that there had been whites in the neighbourhood. As they travelled on, over high sand-hills, the natives informed them that those at the east lake had murdered the white man who had been ill. At twenty minutes past two o'clock they reached the Lake Kadhi-baerri, and then proceeded northward along the side of a large, beautifully timbered, grassed, and clovered swamp or creek, about a mile and a half across, where they found a grave rudely dug by the natives, which, from its being negligently made, they suspected to be that of a white man. Mr. Hodgkinson also in some old deserted huts of the natives found an old flattened pint pot, with no marks upon it. There was abundance of clover and grass for the camels, but no natives were visible, though trees which they had set on fire were still burning. Circumstances afterwards noticed confirmed the idea now entertained that the natives of this lake district are very nomadic, moving about to great distances as their supplies of food and fish may change with the season.

In the morning they hastened to the suspicious grave, taking a canteen of water with them, and their arms. They soon found a body, or, rather, a skeleton, wrapped in a flannel shirt with short sleeves, a piece of which they took. The flesh had evidently been cut from the bones, and very little hair was found, some of which, however, they discovered and took. The skull was severed from the body, and was marked with two apparently sabre-cuts, one over the left eye, the other on the right temple. Some of the teeth were decayed. They reburied the bones, and marked on a small tree near the place " M. K., Oct. 21, 1861." The native with them, namely, Bullingani, told them a fine story of a battle between the whites and blacks, and of the manner in which the white man was killed. He said the blacks had surprised the whites when in camp. They saw, however, no traces of any such skirmish, and thought the whites had chosen a very bad camp, if that were true, in a thick scrub, and within 150 or 200 yards of a black camp. It will be seen that all this story was false, and shows how little dependence can be placed on native accounts of such things.

They soon found another grave, evidently dug with a spade or shovel, but no body in it, and near this they found the dung of camels, a piece of light blue tweed, fragments of paper, small pieces of a nautical almanac, and an exploded " Eley's cartridge." They found also a tin canteen in the blacks' camp, where the pint pot was found, and were told that at the last lake they had passed the natives had the iron-work of saddles, and in another place a pistol, a rifle, etc. A number of natives coming in sight, they were pursued, and one of them captured. On seeing him Bullingani desired them to shoot him, as he was one of those who murdered the whites. They brought him, however, to the camp, and he then took them to the natives' old camp, and dug up some baked horse-hair for stuffing saddles, but said the saddles had been burned, and the bodies of the white men eaten.

On all this evidence McKinlay and his party concluded that Burke and his party had been surprised, massacred and eaten on this spot. They were the more confirmed in this idea by seeing the native whom they had sent for the pistol the day before coming, just as they were rising in the morning, at the head of about forty others, bearing torches, shields, etc., shouting and making a great noise. Satisfied that the blacks meant to attack and massacre them, as they had done Burke's party, McKinlay ordered them back, and told Bullingani to tell them that if they advanced he would fire upon them. As they did not appear to notice this warning, the word was given, and the blacks were fired upon, and several rounds were discharged amongst them, when they fled.

It was not till some time after, when a party had been sent down to Blanche-Water with despatches, and to bring up more provisions, that they received the real news regarding the fate of Burke's party, and the discovery of the bodies of Burke and Wills, and of King still alive amongst the natives of Cooper's Creek; when the truth flashed upon them, and they saw how much they had been imposed upon by the natives. That there had been no fight at all: that the fragments of things found had been picked up about the camp at Cooper's Creek, and that the skeleton which they had found was clearly that of poor Gray, whom the natives had dug up and eaten, burying the bones, not in the original grave, but in the poor, scanty one scratched in the earth by themselves. The regret of Mr. McKinlay must also have been great when he afterwards read the journal of Mr. Alfred Howitt, and discovered that the troop of natives whom he imagined were coming on so hastily were, in reality, the very men who had so hospitably treated King, and, in fact, kept him alive till discovered. That Mr. Howitt had rewarded them for their kindness by a present to each of them, and had promised them the friendship of the whites when they came there again. That they were, in truth, now coming on in their noisy joy, believing that these were the same friendly whites, but were astonished at so different a reception. Such are the results of false information, and it must be confessed that the natives had chiefly themselves to blame, for boasting of having killed and eaten the white travellers.

Immediately after the fight the party went to breakfast, and under the vivid impression of having defeated a deadly attack of hungry cannibals, Mr. McKinlay wrote and buried a memorandum, warning any future white visitors of the hostile nature of the natives here. That they had evidently killed and eaten Burke and his party; that the graves, the hacked skeleton, the panikin, oil can, saddle-stuffing, etc., all confirmed the tale, and that he had been only saved from their designs upon him and his party by firing upon them. After, as he thought, naming the lake most appropriately Lake Massacre, they set out on their return to Lake Buchanan. They first struck off on a bearing 197°; at eleven o'clock reached a richly grassed, recently flooded flat, surrounded by a margin of trees. A-while after they crossed the north end of a dry lake or clover flat, and about one o'clock they came upon a large box creek, from fifty to sixty yards wide, and eighteen or twenty feet deep, with sandy bottom. McKinlay imagined it a branch of Cooper's Creek, the creek connected with it being called Werridi Marara. The next day, October 24th, in the afternoon they regained the camp at Lake Buchanan.

Having now satisfied himself that he had discovered the real catastrophe of Burke's expedition, McKinlay resolved to send Mr. Hodgkinson, accompanied by Bell, Wylde, and Jack, a native, down to Blanche-Water with despatches, notifying this discovery, and the healthy and satisfactory condition of his own party. The detachment was started, with four saddle-horses, and twelve pack-horses, four days afterwards, namely, October 28th. It was calculated that they would make the journey and back in three weeks, and in the mean time it was the leader's intention to examine the country well around. From the number of the natives, and their excellent condition, he was persuaded that there were many lakes and creeks in the district that were permanent. As to the country generally, it was as dry as tinder; there had evidently been no rain there for many months, and they themselves had not seen a drop of rain since they left the Torrens, nor had a drop of surface water been found all the way. His idea was, that if this country had its fair share of rain it would be a good stock-country. He concluded that Mr. Howitt had not yet been able to push his way to Cooper's Creek for want of rain, and, on the other hand, he felt satisfied that Burke on leaving Cooper's Creek, in December last, northwards, had found himself much inconvenienced, and often driven far round by too much water. That, nevertheless, he had reached, probably, the north coast, and was thus far back when he and his party were massacred near one of their old camps.

During his absence, McKinlay had ordered his men to dig a well near the Lake Buchanan, which seems to puzzle Mr. Davis in his journal very much, what the leader could want with a well close to the lake where there was plenty of water; but the intent was, plainly enough, to prevent them getting into disorder or ill-health through inaction. Mr. Davis also gives us a repulsive description of Keri-Keri, the native sent to bring in the pistol to Lake Massacre, and who returned at the head of the supposed hostile multitude, whose hostility Mr. Hodgkinson conceived was much instigated by the rancorous Keri-Keri. He also describes to us the "nardoo" seed on which the natives there so much subsist.

Hodgkinson and his party did not get back from Blackwater till the 29th of November, during which interval the hot, dry weather prevented Mr. McKinlay from getting over to Cooper's Creek, or anywhere far from the camp, and himself and Middleton were very unwell. On Sunday, December 1st, they had a little rain, with the temperature at 110°. This day they observed a spring of one of Terry's breech-loading rifles, suspended from the neck of a native, who said that the remaining portions of the rifle were out north-east, about the course Mr. McKinlay was now about to take, for he determined to make the trip to Cooper's Creek. The next morning they started, taking two camels, five horses, and sufficient food for ten or twelve days. Middleton, Poole, Frank, a native, and a native of the place, made, with the leader, the party. "My object," says McKinlay, " in going out now, is, firstly—to ascertain if there is a likelihood of a flood down Cooper's Creek, this season, after all the rain that had fallen along the eastern side of the continent some months back, and which I thought might have fallen along the eastern side of the west coast range, so to secure us an open retreat in the event of our being able to make some considerable advance northward :—secondly, to ascertain if anyone was as yet stationed at Cooper's Creek, to intimate to them my intention of proceeding northward for some distance, and the almost certainty of crossing any track which either of the search-parties from the northern coast could possibly make *en route* to Cooper's Creek, or even Eyre's Creek."

They started at 9.15, A.M., December 2nd, and reached Cooper's Creek on the 6th. On the way, chiefly over sand-hills, with occasional salt-bush and grassy flats. They passed also several creeks of more or less capacity; first, Tae-Wilton Creek, fast drying up; another creek, at the distance of twenty-five miles from their setting out, unfit to drink ; then to a large creek, called Agaboogana, still over alternate sand-hills and flooded plains. On the 4th Middleton wounded his foot on a sharp stump, and caused the party considerable delay and inconvenience. That day they were at a creek, called Moolany, and the next went on sixteen miles to another, named Goonooboorroo, with but little water in it. Here, however, they found a junction of two considerable creeks.

coming from the south. There were abundance of bronze-wing and crested pigeons there, some beautiful parrots, black ducks, teal, whistlers, painted widgeons, and wood-ducks, in small numbers; also paroquets and quail. There was fish in the water, though it was fast drying up. The next morning, in looking for the horses, they came upon a camp of Burke's, in the dry bed of the creek, and McKinlay, riding up the main creek, soon found himself arrested by an object which told him that he was at Cooper's Creek. "In the camp a little above Pardulli, we saw a gumtree marked 'W. J. WILLS, N.N.W., xlv. yds., A.H.' Turned out our horses here for some time: between the last crossing in the creek and this, I got a view of a couple of red sand bluffs, and distant sand hills or hills of some kind to north-west. Started from Wills's grave at 4.10, and crossed creek; struck the creek again at 5.35, with plenty of water to Howitt's Camp xxxii, thence on to Burke's grave, striking dry creek, and followed it to Yarrowanda; arrived there at 7.10 p.m., Saturday December 7. Started at 7.7. a.m. and came to Burke's grave, about two miles on south bank of creek. On the north-east side of a box tree at upper end of waterhole, native name Yae-ni-mengi, found marked on tree 'R.O'H.B., 21-9-61., A.H.' Deposited a document in case of the return of any party. Saw a cobby horse on arrival here last night; tried to catch him. Saw the track of cattle up the creek, short distance from him: they had gone further up the creek to a water Culli-muno."

The cobby horse here seen by McKinlay, was one turned up by Sturt seventeen years before. It was afterwards caught by Howitt's party. The document deposited at Burke's grave was to the effect, that McKinlay, the leader of the South Australian Burke Relief Party, had received the intelligence from Adelaide, that the Victoria Government were intending to send up a party to convey down to Melbourne the remains of Burke and Wills, and of its intention to establish a depôt on this creek, to await the arrival of one or other of the parties in search of Burke and Wills, from Rockhampton, or from the Albert on the Gulf of Carpentaria. That he was going northward, and at every suitable camp on his route, would bury documents informing either of these parties of what had taken place, and of the intended depôt at Cooper's Creek, so that they could either return to the Albert, or go on through Adelaide, the route to which would be for some time easy of access, and clearly defined, by the tracks of his cartwheels. That his own intended course would intersect any course which either of the parties from the northward could make between Eyre's Creek and the late Burke's depôt on this creek.

This done, McKinlay turned back again, December 8th, and reached his camp at Lake Buchanan on the 11th. About this lake they planted freely various seeds, those of melons, peach, apricots, plum, and pumpkins. Having spent two months at this lake and in exploring the country round, on December 17th they moved forward in a north-east course, still through a country of barren, sultry sand-hills, and of lakes. The whole district round that part is a district of lakes. The blacks turned out in crowds to say good-bye to the whites, who had sojourned so long amongst them. They proceeded about fourteen miles through burning sands, and then camped till the 20th, at a creek named Gunani. On the 20th they made a dreadful journey over rotten flats, in which the wheels of the cart sunk to the axle, and the horses and camels up to their knees. One of the bullocks died on the way from the heat of the sun. In the evening they encamped on a lake which they found ten and a half feet deep, three hundred yards from the shore, and named it Lake McKinlay. Frank the native being found by the leader asleep at night on his watch, was sharply reprimanded, and refused to go further. McKinlay paid him for his six months' services, and dismissed him. The next day they travelled on to another lake named Moolionboorrana, about three miles long by two wide, but nearly destitute of shade. The heat was so intense, that the horses were all in a lather before starting; the camels perspired, which they had not done on the whole journey hitherto; and the men were jaded at the outset. The way was still over flooded flats and sand-hills. On arriving at the lake the cart containing their commissariat was all behind, and they had nothing but a little flour and water boiled for supper. They remained the next day at this shelterless lake to rest. The following day, December 23rd, they made twenty-five miles, through a good grazing country, but the heat was intense, and the thermometer broken, so that they could henceforth make no record of the temperature. They found plenty of pelicans, ducks, and fish at this lake, which was nine or ten miles round. They named it Lake Jeannie; and resolved to spend Christmas Day there. Numbers of natives were there, amongst whom they recognised many who had visited them at Lake Buchanan. Here they saw the process of preparing and cooking the nardoo seed, which the natives pounded betwixt two stones, then winnowed it, and then in a wooden trough kneaded it into paste, and baked thin cakes of it in the ashes. The mode of mixing the water with it was by no means inviting, for it was not poured on the flour out of a vessel, but squirted by mouthfuls upon it. These cakes are represented to have a strong astringent taste, and as leaving a hot sensation in the throat. There was plenty of feed for the cattle all about this lake, and the natives caught and brought them plenty of fish. As the natives were making a great noise in their camp at night, a rocket was sent up, which struck them into instant silence, which was not again broken till morning. On Christmas Day they indulged in roast mutton and plum-pudding, sung their songs, and solaced themselves with tea, as cool as the weather would permit.

The next morning they deposited documents under a tree, which they marked "M. K. Dec. 23, 24, 25; 61 Deg." They then made a short stage to another lake named Appam-barra, the country around hard and bare, with next to no vegetation, except plenty of salt, polygonum, samphire, and other bushes. There were many natives, who smelt strongly of fish; and fish, including craw-fish, was abundant. The horses having strayed back in the night to the better pasture of the last lake, another day was spent here, and McKinlay set the men to clear away the polygonum scrub on each side of the creek, he said, to prevent a surprise, but equally no doubt, to keep the men employed. They found it terribly hot work. On the following morning, at only the distance of five miles they came upon a magnificent lake, which the leader named Lake Hodgkinson, after his second in command; its native name being Watti-Widulo. Mr. McKinlay freely distributed amongst the women bead necklaces and showy bracelets. Here they killed a sheep to jerk, but they were all so fat, that they were obliged to hunt over the flock for the leanest.

Whilst lying here, the natives brought in one of those reports which they are ready to invent, that a party of white fellows, some six or eight, had arrived at Lake Buchanan, and were coming on to overtake them. This at first, greatly surprised them, but they soon came to a true idea of the story. On the 30th, McKinlay with Middleton, Hodgkinson, and Wylde, set out to explore still other lakes which they were told lay to the east, and in a three days' ride they discovered a number of lakes dry or full of water, creeks and sand-hills. The first day they came upon a large creek, shaded by gum-trees, on the banks of which were not less than from 200 to 300 natives, all well armed with spears and boomerangs. Some of them had hair and beards perfectly white. They called the creek Cariderro, but McKinlay named it Browne Creek after a friend. Further on they camped for the night on the margins of two extensive dry lakes, splendidly grassed. From the top of a conspicuous sand-hill, which they named Mount Macdonell, they saw the next day two beautiful

lakes connected by a small channel, which they named
Blanche and Sir Richard, in honour of the Governor and
his lady. Lake Blanche was nearly eight miles and Sir
Richard nearly seven miles in circumference. They
descended to them on the New Year's day of 1862;
found plenty of wild fowl, tens of thousands of pelicans,
and one solitary swan, gulls, ducks, cormorants, avocats,
white spoonbills, crows, kites, pigeons, and magpies of
various kinds. The number of pelicans proved the
abundance of fish; and the natives were calculated at
150. To the northward of these lakes was a fine chain
of ponds, which they named Sturt's Ponds, wondering
much that he did not discover this wonderful region of
lakes, as he passed near them.

Having returned to camp, they celebrated New Year's
Day on the 2nd, not having been altogether on the 1st,
again enjoying their roast mutton and plum-pudding.
The following day McKinlay and a party of whites and
blacks, rode westward to other lakes, the largest of
which they named Lake Strangways, after the Commissioner of Crown Lands. On Sunday, the 5th, McKinlay
with Poole and a black, rode north towards the Stony Desert, to get a glimpse of the country. All was dry and
desolate, they saw a succession of flooded basins, all
parched now, sand-hills, and regions covered with
stones. On their return they passed and named Ellar
Creek.

The party had now spent nearly four months in this
world of lakes, full or dry, of creeks and sand-hills,
flooded flats and hollows, now splendid grass and clover
fields. Mr. McKinlay, having had a renewed supply of
provisions, was thus enabled thoroughly to explore a
region so little suspected in this situation, bordering so
closely on the desert of Sturt of terrible fame. But
another reason for the long sojourn here was the fact
that this renowned desert lay a-head of them on their
northward course, and there was no possibility of passing
it until there had been a good deluge of rain. The
lakes, which the leader had now discovered north-east,

enabled him to draw a step nearer, and accordingly, on the 6th of January, they struck their tents at Wattiwidulo, or Lake Hodgkinson, and went on to Lakes Blanche and Sir Richard, but they did not find that they had mended their quarters. The weather was intensely hot; there was no shade, and all the people became very ill. The cattle suffered greatly too, and there was a determined attempt by the blacks to drive off the bullocks. From the 6th to the 18th, they stood out the torment of this oven-like abode, when they quitted it for the Ellar Creek. During this sojourn at Lake Blanche, McKinlay had made an excursion of three days to the east, through a wretched country of sand-hills and spinifex, or needle grass, to a lofty hill, which he named Mount Wylde, and back by the lakes. After moving camp, on the 18th, to Ellar Creek, through dreadful heat, they found the water so bad that they were compelled to retreat to Lake Hodgkinson; but this lake, of late so abundant and sweet, had now nearly dried up, and the water left was become quite bitter. They, therefore, were again compelled to remove to Hayward Creek, which flows into Lake Hodgkinson, and there found plenty of good water, beautiful shelter of trees, and good feed for the cattle. There they resolved to wait for rain. They cut rushes on the creek sides to prevent any surprise from the natives, and made comfortable beds of them. They made shades of boughs over their tents, and waited for rain.

But the indefatigable McKinlay did not rest. On the 23rd, he took Wylde, Hodgkinson, and two natives, and proceeded northwards to get a peep at the Desert, and judge whether they might venture to plunge into it. He left word at the camp that he might be away three weeks, and took provisions accordingly, but four days of it perfectly satisfied him. It was a scene of dry lakes, dry creeks, red sand-hills, bare of everything but an occasional patch of spinifex; to the north-east and south, all stones. The natives with him said that, still onward, was all the same dreary, lifeless desolation, but he did not put full faith in their report. The reality itself, however, soon drove him back, and he was compelled to make haste, or the little water he had passed on the way would have disappeared. He seems to have penetrated fifty-seven miles into this stern desert, and Davis says, on their return:—"The horses looked very badly, having hardly had a drink since they left this on Thursday; the men too did not look well, having had very little themselves."

They were, therefore, compelled to remain at Hayward's Creek to wait for rain. The sun continued at 120° to 130° daily. Their stores, and especially their flour, were fast decreasing. The natives, who at first were so polite as to come and ask leave to fish in their own waters, now began to want them away, and, as they did not move, reported that a great "aramitha," or flood, was coming down, and they would all be drowned if they did not get away. McKinlay rode up the creek as far as Browne's Creek, where the natives said the flood had arrived, but found it all, as he suspected, fiction. They saw him riding in that direction, and, no doubt, understood his errand, as they kept at a distance on his return: but, on this ride, he reported that he saw as many as 400 or 500 of them on the creek. The water in the creek was falling three-quarters of an inch per day. The natives passed them continually with large quantities of fish, but did not seem disposed to let them have any. No doubt, they considered it bad policy to feed them when they wanted them away. Here, however, they were compelled to remain till the 10th of February. Nearly all of them ill from disordered stomach and bowels, and growing very discontented, and tormented terribly by the flies. Some of the men were sent out to examine the water of the neighbouring lakes, but reported them undrinkable. McKinlay set them to dig a well near the creek, but fifteen feet deep it was salt as brine; and Davis despondingly sighed for rain, "as this sort of life is worse than hard work on the constitution."

At length, on the 6th of February, came thunder and lightning, and, though it did not rain there, they hoped that it had northward. Middleton and Hodgkinson were sent off to see if Lakes McKinlay and Moolionboorana had water enough to warrant a start so far. On the 8th, rain came plentifully; the men returned reporting abundant rain onwards, and now all was alive with preparations of departure direct north; shoeing horses, fetching up camels and bullocks, and packing of tents. On the 10th, they were on the way; but the rain which had set them free had, on the other hand, made the country so soft that they had to wade and drag along up to the knees in mud. McKinlay says that not a green blade of grass was to be seen, yet the creeks were now full. The whole country looked as if it had been carefully ploughed, harrowed, and finally rolled, the farmer having omitted the seed.

On the 13th they passed a camp of Burke's, noticed the camel dung about it, and saw the remains of Burke's horse Billy, which he had killed there, and the saddle. Both the leader and others still suffering severely from dysentery. The country so soft they are obliged to leave the cart and pack the stores on the camels and horses. Thus they struggle on in continual rain and sickness, losing some of their bullocks by the way from fatigue. The flies unremittingly intolerable. But now, instead of drought and dried-up lakes, they found themselves in the midst of vast floods, and were in danger of being surrounded by waters and drowned. On the 30th of March they obtained a wide view from hills which they named the Hamilton Ranges, whence the country appeared literally torn into stripes by the suddenly rushing torrents. Other hills stood at a distance, and between them ran a creek through the gorge. The Hamilton Hills the leader named Hamilton's Tabletops, being square-headed limestone hills, and the others Goyder's Table-tops. The gorge, and an island in the flooded creek, he named Hunter's Gorge and Island.

On the 4th of April they were at a lagoon, which

they named Jeanie Lagoon, with Kangaroo Ranges in full view, tier after tier, and a timbered country. "I never," says McKinlay, "in all my experience found the flies so thoroughly a pest as they have been for the last week or ten days." On the 6th they saw and named Euro Hill, because they there killed an euro, or small species of kangaroo. By this time they were across Sturt's famous Stony Desert. To them, instead of a scene of drought, it had been one of floods and mud. Such are the uncertainties of this perilous region. The summers of 1844—5, when Sturt found all this district one of burning sand and loose stones, was one of great drought through Australia generally: this of 1861—2 was unusually wet. In a dry season, therefore, the traveller is in danger of perishing from heat and drought, in a wet one from floods. On the 28th of February, having reached a creek which he imagined not far from Eyre's Creek, McKinlay says—"We are now in that position not far from the place where Captain Sturt dreaded being overtaken by rain;" and on the 2nd of March, having passed with much difficulty a swollen creek, and camped on an elevation which he called "Escape Camp," he says—"A great portion of the flat is covered by water. Beyond the creek there is nothing visible but lines of trees, marking the course of the lesser channels, and stone hills, all else is perfect sea. We were very fortunate to be caught in it where we were, or to a certainty we should all have been washed away, or perched up on a small island of sand, with nothing but starvation staring us in the face, as there is no vegetation on the sand-rises down the creek."

A new idea here presented itself of the fate of Leichhardt, that he might be suddenly surrounded in some low part of this country, and buried in the waters, without possibility of escape: and this idea was strengthened in the minds of the party from quantities of goats' hair being found amongst the natives of this part of the country, goats being never seen in the interior, except those taken there by Leichhardt. The idea is not an improbable one.

Towards the middle of March they came upon occasional patches of country well grassed, and on the 16th McKinlay says that he has called Ellar's and Warren's Table-tops "the Downs of Plenty," because there was everything that one could wish on travelling over a new country. Some Australian writers, therefore, have indulged in actually Arcadian descriptions of Sturt's Desert, and assert that it is as good a country as the average of Australia. But such partial spots as these hills are but oases in the desert, which may be called into brief and isolated scenes of verdure by the occasional falls of rain, but these are merely fitful, and where they occur transient as a dream. No man could trust himself there with flocks and herds without certain destruction as his fate. If he lived through the scant time of rain and flood, he would soon find himself alone amid burning sand-hills, and stony, black wildernesses, where neither animal nor vegetable life could endure. Towards the end of March they had emerged from the Stony Desert into a region of creeks, ranges, swamps, and finely grassed and flowery plains, yet the spinifex on the hill sides still denoted that the general character of the country was poor, and that the efflorescence was the effect of the abundant rains and tropical warmth, and would not last. It was now the autumn of that hemisphere, and the nights they record as cold. On entering this region we should not, however, quit the Stony Desert without remarking that, contrary to expectation, the camels stepped along over the stones, and appeared to suffer nothing from them.

On the 6th of April, to which we have brought the travellers, from Euro Hill they reached the Daly ranges and creek, and were amongst thousands of wild fowls of various kinds. On the 8th they passed through myal and stony country, and were on a fine creek, which was named as well as some ranges near, after Dr. Müller, the government botanist of Melbourne. On the 9th named another creek the Manserg, the country pretty, with plenty of emus on the plains, and thousands of other birds. This day Mr. Davis records the rare incident that he helped the leader to calculate their position, when they found that they were somewhere about 20° 17′ S. latitude, 142° 17′ E. longitude. This is almost the only observation of the kind through the whole journey. On the 13th Kirby and the sheep were lost, and occasioned much hunting and anxiety, for they were not rediscovered till the 19th.

On the 21st they named various ranges and creeks, as Middleton's Creek, Hamilton's Creek, Warburton's Creek, Crozier's Ranges, William's Ranges, Kirby's Ranges, in memory of the shepherd being lost in them, and McKinlay's creek and ranges.

From this point the travellers may be said to have entered the tropical regions of Australia; the palms, the broad prairies with grass up to the neck, the new trees and fruits, the ant-nests like tall decaying columns, the still more numerous natives, shy and retiring, but hostile, by continually firing the grass around them to drive them away, and destroy the support of their cattle, the streams augmented to deep and large rivers, were all new, and, as it were, more Indian features. On the 22nd of April they saw trees that the leader, who had been in the colony more than thirty years, had never seen before. Copper was found in the bed of a creek, and mica and quartz abounded. The horses having strayed, and a delay occasioned, McKinlay rode to some hills about seven miles off, and ascended one, as he calculated three thousand feet above the level of the creek. Higher ones were visible. This was one mass of quartz, mica, and slate, lying on pipe-clay, all indications of gold. He named them Sarah's Ranges. The next day their bullocks wandered, occasioning another delay. The country passed through showed strongly auriferous features. The natives were busy burning the grass in the ranges, according to their wont for hunting purposes. On the tops of all the ranges the decaying red ant-hills

appeared like sharp spires, and washed by the rains into
all sorts of shapes. The creek at which they camped
they named the Marchant, after a friend of the leader's.
Soon after they crossed another fine creek, which they
named the Williams, after another Adelaide friend. On
the 27th they crossed a splendid creek, where they
noticed bushes, logs, and masses of grass, etc. brought
down by floods, lodging forty feet above them in the
trees, and large trees snapped off thirty feet from the
ground, and others torn up by the roots, evidencing
that these floods must occasionally be tremendous.

In the course of the 28th they passed several watercourses, and named a considerable creek Poole's Creek,
after the father of one of the party. The leader and
Middleton also ascended a rocky hill on the plain,
whence they saw other open plains to north and west as
far as they could discern, to the north north-east were
lines of dark timber. They named the hill Margaret,
and two others at a distance, Mount Elephant, and
Mount Macpherson. Their way now lay over extensive
stretches of undulating country, with frequent streams,
the blacks burning the grass to the east of them. Two
creeks they named the Jessie and the Jeanie. The
country finely timbered, but not densely. No game
visible but a single turkey. They saw various climbing
plants, bearing fruit some like hard peas, others like
little green cucumbers, but bitter, and a third species of
the size of a walnut.

On the 1st of May they observed a black following
the tracks of the party, but on being observed he decamped. They shot a bird resembling a pheasant, with
a large tail, which appeared to be an encumbrance to it.
A large creek crossed they named the William. Game
now became plentiful near a creek named the Dugald.
Here they crossed the track of Burke and Wills, on the
Cloncurry of Burke, their Dugald being probably the
Cloncurry. Soon after they named another creek the
Davis, after one of the party, and then held their course
over forest land and swampy plains to the Leichhardt,

which they struck on the 9th of May. "Its bed vast sheets of stones—rocks and small stones on the opposite side lower down;—the water in its bed is about, or upwards of 150 yards wide. At two miles, bearing of about 210°, struck the river at a stony and rocky fall, and went westward half a mile to avoid the bend; struck river again at three miles on same course as above, then, at four miles struck a lagoon to the south; then, at four and a half miles struck the river, the water in its full width now upwards of 250 yards, a splendid-looking place, and lined on its banks with splendid timber of various kinds, with a variety of palms, etc.; then to the southward of south-west for betwixt six and eight miles. But the rugged banks were so intricate that it was impossible to calculate the distances correctly. In many places, half a mile from the river banks, the plains drop off precipitately from three to ten feet, and slope off in undetermined, deep, earthy creeks, finishing at last in deep, reedy creeks, close to the river. Water in nearly all the side creeks, and compelled us to keep out, but sometimes we were caught in them, thinking the timber we were advancing to was a lagoon, or belt of timber, and then we were compelled to go round it; then cross a very fine creek running into the river, the same, I believe, we crossed yesterday about six miles from camp on our outward course. From this to our camp I make out about thirteen miles, on a bearing of about 200°."

The number of Sturt's pigeons in the neighbourhood of the Leichhardt is described as prodigious. The weather beautiful, the nights cold, the autumn now verging on winter. A native woman with her child were seen, but she made a desperate noise, and fired the grass round McKinlay, and raised her digging stick menacingly as he attempted to approach, and it was with difficulty that he could get near enough to offer her a fish-hook. His object was to learn how far they were from the coast but she could not comprehend the question. The country is described as very pretty, and the grass up to their necks. The leader ordered them to burn this tall grass round their camp to keep it clear, but in doing this, their baggage was set on fire. Davis describes the scene with much humour, which is his vein:—" We had finished, and I thought the fire was all out and secure, the wind at the same time being very still, hardly a breath, when all of a sudden we were perfectly astounded. Bang! bang! bang! Fiz! fiz! We ran down as fast as our legs could carry us, and found, to our dismay, that some fire that had been smouldering had been fanned into a flame, and communicated with the pack-saddles, in which was our ammunition, to say nothing of fireworks; so that rockets and blue lights were vieing with each other in their praiseworthy endeavour to celebrate our arrival at the Falls. It might have been worse had we been farther a-field, as the packs would have been inevitably destroyed. As it is, every rocket is 'absent without leave,' which is a great pity in case we should want to signalize the Victoria, should she be in the Gulf." At this point their camels strayed away, and cost them three days' arduous hunting and much anxiety. They were now in Stokes' "Plains of Promise."

The 18th of May was a memorable day to them, for on that they reached the tidal part of the river, and within a very few miles of the sea, which, however, they could not approach for the dense mangrove swamp. We may quote McKinlay's own account of this event:— "After getting amongst a number of swamps and large lagoons, we struck a fine large mangrove creek, a very pretty spot, like an orange grove. Bearing of $321\frac{1}{2}°$ for two miles; then bearing of $35°$, crossed the sea running in through mangrove creeks into the flats like a sluice, and camped at a lagoon and couple of fresh-water holes, close by the river. We are now perfectly surrounded by salt water, the river on one side and the mangrove creeks and salt flats on the other. I question much whether we shall be able to get to the beach with the horses. Since noon wind changed to the N.N.W.; country very much burnt by the natives—it was dry enough as it aws, without the additional use of fire. Lots of water-lilies in bloom, in all the deep water-holes and lagoons; and a very handsome tree, with dark-green foliage and a beautiful yellow blossom, and completely loaded with a round fruit of the size of a crab-apple, now green, and containing a number of large-sized seeds.

"Monday, May 19. Camp 60. Started out this morning with the intention of going to the beach, taking with me Middleton, Poole, Wylde, and Kirby; but was quite unsuccessful, being hindered by deep and broad mangrove creeks and boggy flats, over which our horses could not travel. I consider we are now about four or five miles from the coast. There is a rise in the river here of six and two-third feet to-day, but yesterday it was a foot higher. Killed our three remaining sheep, and will retrace our steps on the 21st.

"Tuesday, May 20. Camp 60. Sent Hodgkinson and Poole to the salt flats to collect what will be sufficient for our homeward ramble, or rather to the Queensland settled districts, where we hope to arrive in due time; the state of the clothing of the party, and want of various things—the principal thing, food—has prevented my directing the steps of the party to the settled districts of South Australia. A few of the natives came to the opposite side of the river this morning during the flood tide, and got up in the trees, and I was a long time in getting any of them persuaded to cross. At length two of them, and then another middle-aged man, ventured, on my displaying a tomahawk to them. They were of the ordinary stamp, and strange to say, were neither circumcised nor had any of their front teeth out, but were marked down the upper part of the arm, and on the breast and back. After making them a few presents, they recrossed; no information from them, but perhaps we may see something more of them on a future day. Hodgkinson and Poole returned with from forty to fifty pounds of good salt, sufficient for our purpose; and we start in the morning to proceed as far as the Falls, and cross the river there, in the event of not finding a crossing earlier, which I don't expect. The camels, I am sorry to say, are getting lame by the burnt stumps of reeds and strong coarse grass entering the soles of their feet. I hope they will soon recover. If the bar at the mouth of the river will permit vessels to enter, there is a sufficiency of water at all tides to ship horses or stock from alongside the banks, without any wharf or anything else, and good country to pasture upon, but the grasses too strong generally for sheep.

"Wednesday, May 21. Camp 60. Commenced our journey for Port Denison."

And this is all the observation which the leader of this successful expedition makes on having crossed the continent from Adelaide to the Gulf of Carpentaria, without the loss of a man. Here he was on the margin of the sea, and prevented seeing it by the matted mangroves, yet he expresses no disappointment at this obstruction, and on the other hand, no triumph in such an achievement accomplished, the second time that it had been accomplished in the full breadth of the land by any man. The thing is done; and as if it were a trifle of ordinary life, he coolly collects his salt, and says, "To-morrow we are off homewards, though rather in a circuitous course." It is a striking example of—what? Is it philosophy, or want of enthusiasm? Let Mr. McKinlay himself say; we can only record that the important transit is made for the second time, and the party is quietly departing for an eastern port, having long since eaten all their flour, now killed their last sheep, and before they reach Port Denison, will have eaten up their camels and most of their horses. The great journey across being made, we may pass cursorily over their return, as it is chiefly through regions the general character of which is known to us from the expeditions of Leichhardt, Mitchell, Kennedy, and Gregory.

We learn from Davis that, in the attempt to reach the shore, they lost one of their horses, and that they lost three of their sheep at this camp, besides the three killed and jerked for their homeward journey; that they had only two bullocks left, and all their flour, tea, and sugar exhausted, so that the prospect before them was none of the most flattering. On the 21st of May, they started punctually on their return. They had to travel back to the falls on the Leichhardt before they could cross the river. On the 23rd they came upon three trees near the falls, marked by Landsborough with the broad arrow and "L. F. E. 15. C. 5." Instead of following his track reversed down the Flinders, McKinlay struck more directly east. They soon found the feet of the camels so sore from treading on the stumps of reeds burnt by the natives, that they had to make them boots of leather. Several of the men became strongly affected with symptoms of fever. They observed plenty of the runners bearing beans which Leichhardt burnt for coffee, but none of the party were disposed to try this coffee, though they had nothing but meat to subsist upon. The country was pretty level and fit for pasturage, though rather too woody. They now began to lose their horses fast. The first was poisoned or bitten by a snake, and died. On the 7th of June they crossed the Flinders River, crossing at the same time Walker's route shortly afterwards, on what he called the Norman River. From this point they left the level pasture country, and were met by rugged ranges, such as all the travellers in that quarter of Australia have encountered. They now killed their last bullock. The natives were everywhere burning the grass. The farther they now went, the more difficult and lofty became the ranges, and the exhaustion of their horses extreme. Some of the hills were 3000 feet high, and McKinlay named several Gregory, Wildash, Hawker, and Murphett, after Augustus Gregory, the explorer, and other gentlemen. The silk cotton was growing freely. They crossed many times the same river, which they supposed to be one branch of the Flinders, which it may be, or perhaps the main stream of the Carron. On the 15th, McKinlay says:—" I ascended the hills, and never beheld such a fearfully grand country in my life—nothing but towers and pinnacles of sandstone conglomerate, fit for nothing but wallaby and euro; and for a thousand years' hence it can be used for nothing but them and the natives. It is a terrible country." They had now struck the River Gilbert. They were still losing their horses from fatigue, and began to kill their camels from the same cause. Several of the men continued very ill, no doubt from the same fatigue, and from living entirely on jerked meat.

On the 5th of July they reached the Burdekin, the bed of which was nearly a hundred yards wide, with a strong stream running in it, and splendid timber on its banks. They were still killing their horses for food, or leaving them behind because they could not keep up. The nights were now very cold, and strong ice in their tins in the mornings. They now came upon horse tracks in the sand of the river bed, and soon after discovered an old camp, and the letter K cut on a tree recently. They were approaching the settled country. On the 24th of July, however, they had only two packhorses and one camel left, and were yet ninety miles from Port Denison. On the 27th they crossed the Burdekin on a raft, in close company with a number of alligators. On the 30th they killed their last camel, but on the 2nd of August they came in sight of a herd of cattle, and two men "tailing" them, as it is termed, or tending them as is the phrase at home. This was a joyful sight, and they were soon hospitably received at the station of Messrs. Harvey and Somers. Their troubles were now all over, and here, singularly enough, they met with Mr. Brahe, who had gone out with Burke and Wills, and had left the depôt at Cooper's Creek to return, unfortunately, only seven hours before these unfortunate travellers arrived there in their last state of exhaustion. Brahe was in no degree to blame, having stayed long over the time fixed by Burke, his provisions were growing scarce, and his men becoming ill. Moreover, Burke had talked of returning by Queensland. So satisfied was Howitt of Brahe's trustworthiness, that he engaged him to accompany him on his expedition in search of Burke and Wills, and he had the melancholy duty of assisting at the burial of the scattered remains of his former ill-fated leader. He had now come to Queensland to join Mr. Byerley, the son of the late Sir John Byerley, a thoroughly practiced bushman, in a station. From Port Denison they sailed *en route* for Rockhampton, Sydney, Melbourne, and finally, Adelaide, in all which places they were welcomed, as their successfully managed and important expedition deserved.

CHAPTER XIII.

LANDSBOROUGH'S EXPEDITION FROM THE GULF OF CARPENTARIA IN QUEST OF BURKE AND WILLS, 1861.

Mr. Orkney sends his yacht, Sir Charles Hotham, to look out in the Gulf of Carpentaria for the lost explorers.—Disabled on the voyage.—The Government of Queensland send out Landsborough and party.—The Firefly carrying the expedition stranded on Sir Charles Hardy's Island.—Lose five horses.—Assisted to the mouth of the Albert by the Victoria.—Anchored in the Albert. —Mr. Landsborough explores the Albert 120 miles.—Driven back by natives and want of water.—Finds Mr. Walker had been at the Albert, and gone back on the traces of Burke and Wills.—Insists on going too.—Sets out on the 10th of February, 1862.—Sees tracks of Walker, but does not follow them.—Ceases to speak of Burke and Wills, but strikes eastward in quest of good lands.— Follows the Flinders 200 miles to the south-eastward.—Crosses the Jardine Creek and Ranges.—The Thomson.—Follows it, and crosses the Barcoo and Warrego.—At Williams's Station on that river hears of the death of Burke and Wills.—Descends the Darling, and thence to Melbourne.—Visits London. —His skirmish with Mr Crawford about the growth of wool.—Mr. Landsborough's real service is to have found a good track to the Gulf from Queensland, and good land for squatters.—Comments of the *Melbourne Argus* on his tour.

We have seen that whilst Mr. Alfred Howitt was despatched with an expedition directly overland in quest of Messrs. Burke and Wills, a party was engaged under Mr. Landsborough to proceed from Brisbane in Queensland by sea, in company of the Victoria steamer, Captain Norman, to the Gulf of Carpentaria, and thence to set out S.W. in quest of the lost explorers; another, under Mr. Walker, to set out overland from Rockhampton, and to proceed to the Gulf from that point. Besides these, as we have seen, Mr. Orkney, member of the Legislative Assembly for West Melbourne, volunteered his little steamer the Sir Charles Hotham, of only sixteen tons, to proceed instantly to the Albert River, Gulf of Carpentaria, to look out for the missing expedition. This little vessel, built by Mr. Orkney himself, from a model of the Great Eastern, was commanded by Mr. Wyse, the skipper of Lord Dufferin's yacht in his voyage to the Arctic Regions. It was taken in tow by the "Sydney" steamer, and left Hobson's Bay on the 6th of July, with only the Captain and two men on board. The weather setting in stormy, the "Sydney" was soon obliged to cut her adrift, but she made her way safely to Sydney, and again setting forward on her voyage, had the misfortune soon after in being brought to in shallow water for the night, to run upon the peak of her own anchor, knocking a hole in her bottom, and thus incapacitate herself for the voyage, so that Mr. Orkney was disappointed in his generous hope of being of service to the lost explorers.

The Government of Queensland patriotically voted £500 to send out an expedition, and Victoria voted £2000 for a similar purpose. This being the case, the two expeditions organized in Queensland were to be considered the joint enterprises of the colonies of Victoria and Queensland.—Despatch of Governor Barkly, Parliamentary Report, p. 28. Ditto of Governor Brown of Queensland, Parliamentary Report, p. 88, and Colonial Secretary Herbert; Ibid. p. 90. That entrusted to Mr. Landsborough, however, was to be considered "more immediately the contribution of Queensland."—Sir G. F. Bower's Despatch, Ibid. p. 88. This, the Queensland Governor in the same despatch to the Duke of Newcastle, informs us, had been organized at Brisbane with especial care, under his own surveillance, and by the experienced advice of Mr. Augustus Gregory, then residing there. The expedition consisted of eight persons :—Mr. William Landsborough, the leader, Englishman, and four aboriginal blacks, including two troopers of the native police. These persons were all selected by the leader himself, and they had thirty horses, with an ample supply of arms, provisions, and other necessaries. Captain Norman, of the Victoria steamer, was judiciously made Commander-in-chief of both these expeditions, to secure harmony and proper co-operation; and the Victoria proceeded to the Gulf of Carpentaria from Moreton Bay on the 24th of August, 1861, accompanied by the tender, Firefly, of 200 tons, in which the expedition of Landsborough, with its horses, was embarked.

On Sunday, the 1st of September, the Firefly lost sight of the Victoria in a gale near the Raine Island passage on the eastern coast of York Peninsula, and on the 4th they ran on the reef of Sir Charles Hardy's Island. They managed to land, however, safely, twenty-five out of their thirty horses on board. On the 7th the Victoria again hove in sight, and Captain Norman, with great energy, repaired the damages done to the Firefly, saw the horses and stores re-embarked, and conducted the expedition successfully to the mouth of the Albert river in the Gulf of Carpentaria. Here the Victoria had orders to remain six months to afford all necessary aid to the different exploring parties on land.

The Firefly was taken up the Albert river about twenty-six miles, to a point near which another river from the south falls into it, called the Barkly. Beyond this distance the Albert was not navigable, on account of snags, and the Barkly was much in the same condition. There the Firefly was anchored at a depôt, and the horses put on shore. The downs and plains on the banks of the Albert have but little wood, and that very stunted, but still Mr. Landsborough thought they would make good sheep farms. At that season the temperature on the boat ranged from 74° to 94°. The nights were agreeable, and they were not troubled by mosquitos or sand-flies.

On the 14th of November, Mr. Landsborough and his party had set out in conformity with his instructions towards central Mount Stuart, on which route it was hoped that he might fall in with traces of Burke. Mr. Landsborough traced up the Albert River for about 120 miles under the different names of the Albert, the Gregory, and the O'Shanassy, with various creeks falling into it, and about midway, running through considerable hills, which he named Premier Hills, and Barren Ranges, Mounts Kay, Heales, etc., Table Hill, and others. Amongst these ranges were Fullerton, Pratt, Seymour, and other creeks, but many of them were at that season destitute of water, and the grass on the ranges so dry as to have very little nourishment in it. In latitude 19° 54' they came on a considerable sheet of water with plenty of fish and water-fowl, which they named Mary Lake. and into this a river ran which they named the Herbert River. A little farther they found also two other pieces of water which they named Francis and Kenillan Lakes. But water soon disappeared altogether, and a number of blacks, 100 or more, collecting on their track, they thought it best to return, both to avoid a collision, and to seek for Burke and Wills, "in a better watered country." Accordingly, on the 29th of December, they turned their faces homewards, and reached the depot on the Albert on the 19th of January, 1862. In this tour Landsborough advanced a little beyond the 20th parallel of S. latitude. In some parts of the country there were grass and water, and he seems to consider it a good country, but the idea derived from his journal is that of a thirsty land. In the wet season, and for a brief space after, it is probably, a pleasant, grassy country, the river bearing marks of great floods, but for the greater part of the year, it would appear in the explorer's own language, to be "so parched up as to be quite worthless."

The character of the Gregory River is quite tropical, according to Mr. Landsborough's entry. December 3rd, "The bed of the river we had found perfectly dry for some distance back. It is badly watered along the course we have come to-day. Above our camp it is quite of a different character. There are now only gum-trees in the bed of it, when lower down it was crowded with green trees, consisting chiefly of fig, Leichhardt, drooping tea-tree, cabbage palm, pandanus, etc. All the country above the camp, on the banks of the river, is composed of barren, rocky, basaltic ridges, which are slightly timbered with stunted bloodwood trees, and are overrun with desert grass, with the exception of the narrow strips of flooded country on each side of the river, on the lowest parts of which there is coarse grass, and on the highest parts, tufts of the best description of grasses."

They lost two of their horses by drowning on the journey, their intense thirst urging them to rush into the water, where they did find it, incautiously.

On the return to the mouth of the Albert, Captain Norman announced to Mr. Landsborough that Mr. Walker arrived at the depôt on the 7th of December. That he had seen traces of Messrs. Burke and Wills on the Flinders, and that, having supplied himself with the necessary provisions, he had set out to follow up those traces, wherever they might lead him. This being the case, Captain Norman did not deem it at all necessary for Mr. Landsborough and his party to return overland, but that "he ought to return by the Victoria to Queensland, in accordance with the instructions of the Royal Society." Captain Norman added, "that having had to supply Mr. Walker's party, he should only have limited stores for his party should he go overland, and no tea, sugar, or rum whatever. That this was an additional reason why Mr. Landsborough should not risk the safety of his party by returning overland, especially as Mr. Walker would do everything that was necessary or possible to follow up Mr. Burke's tracks. He, therefore, recommended him to return by the Victoria, yet left it to his discretion if he felt impelled to go overland.

Mr. Landsborough thought it absolutely necessary that he should go after the tracks of Mr. Burke, though Mr. Walker was gone already, giving as a reason that "Mr. Walker will not be able probably to follow the tracks of Mr. Burke and his companions, *as too long a time has elapsed since they were made.*" A reason which surely applied to Mr. Landsborough still more than to Mr. Walker, as it was now still longer since they were made. In short, Mr. Landsborough was resolved to make the land journey, and declared that he would not have come at all, had he thought that he should not be allowed to make it. That is, apparently, whether it was necessary or not. "All along," he asserted, "he had thought that that would be the way that Burke's tracks would be found, and more particularly after he learned that Messrs. Cornish and Buchanan had seen what they believed to be tracks of Burke's party, about 200 miles to the westward of Mount Narrien." These reasons were certainly by no means complimentary to the abilities of Mr. Walker. We shall see how Mr. Landsborough justified his own acumen in following tracks.

On the 10th of February, 1862, he set out from the Albert in the professed pursuit of the traces of the original explorers. He directed his course first to the Flinders, because it was on that river that Walker had seen their tracks returning southward from the Gulf. On the 11th, the second day of their journey, they perceived traces of Walker's party, but already so faint that none but the natives could see them distinctly. "As the tracks of Walker's party," says Landsborough, "were so indistinct that I could only see them when they were pointed out to me by the aborigines of our party, I foresaw that it would be tedious, if not impossible, to follow them to where Mr. Walker said he had left the tracks of Mr. Burke's party." On the 12th he says, "In our journey to-day, although we often got off the tracks of Mr. Walker's party, we did not altogether lose them. Near where we encamped to-night, Jemmy saw a dead horse." On the 13th, however, they gave up the tracks of Walker altogether. "We started on our journey at 9·6, and having passed over rich, lightly-wooded plain, about eight miles, we reached the Leichhardt River at a part where the tide reaches. This river seems to be fully larger than the Albert. The tracks of Walker's party were so indistinct on the rich plains, from so much rain having fallen, that I gave up all hope of being able to follow them."—Landsborough's Journal.

Thus, so far from following Burke and Wills where Walker could not, the plea on which Mr. Landsborough insisted to Captain Norman on undertaking this journey from the Albert River southward, he could not follow the far more recent tracks of Walker for more than three days. He then gave up tracking even Walker altogether, and as to tracking Burke and Wills, there is no evidence in his journal that he attempted to do that at all. From this moment to the time when Landsborough reached Mr. Williams's Station on the Warrego, and there learned the fate of Burke and Wills, there are but two mentions of Burke and Wills, and the second is only an incidental one, occurring on the 10th of April, when Landsborough's party were on the Thomson River. The statement is a remarkably confused one. He was on the Thomson River, but did not, according to his account, know it to be that river, yet it was flowing exactly in the direction of that river, and he ventured to seek the Barcoo by crossing S.E. from it in search of it, which he could only have done in the confidence that he was on the Thomson. "April 10th. As I imagined, Gregory's party had traced the Thomson to its head. I did not suppose this river was it. I determined, as we had used the most of our stores, to leave the river if possible, and start for the settled districts. It was very vexatious to come to this resolution, as the river was flowing almost in the direction of Burke's starting point on Cooper's Creek." The blacks, he says, "told us of two practicable roads to the Barcoo," and they found the Barcoo by following up Dunsmore Creek. This is the second and incidental mention of Burke after giving up Walker's tracks. The first was on the 19th of February, just nine days after leaving the Albert, and is the only indication in the whole journal of the return journey, that Mr. Landsborough meant to look out for Burke and Wills at all. "Feb. 19. At 9·30 having come over the plains on our old course for five miles from the isolated hills, we reached the Flinders River. The river, we were glad to find had been recently flooded; in crossing, we ascertained that it had four channels, one of which was running. As this was the river on the banks of which Mr. Walker said he had found the track of Burke's party, I thought it would be a good plan to follow it up, and resolved to do so."

Here, with the exception of the incidental mention just adverted to, all evidence ceases that Mr. Landsborough was ostensibly in search of Burke. We have no expression of the fact that he was on the look-out for traces of the missing travellers, no expression of anxiety that he neither discovers the track of Walker nor theirs. The subject is never recurred to with a sense of care and regret that he was obtaining no indications of the lost explorers. If ever their image or the anxiety to find them was in his mind, it never came into his pen; for anything the reader can discover, Mr. Landsborough is bent solely on an expedition in quest of good lands and of future stations. There is not a trace even of a desire to justify the expectations which he had held out to Captain Norman, that his sagacity and penetration in following up a trail would be found superior to those of Walker. What is more extraordinary is that, having struck the Flinders at about 100 miles from the sea, following it up, at no great distance onwards, he actually crossed the track of Burke and Wills without at all discovering it, and ran parallel with it, only on the opposite bank of the river, to the junction of the Flinders and Cloncurry. From that point, having missed their traces altogether, he entirely quitted their route, and pursued the river for nearly 300 miles south-eastward, without, so far as the reader can discover, any further thought about the grand object of his journey. When he left the Flinders, it still presented a bed of 120 yards wide, the stream itself then being low. Nearly about the 144th parallel of longitude and about 20° of latitude, he crossed the Jardine Creek and Ranges, and found himself at the source of the Thomson. He then followed down that river nearly to 25° S. latitude, where he crossed at the Dunsmore Creek to the Barcoo, and ran still more eastward to the Warrego. Every step of this route, from the time that he left the junction of the Flinders and Cloncurry, led him farther and farther from the traces of Burke and Wills, as well as from that point towards which, by his own statement (See Victoria Report of Landsborough and Walker's Expeditions, 1861—2, p. 8), both Mr. Gregory and himself had agreed that his course should be held, namely, Mr. Burke's starting point, Cooper's Creek, where Mr. Howitt was waiting with supplies to receive him, and there he would have learned the whole fate of the missing party. From Mr. Williams's Station, on the Warrego, where he learned the result of the Burke and Wills expedition, he ran down to the Darling, and thence to Melbourne, which he reached in August, the Exploration Committee, on the 27th of June, having despatched an order to him at Menindie to dispose of his horses and material, and to proceed to that place.

As it regarded the great object of the expedition, the discovery of the missing party of Burke and Wills, Landsborough's journey was an entire failure. After his disparaging remarks to Captain Norman of Mr. Walker's ability to follow a trail, it appeared like a Nemesis that he should actually run a geographical degree, at least, parallel with Burke and Wills' track along the Flinders, and still more so as these gentlemen made two tracks, one outward and one returning—should, as it were, almost touch one of them, and really cross both, without discovering either. It would appear, indeed, that he had early given up all hope of tracing Burke and Wills. His heart was clearly set upon the charms of good land, of which he reported extensive districts along his course. His enthusiastic speculations on the Arcadian promises of the far north and the interior, and on the plenteous growth of wool in those torrid regions, led, on the 11th of May, 1863, to a brusque encounter in the meeting of the Geographical Society in London :—

"Mr. Crawfurd was of opinion that wool could not be grown in the tropics. Sheep were intended for a temperate climate, and the fleece given them to protect them from the cold. In the tropics, the fleece was not required."

Mr. Landsborough—" You are theorizing. Who, of all the human race, have the most wool on their heads? Is it not the inhabitants of the tropics?"

The retort was as smart as it was brusque; but a clever hit does not decide a statistical fact. Whatever time may determine, when flocks have been, for a tolerable period, depastured in the interior and the far north, the experiences of Captain Sturt during his six months' detention in the Stony Desert, is altogether opposed to Mr. Landsborough's assurances. Negro wool is not sheep's wool. Neither the wool of the sheep, the hair, nor nails, of the men, grew in the least degree during the whole of that time. The sheep became fat, as they did on McKinlay's journey through the same regions, and still on to the gulf, but their flesh was tasteless. No doubt, however, Mr. Landsborough's journey, and his reports, and descriptions, will have helped to stimulate the tide of pastoral colonization northwards in Australia, and the question of the growth of wool, and of the fitness of particular parts of the continent for different purposes, of pasturage of sheep, of cattle, the cultivation of corn, cotton, coffee, or other produce, will be decided by actual experience. No doubt a great deal may be done towards rendering the tropical regions of Australia habitable and useful, and, in particular, by the conservation of the waters, which fall occasionally in such abundance, by extensive and numerous tanks and reservoirs, as in India. The way in which stations have crept into the torrid and arid regions for 500 miles north of Adelaide, shows how they will by degrees advance themselves into the interior, which now seems, in many places, wholly opposed to human and pastoral life. Nothing will contribute to this so much as the throwing of embankments across valleys, so as to detain the deluges of rain water. In such regions the inhabitants will gradually become a tropical race in habits and appearance, as the Spaniards and Portuguese in the tropical regions of South America. In the mean time, every successful explorer renders a substantial service to the country by opening up the vast regions of this new world, and hastening the solution of these problems of life and rural economy. The late passages across the Australian continent have given a wonderful stimulus to the spread of population towards the north. South Australia has already proceeded to found a new colony on the northern coasts, the first of the three ships appointed to convey settlers, the Beatrice, having sailed on the 16th of April, 1864, followed by the Henry Ellis and the Yatala; and Queensland proposes to make a settlement on York Peninsula. These, undoubtedly, are the nuclei of great populations in the northern regions of Australia. Another service, therefore, which Mr. Landsborough has rendered, is to have opened up a more direct and easy highway overland from Queensland to the Gulf of Carpentaria than any of the former tracks of explorers. His course from the Albert to the settled districts of Queensland is almost a continuous line of rivers, and as future travellers will, no doubt, strike a straight line of route from the bend of the river Barcoo, west of the Alice, on the 24th parallel of latitude, in a north-west direction, to the Thomson, exactly on the line of the tropic of Capricorn, it will then be in no part very circuitous. This line, through its whole course, from the source of the Barcoo, near Mount Playfair, to the gulf, is singularly free from difficult hills, the Jardine Ranges, at the source of the Flinders, scarcely forming an exception. Mr. Landsborough's journey was nearly destitute of incident, though it is to be regretted that he thought himself necessitated to fire once or twice on the natives. So easy was the travelling that a foal, dropped at an early part of the journey, followed the mare the whole way to the settled district. The opening up of this route and the report of the grazing lands upon it may be regarded as the real benefit of his expedition.

Since writing the above, I have met with the following remarks in the files of the *Melbourne Argus*, which fully accord with my own impressions on reading Mr. Landsborough's report of his expedition, and show that my opinion, formed from an impartial consideration of his own statements, at this distance both of time and space, are not peculiar to myself:—

"Great credit must be given to Mr. Landsborough for the celerity with which he has accomplished the expedition. At the same time, its object seems to have been lost sight of at a very early stage of the journey, as there was not the remotest probability of striking Burke's track after quitting the Flinders River, and taking a S.S.E. course for the remainder of the way. In fact, from that moment all mention ceases to be made of the ostensible purpose for which the party was organized, until Mr. Landsborough reached the Warrego, and received the intelligence of Burke and Wills having perished, at which great surprise was expressed. But supposing these gallant men to have been still living, and anxiously awaiting succour at some one of the ninety camping places at which they halted, on their arduous journey between the depôt and the Gulf, what excuse could Mr. Landsborough have offered for giving so wide a berth to the probable route of the explorers, and for omitting to endeavour to strike their track, traces of which had been reported on the Flinders by Mr. Walker? We may be reminded that 'all's well that ends well,' that the lamented explorers were beyond the reach of human assistance, and that Mr. Landsborough has achieved a most valuable result in following the course he did; but we cannot help remarking that, in so doing, he seems to have been more intent upon serving the cause of pastoral settlement than upon ascertaining if it were possible to afford relief to the missing men. The impression produced by a perusal of the despatch which we published on Saturday last is, that the writer was commissioned to open up a practicable route from the Warrego to the Flinders, and not that he was the leader of a party which had been organized and despatched 'for the purpose of rendering relief, if possible, to the missing explorers under the command of Mr. Burke.' We do not wish to detract one iota from the credit due to Mr. Landsborough for what he has actually effected, but we must not lose sight of the 'mission of humanity' in which he was professedly engaged, nor the fact that this mission was replaced by one of a totally different character, strengthening as this circumstance does the conviction, which is gaining ground in the public mind, that we have been deluded in expending large sums of money in sending out relief expeditions, which were chiefly employed in exploring available country for the benefit of the government and people of Queensland. The cost and the empty honour have been ours, but theirs has been the substantial gain."—*Melbourne Argus*, quoted by the *Australian and New Zealand Gazette*, October 4, 1862.

With every desire to do justice to the ability with which Mr. Landsborough conducted his expedition, and to the valuable track and valuable lands which he opened up, no one, I think, can read his report of his journey without feeling that there is much truth in the remarks of the *Argus*.

CHAPTER XIV.

MR. FREDERICK WALKER'S EXPEDITION IN QUEST OF BURKE AND WILLS.

Mr. Walker celebrated in Queensland for explorations attended by blacks.—His prompt attention to the calls on him to go in quest of the missing explorers.—Started from Dutton's Station on the Dawson, September 7th, 1861.—By the 16th reached the Nogoa.—Went north to the Poma.—Crossed the Ranges by his own, Walker's Pass.—Began to mark trees where the new country commenced.—Crossed at the Barcoo on the 27th.—October 15th, found a tree marked by Gregory.—Found two trees marked by Leichhardt.—Went north-west for the Alice.—Saw tracks of horses, which they thought Leichhardt's.—Advanced over ranges to the Thomson.—Saw other traces of Leichhardt.—Remarks of Patrick, the native, on a vast view from Mount Macalister.—Head waters of the Barkly.—Camlaroy and Houghton Creeks.—Mounts Gilbeo and Castor and Pollux.—Basaltic country on the Barkly, with good grazing land.—Struck a tributary of the Flinders, the Norman.—Numerous rivers and creeks, chiefly dry.—A fight with the natives.—Their horses scarcely able to travel.—Blacks say water all the way now.—They must stick to the river.—The junction of the Norman and Flinders.—Traces of Burke and Wills.—Second time traces of them on their return.—Walker zealous to get supplies from the steamer, and follow these traces.—Leaves of a memorandum book.—Morning Inlet.—Another fight with the natives.—Other natives tell them of whites on the Albert River.—Pushed over the box flats.—Saw a tree marked V, and a broad arrow.—Blacks try to cut them off from the Albert.—See a tree marked "Dig," and find a paper in a bottle directing them to the Victoria.—Arrived at the vessel in a storm of rain.—The journey from Rockhampton thus made in three months and twelve days.—Returns to track Burke and Wills.—Lost them on the flooded flats of the Flinders.—Burke's last camp.—Believes Burke gone towards Queensland.—Follows along the Norman.—Recovers a horse.—Jardine Creek.—Mount Barry.—Mounts Pylades and Orestes.—Mount Picken.—Numerous flooded creeks.—Very mountainous region.—On the Gilbert.—Mounts Mica and Granite.—The Cordilleras or dividing range.—The Lynd.—All boots worn out and horses lamed by the sharp slates.—Enormous quartz reefs.—Quartz Creek.—The Yananoa.—The Clarke.—The Burdekin and a large tributary.—A very bad grass.—Halt on account of the knocked-up horses.—A light party goes on to seek provisions.—A bad country.—Reach the station of Messrs. Wood and Robinson.—Reach Rockhampton June 4, having done the journey from the Gulf in five months and two weeks.—Great promptness and merit of Mr. Walker.

FROM a letter of Governor Barkly, of Victoria, to Governor Bowen, of Queensland, dated July the 19th, 1861, we learn that through Captain Mayne, of Sydney, the Victoria Government had arranged with Mr. Frederick Walker to proceed from Rockhampton, in Queensland, to the Albert River, in the Gulf of Carpentaria, with his party of mounted aborigines, to search the intervening country, and co-operate with the steamers on the Albert for the discovery of Burke's tracks. Mr. Walker was already celebrated as an explorer in the interior of Queensland, and for his friendly relation to the natives. Captain Mayne had ordered Mr. Jardine, of Rockhampton, to buy twenty-seven horses for the journey, and hoped to have all the necessary stores ready to forward by the steamer which left Sydney on the 25th of that month. The promptitude and alacrity with which Mr. Walker commenced his operations for this enterprise, is shown by his journal, Victoria Report, 1861—2, in which he gives a hasty sketch of his proceedings, on receiving the news of his appointment to this arduous office. He was somewhere up the country, but he says:—"I received Captain Mayne's letter on the 6th of August. I returned that day forty miles to Bawhinia Downs; stopped there the next day to arrange matters with my friend, Mr. Chas. B. Dutton; sent Patrick to collect my men, and gave directions to Jack Horsfeldt to cure the meat for the expedition. I then started for Rockhampton, but when I reached the Dawson, I could not get the horses within twenty yards of the banks. Patrick cut a canoe, and I crossed. Finding Mr. Govan at Rio, I exchanged horses with him. I rode his to Rockhampton, and he mine to the station. I hastened to get everything in readiness, but found that only twelve horses had been purchased. With the assistance of my friends, Mr. Hutchinson and Captain Hunter, I made up my lot in a few days, and started my whole party on Saturday, August the 25th."

He waited till the next day to get the English mail, and to see Captain Norman, who, he understood, would put in at Rockhampton; but hearing that he could not, he instantly started to join his expedition. "Some delay took place, owing to the heaviness of the ground, on my way up to Mr. Dutton's. We, however, managed to cross the Dawson safely, stopped two days at Mr. Dutton's, packing the meal, and preparing everything in proper order for the final start, which, to my great joy, took place on the 7th of September. The horses are not in as good order as I could wish: I must get them in proper trim before I can go a-head full speed. So, for the present, short stages and good camps are the order of the day."

In just a month he had received the commission up the country, had been down to Rockhampton, and back to Albinia Downs, the station of Messrs. Hope, Dennistoun and Rollestone; had his stores prepared, and was ready for a start. At this station he purchased the wanting number of horses, and made better arrangements; and from this point his journal may be said to begin. By the 16th he had reached the Nogoa, which he crossed on the 19th, and then, to avoid a dense brigalow scrub, he made a detour north to the Poma, and crossed the ranges by his own pass—Walker's Pass, which he went through, to the Neville. He began marking trees on Emerald Downs, on the Poma Creek, as that was new ground to him. On the 27th they crossed over to the Barcoo, and on the following three days pushed on down that river—the horses daily improving. In latitude 24° 34', longitude 146° 1', on the 5th of October, they found a tree marked by Gregory, XXII., and on the evening of the same day, one on the south bank, marked L., that is, Leichhardt. Gregory had seen a tree marked by Leichhardt seven miles below this. Leichhardt's track there was quite obliterated.

Quitting the Victoria, after having seen another tree marked by Leichhardt, they advanced in a north-west direction for the Alice, passing over downs and sandy land infested with the needle-grass. As they approached the Alice, they noticed very old tracks of horses going down the Patrick, which they believed to be Leichhardt's. They left the Victoria, or Barcoo, about thirty miles south of latitude 24°, and on the 146th parallel of longitude, and struck the Alice near latitude 23° on the 13th of October. Various creeks fell into it, and the country improved. The next day they passed over the downs, which form the watershoot betwixt the Alice and the

Thomson, and ten miles further came on a fine tributary of the Thomson, which they called the Coreena. On the 16th they were amongst mountains and high peaks, one of which they named Mount Macalister, and another Mount Horsfeld, where they were astonished to see the blacks having iron tomahawks, and one of them a broad axe, while the blacks near the settlements had only stone tomahawks. Both here and on the heads of the Thomson, the next day, they saw traces of Leichhardt's expedition. In one place they had camped on a fine lagoon. This was near the junction of latitude 22°, longitude 145°. Looking from the peak of Mount Macalister, the native, Patrick, though accustomed to the immense plains of the Edwards and Murrumbidgee, was struck with consternation, and remarked—"There is no t'other side this country!"

Mr. Walker now advanced through a hilly country to latitude 21°, in a N.W. course, when he fell in with the head waters of the river Barkly. On this track they saw great plains amongst the mountains, crossed fine downs, and several creeks, the Camlaroy and the Houghton in particular, and named Mounts Gilbee, Castor, and Pollux. Here they were obliged to leave a horse. The river Barkly appeared as large as the Dawson, and Mr. Walker had an idea that Eyre's Creek flowed into it—a notion, it is needless to say, incorrect, the Barkly being a tributary of the Flinders. The Barkly was running a nearly westerly course, through a rough, hilly, basaltic country, but the downs so well grassed, that Walker thought, if the country were not too hot, it would be as good sheep country as any in Australia.

They quitted the Barkly about ten miles beyond latitude 21°, and near the 144th degree of longitude, taking a more northerly course till Sunday, November 10th, when they came upon a river on the 143rd parallel of longitude, and about twenty miles south of latitude 19°, which they supposed to be the Flinders, but which turned out to be a large tributary of it, running between that river and the Gilbert, which they named the Norman. In this course they passed over downs and sandstone ranges, and several considerable rivers, the Macadam, Dutton, Stawell; the Woolgar, Despond, Patience, and Grateful Creeks. Many of these rivers and creeks, however, had no water in them, and the thermometer sometimes stood at upwards of 100° in the shade. They now began to fall in with blacks, armed with very long spears. On the 30th of October, so many were coming on them armed, that Mr. Walker deemed it necessary to fire on them, and he reports twelve killed, and numbers wounded.

Again following up this unknown river, they had to dig in its bed for water. At the Stawell and Woolgar they still were severely distressed for want of water. The horses began to give in, and one or two had to be left behind. On the 6th they were again attacked by blacks, and shot one of them. It is to be feared that the native troopers, as is but too characteristic of them, led Mr. Walker into these frays, so contrary to his usual manner with the blacks, by their over-readiness to attack their fellow blacks of other tribes. At length, on the 10th of November, they began to feel sure this river must be the Flinders, from the size of its channel, which had some considerable water holes in it. It was in fact, as observed, the Norman. The intense heat and shortness of feed and water so completely knocked up their horses, that they contemplated leaving seven or eight behind, and pushing on with the rest, lest the steamer should have left the Albert. Thermometer ranging from 103° to 105° in the shade. The ground was hard, and covered with spinifex. On the 20th other blacks appeared, but were peaceable. They told him that he would find water now all the way to the gulf; in the river, at present, however, only by places. That he must stick to the river, and not go west, as the country was bad. That this river joined another running more west, and they were correct, the Flinders. But Walker now began to imagine this unknown river, the Norman, a tributary of the Gilbert. They now began to get out of the heavy, sandy country of spinifex, melaleuca brush, and other rubbish. They still went on, wondering what river it was, and why, by their calculations, they did not fall in with Gregory's camps; neither could they make the country, now beginning to show large flooded flats, agree with his descriptions. On the 23rd of November, they came to a lagoon, which Mr. Walker imagined must be the place where Gregory camped on September 11th, 1845; and he adds, " My map is right, after all, and this, I suppose, is the river marked on the maps as Bynoe—what the devil is Bynoe?" Gregory never was on this river, however, for this was not the Gilbert.

On the 25th they really came upon the junction of the Norman and Flinders, the latter a beautiful large river, with high banks, and a delicious breeze blowing up it, and water in it, I suppose, for they got a good many ducks, which were very acceptable, their meat that very day being finished. And here they made a grand discovery, the trail of Burke and Wills. " At this camp, latitude 18° 7', were found by Jingle, the well-defined trail of either three or four camels, and one horse. They had come down the Flinders. This evening we supposed Burke had gone down on Leichhardt's track, intending probably to follow Gregory up the Gilbert. This night we had a tremendous thunder-storm, the first heavy rain we have had since starting from Bauhinia Downs, Mr. Dutton's station.

"Tuesday, 26th November.—This morning Jemmy Cargara, in collecting the horses, found Burke's trail returning across the plain, and going S.S.E. He has, therefore, I conclude, made back after having seen the Gulf of Carpentaria, towards the south again. It is to be hoped Mr. Howitt has pushed far enough to meet him with supplies. I hope to get rations from Captain Norman to enable me to run his trail now I have found it. I shall be dreadfully disappointed if the steamer has left, for I have barely enough to carry me back, and it would be madness to follow Burke south without an ample supply. Grateful Creek, and the three large creeks crossed upon leaving it, are evidently the heads of the Flinders, but the southerly bend which the main one took, caused me to cross it. The table-land is therefore the dividing range. I suppose that Burke followed up the Barkly and Stawell, and then cut across to the Flinders, not more than twenty or thirty miles to the west of my course."

Such were Walker's speculations, as they regarded Burke's course not very exact. On Wednesday the 27th they picked up two blank leaves, most likely out of Burke's memorandum book, from which he was in the habit of tearing leaves. The next day, after crossing some sandstone ranges, they saw vast plains extending north and west, and felt that they were those described by Captain Stokes. The following day, the 29th, they reached Morning Inlet. "Night very oppressive. Mosquitos triumphant." On December 1st they were on Leichhardt river, and, I regret to record, had another skirmish with the natives. These were stretching themselves across their way in the shape of a half moon. This movement being what the squatters term "stockyarding," from the way in which their men drive their wild cattle into the stock-yard, is regarded by them as peculiarly hostile, and intended to concentrate their showers of spears on the assailed party. There does not appear to have been any endeavour used to warn the blacks by signs to disperse, as I should have expected from Mr. Walker's general humanity to the natives. He ordered their left wing to be charged by his mounted followers, the result of which, he says, was, that "the circular line doubled up, the blacks turned and fled, but their centre and left wing suffered a heavy loss."

The next day they saw more blacks, and more signs of civilization, namely, a sailor's jumper, and an empty cognac bottle in a black's camp. The blacks, whose language was understood by one of the black troopers from Edward's River, informed them that they had seen a large party of whites on the Albert River. This was good news. The following day, December 3rd, they went twenty-two miles to the Albert River, crossing a succession of plains and flooded box flats. They now left six horses on the grassy plains, and pushed on without them. Their camp at this place was Gregory's camp of September 3rd. In following down the river next day Mr. Walker and Jingle, a native, found a tree marked with a chisel "Victoria, Dep., 8 miles," and four miles further down another marked V and a broad arrow beneath it. These were cheering signs, and their only anxiety now was lest the Victoria should have left. At this moment of great interest, Mr. Walker and Jingle found themselves in serious jeopardy. They saw the blacks attempting to cut them off from the river. Jingle's horse gave in, and he was obliged to fly on foot. At the same time he informed Mr. Walker that he had only two cartridges. However, by taking advantage of a belt of timber, and by alternately riding and walking, they eluded the enemy, and arrived safe in their camp.

They now found a marked tree of Gregory's, and another of Captain Norman's, marked "Dig," and under ground they found a bottle in which was a paper informing them that the camp was twelve miles lower down, on the left bank of the river. The note being dated November 29th, they felt pretty confident that they should find the Victoria still there; and the next day, December 7th, 1861, they reached the depôt in the midst of a pelting hurricane of rain, and had the pleasure of shaking hands with Captain Norman.

Thus had Frederick Walker made this journey from Rockhampton in three months and twelve days, having left Bawhinia Downs on the 7th of September. A more prompt, well pursued and successfully conducted expedition of the same extent, does not occur in the annals of Australian exploration. He had discovered the traces of Burke going southwards, that is, homewards, and having rested and reprovisioned his party, he again set out on the 20th to follow up those traces, having remained thirteen days, that is, from the 7th to that date.

Walker returned actively to the Flinders, and commenced retracing the tracks of Burke and Wills as they led southward, that is, homewards from the gulf. These tracks, which he had seen in making for the Victoria steamer on the Albert, he now followed down to his 9th camp; but here he lost them on the splendidly grassy plains, for the rains had not only flooded the Flinders but soaked the great plains along its course, and the sun had brought out such a growth of new grass as completely obliterated all further traces of the route taken by Burke. Walker's chart shows the Flinders River from its mouth to a point some fifteen or twenty minutes south of the 19th parallel of latitude. It presents a succession of low sandstone ranges, alternating with salt lagoons and creeks in about latitude 18°, as far west as the Leichhardt River, or to the west of the 146th degree of longitude. It places Burke's last camp, 119, on the Flinders, considerably to the north of the 18th degree of latitude, and shows his return route, as traced by the blacks, along the banks of the river, over fine plains, to a point considerably south of the 19th parallel, and, as observed, as far as Walker's 9th camp. These plains appear subject to much inundation, and hence the failure of further trace of the track; but, from what he had observed, Walker felt now convinced that Burke had struck off eastward towards Queensland, and he determined to follow in that direction, anxiously scrutinizing the country for fresh indications of the travellers.

Near this place, he must have crossed the future track of McKinlay. He appears to have followed the river which he called the Norman, and which will, no doubt, prove to be a branch of the Flinders. Here he fell into his former outward-going track, and marked on a tree, under his former date of November the 16th, 1861, January the 26th, 1862. He congratulated himself on having escaped out of the flooded box flats of the Flinders, the Norman being there bank full.

On the 29th of January, they came upon a horse, which they had been obliged to leave as they went out;

and the next day they recovered two more. On the 1st of February, despairing of finding the tracks of Burke on this course, Walker quitted it at his 36th camp, marking a tree with the dates of his first and second visits to the place, and then took a direction 33° east of north. They soon came upon a creek much larger than the Norman, with a bed 100 yards in width, and a running stream of half that breadth. He imagined it to be Gregory's Creek of the 13th and 14th of September, but named it the Jardine. From the sandstone ridges which they crossed, they could see the Gilbert River Ranges and the table-land at the head of the Flinders. They continued to pass over hilly country with rocks of porphyry, or basalt, and fine valleys, with running streams, till February the 5th, when Mr. Walker took his bearings as follows:—"A very high table-land, the northern end of which bore by compass 15° E. of N., he called Mount Barry, after Sir Redmond Barry, of Victoria. Two remarkable peaks, one bearing 52° E. of N., Mount Orestes, the other bearing 55° E. of N., Mount Pylades. A queer looking range, which we accordingly named Mount Queer, bore 65° E. of N. A range in the middle of the valley, 35° E. of N., and a remarkable peak in the distance, Mount Picken, after an old friend, Captain Picken."

The straying of their horses and heavy rain detained them some days in this place, and the creeks began to run on all sides of them. They imagined the main stream the Carin of Leichhardt. Passing Mount Omer on the 10th of February, they found themselves at the back of Mount Orestes, and were compelled by a wall of rock to ascend higher. They soon found themselves on the summit of Mount Barry, over a series of terraces of red rock, and saw the valley of what they thought the Carin stretching far to the W.N.W., and as far as they could judge, a good pastoral country. At an immense distance E. of S., were very high mountains, from which they supposed the main head of the Flinders came.

From hence they proceeded about N. of E., and

through rocky country, with deep ravines and running waters. The rocks appeared to be of sandstone, and in the valley were detached masses of most fantastic shapes. Amidst this country lay green ridges and rocks of basalt. They imagined themselves on the Gilbert, according to Gregory's description. As Mr. Walker seemed to be making a hasty progress home, and took few observations of latitude or longitude, it is difficult to ascertain exactly his position at many points of his journey, and he felt a good deal of uncertainty himself, though always confident of the main direction of his course. On the 14th of February, he felt satisfied that he was on the Gilbert of Gregory. His way lay through a country of slate, porphyry, and granite, with many quartz reefs. He named a hill Mount Mica, and another Mount Granite, from the predominant rock. The slate so much injured the feet of his horses that he was obliged to make short journeys.

On the 16th of February, Mr. Walker considered that they were in the great dividing granite range, called the Cordillera by the Rev. W. B. Clarke, which terminates at Cape York. A valley to the north he believed to be the valley of the Lynd. The horses were now all completely lamed, and the boots of the party were worn out; the leader himself had only an old pair given him by Captain Norman. The next day they were obliged to abandon ten horses: they could travel no further.

Steering S. of E., they came on the 20th of February on the river which they believed to be the Lynd of Gregory, but which bade fair to join the Burdekin. Here they got two good observations, and found themselves in $18°\ 57'$, or $1\frac{3}{4}°$ above the 19th parallel. As they neared the valley of the Burdekin in $1\frac{3}{4}°$, they reached a tributary of the Copperfield, which the leader called the Quartz, on account of the enormous reefs of quartz. Mr. Walker thought the valley to the north, a basalt country, must be a good sheep country, if the climate proved suitable. They here procured three ducks, the only fresh meat they had had, except two opossums, since they left camp 24. The men, however, had continued healthy, having had the use of dried apples; but now one of them showed symptoms of scurvy. Their course lay still over a succession of ridges, all of which are laid down on Mr. Walker's map. The rain fell in torrents. They went now E.S.E. amongst what appeared the extinct craters of volcanoes, with deep basins of water, and crumbling granite with mica, and alternate layers of granite and ashes, covered by the black soil of the plains.

On the 24th of February, they reached a river which his blacks called Yananoa; its course N.E. After being delayed by the torrents of rain, the lameness of their few remaining horses, and their own shoeless condition, passing still over rocky ranges and boggy vallies, they came on the Clarke, and, on the 8th of March, reached the Burdekin. On the 10th, a river came from S.W. as large as the Burdekin, which they had some trouble in crossing, the horses stumbling over the basalt and porphyry rocks. Soon after they reached a small river full of slate, and, therefore, named it the Slate River, where they made their 47th camp. On the other side of the river rose Mount Welcome, where they observed some good little plains. "But on the Burdekin," observes Walker, "I noticed a very bad description of grass growing wherever the slate is. It reached a height of from six to nine feet, and is surmounted by the worst grass-seed I have ever seen. The pain caused by a wound from this grass-seed is exactly like that from the bite of a soldier ant."

Their course was exceedingly rough down the Burdekin, over granite, porphyry and slate rocks, shoeless, their horses all but incapable of moving, from their worn-down hoofs, and their provisions exhausted, except a few dried apples, and some damaged flour, which they had to sift through a veil in order to make it at all tolerable. The scurvy in Macalister still only kept down by the dried apples and native cucumbers, which, fortunately, were there abundant. Course E.S.E. Their sugar was nearly out; their peas, which they had roasted for coffee, were finished, and yet they were compelled to halt amongst the rocky cliffs which shut in the river, because the horses were completely done up. It was, therefore, necessary to make a strenuous effort, and Mr. Walker sent on part of his people, with seven of the best horses, to seek provisions wherever they could find them. He himself moved on after them as well as he could. They now caught plenty of fish, and shot a young emu. They crossed a river on the 24th, which they believed to be the Fanning. The trees were marked B., which they supposed meant Blacks, and numbers of these were around them. They found a tree marked by Dalrymple, and saw a range which they deemed Roley's Range, in a direct eastern course for Port Denison. The country still continued bad, and Mr. Walker felt persuaded that any persons settling in it would suffer great losses in sheep. On the 4th of April they overtook Macalister, who reported that they were only four miles from Strathalbyn, the station of Messrs. Wood and Robinson on the Burdekin. There all their troubles ended. Mr. Walker proceeded to Port Denison for supplies, that he might send a number of his people back to collect the horses, twenty in number, which they had been obliged to abandon. This done, he reached Rockhampton on the 5th of June, having performed the journey from the Gulf of Carpentaria in about five months and two weeks.

The celerity, ability, and unassuming modesty with which this arduous journey from the coast of Queensland to the Gulf of Carpentaria, and back again, in about nine months, with loss only of a few horses, confer the highest credit on Mr. Frederick Walker and his band, chiefly of natives. He performed his mission with a singleness of purpose most praiseworthy. No temptation to seek new pastoral lands diverted him from the anxious search for the missing explorers. Perhaps none of the distinguished body of explorers of this period did their work more ably; certainly none received less commendation for it. If we may judge by his conduct, he appears to possess less worldly ambition than sense of duty. He seems to have sought no applause, no presentations of plate or geographic medals; hastened to no capitals, imperial or colonial, to wear his laurels, but having discharged his mission with great promptness and mastership, he retired to his private duties with the same unostentatious quietness which he had displayed in his public ones. At least, knowing nothing of Mr. Walker but what appears connected with his expedition, this is the impression which it has left with myself.

CHAPTER XV.

EXPEDITIONS OF DISCOVERY IN SOUTH AUSTRALIA IN 1856—7—8, and 9.

Renewed spirit of discovery in South Australia.—The causes.—Mr. Babbage sent to examine the country, Tanunda and Angaston, etc.—Collected 300 geologic specimens.—Captain Cadell reports gold in Kangaroo Island.—Tolmer's like report.—Tolmer despatched to find it.—Mr. Babbage sent to search for gold farther north.—The Adelaide Philosophical Society recommends exploration N.W.—Mr. Babbage discovers Blanche-Water. etc.
MR. BABBAGE'S THIRD TRIP, NOW IN QUEST OF LAND.—Mr. Babbage's objects.—His party and equipment.—Set out in February, 1857.—Difficulties from drought.—Dromedaries recommended.—Discovers the remains of Coulthard. —Coulthard, Scott, and Brooks, land-hunters.—Coulthard lost.—Generous offer of Mr. Swinden for his discovery.—Mr. Babbage finds his remains.—Affecting account of his death.—Babbage proceeds westward by Lake Gairdner and other salt lakes.—Lakes Hart and Younghusband.—Returns to Elizabeth Creek. —Dissatisfaction in Adelaide at Mr. Babbage's progress.—Mr. C. Gregory sent to assist him.—Finds Mr. Babbage absent, sends back part of his horses and drays, and goes to seek him.—Mr. Babbage's resentment.—Major Warburton sent to supersede him.—The Major finds Mr. Babbage gone north-west.—Overtakes him, and turns him back.—The Major returns himself, without further progress.—Mr. Babbage's real services.
EXPEDITION OF MR. HACK FROM STREAKY BAY. ALSO OF MESSRS. MILLER AND DUTTON from the same point.—Mr. Hack sent to examine the country north and east of Streaky Bay.—His explorations amongst the salt lakes.—Indifferent country.—Goes by the Gawler Ranges and Baxter's Range to the head of Spencer's Gulf.—Messrs. Miller and Dutton proceed N.W. from Streaky Bay into the interior.—Return for want of water.

FROM the year 1856 a very active spirit of exploration seized on the public of South Australia. In this year Augustus Gregory was making the great Australian expedition ; in Western Australia the spirit of exploration was actively afloat, and South Australia could not lag behind. The gold discoveries of the other colonies, especially of the bordering one, Victoria, made it most important that South Australia should have all possible inducements for keeping her working population at home. It was equally desirable to extend the space over which the squatters could spread their flocks and herds, and speculative enterprise was turning in that direction ; but the first attempt was to open up a gold and a coal field.

For this purpose Mr. Benjamin Herschell Babbage, the geologist of the colony, was sent out, in consequence of a memorial to the Governor, signed by nearly the whole of the commercial houses in Adelaide. Mr. Babbage examined the country to some distance north and east of Adelaide, about Tanunda and Angaston, the Kaiser Stuhl and Jacob's Creek, the Gawler river, and the basin of the North Rhine, Evan Dale, Flaxman's Valley, the Barossa Range, Mount Crawford, etc., returning by the South Rhine and Mount Torrens to Adelaide. In this tour Mr. Babbage collected 300 specimens of stones generally found in gold districts, felspar, trap, basalt, soapstone, conglomerates, horneblende, opal, chalcedony, etc., without coming on the gold itself.

In August of the same year Captain Cadell, the great navigator of Australian rivers, reported to the Secretary of the Gold Searching Committee, that while on a visit to Kangaroo Island, a native woman named Betsy, who had lived on the island thirty years, on being shown some nuggets from the diggings, said that when her son Nat, then a sailor in England, was a piccaninny, she had "seen plenty like it that yellow-fellow tone," and that she and another lubra had beat them out, or "made them long," as she expressed it. Captain Cadell recommended that the district, the Stringy-bark Ranges west of Cape Willoughby, should be searched, and that in case it turned out a gold-field, Betsy and himself should share the reward.

Another claimant, however, quickly appeared for this same district, Mr. Alexander Tolmer, who stated that being sent by Governor Grey, in 1844, to Kangaroo Island to capture a desperate gang of bushrangers, he had seen quartz with yellow metal imbedded in it, which he was now convinced was gold. The place where he had seen it was about twenty miles S.S.W. from Western River. The Gold Committee agreed to send out Mr. Tolmer with a party to examine the spots where both he and the lubra, Betsy, had reported gold.

In the mean time Mr. Babbage, assisted by Mr. Bonney, was directed to return and prosecute the search for gold farther north. They were to have the assistance of three practical miners, and all necessary apparatus and supplies. They were to proceed to Mount Remarkable, and passing beyond the head of Spencer's Gulf, to Mount Arden and Mount Serle. From Mount Serle they were to return home by Black Rock, following a line to the eastward of the outward journey.

The committee of the Adelaide Philosophical Society also recommended an expedition into the north-west interior. That it should be provisioned for six months, be conveyed to Fowler's Bay, and recommended to proceed north-west as far as the north-west angle of the province, diverging east and west as they went, so as to ascertain the general character of the country. They were then, if possible, to make their way by a south-easterly course to the head of Spencer's Gulf. For this purpose they estimated that a grant of £3000 would be sufficient, and they recommended that it should be made.

But little discovery of gold was made by Mr. Babbage in his second journey, and Mr. Bonney had soon abandoned the search. As Mr. Babbage pushed on into the neighbourhood of Mounts Remarkable, Serle, and Hopeless, the indications of gold did not improve. Mr. Babbage, though discovering the much desired trap rock, saw nothing to warrant the conclusion that he had traversed an auriferous country. But if he failed to discover gold, he discovered what to the stock-holder and sheep farmer was still more valuable, namely, water. In the early part of October, 1856, when about twenty miles north of Mount Serle, he struck upon a large creek, which he followed for about sixty miles. In connection with this creek were large lagoons, or deposits of fresh water, some of them 200 yards in length, and 100 in breadth. One of them was fully a mile long. On those sheets of water, large quantities of water-fowls of various kinds were seen, plainly evincing their permanent character. Mr. Babbage named the creek Macdonnell Creek; one of the finest pools St. Mary's Pool, and the long reach of water he designated Blanchewater. In connection with this discovery was that of a much finer race of blacks than had hitherto been met with, affording promise of a better country beyond. Speedy applications were made to the government for the land including the creek and the fresh water reaches.

MR. BABBAGE'S THIRD TRIP; NOW IN QUEST OF LAND.

In 1857, Mr. Babbage's proposal, or rather that of the Adelaide Philosophical Society to the Crown Lands Department of South Australia, to make an expedition to explore the country about Lake Torrens, was accepted. He proposed to take out only a light party, and form a depôt in the neighbourhood of Mount Nor'-West. Thence he meant to examine the country thoroughly along the inner margin of Lake Torrens, from the 135th to the 140th parallel of longitude. In this, as yet unvisited district, he expected to find sheets of permanent water, more extensive even than Blanchewater on the course of the Frome, and prior to its junction with the lake. He proposed to obviate one of the difficulties of former explorers, by carrying a small still with him, so as to procure fresh water from water salt or brackish. Having made his way round the interior of Horse-shoe Bend to a point on the eastern arm in the same parallel of latitude, on his starting-point on the western arm, he hoped to cross the lake at the point at which he formerly indicated the probability of finding a sound bottom. The practicability of this passage was, however, before Mr. Babbage's arrival, proved by Mr. Ball, who was engaged by Mr. Jacob as surveyor in the north, crossing the lake twice in that part, and proceeding towards the northern portion of the Barrier Range and to the Grey Range, through a scrubby country without water, afterwards crossed by Mr. A. C. Gregory.

The South Australian papers of February 11, reported

Mr. Babbage as ready to start. He was taking with him nine companions, sixteen horses, about 150 sheep, and provisions for eighteen months, exclusive of a ton of flour to be stored for him, in case of need, at Port Augusta. His party consisted of himself, as leader; Mr. W. G. Harris, surveyor and second in command; Mr. T. Warriner, as general assistant; Mr. Herrgolt, botanist; J. Jones, teamster and saddler; S. Thompson, teamster and wheelwright; H. Kornoll, teamster; G. Nason, teamster; H. Lewis, cook and wheelwright; J. Stringer, shepherd. They had one heavy and two spring drays, and a tank cart. Each member, it was finally determined, should carry with him a small still which would distil a quart of water in an hour. Very simple boring apparatus was also provided to seek for water below the surface, where it was supposed likely that it might be found.

The Adelaide papers of March 11, reported Mr. Babbage on his way, but waiting at Port Augusta for reinforcements. By despatches from him to the 30th of April, it appeared that he had encountered much difficulty and delay from drought, and this had led to much discussion in Adelaide on the advantage of employing dromedaries on expeditions into the interior, as recommended by Mr. Horrocks, who said he had travelled with one from Gawler Town to Penwortham, fifty-three miles in a single day, and that stony ground did not appear to distress him. That in the hottest weather when eating only dry straw, he required only to drink once in nine days; that when he could get the oak, honey-suckle, or green food, he never drank at all. That as a beast of burden he was able to carry eight hundred weight, but on a journey his load was only half that amount, and with that load he was able to travel twenty days without water, through a country destitute of vegetation. Like the camel, the horse was averse to him, but grew reconciled by custom. The drawback to the dromedary was, that he was treacherous, and required muzzling. Mr. Horrocks, from his own experience, contended that a party of fifteen men with ten dromedaries, might travel from Port Augusta to Port Essington in two months at any period of the year and examine the country for 100 miles on both sides of the line of march.

The main incident of Mr. Babbage's progress up to April 30th, was his advancing as fast as possible towards Swinden's country. He had made a trip on foot with Jones, in search of the remains of the unfortunate Coulthard, and also for the purpose of finding an easy dray route towards Swinden's country. This Mr. Coulthard was one of a squatter projecting party. A correspondent of the *Adelaide Observer*, May 11th, 1853, gave this account of his loss. "At or about the beginning of March, Mr. Salter, Mr. Sleep, and myself, had just returned from Pernatty to Mr. Sleep's station, where we found Messrs. Coulthard, Scott, and Brooks, awaiting our return, with the intention of going in that direction themselves. We most earnestly persuaded them not to venture on the journey at that time of the year, and assured them that it was impossible to travel the country, from want of water. We determined not to give the least encouragement, and did our utmost to dissuade them from the undertaking. We had just returned from a distance of about 100 miles from the north-west, and but for the occurrence of a thunder storm, our horses must have died from want of water. At this time, Mr. Swinden was away at Mount Deception, about 400 miles northward of Sleep's Station. On his return, Messrs. Brooks and Scott had gone back to the station with the intelligence of the loss of their travelling companion, Mr. Coulthard. Mr. Swinden, hearing this, used his utmost endeavour to induce the men who were encamped at the station at that time, to go in search of Mr. Coulthard, and even promised Mr. M. Campbell, in my hearing, who was acquainted with the country, 100 guineas if he succeeded in finding the body, or 200 in the event of finding Mr. Coulthard alive. He also promised to pay any losses the party might sustain by the death of their bullocks, or otherwise. Mr. Campbell and his party accordingly started on the search, but were obliged to return, from want of water for the cattle. At the commencement of this week, Mr. Campbell again started from Mount Remarkable, with the intention of attempting the journey from Sleep's Station on foot, with the determination of ascertaining the fate of the unfortunate Coulthard at any cost, before his return."

Though Pernatty lies only on the western side of the lower extremity of Lake Torrens, yet all these and other attempts proved useless, in endeavouring to reach it. Three natives who were now sent out professed to have found the body of his horse, but not Coulthard's own remains.

Mr. Babbage's pedestrian attempt with Jones occupied eleven days, and resulted in no trace of the missing man. His companions represented him as much weakened when he parted from them in search of water, and all their endeavours to discover him whilst he might be alive, had been utterly vain. Mr. Babbage, however, persevered in his endeavours, and by a despatch from him, dated June 16th, it was announced that he had discovered the remains of Coulthard under very affecting circumstances. The body of the unfortunate man lay under a scrub bush, and at a short destance from him his canteen and other bush accoutrements. Upon one side of that canteen, offering a convex surface of tin of about twelve inches long and ten inches deep, was scratched with a nail, or some other rough pointed instrument, the following inscription:—" I never reached water. I do not know how long it is since it is that I left Scott and Brooks, but I think it Monday bleeding Pomp to lieve of his blood I took his black horse to look for water and the last thing I can remember is puling the saddle off him and letting him go until now is not good. I am not th shure how long it may be wether 2 or 3 days I do not know. My Tung is stiking to my mouth & I see what I have rote I know it is this is the last time I may have of expressing feeling alive & the feeling exce   is lost for want of water My ey Dazels My tong burn   I can see no more God help."

The *Adelaide Register* observes of this affecting document:—" As we traced off this inscription, we could plainly see the growing feebleness of the unhappy writer. The early words are firmly and clearly marked, but as the writer advanced, his strokes became less and less distinct, the form of his letters less perfect, his hand wanders from the direction of the writing, and some of his words are almost illegible. For instance, the space between the words 'feeling' and 'for want of water' is covered with vague scratches, some of which it is impossible to form into words, and the filling up of the sentence which we have given, 'exce   is lost,' is rather an approximation to than a faithful version of the original. The word 'burn' is not finished, for the vital powers were evidently exhausted. A long blank interval follows. Then the dying man rallies for a moment, and applies himself to his sad task, and in larger characters, and with more vigorous expression, come the words, 'I can s,' but the rest of the sentence, 'ee no more,' is small and faint, and extends far beyond the ridge at the junction of the metal which had bounded the previous lines. The prayer for help with which this most touching relic closes, is placed at the beginning of the subsequent line, and terminates all that can be deciphered of the inscription. Once more, however, the desire to communicate some last thought seems to have seized the blinded and bewildered writer, and led him to apply his instrument again to the surface on which he had written. But his hand failed him, and a few faint and incoherent scratches are all that appear to indicate his unaccomplished desire. To the Omniscient alone the last thought of poor Coulthard is known."

Of the many who have perished in the arid wildernesses of Australia, few have left us a memorandum of their dying thoughts, their failing life. Burke and Wills are amongst the few besides Coulthard who have done it. Such efforts are amongst the most pathetic records in the whole wide history of human suffering. In this sad tracing we see not only the failing of the strength, but of the memory; the mind falls into confusion, and even the power to spell drops like that of recording the flight of time.

Further letters from Mr. Babbage down to July 27, detail his excursion westward into the neighbourhood of Lake Gairdner, and a whole group of salt lakes. It must be confessed that he spared no pains in traversing this part of the country, and endeavouring to determine the boundaries of these lakes. In his labyrinthine course, which may be traced on the maps, he visited the whole eastern shore of Lake Gairdner, Lake Finnis, Lake Blythe, Lake Macfarlane, traversing both the eastern and western shores of the Island Lagoon, showing the connection of the Island Lagoon, or Great Salt Lake as he appears to call it, with Red Lake, and, as he believed, with Lake Gairdner. Five miles to the north-west of Island Lagoon, he went round and named Lake Hart, which he computed to cover 120 square miles of country, whilst Island Lagoon covered 480 square miles. An arm from Lake Hart, he states, running to the west, nearly joins Lake Hanson, a third lake of much smaller dimensions. Ten miles further on to the north-west is Lake Younghusband, a singularly shaped lake, covering about 50 square miles, having many bays and promontories, especially on the northern side. To the north of Lake Younghusband is a small lake marked on the plan as Lake Reynolds, distinguished for the beauty of its blue waters, surrounded by wooded sandhills running close down to the shore. The stony table-land in which Swinden's country is situated, extends to the north-west, along the northern shores of this chain of lakes, forming bluffs and headlands, which project out into the Great Salt Lake, Lakes Hart and Hanson. The northern shore of Lake Younghusband is about five miles S.S.W. of the edge of the stony land, and between them is another small lake, apparently of about the same size as Lake Reynolds.

All these lakes were salt, and affected by mirage, which gave a flattering but delusive appearance of cliffs and picturesque scenery. The eastern shores were low, the western formed of lofty sand hills, and marl cliffs covered by scrub. From the Great Salt Lake to Lake Younghusband they saw few blacks; on the northern shores of Younghusband they saw numerous signs of them. There were few creeks anywhere, and where there was land at all promising, there was a total want of water. He had only advanced northwards as far as latitude 30° 45′, and westward to longitude 135° 41′. At the time of his writing he was camped on the Elizabeth Creek, on the western side of Lake Torrens, which was his advanced camp.

His progress had, meantime, created much dissatisfaction at Adelaide, and Mr. Charles Gregory, who had arrived there in his brother's expedition from Moreton Bay in search of traces of Leichhardt, was sent to reinforce him with additional pack-horses, and with instructions to send back the useless drays, and the horses belonging to them, and to assist Mr. Babbage in making a progress northward into the unknown country. On arriving at the advanced camp, Mr. Gregory found Mr. Babbage absent, and on his own responsibility sent off the surplus horses, according to his instructions, retaining only what he deemed sufficient. Then, being alarmed for Mr. Babbage's safety, who had been absent far longer than he had intended, Mr. Gregory set of in search of him, instead of pushing forward, as he otherwise intended, to look for some permanent water to camp the party for the summer.

But Mr. Babbage was in no danger. In his despatch of July 27, he had announced that in a few days he was about to start with Warriner and a pack-horse to follow down the eastern shore of the Great Salt Lake, until he reached Lake Gairdner, and thence across the scrub by Lake Dutton to Beda. In pursuance of this design he had ultimately returned southward to his original starting place at Port Augusta, on Spencer's Gulf. Thus he heard of the return of the surplus horses, and men despatched by Mr. Gregory, and resenting this interference with his authority, he ordered the men to go back, which they refused to do, and he had them imprisoned in the lock-up at Mount Remarkable, and wrote to Adelaide, complaining of the measures taken by Mr. Gregory in his absence. The commissioner of Crown Lands, however, forwarded a very severe despatch to Mr. Babbage, blaming him strongly for wasting a month rambling about over country already explored, reminding him that though his expedition had already cost nearly £5000, he had not penetrated more than 100 miles beyond the settled district, and stating that he would have been immediately recalled, but for the hope that he would advance northwards promptly.

The disappointment of the Adelaide public arose from the desire which had been felt that Mr. Babbage should push into the north-west districts, and send news of good grazing lands there, whilst Mr. Babbage himself had entertained an idea that the west, which Messrs. Hack and Harris had rather made known than thoroughly explored, required further research, and that this might open up available grazing country as well. He had been doing this in a very systematic and scientific manner, and certainly gave a far more definite knowledge of the salt lake country than was before possessed. Unfortunately for him, it was not precisely the service which the public was just then anxiously expecting from him. Had he found a broad tract of good country, that would have healed all sores, but again, unfortunately for him, the country did not prove such; and the upshot of the matter was a reprimand for what every one now must admit to have been real service to the geography of the colony, and the sending out of Major Warburton to supersede him, and to proceed northward, Mr. Stuart and Forster having now reported that there was permanent water with fish in it to the north of Mr. Babbage's farthest point.

BABBAGE AND WARBURTON.

Before following Major Warburton on his route, it is simple justice to Mr. Babbage to say that even his opponents admitted that his proceedings were warranted, and as he afterwards contended, demanded by his instructions. The expedition was fitted out for eighteen months, and the instructions were to survey and map the further portion of the known territories before penetrating into the unknown. Six months had only elapsed, and could scarcely be said to be too much for the accomplishment of this object in the effective manner in which Mr. Babbage was performing it.

In Major Warburton's party, Mr. Charles Gregory, already up the country, was named second in command. He was also accompanied by Sergeant-major Hall and another police trooper, as well as by Baker, one of Babbage's men, who had returned to Adelaide shortly before with Mr. Harris. As many of Mr. Babbage's party as, on their overtaking him, were willing to go on with them, were to be attached to the expedition. Major Warburton lost no time in embarking on board the Mariner for Port Augusta, which he reached on the 29th of September, 1858, and the very next day he met Mr. Charles Gregory, returning to Adelaide in company with Phibbs, one of the New South Wales party. They turned back with the Major for the camp on the Elizabeth, which they reached on the 3rd of October.

The rumour of his probable recall had, however, reached Mr. Babbage, at the Elizabeth, through some stray newspaper; and acting on the last injunction of the Crown Lands Commissioner, he had instantly made up a light party of four men, eleven horses, and provisions for three months, and had been gone northwards eight days when the Major arrived at his camp. The very same day Major Warburton sent off Mr. Gregory and a man in pursuit of Mr. Babbage, with his recall in Mr. Gregory's pocket.

Having despatched his messenger after Mr. Babbage,

the Major found himself greatly embarrassed by the large amount of stores in the camp, and proposed to sell them —but to whom? Not finding customers in that wilderness, he determined first to pursue after Mr. Babbage with a light party, and three months' provisions; then he re-determined not to follow him, as the water was fast drying up, and Mr. Babbage had taken all the water bags with him. When three weeks had passed and no tidings of Mr. Babbage, the Major concluded, after all, to go in search of him, having stored 300 gallons of water at Yeltarowie. He hoped to overtake Mr. Babbage in three weeks, and bring him back. In fact, his great idea appeared the stopping Mr. Babbage now actively on the track of exploration, not that of exploration himself. He, in fact, declared the country unfit for stocking, and further exploration useless. At length the Major came up with Mr. Babbage, who had reached about the 292nd parallel of latitude. He had entered on Stuart's new country, and found it as he represented it. He was on the western shore of Lake Gregory, and north of Lake Bowman. He had found an abundance of springs of fresh water, one of them a hot spring, pouring out 170,000 gallons daily. He was busy mapping the country, and taking valuable geological notes, when the Major came up with him and ordered him home. It was a proceeding more natural to an officer of police, than to an explorer. The country was now promising to reward the search; there was every facility for proceeding; grass and water in abundance, and stores in such quantities as to embarrass the Major: but he would neither allow Mr. Babbage to proceed, nor proceed himself! And that on the most extraordinary plea, that "there was already as much country discovered as could be stocked in twelve months."

The sending of Major Warburton after Mr. Babbage, when this gentleman had received stringent orders from the Crown Lands Commissioners to press rapidly northward, and when he was actually obeying this order, must be regarded as more hasty than prudent, or just to

Mr. Babbage, and seems to have produced a check in the enterprise of a most disastrous character: a stop to discovery when the expedition had arrived at the very portals of it, and an enormous waste of supplies which might have conducted a well regulated expedition and a carefully adventurous leader to the most advantageous results. To myself, calmly contemplating these proceedings at this distance of time and place, Mr. Babbage seems to have been a zealous and painstaking officer, desirous to do his duty in the best manner; and though he might perhaps have left his detour westward till he had made further progress northward, yet he was ready to receive a fresh prompting from head quarters, and had that been allowed to operate without further interference, there is every presumption that the whole expedition would have been a very satisfactory one. As it was, Mr. Babbage, though literally *arrested* in the course of his legitimate duties, rendered great services to the geography of the colony.

Major Warburton, however, did not return from his Babbage hunt without having acquired some useful ideas regarding explorations. In 1859, he addressed a letter to the South Australian Government suggesting an economical mode of exploring the interior by means of the police. He recommended that an expedition should set out from Mount Serle to cross the continent to the Victoria River, or the Gulf of Carpentaria. The former route, however, was at the very time in process of attempt by Stuart, and ended in his not reaching the Victoria, but the Adelaide. The latter has since been accomplished by McKinlay, and from other points by Burke and Wills, Landsborough and Walker.

MR. STEPHEN HACK'S EXPEDITION FROM STREAKY BAY. MESSRS. MILLAR AND DUTTON FROM THE SAME POINT.

Mr. Hack, in 1857, was sent out with an expedition equipped for six months, to start from Streaky Bay, and to examine the country north and east of that point.

By a letter received from him on the 29th of July, he was then at Kondoolea, in latitude 32° 30', himself, party, and horses all in good health. He had proceeded by Porla and Minera through the mallee scrub, west of Mount Sturt, and then struck northward to the west of the Salt Lakes. He had made no startling discoveries, but had passed over a considerable quantity of good pasture land, and found a tolerable supply of water.

From Kondoolea, Mr. Hack proceeded by Warna to Warrea, at the north point of the Salt Lake, through what he calls second-rate salt bush country, more or less mixed with grass and patches of forest oak. From Warrea, on the 3rd of August, he advanced to Moonaree, fifteen miles, through useless scrub. About Moonaree was some good grass country, and then scrub again to Mendea, lying between the Salt Lake and what Mr. Hack calls the Great Salt Lake, namely Lake Gairdner, where they came on Major Warburton's track. At Murnea, ten miles farther, they found a good rock water, and ascended a hill, whence to the north the whole scene was white with salt; and sixty degrees east of south, they saw a high range, but to the north of that range no high land could be seen. From thence to Kundery, at the southern point of Lake Gairdner, Mr. Hack pronounced the country first rate, salt bush mixed with grass. The natives told them there of large herds of wild cattle north of the lake.

From Kundery, Mr. Hack went southward in the scrub at the foot of the Gawler Ranges, and speaks of much good country about Koleymirrika, Pondanna, Kodondo, Puttamaring, with large permanent water towards Eureka Bluff and the Conical Hill. He heard from the natives of various lakes with wild fowl, and found the good country running nearly to Mount Sturt. From a permanent water called Muddera, Mr. Harris took a ride through the country round, finding good land, permanent water, and ranges of hills, one of which he called the Hill of the Plain. Leaving Kundery, he proceeded south to Mount Nott, thence eastward by Mount Ives to Freeling Range, finding good salt-bush country with patches of grass, with springs and rock waters. From Lynch's Creek, some miles north of Freeling's Range, they steered N.E., and again crossed Major Warburton's track, proceeding towards Lake Gairdner. From this point Mr. Hack proceeded to Rockwell Creek, near the S.E. quarter of Lake Gairdner, to Mount Separation, on to and through Baxter's Range to the head of Spencer's Gulf, and by Mount Remarkable to Adelaide. In this journey, Mr. Hack did not penetrate so far north as it was hoped that he would; but he found a considerable extent of available country. On his return to Adelaide, it was proposed that he should set out again to endeavour to penetrate northwards west of Lake Torrens, whilst Mr. Babbage proceeded to the N.E. of that lake.

Mr. Miller, the overseer of Mr. Price Maurice, who was out with Mr. Hack, on his return to Mr. Price's Station, had a strong conviction that, by deviating somewhat from the line of route Mr. Hack had pursued, he should find new and valuable grazing country. He united with Mr. Charles William Dutton; and these enterprising young men determined, without other help, to enter on a fresh search. Providing themselves with rations for a month, they started for Streaky Bay, and thence struck off for Belama Cappe, lying 100 miles along the coast. Thence they travelled in a N.W. direction for about twenty miles through dense scrub; thence N.N.W. by N. about thirty miles through good grazing land; thence N.E. for about twenty miles, through still good grazing land: thence E. about twenty miles to water, through grazing land not so good. At this point they were obliged to return through want of a native guide to point out water, as well as from the want of a commissariat to carry them further. These two adventurous young men were actually separated from each other for three days, whilst seeking water, and travelled more than 100 miles singly before they met again. What they saw, however, convinced them good country is to be found more westward than it had before been sought for.

The greater portion of what they saw was open, grassy plains, without timber, but with low brush in places, and salt bush on the flats mixed with abundant grass. Kangaroos in abundance were seen. The great want, however, would appear to be water, and before driving flocks or herds thither, the possibility of obtaining this is an indispensable requirement.

The expedition of Major Warburton and Mr. Davenport into the same part of the country as Mr. Hack, and which is referred to in the Major's narrative, took place immediately before Mr. Hack's in the same year. These gentlemen left Adelaide in May. Mr. Hack gave a description of Lake Gairdner, which he discovered in the course of his expedition, but the extent of which he had not the opportunity of exploring. Mr. Davenport traced this lake sixty miles farther.

CHAPTER XVI.

EXPLORING EXPEDITIONS IN SOUTH AUSTRALIA IN 1856, 57, AND 58, CONTINUED.

EXPEDITIONS OF MESSRS. GOYDER AND FREELING IN 1856-7-8.—Mr. Goyder sent to examine the country about Blanche Water, and make a trigonometric survey of it.—His marvellous report.—Great sensation in Adelaide.—The possessors of flocks and herds already on the way to this Goshen.—Those of Victoria on the same march.—Captain Freeling sent to ascertain the truth of these tidings.—Find all the results of mirage.—His report.—Close examination of Lake Torrens.—Its old character restored.—Mr. Swinden's discovery of available land west of Lake Torrens.
MAJOR WARBURTON'S EXPEDITION TO LAKE GAIRDNER WITH THE HON. S. DAVENPORT.—Proceed from Streaky Bay to the Gawler Ranges.—Thence to Lake Gairdner.—Theory of the country.—Low estimate of it.—Mr. Davenport's progress west.—Major Warburton's examination of the lakes.
MR. PARRY'S SURVEYING EXPEDITION NEAR LAKE TORRENS.—Reports all barren.
EXPEDITION OF GOVERNOR MCDONNELL TO LODDON SPRINGS.—His voyage up the Darling in 1859.

IN consequence of the reports of Mr. Babbage of some good country in the district about Blanche Water, Mr. Goyder, the deputy surveyor-general, was despatched in 1857 with a small party to make a trigonometrical survey of that neighbourhood. Mr. Goyder measured his base line, and penetrated to the southern bank of Lake Torrens, in about latitude 29°, or thirty miles N.E. of St. Mary's Pool, this being about the northern extent of Mr. Babbage's explorations. Mr. Goyder returned with tidings which put the whole of the colony into a trepidation of delightful surprise. He declared that, in those parts of the country where former travellers had discovered only arid deserts and salt lakes, he had found Lake Torrens to be a fresh water lake, and the country about it abounding with romantic scenery, grassy plains, noble hills, vallies watered with fresh creeks, abounding with birds and flowers. What was most surprising, was that Mr. Goyder asserted that the southern banks of Lake Torrens showed no flood-marks, a proof that there was *a constant level*, and that the lake had other outlets for the floods. This was so totally contrary to the reports of Eyre, Stuart, and others, who represented the lake as lying in a basin bare of water over a vast extent, and the bed of it encrusted with salt, that it should have excited some misgivings in the public mind.

Mr. Goyder said he could see that the opposite banks of the lake were precipitous; that he noticed several islands at five miles' distance with rocky, precipitous sides, indicating deep water; and that the water itself was clear and perfectly fresh, showing no salt incrustations whatever. "Some of the creeks," he continued, "which flow into the lake are broad, but shallow. There are no deltas at their embouchures. The most important of them is the continuation of the McDonnell, described by Mr. Babbage. That and several others are much finer waters than the Blanche. One of the most romantically beautiful—probably a portion of the McDonnell—Mr. Goyder has named the Freeling, in latitude 29° 45′ 42″, about six miles north of Mount Freeling. The stream, for a length of several miles, flows between rocky walls of from sixty to seventy feet high, apparently cut by the action of the water; but it is fringed by gigantic gum-trees, springing from alluvial deposits between the channels and the rocks. It abounds with all kinds of water-fowl, ducks, geese, and cranes, which are common upon the lake and creek; as also cockatoos, quail, and pigeons. Another, the most useful water seen by the party, is between St. Mary's Pool and the lake, fourteen miles N.E. of the former. This has been called the Werter Water, from the native name of the country."

Mr. Goyder also described a number of very large springs to the north of St. Mary's Pool, but all perfectly fresh, and though there was a white substance on the ground about them, it was only ammonia, not soda, or salt. As for the saline water described by former travellers, Mr. Goyder regarded them only as springs in some of the creeks on the outskirts of Lake Torrens, and not at all affecting its waters, which he represented as deep, pure, and permanent; the country full of grassy valleys, with steep rocks, numerous streams, and *occasionally*, arid plains. The rivers and creeks were so numerous that he reverted to the idea of an inland sea, which received their waters. These elysian fields, and the report of Mr. Babbage of good lands in the far north of the colony, put the possessors of flocks and herds into immediate motion. They were doomed to a severe disappointment. The government wisely determined to send out the surveyor-general, Captain Freeling, to test the discoveries of Mr. Goyder. In the mean time, not only were the squatters of South Australia making vast preparations for taking possession of the new Goshen announced by Mr. Goyder, but they were threatened with active competition from the squatters of Victoria. The *Ballarat Star* stated that some dozens of flocks and herds were already on the way for Lake Torrens, and the imaginations of the diggers were excited by reports that there were three splendid copper mines in the same favoured tract of country, two of them equal to the famous Burra-Burra.

Scarcely had Captain Freeling set out towards the country of Mr. Goyder, when another exploring party returned to Adelaide with intelligence of a fine pastoral country to the west of Lake Torrens. This party consisted of Mr. D. Thompson, of the Tariara, Mr. Murdoch Campbell, of Mount Remarkable, and Mr. Charles Swinden, of the Gilbert. Mr. Edwin Stocks was also for part of the way a companion. They reported favourably of the country to the west of the Torrens. Corporal Burt, of Mount Serle, and a party, had ridden as far as the Freeling, and confirmed Mr. Goyder's statements of the country, and that the Freeling was running strongly. Captain Freeling had reached Karrazaka on the 6th of August.

A despatch from Captain Freeling, dated fifteen miles south of Lake Torrens, September 6th, commenced thus:—" I much regret that what there is to relate is decidedly unfavourable to the extension of discoveries in the direction mentioned, and by the means proposed. The extensive bays described in Mr. Goyder's report, the bluff headlands, between the north and south shores, the vegetation covering them, and their perpendicular cliffs, have been all the result of mirage, and do not, in point of fact, exist as represented. The conclusion drawn in that report, that the lake is subject only to the most trifling variation of level, is also proved to be an erroneous deduction. I give the grounds for this statement:—

"We arrived at the present camp in the afternoon of the 2nd instant. I had observed a very marked difference in the country after leaving Mounts Distance, Gairdner and Freeling, the ranges merging into hummocky hills, sometimes isolated, and having extensive plains of an alluvial character, rapidly opening into fissures under the sun's heat, and having very little perceptible fall towards the north: also drift timber being seen for miles over these plains was evidence of floods, and that a vast body of water is poured down by the McDonnell, and other streams running northerly, after a heavy fall of rain. These indications made me conceive that the lake, when observed by Mr. Goyder, was merely an accumulation of such flood waters. We proceeded on the 3rd instant to Lake Torrens on horseback, and made the exact spot from which Mr. Goyder saw the water. From the statement of William Rowe, who accompanied us, and who also was with Mr. Goyder, the water of the lake had receded half-a-mile. For six miles back the ground was nearly a dead level, and had at times been covered with water, probably as much as one foot deep. The soil over this part, and at the water's edge, was the same—a mixture of clay and sand, destitute of stones. On the margin, where the water had receded, slightly saline incrustations remained on the ground, the water itself, however, might be called fresh. The Mount Hopeless range was clearly visible to the south, a distance of twenty miles, and northerly were apparent islands, with cliffs and vegetation, but presenting so marked a difference in appearance as to render their character a matter of mere conjecture."

On proceeding to put these rocks and hills, and the depth of water, to the test, they found them a great delusion. They brought up to the lake a boat, which had been carried along with them for the occasion, and a small folding iron punt, but there was no water to float them. They pushed the punt through the mud for a quarter of a mile, by the united exertions of six men, but still there was no depth of water to float it. Still before them they seemed to see rocks and land, and one of the islands with steep cliffs; but, on looking back to the level shore which they had left, they saw exactly the same appearances, where they knew that there was not a single cliff in reality.

The next day, accompanied by Messrs. Southon, Smart, and Roberts, three settlers, they attempted, eight in number, to wade across the lake to the other shore. The whole way was through mud, and more or less water, but never enough to float a boat. They came to some islands, which were flats only a foot or so above the water, the water never being more than six inches deep. A native guide gave up quite worn out, and remained on an island whilst the rest went still further, when another man became quite exhausted. When three miles from the starting point they turned back, satisfied of the impracticable nature of the water for navigation. The view from the point farthest reached was desolate in the extreme, the same shallow waters, low islands, and mud, extending round three parts of the horizon. Captain Freeling returned satisfied that the views of Mr. Eyre, Captain Sturt, and Captain Frome, were quite correct, and that the character of the country bordering the lake was everywhere the same, and that of a most desolate and unprofitable kind. It is plain that Mr. Goyder had been deceived by a mirage, and also had taken a flooded state of the Lake Torrens from heavy rains for the lake in its ordinary condition. He thought this was its normal state because he saw no flood-marks, the fact being that it had inundated the country beyond the average flood-marks, and by the time that Captain Freeling arrived, had subsided again to its usually shallow condition. The freshness of the water, too, so different to what former explorers had found it, was owing to these recent floods.

The immediate consequence of the report of Mr. Goyder were applications to the South Australian Government for leases of nearly five millions of acres of land for pastoral purposes, many of these coming from neighbouring colonies; nor did the discouraging report of Captain Freeling entirely damp out this bucolic ardour, for it was not long before the greater portion of the peninsula formed by Lake Torrens was surveyed, and leased for squatting stations.

Simultaneously with the expeditions of Goyder, Freeling, and Hack, several stockholders pushed their way to a considerable distance north and west of Lake Torrens, and discovered much country which satisfied them, and which appeared to possess permanent water. When these gentlemen had legally secured their runs in that quarter, one of them, Mr. Swinden, published a narrative of his expedition.

MAJOR WARBURTON'S EXPEDITION TO LAKE GAIRDNER, WITH THE HON. S. DAVENPORT. 1858.

Amongst the many exploration trips about this time into the country north and north-west of Adelaide one was undertaken in May, 1858, by Major Warburton and the Hon. S. Davenport to Lake Gairdner. We find them at the Wedge, a station of Mr. Tennant's, somewhere on Streaky Bay, on the 17th of June. They proceeded N.E. through Hope Downs towards the Gawler Ranges, through a rocky, scrubby country, and so on to Kundery, at the south-west point of Lake Gairdner. On this route they crossed the tracks of Eyre and Baxter, both still quite distinct. Major Warburton represents the country as one of granite formation, with an underlying stratum of limestone, more or less oolitic. That the granite, or porphyry having a perpendicular cleavage, lets down the rain water to the limestone stratum, which passing away on its bed, underdrains the whole of that country. This he believes is the cause of its general want of springs and creeks, and that this can only be remedied by sinking wells to the bed of limestone. He casts great doubts on the availableness of the Gawler Ranges reported by Messrs. Hack and Harris, and thinks the 4000 or 5000 square miles might carry perhaps a sheep to a square mile, but that even that would be a hazardous experiment.

At Kangaroo Flat, about ten miles E.N.E. of Moonaree, on the S.W. coast of Lake Gairdner, Mr. Davenport advanced along the western shore of the lake, sixty miles farther than the longitude of Yarlbinda, the farthest point of Mr. Hack, and seems to agree very much in opinion of the country with Major Warburton, and that its only resource is the sinking of wells. Accompanied by Police Sergeant Hooker and Police trooper Daune, Major Warburton advanced westward to Daddy's Hill, and in about thirty miles further, found he had been traversing a narrow peninsula, and was now surrounded by the lake and compelled to turn back. The rounding of this water and the neighbouring hills, had sent him from 130 to 150 miles about. He still pursued the circuitous shores of the lake to longitude 134° 15′, latitude 31° 15′, and this was the farthest point that he could attain from want of both water and provisions. On the morning of the 11th he directed his course S.W., and struck into Police-trooper Geharty's track, which led him to Belemah on the sea-coast, a little to the west of Denial Bay, which he reached July 19. From Streaky Bay, Major Warburton rode to Port Lincoln, 200 miles, observing Eyre's wheel tracks of 1845, which, as well as the prints of the bullocks' hoofs, remained perfectly clear. He had also seen Darke's tracks in Gawler's Ranges. From Port Lincoln he sailed to Port Augusta, and thence to Adelaide, where we find him writing his report on the 9th of August.

In his general remarks, the Major gave the preference to the country from Streaky Bay to Belemah over the Gawler Ranges, because water, he felt confident, could be got in their part of the coast country by sinking. He considered Fowler's Bay and the most northerly crossing place on Lake Torrens as the two best points of departure for any further expeditions into the interior; Fowler's Bay for western examination, and the north of Lake Torrens for north-western.

MR. SAMUEL PARRY'S SURVEYING EXPEDITION NEAR LAKE TORRENS.

Simultaneously with Major Warburton and Mr. Babbage's expedition westward, Mr. Parry, the Government Surveyor, made a journey into the country lying within the sweep of Lake Torrens, Lake Gregory and Blanche Water from Mount Serle to Illusion Plains and Angipena. In this trip he reported much good country, but a correspondent of the *Adelaide Register* says that he went with Mr. Parry on part of his expedition, namely near Gill's Station, thence to Shamrock Pool, and thence to the distant range, and that he never saw such a barren country. The plain was much better; Shamrock Pool was rain-water, and would serve one or two hundred head of cattle during the winter. Want of water appears the great defect of most of this region.

EXPEDITION OF SIR RICHARD MACDONNELL, GOVERNOR OF SOUTH AUSTRALIA TO AND BEYOND THE LODDON SPRINGS.

About the same period Sir Richard Macdonnell the enterprising governor of this colony himself with a large party, made an expedition to the neighbourhood of the Lake Torrens, and to the west of it, in the same direction as the late explorers. He first inspected the newly explored districts north of Mount Serle, and found the country very much burnt up south of Angipena. He examined the numerous mines, including the Appealina, Chambers' and Finch's, and the copper-mine near Mount

Rose. He then started upon the more adventurous part of his journey, suffering everywhere from the extreme drought of the season. He went on to Lake Weatherstone, Mount Attraction Springs, Blanche Cup, Strangway and Loddon Springs. He still pushed on beyond these, till stopped by utter desolation, and burning sand-hills. Both men and horses turned back thoroughly exhausted. In 1859, his Excellency accompanied Captain Cadell in the steamer Albany 600 miles up the Darling, above the junction with the Murray. The voyage of Mr. Randell still further up the Darling in the same year will be mentioned hereafter, with the other steam voyages up the rivers.

CHAPTER XVII.

AUGUSTUS C. GREGORY'S EXPEDITION IN QUEST OF DR. LEICHHARDT'S REMAINS.

A convict reports Leichhardt alive and in captivity in the interior.—Mr. Hely's journey to ascertain the fact.—Reports Leichhardt murdered by the natives.—In 1858, the New South Wales Government sent out Mr. A. C. Gregory from Moreton Bay to seek for traces of Leichhardt.—Traces of Leichhardt on the Barcoo near Mount Inniskillen eighty miles beyond Hely's farthest point.—Proceeds to the Alice.—A terrible country.—Loses all traces of Leichhardt.—Imagines him gone west.—Traces down the Thomson.—Return to the Barcoo.—Follows down that river to ascertain its real course.—Arrives at Cooper's Creek, thus identifying the two waters.—Traces the course of Cooper's Creek by Strzelecki's Creek to Lake Torrens.—Thus demonstrates the flow of this water from the Mountains of the east to Spencer's Gulf.—Crosses Lake Torrens on solid bottom.—Arrival in Adelaide.—The fate of Leichhardt still a mystery.

In 1857, a convict named Garbut, then in confinement on Cockatoo Island, near Sydney, created a great sensation, by stating that he actually knew Dr. Leichhardt to be alive and in captivity. His account was substantially this:—"That far in the interior, beyond even the bounds of pastoral enterprise, was a tract of rich, well-watered country, peopled by a colony of runaway convicts, who had married native women, and kept up a communication with the settlements by means of pack-horses, obtaining by this means not only new recruits of their own stamp, but supplies of necessaries and even luxuries. Dr. Leichhardt and his party, he said, came suddenly upon this colony, directly after leaving the settled district, and for fear he or they should divulge its existence, were forcibly detained. Garbut offered, if liberated, to lead a party to the spot, but stated that his brother and uncle, also convicts, had been there as well as he, and sought, we believe, their liberation also. He asserted, that the last of Leichhardt's camps, discovered by Mr. Hovenden Hely, during his expedition in 1853, was within two hundred miles of the settlement which he professed to describe.

The story had an air of fiction upon it altogether. Such a convict settlement, with a traffic carried on between it and the people of the colony for supplies, could not possibly remain a secret. Not only would the track made by such traffic have betrayed it, but the convicts could not have possessed the money necessary to purchase a regular supply of necessaries. It was clearly a scheme of Garbut to get himself, his brother, and uncle sent out on such a search, when they would have escaped into the woods. A little enquiry dissipated the fable, but left a renewed desire in the public mind for some further endeavour to trace the fate of Leichhardt.

The public has never indeed at any time rested satisfied with the mystery still hanging over the disappearance of the expedition of Leichhardt. The search of Mr. Hovenden Hely, though continued for 300 miles, and to a spot where the natives declared that the unfortunate traveller and all his party had been murdered, did not remove this dissatisfied feeling. Of late this sentiment instead of growing weaker, had gained strength, and Mr. A. C. Gregory, who had made so successful a journey across the north of the continent in 1856, offered his services to the New South Wales government for another search. This was accepted, and the party, consisting of Mr. A. C. Gregory, his brother, Mr. C. F. Gregory, an overseer, and seven experienced bushmen, having ten saddle, and thirty pack horses, and provisions for five months, started on the 12th of January, 1858. From the 27th of March to the 1st of April the party were occupied in traversing the district occupied as stations by the Moreton Bay settlers. As an acknowledged state of war exists along the settlements between the blacks and the whites, the former never show themselves except when they feel confident of victory, and as they did not like the looks of Mr. Gregory's party, they kept at a respectful distance for the first 100 miles; and from Moreton Bay, indeed, to Mount Serle, he did not see 100 of them in all. On Cooper's Creek he saw very few.

After clearing the Moreton Bay district, they struck

the Victoria, and found at the bend of that river the last traces of Leichhardt. The spot is a little north of Mount Inniskillen, and in longitude 146° 6′. These traces consist of a letter L cut in a tree, which is of immense size, being fully eighteen inches long, and four inches broad, the incision being also of a great depth. A few cut poles were lying about, evidently the remains of a camp. This spot is eighty miles beyond the traces found by Hely, though he was informed by the blacks that Leichhardt had been murdered where Hely found them. The traces now found by Gregory show that Leichhardt could not have been murdered where Hely was, he had been at least eighty miles beyond that spot, and the goat's hair and human hair discovered amongst the blacks of Cooper's Creek since by McKinlay, seem to prove his advance still farther. Walker, in 1862, saw trees marked by Leichhardt in the same longitude as Gregory, but still more northwards, in latitude 22°.

After leaving these indications of Leichhardt's former presence, Mr. Gregory never once discovered the slightest trace of him. By the latter end of April Mr. Gregory reached the Alice Creek, but found the country to the north and north-west a frightful and impenetrable desert. It is his opinion that when Leichhardt was there, rains had fallen, filling the clay pans that abound in that region. That lured on by these shallow pools of water, Leichhardt had pushed forwards, until the unceasing heat of a tropical sun evaporated the water both before and behind him, leaving him without means of existence to perish in the desert. Mr. Gregory then proceeded down the Victoria river to its junction with the Thomson. This was early in May, and heavy rains had just previously fallen. Quitting the Victoria, they pursued the course of the Thomson upwards of 100 miles, in the hope of intersecting Leichhardt's tracks, but, as observed, without success. Having advanced to within ten degrees of the tropic, they found it impossible to proceed further, no trace existing of rain having ever fallen there, the earth being baked as hard as a brickkiln, and without a trace of vegetation. Mr. Gregory retracing his steps down the Thomson, after a fortnight's absence, regained the Victoria.

All hope of finding the remains of Leichhardt having vanished, Mr. Gregory, holding *carte blanche* from the New South Wales Government, resolved to trace down the Victoria River. He found it, as he advanced, gradually widen, till it became thirty-five miles in width. Our readers, however, must not delude their imaginations as to this so-called river. It contained no water, except a few pools here and there in its course, the bed of the river consisting of immense deposits of sand and stones. This, however, shows what must be the floods which come down it at times. In this part of their march, the party often found great difficulty in supplying their horses with food, no living vegetation appearing for three or four days together, the poor animals being reduced to eat rotten weeds, and whatever dead and decaying rubbish they could find. The country is stiff clay, and full of deep fissures. One horse, completely exhausted, was obliged to be left behind.

The Victoria eventually opened out into a vast plain of a desert character, covered with stone, chiefly sandstone, and where the pools in the river bed had nearly all disappeared. A few dwarf gums were occasionally seen in the Victoria, but none that indicated a steady flow of water. The party, however, continued their course, resolved to see what became of the river bed, even though they had lost the river. At length they arrived at a solution of the question. The Grey and Barrier Ranges are continued northward in a low mountain chain, and this chain, meeting the Victoria at nearly right angles, forces its waters into a narrow channel, this channel being the well-known Cooper's Creek. Here Mr. Gregory rested awhile to recruit his horses, feed and water being plentiful, and here, we may conclude, he paused to congratulate his companions upon the interesting geographical discovery they had made. It was now proved that the Victoria River and Cooper's Creek were one and the same. Following the creek about 100 miles, Mr. Gregory found that it radiated into a number of small streamlets, which were crossed by numerous sand-hummocks of twenty or thirty feet high, and by which they were absorbed. One, however, of the arms or branches of Cooper's Creek, escaped, namely, the most external one, to which Sturt gave the name of Strzelecki's Creek. Pursuing this creek, Mr. Gregory never lost sight of it until he traced it into Lake Torrens. The termination of Strzelecki's Creek he found to be the Salt Creek of Sturt. Mr. Gregory has thus demonstrated that the Victoria (Barcoo), Cooper's Creek, Strzelecki's Creek, Salt Creek, and Lake Torrens all constitute the pathway or receptacle of the same flood of waters, proceeding from the mountains of the east coast to the Gulf of Spencer. Other travellers have touched at particular points of this long and winding path for the rains of the desert, but Mr. Gregory alone has followed it mile by mile, step by step, demonstrating what some have fancied, but what no one could have possibly affirmed.

Mr. Gregory crossed Lake Torrens by a firm and well-defined isthmus, about five miles broad, in a north-easterly direction from Mount Hopeless; being probably the same crossing indicated about two years before by Mr. Babbage, and more recently by Mr. Ball. The party arrived in Adelaide at three o'clock on the 31st of July, and as Mr. Gregory stepped from the railway carriage upon the platform, he was received with three cheers by about forty persons who had assembled, and the Town Clerk informed him that the Corporation had an address to deliver him, but that he had arrived earlier than they expected, and were, therefore, not present. Mr. Gregory, in his rough bush costume, was evidently no more prepared to receive the Corporation than they were prepared to receive him; and the Hon. F. S. Dutton appearing, drove him off in his carriage amid the cheers of the people. The explorer's reception in Adelaide was most enthusiastic.

Successful and most important as this expedition of Mr. Gregory's has been in ascertaining the real character of the Barcoo, and the course of the waters from the north-east to the south-west of Australia, still the public mind does not abandon the desire to trace farther the progress of Leichhardt. On the 22nd of November, 1858, a paper by the Rev. W. B. Clarke, of Sydney, was read at the meeting of the Royal Geographical Society, urging further searches for traces of his route from the Barcoo westward, which was supported by Sir Charles Nicholson; and the instances shown by McKinlay of the probability of his having passed westward of Cooper's Creek, may yet lead to a successful discovery of his remains; thus solving this long-continued mystery.

CHAPTER XVIII.

EXPEDITIONS IN WESTERN AUSTRALIA IN 1858 AND 1861, BY MR. FRANK T. GREGORY.

EXPEDITIONS IN WESTERN AUSTRALIA, 1858.—Frank Gregory and party examine the country between the river Gascoyne and Mount Murchison.—Proceed to the Geraldine Mines.—Mount Nairn on the Murchison.—Reach the Gascoyne.—Country well grassed.—Lockyer's Range.—Lyons River.—The Alma.—Mount Augustus 3,000 feet.—Good country.—Proceed S.S.E.—Mounts Gould and Hale.—Extensive tracts of good country.—Return to the Nairn and Geraldine Mines.—The natives numerous, and sometimes troublesome.—New pigeons and new vegetables.—Melons and sweet potatoes.—Geologic character of the country.—Babbage Island.—New yam.

EXPEDITION OF MR. F. T. GREGORY INTO THE INTERIOR OF DE WITT'S LAND, IN 1861.—Land at Nickol Bay.—Discover the Fortescue.—The Hammersley Ranges.—Mounts Augustus, Phillips, Samson.—The Barlee Ranges.—Neighbourhood of the Lyons.—Second progress eastward.—The Sherlock, Yule, and Oakover Rivers.—Ranges in the interior.—Great extents of pasturable land.—The rivers Strelley, Shaw, and De Grey.—Great sea-flats.—Sufferings in the last journey.—Character of the climate and country.—Pearl oyster-beds.—Natural productions.—Return.

The newspapers of Western Australia, of the 7th of April, brought the intelligence of an exploring expedition for examining the country betwixt the Gascoyne and Mount Murchison. It was under the command of Mr. Frank Gregory, and was equipped at the joint expense of the settlers and the government. The final point of departure would be the Geraldine mines; and it was on the eve of starting. It consisted of the Messrs. Gregory, J. Roe, W. Moore, C. Nairn, Mr. Gregory's chainer, and a native. The number of horses was ten, the government contributing to the expedition the services of Mr. Gregory and his chainer, three horses, implements, two tents and pack-saddles. The settlers had subscribed £40 towards it, and the party was provisioned for two months.

Subsequent advices stated Mr. Gregory and his party to be at the Geraldine mines all well, and intending to start on the 16th of April. From this expedition Mr. Gregory returned within the proposed period, having arrived in Perth on the 10th of July, and having, according to report, discovered millions of acres of good land, growing melons and potatoes indigenously. He had given to the new country the name of Lyons.

After leaving the Geraldine mines they followed the Murchison till they came to a hill, which they named Mount Nairn, principally in a N.W. direction. The banks of the river had grassy lands, backed by acacia scrubs. At Mount Nairn the party left the Murchison, proceeding N.W., and crossed a tributary of the Murchison, through a stony country, with short grass. Pursuing the same course, they struck the Gascoyne an hour after leaving the tributary of the Murchison. Still pursuing the same N.W. course, they followed the Gascoyne, the river increasing in size as they advanced. The country near its banks was beautifully grassed, and timbered with the flooded gum, far finer than any they had seen on the Murchison, but there was no timber of any size in the country farther back. They occasionally met with flats of rich country from two to three miles wide. The river took a southerly bend from some hills named Lockyer's Range, and then pursued a N.N.W. course till it reached the sea. The country continued of the same good description on the banks, but deteriorated upon approaching the coast. The party returned from the mouth of the Gascoyne on the north bank, and about eighty miles from the coast struck a large tributary, which they named the Lyons River, taking a northerly course, which they followed. Both the banks of this river were well grassed, but the neighbouring country was, generally speaking, poor. At the extreme northerly point attained by the party, the Lyons is joined by a river, named the Alma, the Lyons taking a bend, first easterly, and ultimately south-east. The river was still followed, until they reached a hill, nearly 3,000 feet above the level of the sea, and which they named Mount Augustus. Here there were several large flats, the most extensive being about twenty-eight miles long, and three or four wide. From Mount Augustus they had a good view of the surrounding country, which appeared to be of an excellent description. Departing from Mount Augustus, they left the Lyons, and pursued a S.E. course, till they again came upon the Gascoyne, the country being stony, and slightly grassed. They crossed the main Gascoyne, and proceeded S.S.E., until they reached a tributary of the Murchison, the country being still stony, but somewhat better grassed. From this spot, where there is a hill named Mount Gould, to another hill named Mount Hale, and still following the tributary of the Murchison, the exploring party discovered a succession of rich flats. They then proceeded almost due west, until they reached Mount Nairn, the point whence they diverged from the river on their outward trip. From thence they followed the Murchison to the Geraldine mines.

The *Perth Enquirer* says of this expedition :—"The country is described as well watered, and no wonder, for there appears a perfect network of rivers connected with the Murchison and Gascoyne, some of them of considerable size, fifty or sixty yards wide. The quantity of good land seen is estimated at a million of acres, the best of it distant some 300 miles from the settled districts, but the intervening tract will support stock *en route*. There were evidences of great and recent floods, and the water was estimated to have risen forty feet. A sand deposit of about two inches depth had been left. It is conjectured that a heavy flood had taken place during the present year. The natives were numerous, especially on the banks of the Gascoyne, and at times became so troublesome that Mr. Gregory on one occasion fired his gun at them. It was loaded with shot, and did no further harm than to induce them to keep at a respectful distance. On another occasion, near the mouth of the Gascoyne, the natives again became so troublesome that the party charged them on horseback, a proceeding which created much alarm amongst them. They were followed for some time by these natives, but apparently for the purpose of warning others not to get in the way, for they shouted, and with their hands waved off any who attempted to approach. Game was not plentiful, and they only saw two natives with kangaroo-skin cloaks. One kangaroo and one emu were shot during the trip, and some ducks and pigeons. The party also obtained fish, but on the whole their supply of provisions was short, especially meat, the flour lasting out pretty well. We do not hear of many additions to our natural history. There was seen a new species of pigeon, slate-coloured, and several varieties of vegetables, some resembling our water and sweet melons, sweet potatoes, and a few new grasses. The melons were small, and the leaves similar to the sweet and water-melons. Seeds of grass were saved, amongst these some resembling oats, which the natives use for food. A small, gourd-like fruit, filled with seeds, to which down is attached, like the dandelion, was also preserved. When at Shark's Bay, the expedition crossed to Babbage Island, the southern mouth of the Gascoyne being dry. The stone of the country appears to be chiefly sandstone and oolitic limestone, and in the hills granite, quartz, and variegated jasper. In some places there were gypsum and clayey shales, indicating the probable existence of coal. They discovered, also, a new vegetable, a convolvulus, having roots some of them of a pound weight or more, and eating like a sweet potato. Mr. Gregory considered, however, that the Upper Gascoyne and Lyons could not be advantageously settled without the discovery of a near port.

THE EXPEDITION OF MR. F. T. GREGORY INTO THE INTERIOR OF DE WITT'S LAND, IN 1861.

It appears that this expedition was undertaken at the recommendation of the Royal Geographical Society, but chiefly equipped by the Government of Western Australia. The persons of the party were—

> F. T. Gregory, Commander.
> J. Turner, Assistant and Storekeeper.

E. Brockman, ⎫
W. S. Hall, ⎬ Assistants.
J. M'Court, ⎭
A. James, Farrier.

These set sail from Fremantle, in the barque Dolphin, Captain Dixon, on the 23rd of April, and were afterwards joined at Champion Bay by—

J. Harding,
M. Brown, and
P. Walcott,

as volunteers, bringing with them additional horses. They were provisioned for eight months; ten horses were taken from Fremantle, and ten more from Champion Bay, thus twenty horses, and a small number of sheep, it would appear twenty-two, but the account is by no means clear. Mr. P. Walcott, who joined them at Champion Bay, proposed to collect specimens of natural history.

They reached Dampier Archipelago on May the 11th, and observed that what is shown on the charts as a promontory, extending to the north of Sloping Head, is an island with a channel nearly half-a-mile wide, separating it from the main, and they gave it the name of Dolphin Island, in honour of the ship. On anchoring in Nickol Bay, they found the dry channel of a river, which they named the Nickol River. They had much difficulty in landing their stores, horses, and sheep, on account of the low, swampy ground abutting on the Bay, and the distance they had to swim the horses from the ship, the water not being deep enough to bring the vessel nearer to the shore. It was the 21st of May before they had landed everything, and the 25th before they could make a fair start. In the course of disembarking they had the misfortune to have Mr. Hearson, the second mate of the Dolphin, severely wounded, by the going off of one of the guns in passing it over the gunwale of the boat. Escaping from the swamps, and taking a westward course, they fell in with the channel of a river eighty yards wide, having pools of water in it, and fine grassy banks. This river, which they called the Maitland, came from the S.E. After crossing the beds of other, now nearly dried-up streams, they entered vast plains, and found a larger river, which, on the 30th, turned suddenly north-east, through a rocky defile. This river they named the Fortescue, and on account of the rocky country on each side were obliged to travel along its bed, which had occasional pools, with reeds, ducks and fish. The water, however, was saline to the taste. The river led them on to ranges of hills, one of which, running at some distance parallel with the river, left some fine open plains and valleys at their feet. They named this range the Hammersley Range, after one of the most liberal promoters of the expedition, and the fertile plains between it and the river the Chichester Downs.

Pursuing their route, the river changed its course, sweeping round from south-east to south-west. They proceeded through ranges 2400 feet above the level of the sea, and in latitude 22° 51′ other hills rose on the east of their track 1000 feet high. For sixty miles the river continued that course, with very little water in it, though the channel was large. Still other ranges of hills were met. A river coming in from the westward they named the Harding, in latitude 22° 58′ 28″, longitude 117° 10′. Another, still larger, coming from the same direction, in 23° 28′ 15″, they named the Ashburton. They could see from the hills near it, Mounts Augustus, Phillips, and Samuel, and, still more south, the Barlee Range. They went on till they could trace the course of a stream running thence into the Lyons River. In latitude 23° 56′ 45″, they, therefore, turned back, and, keeping more westward, they examined the hills which they named Samson and Bruce, the latter having an elevation of 4000 feet. From the great bend of the Fortescue they proceeded N.W., over extensive plains, containing, as they calculated, 200,000 acres of fine pasturage land, and then through a stony country, clothed with short green grass and melons, a country very much resembling that of the Mauritius. They now struck a river of considerable extent, running northwest, which they named the Sherlock, containing pools of water. This, at last, led them out into low, alluvial plains, and finally to the sea between Picard and Depuch Islands. Thence they regained their camp at Nickol Bay.

On the 30th of July, they set out again on an eastward course in the hope of reaching some large river supposed to be out far in that direction. After striking the Sherlock, they travelled over a poor country of red granite rocks, covered with triodia and a few acacias. In latitude 21° 6' 26", they struck another river containing a little water, coming more from the S.E., which they named the Yule. This, they thought, would take them too much E.; therefore, they followed another stream which flowed northward, and which led them out to Breaker Inlet. They named it the Strelley, and another stream, which came in from the S.S.E., the Shaw. This was also joined by a much larger river coming from the southward, 100 yards wide, which they named the De Grey. They followed this river in an E.S.E. course over a very rocky country into another, coming more from the S., which they called the Oakover. This they pursued into some ranges, and then came out in desert, sandy plains, which compelled them to return. They had nearly reached longitude 122° and latitude 22°. They had suffered intensely from heat, thirst, and fatigue. Mr. Gregory describes the effect of this fatigue and thirst on the eyes of the horses as something awful. They were sunk deep into their heads, and the whole head appeared shrunk with them, producing a very unpleasant and ghostly expression. They calculated that they could not be far from the imagined river of their search, and turned back with regret; but to have gone further would have been certain destruction to them all. They had lost one horse after another, and had abandoned their loads and pack-saddles to enable them to do what they had done.

By the 26th of September, they again reached the mouth of the De Grey between the Points Larrey and Poissonier, in the neighbourhood of which lie great sea-flats. After this they made an excursion up the Sherlock and the Yule, finding much hilly country as well as fine grazing land on the latter river; and on the 21st of October they returned on board the Dolphin, and set sail homewards.

Mr. Gregory gives us a summary of his impressions of this great tract of country lying north of that traversed by him before. It is clear that as he was in it from May to October, he enjoyed its autumn, winter, and spring months. During that period, they had very little rain. The beds of the rivers, though large, and their banks bearing marks of great occasional floods, had very little water in them. He gives the maximum of heat in the shade as ranging from 76° to 92°; but he says the thermometer, placed on a sandbank in the sun, in October, rose to 178° Fahrenheit. In fact, as might be supposed from its latitude, the country has altogether a thirsty and tropical character. He himself doubts whether it will produce wheat and barley in perfection, but thinks it most adapted for the growth of cotton. He calculates that it contains two or three millions of acres suitable for grazing, and 200,000 adapted to agriculture. As to wool, time must decide how far it will succeed or degenerate, as it must do in the north of Queensland. The country rises in a succession of steps, as it were from the sea to the farthest interior. First they came to wide plains; then to hills of from 40 to 100 feet; next to others of from 500 to 1000 feet; and afterwards to ranges of 2000, and finally, 4000 feet. Not many minerals were found. Quartz reefs traversed the hills; but they could discover no traces of gold. The most valuable discovery was that of pearl-oyster beds on the coast of Nickol Bay, the crew of the Dolphin having collected separate pearls of value, one rated by competent persons at £26, and the pearl-oysters altogether of the value of £500 to £600.

Cotton plants grew luxuriantly, but were burnt by an accident. They saw many beautiful flowers of new kinds. An elegant shrub, bearing deep crimson-dragon flowers, they regarded as the most beautiful they had seen in Australia. Palms grew to forty feet of height on the Fortescue, and amongst the indigenous fruits were that of the adansonia, or gouty-stem tree, of Sir George Grey, nearly allied to the baobah, or monkey bread-fruit of South Africa, sweet and water melons, a wild fig well tasted, and a sweet and palatable plum, in considerable abundance. Several birds were seen new to them and of beautiful plumage; one of them, a paroquet, supposed, however, to be the golden-backed one of Gould; and there were large flocks of the white cockatoo with the orange-tinted crest. The natives were a finely grown race, and though inclined, as usual, to be thievish, not very formidable either in temper or numbers.

CHAPTER XIX.

EXPEDITION FOR BRINGING DOWN THE REMAINS OF BURKE AND WILLS.

Wonderful progress of Australia since this history commenced.—The expedition to bring down the remains of Burke and Wills sets out from Melbourne in December, 1861.—The party and equipment.—Vary the route from Menindie.—Proceed more eastward.—The country better.—Mount Babbage.—Boally and Bultilla Creeks,—Intense heat and flies.—Cadell's Range.—Take the old route at Altolka.—Rains and grass.—Getting Camels over Wilkie's Creek.—February the 27th, reach Wills's grave —Mr. Howitt starts to examine the route towards Mount Hopeless.—Find McKinlay's mark at Burke's grave.—A wilful guide.—Return to camp.—On March 5th, set out to reach Mount Hopeless.—Strzelecki's creek.—Gregory's camp.—Miserable country.—Reach Blanche Water.—Baker's Station.—Blacks eating poisoned sugar.—Barren cattle stations.—Return by Lake Hope.—Still very wretched country.—Lake Hope.—Idea that the waters from Cooper's Creek pass this way.—McKinlay's Guide.—Reach the Depôt.—Coming down of a great flood.—Remove the remains of Wills out of its reach.—Explore the country northwards.—High rocks and red sand-hills.—Bateman's Creek.—Frightened natives.—Other creeks.—Natives say McKinlay's party detained by floods.—Search for McKinlay's party.—Teniel Ranges.—Lake Lipsom.—Kycjoran Creek.—William's Creek.—A funeral oration.—Regain the Depôt.—Hunt down a cow and calf.—Catch Sturt's roan horse.—Much frying of beef.—Dishonest black guide.—The flood still coming down—Arrival of Corporal Wauchope with despatches.—Howitt returns with him to Blanche Water.—Returns to the Depôt.—Orders to wait for arrival of Landsborough from the gulf, and to look out for McKinlay.—Journey northwest across the Stony Desert.—Appearance of the desert at the time.—Very passable.—Lake Short.—Odd conduct of the guide.—Tracks thought to be of McKinlay's party.—Vain search for the party.—Terrible country.—Other horse tracks, supposed of land-hunters.—Sampson's Range.—Rumours of McKinlay.—A camel lost.—Another journey to Blanche Water for supplies.—Angipena Police Station.—Singular scenery.—Wilpena Pound.—Striking scenery of Jacob's Station.—Constant war with the blacks.—Try to kill Howitt's black boy.—Bloodless affair with them.—Their language imitated by the settlers in their converse with them.—Evident fate of the aborigines.—Seventeen years' residence of a sailor amongst them.—His desire to mediate between the blacks and squatters.—Opinion of Mr. Wentworth, that the whites are always the aggressors.—Before setting out with the remains of Burke and Wills, Howitt buries supplies of food and clothing at the Depôt, should any exploring party arrive there.—Journey down to Adelaide.—An attempt made from Jacob's Station to open up a route eastward to the Darling.—Found impracticable.—Arrive at Adelaide.—Dinner to McKinlay.—Honours to the deceased at Adelaide.—Arrival of the remains at Melbourne.—Their reception by the committee.—Lying in state.—Meeting to receive the explorers.—The funeral of Burke and Wills.—Addresses of satisfaction presented to Howitt and his party, Captain Norman and Mr. Kyte, the originators of the expedition.—Grants by government to the relatives of Mr. Wills, to the nurse of Burke, and others.

ONE more enterprise and we have arrived at the close of

this eventful history. When we commenced it, Australia was a terra incognita. It is now a populous land, boasting no less than five states or colonies, with its swarming cities and cultivated farms. It has become the greatest grazing and wool-growing country in the world. Its gold is poured into Europe with a Pactolian profusion, and already it is planning the foundation of new colonies. The swarm which fled the paternal hive but the other day is now casting off new swarms of its own. But all this marvellous developement of energy and life has been produced by the labours of self-sacrificing explorers and bold adventurers on sea and land, in discovery and commerce, many of whom have laid down their lives in the desert. It was decreed, however, that the remains of the last martyrs to discovery should be brought from their far off graves to receive the public honours of a great funeral and a monument. The same leader who had so successfully conducted the expedition, which sought and found the remains of this brave but unfortunate party, was again selected for this melancholy duty.

Mr. Alfred Howitt quitted Melbourne on this service on the 9th of December, 1861. His party this time consisted of twelve persons, including Messrs. W. F. Welch, surveyor, Dr. Murray, who volunteered to go as surgeon to the party, and for which purpose the Melbourne Hospital Committee had freely allowed him six months' absence; Weston Phillips and A. Aitkin, both of whom had been with Howitt not only on the last journey to Cooper's Creek, but also in the Gippsland mountains; Henry Burrell; and H. L. Galbraith. They were provisioned for five months from the time of leaving Menindie, and if they fell short, were to seek additional supplies in the northern regions of South Australia.

On reaching Menindie, instead of taking the direct northern track followed by Burke and Wills, and by himself on the last journey, in consequence of information from squatters that better country could be found more eastward, and which proved quite true, Mr. Howitt ascended the Darling to Mr. Jamieson's station, near Mount Murchison. January 28th, they camped near Mount Babbage; on the 30th, they followed up the Butto or Boalley Creek, and then down the Bullilla Creek. The weather was intensely hot, the flies intolerable. They passed Cadell's Range, and over inferior country to Youngeanya, where there was plenty of grass and portulac. From this point the leader reconnoitred the more westward direction to Torowoto, but found all dry, and returned and pursued his previous course to Cooper's Creek. The Macadam Range, which they reached northward, appeared 700 or 800 feet high. At Altolka they fell into their old route, and upon better country, but bad to travel, in consequence of rain. The country around Stokes' ranges looked like an immense field of young oats, from the recent rains. On February 18th, they reached Cooper's Creek, half a mile from camp sixty of Burke. The water at Burke's camp was dried up. This had not been the case a few days before at Wilkie's creek, where they found the camels very troublesome in crossing. "This," says the leader, "was as disagreeable a job as any one could have. I have never seen animals so afraid of, or so helpless in the water. We had to make them lie down on its margin, and then push them in bodily, some of the party on the opposite side towing them over by a rope. I was thankful when they were all safe across." They had now frequent showers, and caught a good deal of fish. On the 27th of February they reached Wills's grave, and the same day at eleven A.M., Mr. Howitt left the depôt, with Galbraith, O'Donnel, and M'William, with six horses and five days' rations, to ascertain whether water was to be found on the way to Mount Hopeless, so as to know their chance of obtaining supplies from that quarter, as well as of their being able to return that way and by Adelaide, if necessary. By taking only horses they saved themselves much trouble, for they still complain that the horses are extremely frightened at the camels, and gallop away for miles in different directions, creating much labour and delay in recovering them.

In travelling down the creek, they found McKinlay's mark on a tree at Burke's grave, and about two miles lower down they found MK. again on a tree conjoined with a broad arrow under in a square. Again, at the water-hole at Wills's grave, they found McKinlay's mark, and from the direct manner in which he had gone from point to point, they concluded that one of the natives had directed him to them. Every thing was scorched up by the sun, except the extraordinary growth of green plants in the bed of the creek of which the camels were very fond. The native orange-trees were then covered with fruit and blossom. As they advanced, all traces of vegetation vanished, it was a scene of sultry yellow sand-hills. On the 29th they fell in with a camp of friendly natives, who brought all their piccaninnies out to be admired. Here they took a good deal of trouble in getting their native guide to direct them to water. Amongst other stratagems he turned very lame, but they then set him on a horse, when he set off at such a rate, beating the horse with a stick, that they had much to do to keep him in. At length he found it useless to resist, gave in, and showed them water, when, their object being served, they returned to their camp on Cooper's Creek. At dinner that day the native guide devoured a snake ravenously.

On March 5th, they set out in earnest to reach Mount Hopeless, the party being four in number, with six camels, four horses, a month's rations, and every water-bag and canteen they possessed. Could poor Burke and Wills have commenced that journey with such animals and supplies, they would have accomplished it. On the 6th, at evening, they reached Tungarilla, their previous point, and found Pardue, the guide, and his mate still there, but they refused to go further with the party. On the 8th they found fresh water, and afterwards struck Strzelecki's Creek, but found it perfectly dry, except in one place where was a small quantity of water. The next day they reached a better supply of water in the channels, and the camels drunk at least seven gallons each. Though they can bear the want of water better than horses, they are just as insatiate of it when they reach it in hot weather. The two following days they pursued the course of the creek which ran through red steep sand-hills, the greater part of the bed of the creek dry, and overgrown with polygonum and other bushes. They were of opinion that very little water from Cooper's Creek found its way across these extensive sandy plains. On the 10th they camped by Gregory's marked tree, a small triangle over 77 within a triangle. They travelled on till the 14th, over miserable sandy country, sometimes showing grass, sometimes cotton salt, and other bushes. On the 14th they reached Mount Hopeless, which they were surprised to find the most insignificant hill in the neighbourhood. They were most hospitably received at Mr. Jacob's station, and the next day, they travelled over stony plains, sixteen miles, to Blanchewater, and were very kindly received by Mr. James at Baker's station. Thus they completed this trip of 180 miles through a country which had only once been traversed by white men before, in eleven days. At this station three half-wild blacks were nearly poisoned by stealing the arsenicated sugar put out for the innumerable and all-devouring ants. They just eat the sugar and then went to say they were "poisa, tumble down." They dosed them with about two quarts of soap-suds each, and sent them away relieved.

The manner in which squatting stations were pushed out, one beyond another in this sterile, desert country, where the cattle wandered about seeking for grass amongst the stones, surprised the travellers.

Having ascertained that the way was open to Adelaide by Blanchewater, and that stores might be obtained, the party returned by Hope Lake, a route considerably more to the west. We may say generally that the country was very much like that which they had passed over in going. In fact, we find on the map of their track these notes, till they were once more on Cooper's Creek, "poor stony country;" "rough stony hills;" "dry salt lake;" "very poor country;" "dry lake;" "ridges of drift sand;" "very poor country;" and north of Lake Hope, "miserable country;" "sand ridges;" "porcupine grass;" "thickly timbered scrubby flats;" "open sand country;" "no timber;" "dry lake." The incidents were few. On the 23rd of March they followed McKinlay's track through a very poor country, for about twenty miles. The next day they reached Lake Hope, a large expanse of water, bordered with stunted box-trees, the water rather brackish. The following day they were at Wallpappanina Lake, about eight or nine miles in length, its margin rich with grass, as well as the parts of the lake from which the water had retired. Pelicans, swans, and other wild fowl on the lake. The next day, March 25, they reached Lake Appadeer, the waters of which were nauseous. They had taken native guides from Lake Hope, of whom Boulin-ganne, McKinlay's guide, was one. The leader was of opinion that in wet seasons the waters from Cooper's Creek passed down this way rather than by Strzelecki's Creek to Blanchewater, and Lake Torrens.

At Apparalpa on the 28th, the natives assumed a hostile appearance, not liking the camels, but they soon thought better of it. The next day the natives told them that McKinlay's party were detained up the country by great floods. At Yenbarka, on Cooper's Creek, they sought for a camp of Burke's, but could not find it. Howitt was of opinion Cooper's Creek, which here breaks up in the plains, in flood time runs in this direction to the Hope Plains, and so to Lake Lipsom of Sturt. Arriving at the depôt on the 2nd of April, they found all well, and the three camels left there become perfect curiosities of fat, being nearly all hump, showing that the country suited them perfectly.

The natives asserting that a great flood was coming down the creek, a party was despatched on horseback to see if it were so, and for the first day found no signs of it; but the next morning they observed the stream running, then increasing into a small river, and the back waters and channels all filling. On this they hastened back to report. The water coming down was clear, but very unpleasant in taste, being no doubt the old water which the flood was pushing before it. According to the native account, the flood had travelled seventy miles in about six weeks. On the 12th most of the party proceeded north to disinter the remains of poor Wills, lest the flood should cover the grave, and they were sent up to the depôt. The waters down the creek were fast drying up, but soon to be replenished by the flood. At that time, however, Mr. Howitt was of opinion that all the waters seen by Burke south of the Stony Desert were dry.

April the 15th, Mr. Howitt left the camp with a party for an examination of the country northward. They soon left the good country, and were amongst high, red, sand-hills, several remarkable peaks being visible ahead. This journey, which was continued to lat. 26° 40′ 45″, long. 140° 21′, was chiefly through the same country of red sand-hills, of the colour of red-hot iron, but with creeks and grassy valleys lying amongst them. On the 18th they reached a creek which they named Bateman's Creek. The creek had a well-defined channel, and was lined with box, orange, and bean trees; the valleys were so grassy that it was difficult to imagine themselves still near Cooper's Creek. They found natives friendly, but frightened at them, and glad to steal away unobserved. One old woman suddenly come upon, pretended to be dead, and a boy not finding sufficient bushes to hide him, stuck his head ostrich-like into a single one. As they advanced they found other creeks, Burrell's Creek, Phillips' Creek, and O'Donnell's Creek. The natives still spoke of McKinlay's party being surrounded by water, a fact true in itself, at one time. Numbers of water fowls were about these lakes; swarms of young ducks running about, and young hedgereegors in almost every box-tree. The nights were now cold.

They were now on the edge of the Stony Desert, and their native guide described the country all round from S.E. to W. as a country of that stony character of many days' journey across. He pointed N.W., as the point where he believed McKinlay's party to be. They had followed the stony ranges and table-lands ever since leaving Cooper's Creek, at from ten to twenty miles distance, and they now made a sweep westward in returning, after first visiting some prominent hills somewhat to the N.E., which they named Teniel's Range. Along O'Donnell's Creek they found a wonderful growth of grasses, portulac, and other vegetables, in many places to their saddle girths, but near the ranges the stones appeared again packed like a pavement. After halting to collect native melons, they returned. On the 25th of April they passed three dry salt lakes, and observed McKinlay's dray marks. The next day they rode to Lake Lipsom of Sturt, called by the natives Bando Patchadilly. They found the lake about three miles by four in size, flanked by sand-hills, and without timber, except two or three box-trees. They found McKinlay's camp, but neither marked tree nor any document buried. They saw other lakes to the eastward. The natives were very friendly, and brought them cakes of portulac seed, which tasted rather sweet, and like linseed, but knowing the mode of making it, they simply satisfied themselves with tasting of it. Everywhere the natives were collecting this seed, and Harry Burrell found a bundle of it done up in grass, and daubed with mud, containing a bushel and a half. On the Kyejerou Creek they saw the natives catching large quantities of fish. The next day they camped on a creek which they named after one of the party, Williams Creek. At their next camp they saw the natives encamped near them, and heard an old man make a funeral oration over a boy lately buried. Frank the guide said it was, "big one cry over him, and all the same as preach." "The speaker used much action, and ran his words so into one another," observes Howitt, "that it was only now and then that I could catch his meaning. I heard, however, that the subject of his speech had walked a long way, and would never walk back again, and that he had been a good fisherman, and had collected much bower, portulac-seed. They kept up this amusement, accompanied by the hammering of stones, pounding of nardoo, and the grinding of bower till a late hour. It was a curious peep into native life. One of these natives was white-washed all over."

On May 1st, they regained the depôt. Before reaching the creek they saw the tracks of a cow and a calf, and immediately after occurs this curious entry in the diary: —" Galbraith, three days before, came across the horse which had been known to run here for some years. Gregory was the first to mention the fact. He saw the fresh tracks last year; McKinlay also saw him, but was unable to catch him. Galbraith, after a gallop, got alongside, and passed the halter in a slip-knot over his head. Not being able to pull him in, he fastened the halter to his stirrup-iron, and slackening his pace, in about 100 yards choked him, and he fell. Before he could rise, a turn of the rope was round his lower jaw, and after a short struggle he gave in, and was led to the camp, where he is now hobbled. He is a roan cob, a little under fifteen hands, bald face, off-knee white, near hind leg white, and white streak down inside of off-leg. Brands H C near shoulder ; E T under saddle near side ; I near thigh. I think it is most probable that this is the roan horse mentioned by Sturt as having been left here by him some seventeen or eighteen years ago. The horse has every appearance of being over twenty years old."

The entries of the next two days are of curious interest in that Australian interior, where only the explorers could have conveyed cattle. Was this cow one of Leich-hardt's ? " May 2nd.—The depôt. This morning W. L. Galbraith and Frank, while out after horses, came on fresh traces of the cattle following and crossing our track of last night. Changing their horses, and procur-ing a supply of ammunition, they started in pursuit, and found a cow and a fine young bull in a billibong, about three miles from here. The cattle, on seeing them, started, and Frank shot the cow with a Colt's revolver. Galbraith also secured the bull, when seven miles distant from the depôt, after some hard galloping, being several times hunted by the bull. He at last shot him with a Whitney revolver, when in the act of overtaking and horning his horse. The bull was killed on the spot, and fell completely over, from the speed at which he was going. The two camels have just packed in the cow: O'Donnell and Galbraith are gone out again with rations and water for Frank and Mr. Williams, who are camped by the bull. It may be imagined that frying is going on to a great extent. Our friend Winkely, a black, has been in a state of great surprise at such a supply of meat, and fingered the fat with the eyes of a cannibal. He made no such signs of disgust at a huge junk of beef as he used to do at damper, pronouncing it 'malingkee,'—bad; but roasted it on the coals, and devoured it.

"May 3rd. Commenced at day-break to cut up the cow for curing. The meat excellent, and very fat. Winkely in a state of consternation at the effects of the Colt's revolver bullet, which had broken the shoulder-blade and one rib. I think his report on the 'piccanniny mucketie' to his friends will have a good effect. The bull was brought in about two o'clock, and weighed about seven hundred weight, and is very fat. Frying to an extraordinary extent still goes on, and the conversation here is extremely beefy. Captain Sturt is slightly lame from a strain he got in being caught, but I hope will soon be all right."

The time was now come for Winkely the black to go home, and another native was come to take his place; but at the last moment Winkely disgraced himself. That temptation which the sight of European implements and conveniences must naturally excite in all savages had overcome him, and besides the presents given him, he had secreted another tomahawk, a pannikin, a saddle, and some straps. As the best punishment, the tomahawk given him was taken away, and the new black, who was believed to be an accomplice, was walked off with Winkely. They retired, casting sundry looks behind them, apprehensive of a shot from the terrible revolver.

During all this time the flood was slowly creeping on at the rate of two miles a week. This was in consequence of the flatness of the country, and the number of channels and large backwaters which it had to fill. The water was of a clear olive-green colour, and so far as it reached the creek, became a fine river.

On the 12th of May the party was agreeably surprised by the arrival of Corporal Wauchope and Trooper Poynter, of the South Australian mounted police, with despatches from the Exploration Committee. They had been three days without water on the way; the upper holes of Strzelecki's Creek being then quite dry. On the 17th, Mr. Howitt, accompanied by seven of the party, with nine horses and nine camels, returned with these messengers to Blanchewater for stores, and reached that place on the 30th.

On the second journey to Cooper's Creek, Howitt's instructions were, before bringing down the remains of Burke and Wills, to remain on the look out for the parties of Landsborough and Walker, one or other of which might be expected to reach the depôt from the north, in quest of the missing explorers. He was also to look out for McKinlay's party, and give it any necessary aid. During his stay, he was to receive supplies and despatches viâ Adelaide and Blanchewater. In pursuance of these directions, he had remained at Cooper's Creek from February 18th till the end of May, but not idly. The very day that he reached Wills's grave, February 27th, he set out again to examine the way toward Mount Hopeless, finally set off for that place on the 5th of March, reached Blanchewater in eleven days, and was back at Cooper's Creek on the 2nd of April. On the 15th, he quitted the depôt again, and made an examination of the country in a south-west direction, as far as the edge of Sturt's Desert, and returned to the depôt on the 1st of

May. No news of the exploring parties having yet reached him, but having seen traces of McKinlay south of Lake Hope in returning from Blanchewater, on the 3rd of July, he once more left Cooper's Creek for a more extensive journey N.W., in fact, to cross Sturt's Desert, in the hope of finding the tracks of McKinlay, and giving him aid, if, as the natives asserted, he had been locked up by the floods. The track he followed across the desert was the one made use of by the natives of Lake Hope, Cooper's Creek, and Kyejerou, on their long journeys to procure the "pitchery" so much used by them as a narcotic, and, therefore, he concluded, the shortest known to them. He was attended by Dr. Murray, Messrs. W. Phillips, H. McWilliams, and Black Charley, thirteen horses, and a month's rations. He proceeded on this journey along the track by which he returned from his former northern trip, forming almost a straight line to the N.W. It was now winter, and the rains had produced a wonderful change in the desert; there was plenty of water, and plenty of grass amongst the stones. They had some trouble in a black guide of that district bolting, and having to be pursued and brought back; but they were at Williams's Creek on the 6th, at Kyejerou Creek the next day, at Appanparrow on the 8th, and on the southern edge of Sturt's Desert on the 9th. The first view of the desert showed it as if done in Indian ink and sepia, but when they got into it, although the stones by places were densely packed together like a pavement, in others larger, and loosely strewn on a spongey soil, and following alternate stretches of sand-ridges, grass and salt-bushes, prickly acacias, and a good deal of stunted timber, yet there were clay-pans, and channels of water, and flats covered with as rich a vegetation as the most luxuriant cloverfield. "Taking all in all," Howitt observes, as Wills had done, "the travelling is by no means bad, and far better than our track across the Stokes Range; and thus far the celebrated desert is very little different from large tracts of country in what is known in South Australia as the Far North and the Nor' West."

July 11th. They came upon a flooded creek, which they could not cross, and upon a lake amid sand-hills, about six miles in diameter, which the leader named Lake Short, after Mr. Short, one of the party; and who had also been with the leader in Gippsland. Numbers of emus were feeding on the flats very tamely, and native companions and water-fowl were numerous. Probably Tommy, the native, would have enjoyed a good fat rat as much as a wild duck, for the evening before, he had caught a dozen, pulled off their tails, and tied them in a bunch, and then, roasting the rats in the ashes, devoured them *seriatim*, very much like biting so many sausages. The two blacks this journey were a nuisance. Charley, near this lake, got lost, black-fellow as he was, and was found going in a wrong direction, and having "big one cry," because "lose 'im all about white-fellow." Tommy was frightened at being out of his own district; and Charley was of no use after Perodinna blacks tried to kill him for his clothes. The leader observes that he must certainly be a little cracked, for one very cold night he took off all his clothes, and sat by the fire, having a talk to himself, after which, he put a lot of stones that were round the fire into his blankets, and lay down on the ground, with a charred log to warm him. Williams found him that way, and had some trouble to put him to-rights. Major Mitchell says, that his blacks frequently stripped themselves naked, and lay down by the fire in that state, on very cold nights.

On the 13th of July they crossed the tracks of two horses, going towards the hills, and soon after the same tracks returning. They appeared to be three months old, and they attributed them to some of McKinlay's party. The next day they crossed the tracks of a number of horses, and two or three camels, going up a creek about N.E. This was in latitude 26° 14', longitude 139° 22'. They were now convinced that they were the tracks of McKinlay's party, and were on the *qui vive* to follow them up. About 3 o'clock they came to a native camp, buried in tall marsh-mallows in flower, looking like a field of white hollyhocks. An old native, whose hut they found, shut the door with a bundle of grass, but Tommy held a palaver with him, and persuaded him to come out. He said McKinlay's party were camped "three sleeps" down the creek, with camels, horses and sheep, and counted the three stages on his fingers, naming the places. On this information they turned back. At evening they camped on a billibong, on a clayey plain, covered with herbage, marsh-mallows, and native spinach. There the leader, walking out again, saw the tracks, but only faintly. The next day they saw them again, but indistinct, and nearly drifted up; and there they soon lost them again. They pursued the quest, hunting right and left, over dry plains, and amongst water-holes left by the floods, till near Lake Sturt. If the old native had been correct, they must then have been within a day's journey of the camp of McKinlay, but there was no sign of it. Howitt, who had ridden a-head of the party in this search, now returned to camp 71, and the next morning struck off in a N. course, which he followed to the 26th degree of latitude. They again communicated with natives, but got no clue. They now followed down Wills' Creek southward, and on the 19th came on the track of a single horse, but very old, and with several single camel prints, which they thought probably were made by Burke's party. This was in the neighbourhood of some of the most pleasing scenery which they had seen in the interior. Wood and water, and luxuriant vegetation, marsh-mallows ten feet high, polygonum, and flowering plants. An old native, whom they endeavoured to get some information from, for Mr. Howitt had made himself master of the Cooper's Creek language, ran on, shouting "Amma murda!" as loud as he could, and bolted into a box swamp, and was lost in the polygonum in a few minutes.

Soon after seeing the horse-track they discovered the

fresh tracks of two bullocks, and presently found the animals feeding in a large plain, a mile or two from the creek. They believed them to be two of McKinlay's. They also saw the well-defined tracks of boots. After much looking about they retraced their steps up the creek N.W., still observing tracks of bullocks that had been wandering in different directions. From camp 74, latitude 25° 52', longitude 139° 19', Mr. Howitt rode northward to some sandstone hills, which he named Sampson's Range, after Mr. Sampson of the contingent exploring party, and then forward again some miles, where he saw still before him stony plains, with plenty of grass, and beyond them, mid from east to west, a second stony desert. Returning to the camp, they now set off south again, as their provisions were nearly exhausted. On their way to Sturt's Lake some natives told them that Pinnaron (McKinlay) and the "white fellows" had thrown away their wheelbarrow (cart), and were gone with their horses, camels, and sheep, N.E., and round to E. They could only conclude that this was the case, and that McKinlay had gone away N.E. Ice was in their water-pots now every morning. The desert, in recrossing it, appeared about seventeen miles in the stony part. The Cooper's Creek Depôt was reached August 2nd, and all was found right, except that the lost camel could not be traced, though Messrs. Aitkin, Phillips, and Burrell had tracked him fourteen miles into the stones, where his traces were lost. On this journey they had seen the tracks of a number of horses going towards the desert and back, S.E., which they believed to be those belonging to a party from the Darling, seeking ground for stations.

On the 16th of August Mr. Howitt again set out for Blanchewater for supplies, accompanied by Messrs. Galbraith, O'Donnell, Burrell, and Teniel, with twenty horses. Aitkin, M'Williams, and C. Phillips, attended with the camels to carry water. Everything on the way was dry and burnt up. Blanchewater was reached on the 27th of August, but not meeting despatches there as expected, the leader and light party rode on to Angipena, 120 miles.

A word or two may here be said, in passing, on the curious character of this part of the country. Angipena, says my son in one of his letters, is one of the most picturesque places that I have seen in South Australia. It is in a basin of low, round hills, rising out of the thick pine forest, and surrounded by high and very ragged slate mountains. The pines suit the character of the mountains, and the gums in the creeks break the monotony of the pines. Green grass and flowers, too, are growing up to the top of the low, round hills that rise above the pines, so that it looks very cheerful. This is a police-station, and the conversation is very horsy, and when horse is not the subject; copper is, varied with "Bill So-and-so," and "Jack This and That."

Angipena bears a certain resemblance to Wilpena Pound, somewhat east of Mount Deception, between Lakes Torrens and Blanche. Those who have seen the great circles on the face of the moon through a telescope, may form an idea of how Wilpena Pound looks from the moon. It is an enormous circle, of many miles in diameter, surrounded by high, steep, impassable rocks, and having only one entrance through the rocks, called the Main Gap. From this circumstance it is called the Pound. It contains, it is said, twenty square miles of land of the richest description, has flowing creeks, and is occupied as a joint-stock station, feeding many thousands of sheep.

The scenery of Parallana, Jacob's Station, near Mount Hopeless, is also very striking. "This place," says Mr. Howitt, "is one of the most wild and romantic spots I have ever seen. The station is in a deep ravine, so that you do not see it until you come to the edge of a level, stony plain. Looking up the valley from the house, a high mass of mountain, some two or three thousand feet high, rising in rugged ridges, and peaks; one mass of red slate rock above another, overlook the ravine, and the high peaks are in a sort of transparent indigo-blue haze, and not a tree or branch to be seen. The air looks so clear that you can almost see the texture of the stone; it seems to confuse one's ideas of distance. When first seen, as I saw it, at sunset, when the light and shade is very striking; it almost takes one's breath for a moment. It is, indeed, wild and savage in the highest degree. No rain, however, has fallen for a long time, so that you may imagine it a desert of stone. Our hosts here are very hospitable, but you would think it strange to see rows of fire-arms, all loaded and ready on the walls, as the blacks cannot be trusted; only three days before our arrival there had been an encounter with them at one of the outside stations.

"You may feel pity for the blacks, but they are such an idle, incorrigibly treacherous, lying race, that I am getting into a state of aversion towards them, and sometimes when harrassed by constant watching for three or four days and nights amongst the wild tribes beyond our depôt, I am almost tempted to wish that they would try to surprise us, that we might for once and all have it out with them. I can well understand the feeling of bitter enmity which always subsists between the outside settlers and the native tribes. In my last journey, for twelve days we never knew what it was to have a moment's rest, from constant watchfulness, day and night, except when actually on horseback and travelling."

On one occasion, near Lake Hope, he confesses that he was nearly driven to shooting one of these wild brethren of ours. "We are on the best terms with our black friends, and have had no serious trouble yet with them, except going up last time, with a small tribe near Lake Hope, who tried to kill my black boy. However, I hunted them very quickly, but without having to shoot any. It was very funny, although I was rather 'riled' at the time. One fellow nearly got shot as he tried to grab my revolver, and instinctively I almost pulled the trigger, having cocked it mechanically. But I fortunately bethought myself in time, and contented myself with poking it into his face, and telling him to be off, or I would shoot him. It was very absurd to see how they scampered. I then packed up, and rode through their camp, rifle in hand, to show them that we were not frightened at them. On the contrary, some of them I saw were shaking, and their teeth chattering. I find it a great advantage to be able to speak to them in their own language; and, by the bye, I find now that the curious broken language, spoken with and by blacks as English, is no more than a literal translation of their own languages, which are very simple in construction. Thus, instead of saying, 'Where are you going?' one would say, 'Which way walk?' an exact translation of their 'Woordary tay kana?' In the same way one would not say, 'Is the water dried up?' but 'That one water tumble down?' that is, 'dead.' The same phrase as 'Appa nannya ballena.'"

It is to me a great satisfaction that my son avoided shooting the man, and that he returned from his long and various wanderings amongst these children of the wilderness with hands clear from one drop of their blood. To the many excellent qualities of the Australian natives he, as well as almost every traveller amongst them, bears witness. They are, when you become acquainted with them, generally ready to serve you; but, in common with all wild tribes, they are tempted beyond their strength by the sight of the white-men's superior food, his implements, his sheep and cattle. The white-men have destroyed wholesale their sheep and cattle, the kangaroo, the emu, the wild turkey, and the opossum, to say nothing of usurping their country; and it would be more than human nature, especially untutored human nature, to behold all this with stoical equanimity. Incapable, as they appear, of adopting our civilization, it is their resentment of our encroachments and their reprisals on the white-men's flocks and herds that will, no doubt, pursue them to extinction. The natives, however, in all cases, have been first estranged by firing on them. Mr. Wentworth, in his "New South Wales," p. 116, says that the natives of Van Diemen's Land were irreconcilably embittered by an officer firing on them with grape shot, who thought they were advancing hostilely towards him, when they were only advancing in noisy joy. This was exactly the case with the natives of Cooper's Creek, fired on by McKinlay after they had been conciliated by Howitt.

In 1863, a seaman, named James Morrill, who was wrecked in 1846 on a voyage from Sydney to China, in the barque Peruvian, on the north-eastern coast of Australia, on Cape Cleveland, with several other persons, whom he survived, and who had continued to live amongst the blacks these seventeen years, made himself known to some stockmen in the north of Queensland. He contends that the blacks are a well-disposed people, but that the whites encroach without ceremony on their lands; feuds arise, and the stockmen, as, in consequence of the late discoveries, they advance north and westwards, regard them as universally hostile, shoot at them the moment they see them, and the blacks in return commit depredations on their cattle and sheep. The *Melbourne Argus* of March, 1863, stated that he was gone down to Brisbane to endeavour to have a better understanding effected between the blacks and whites; that the blacks prayed that at least the swamps and saltwater creeks might be left to them undisturbed, and they would give the upper rivers to the whites; that it was his intention to settle himself in those districts where the whites were now coming into contact with the blacks, and endeavour to secure these objects, namely, some remnants of land to the natives and security to the whites. The object is worthy of one who has received so much kindness from the natives, and every one must wish him all success. But the inevitable toils of extermination are gathering round the hunter race of Australia as of America, and, if any traces of it survive the rapid march of the tide of white life, it will be only in desert districts which have no attractions even for the all-grasping European. Blessed, however, be they, who, instead of accelerating the extinction of the doomed race, look kindly on it, and spare the uplifted hand of retaliation as often as possible. Let it be remembered that, as it perishes, it bequeaths to us a magnificent home and empire.

And now let us return from this digression, not without an object. Receiving news of the safety of the parties of McKinlay, Walker, and Landsborough, Howitt, on his return from this journey, made preparations to quit Cooper's Creek, and carry down the remains of Burke and Wills to Adelaide, and to proceed thence by sea to Melbourne. By taking the track to Mount Hopeless twice already, he had ascertained that the outlying South Australia stations were within seven days of Cooper's Creek. He had also ascertained that the route by Strzelecki's Creek was much worse from want of water and grass there than the one by Lake Hope. Already stations in the neighbourhood of Lake Hope were being taken up by Mr. Stuckey and Messrs. Deane and Hack, and it appears that Mr. Howitt had been on the lake with Mr. Deane, and was of the opinion of Mr. Elder and Mr. Stuckey, that Stuckey's Creek connects Cooper's Creek with Lake Hope.

Before leaving Cooper's Creek with the remains of Burke and Wills, he had, according to his instructions, made a deposit of stores and clothing in case any party of explorers should yet come that way. He had deposited ninety pounds of flour, a quantity of sugar, tea, and other small stores in proportion. The quantity of clothing which he had left was sufficient for twelve men, so that any party arriving at the depôt could be fully equipped. The stores were sufficient to support a party of twelve men till they could reach the settlements, allowing a fortnight at the depôt for the purpose of recruiting their strength. He left a notice-board over the cache, containing the discovery of the plant and also all the information which he possessed with reference to the tracks and watercourses between Cooper's Creek and the settlements, and marked the surrounding trees to a considerable distance from the depôt.

This being done early in October, he set forward with his party from this eventful place, bearing with them the remains of the brave men who had perished there. It was a subject of great regret to the leader that he was not authorized by his instructions to proceed to Gray's grave, and bring down his remains also. They took the way by Lake Hope, and he addressed a despatch to the Exploration Committee of Victoria from Blanchewater on the 22nd of that month. In this he states that, before leaving Cooper's Creek, he had collected the natives of that part of it, and given them clothes and other presents, and also the brass plate, stating their kindness to King, prepared for that purpose by the Committee. He also stated that these natives, far from molesting them during their sojourn at the creek, had carefully kept away from the country over which their horses and camels grazed; and even when compelled of late to resort to their waters for fish, the other holes below being exhausted, they never commenced fishing until one of their number had been down to the camp of the strangers to request leave. Before quitting the depôt, the natives came to say good-bye, and to enquire whether they might have the camp and the ground again on which it stood, as well as whether they might fish in the creek again; and, of course, the leader gave them permission to "sit down there again."

About half-way between Cooper's Creek and Lake Hope, about forty miles from the lowest waters of Cooper's Creek, and fifty from Lake Hope, they camped at a native well, called Murdacoloa, ten feet deep, which supplied them with 600 gallons of excellent water on the evening they arrived there, and stood at a level of three feet an hour afterwards. At a second water-hole, the blacks came to entreat the leader to go and shoot their neighbours at Coonaboora, promising to bury them! The creeks were running with water between Lake Hope and Lake Torrens, and this latter lake was full of water. One of their camels had strayed, and was not heard of.

On reaching Blanchewater, they went twenty miles to a spring in the mountains to give the horses a spell, and took advantage of the opportunity to make a short trip with gentlemen from the neighbouring stations, towards the Grey Ranges of Sturt, thinking it possible to find a short cut to the Darling which would have been of great advantage to the Far North. They left the camp in latitude 27°, Mullagan in latitude 30°, and crossed the lake country freshened up by the rains, but very miserable to the edge of the lake—a flat basin surrounded by sand-hills and stony country, and with a loose bed of salt soil containing gypsum. They found a number of springs of brackish water indicated by reeds, the only vegetation for miles, the country being exactly like powdered gingerbread. They pushed on eastward for Sturt's Depôt at Preservation Creek, and when about thirty miles from it, and ten miles within the Grey Range, found the country so frightfully dry, that having been for some time without water, they were compelled to return, the leader pronouncing this track one of the most arid ones that he had seen. The hollows in the dry channels of the creeks were piled with dead sticks and leaves, showing what a long period had elapsed since these creeks ran. Instead of the popular phrase, "as dry as a bone," they thought a more expressive one would be "as dry as the Grey Range."

As the train bearing the remains of the great explorers approached the city of Adelaide, Mr. Howitt and Dr. Murray hastened on before to prepare for their fitting reception in that city. They arrived on the 8th of December, and found the mayor and a company of the most distinguished men of the place doing honour to Mr. McKinlay on his safe return from his most successful expedition to the Gulf of Carpentaria, and across the continent to Queensland. Three hundred guests were assembled at a banquet, amongst them two of Mr. McKinlay's companions, Mr. Poole, and the humorous Mr. Davis, whose journal of the expedition has been published by Mr. Westgarth. In the midst of the feast Mr. Howitt and Dr. Murray walked in, and were received with loud cheers, and were conducted to the top of the room amid reiterated acclamations. They shook hands with the Chairman and Messrs. McKinlay and Davis, and then took their seats, all remaining standing until they had done so. It was a most interesting event, that men who had traversed such lengths of blazing wilderness, for the same object, should meet under such circumstances. The mayor in introducing Mr. Howitt and Dr. Murray, said, that after finding the remains of Burke and Wills, these gentlemen had been anxiously seeking Mr. McKinlay and party, who were then, he believed, 1200 miles away from them. Here they first met, and he might congratulate Messrs. Howitt and Murray on finding their old friends in such comfortable quarters. In reply, Mr. Howitt spoke in the warmest terms of the manner in which Mr. McKinlay had accomplished his arduous task of travel, and said, that if he were inclined to envy any explorer, it was he, for the splendid manner in which he had crossed the continent.

On the 11th, part of Mr. Howitt's party arrived at the railway station of Adelaide with the remains. No ceremony had been arranged, but crowding thousands, in a purely spontaneous movement, thronged the streets to see them conveyed thence to the barracks, which was appointed as their resting place till their removal to the steamer which should convey them to Melbourne. For a time all business was suspended, and the streets were silent, making most audible the slow tread of the crowd who followed the hearse, and the solemn sounds of the military band playing the "Dead March in Saul."

Similar honours were paid to the deceased martyrs of exploration during the time that the remains lay in Adelaide, and they were accompanied by the mayor and many of the ministers of state and distinguished inhabitants to the steamer, on which they were embarked for Melbourne. On Sunday morning, the 28th of De-

ARRIVAL OF THE REMAINS AT MELBOURNE.

cember, 1862, the remains of these great explorers arrived in Melbourne. The steamer Havilah which had brought them from Adelaide was sighted off Cape Otway at 1·30 P.M. on Saturday; and the Exploration Committee having been communicated with by telegram, everything was got in readiness to receive Mr. Howitt and his party, and from their hands the remains. The following is the account of the landing of the remains by the "Illustrated Melbourne Post."

"At twelve o'clock on Saturday night, Dr. Eades, the Mayor of Melbourne, attended by Dr. Wilkie, John Watson, Esq., and Dr. Macadam, members of the Exploration Committee, Dr. James of the Melbourne Hospital, and J. V. O. Bruce, Esq., proceeded to Sandridge in a mourning coach, followed by a hearse. The arrival of the Havilah, however, was delayed till five o'clock on Sunday morning, when these gentlemen, and also Ellen Dogherty, Mr. Burke's nurse, were in readiness on the pier to relieve Mr. Howitt's party from their charge. Mr. Howitt, Dr. Murray, and Mr. Weston Phillips, the paty attending the remains were briefly welcomed by the committee. The remains, which were contained in a very handsome case, inclosed in a strong outer covering, the whole appropriately shrouded by the Union Jack, were removed from the vessel to the hearse, the company following bare-headed. As the public was not aware of the arrival, not more than half a dozen strangers were present, and these remained in respectful attitudes at some distance from the procession. The remains placed at once in the hearse, were conveyed to the Royal Society's Hall in Melbourne, where they arrived at about seven o'clock, when Mr. Howitt handed over the keys of the case to Dr. Macadam, the honorary secretary of the society.

"Mr. Howitt received the congratulations of the committee, for the successful issue of his expedition, and the brave explorer and the whole of the party appeared in the enjoyment of perfect health. At the suggestion of the Mayor, Dr. Eades, the Corporation flag remained half mast high at the Town Hall the whole of the day, and the flag of the Havilah which had been lowered to half mast on her arrival in the harbour, continued so also."

On the following day, Monday the 29th, a meeting of the Exploration Committee was held formally to receive Mr. Howitt and the members of the expedition who had arrived with the remains. At this meeting the most cordial approbation was expressed of the able and satisfactory manner in which the expedition had been conducted. It was resolved that this expression of the sense of the services rendered to the colony by Mr. Howitt and his party should be presented in form engrossed on parchment, and should be presented at a public meeting, to be held on the evening of the day of the funeral of Burke and Wills, at which meeting addresses of recognition should also be presented to Captain Norman of the Victoria, and to Mr. Ambrose Kyte, the originator of the scheme of the expedition, and the donor of £1000 towards its expenses. Photographed copies of the address to the members of the relief expedition, were to be handed by Mr. Howitt to each individual of his party. Wednesday evening was fixed for the ceremony of placing the remains in their respective coffins, at a special meeting of the Exploration Committee.

In the course of the present meeting Mr. Howitt explained that Mr. Aitken and Mr. Charles Phillips had proceeded overland from South Australia to the Wimmera with the camels, and Mr. Williams had remained in Adelaide. He expressed his grateful sense of the most satisfactory manner in which he had been supported on the journey by Dr. Murray and every individual of the party. Dr. Murray stated that the health of the party, had on the whole, been very good, which he attributed to the ample supply of both preserved vegetables, and fresh ones grown in a temporary garden at Cooper's Creek, and to the free use of citric acid and lime-juice. It was reported that Dr. Murray had made a considerable collection of botanical and mineralogical specimens on the journey, and had brought down a series of photographic views of the scenery, etc.

At the meeting, when the case containing the remains was opened, they were found carefully sewn up in two packages. Mr. Howitt stated his belief that these bones were all that had been found on his first journey to Cooper's Creek. The hands and feet of Burke, and the skull, and a portion of the feet of Wills were missing, having, no doubt, been removed by the wild dogs. The shirt in which Wills died accompanied the remains, and was deposited with him in the coffin. The bones were arranged in their natural order by Dr. Wheeler, who had accompanied Mr. Howitt on his first journey, and a winding-sheet from the linen-chest of the Burke family was produced by Burke's nurse, Mrs. Dogherty, and his remains wrapped in it. Plate glass in the lids of the coffins permitted the remains to be seen, and a slide of wood to cover this when the funeral should take place.

The sides of the hall were draped with black cloth during the time that the remains lay in state and open to public inspection. The coffins stood on a handsome catafalque, approached on each side by a flight of five steps, and surmounted by a canopy, the four supports of which represented palm-trees.

On Wednesday, January 21st, the funeral took place. The coffins were placed on an elegant funeral car, and were attended to the Melbourne cemetery, as may be said, by the whole population of the place. The order of the procession was the following:—

The Castlemaine Light Dragoons.

The Band of the Castlemaine Rifle Volunteer Regiment, playing the "Dead March in Saul."

The Castlemaine Volunteer Rifles, under the command of Captain Ryland.

A firing-party of Police, consisting of forty men and officers, with arms reversed, under the command of Mr. Superintendent Lyttleton.

Clergymen on foot.

A mourning coach, conveying the Very Rev. the Dean of Melbourne.

Undertaker, slate lid, and mutes.

THE FUNERAL CAR, WITH REMAINS,

drawn by six horses, each horse being led by an attendant.

The pall-bearers, four abreast: those for Burke being Sir William Stawell, Mr. O'Shanassy, King, the survivor, Captain Standish, Mr. Kyte, Mr. Ireland, and Sir Francis Murphy; and for Wills—Mr. Thomas Wills, Dr. Müller, Captain Norman, the Hon. G. Verdon, Mr. Howitt, the Hon. Richard Heales, and the Mayor of Melbourne.

The chief mourners, three abreast.

The members of the Exploration Committee, three abreast.

Howitt's party.

The men of the Victoria steam sloop of war.

A mourning coach drawn by four horses, and conveying Mrs. Dogherty, Burke's nurse.

Five mourning coaches, conveying the Town Clerk and members of the Corporation of Melbourne.

The Governor's carriage, conveying his Excellency and his aide-de-camp, Captain Bancroft, and followed by three orderlies.

Six private carriages, conveying the Consuls for foreign states, in uniform, as under:—Mr. J. B. Were, Consul for Norway and Sweden, and Consul-General for Portugal; Mons. Truy, for France; Mr. Damyon, for Russia; Mr. J. Ploos Van Amstel, for the Netherlands; Mr. Michaelis, for Prussia; Mr. Schlostein, for the Hanseatic Towns; Mr. Cooper, for Portugal; Mr. S. Rentsch, for Switzerland; Mr. James Graham, for Italy.

A carriage, conveying the Vice-Chancellor of the Melbourne University, and Mr. Justice Chapman.

A carriage, conveying Sir James Palmer, President of

the Legislative Council, and the Hon. Matthew Hervey, M.C.L.

A carriage, conveying the Hon. J. S. Johnson, M.L.A., the Hon. W. H. F. Mitchell, M.L.C., the Hon. J. D. Wood, M.L.A., and Mr. A. J. Smith, M.L.C.

A carriage, conveying Thomas H. Power, Esq., M.L.C., and others.

Other members of Parliament, principally of the Legislative Assembly, on foot, and some in cabs.

Officers of the Police, and of the Army and Navy, including those of the colonial sloop of war, Victoria.

A party of Melbourne Volunteer Cavalry.

Members of Municipal Councils, on foot.

The M.U. Independent Order of Odd Fellows.

The Ancient Order of Foresters.

The Ancient and Independent Order of Odd Fellows.

The Grand United Order of Odd Fellows.

The Ancient Order of Rechabites.

Citizens in carriages, and on foot.

It will be observed by the above that there were several alterations in the order of the procession previously determined upon.

The Geelong Corporation was represented by the Mayor, and only two members of the Council.

The funeral service was performed by the Dean of Melbourne, attended by all the principal clergymen, and by the Governor; and the remains were deposited in the vault, over which it was resolved to erect a monument to the memory of the explorers. The ceremony was concluded by the firing of three volleys over the grave by a select party of police.

The same evening, at the public meeting appointed, the formal thanks of the Royal Society and the public were presented to Mr. Howitt and his party, to Captain Norman, of the Victoria, and to Mr. Ambrose Kyte, by the Chief Justice, Sir William Stawell, the Governor, Sir Henry Barkly, in the chair.

It is gratifying to record that pensions have been conferred by the Victoria Government on the relations of Wills, on King, the sole survivor of the expedition, and on Mrs. Dogherty, Burke's nurse. I find in one of the Melbourne journals the following particulars of this honourable fact:—

"In Committee of Supply various votes of a special character were taken before Parliament broke up. Among them were the following :—£3125 for the purchase of debentures (to remain the property of the Government), the interest of which to be paid as an annuity to King, the survivor of the exploring expedition; £2000 for the purchase of debentures, in a similar manner, the interest to be paid as an annuity to Mrs. Wills, the mother of Wills, the late explorer; £500 to each of the two Misses Wills; £125 to Dr. Wills (to pay his passage to England); £200 to an Indian cameldriver, who lost the use of an arm by the bite of a camel while on the exploring expedition; and a similar sum to Mr. Welsh, whose eyes were seriously injured by a stroke of light while he was taking an observation, while he was a member of Howitt's searching party; and £1000 for the purchase of debentures, the interest on which will be paid to Mrs. Ellen Dogherty, the foster mother of poor Burke, who arrived in this colony soon after the departure of Burke on his gallant but fatal expedition."

And thus we terminate this eventful history, in which the loss of two meritorious men, and one of their followers, has given an impulse to the development of Australia, and to the spread of population over its whole extent, such as could scarcely be anticipated even from its previous unparalleled career, and unequalled in rapidity of progress by anything in the world's history. To a few of these striking incidents I devote a concluding chapter.

CHAPTER XX.

CONCLUSION OF DISCOVERY IN AUSTRALIA.

Introduction of steam on the Murray and other rivers by Captain Cadell, Mr Randall, and others.—Impulse given by the late expeditions across the continent.—Squatters advancing on all the tracks of Gregory, Walker, and Landsborough on the east—on those of Stuart and McKinlay centrally.—Advances into York Peninsula.—Two towns to be built there.—Other squatters on the Belyando, Burdekin, and Lynd.—Advances on the track of Burke and Wills.—In the Stony Desert itself.—Of others on Lake Hope.—In Western Australia the same spread of flocks and herds into new regions.—Nickol Bay.—The De Grey region.—Doubtful Bay.—Camden Harbour.—Applications for islands in Shark's Bay in Recherche Archipelago.—Settlement in Dampier's Land.—Further attempts to explore the country on the Australian Bight.—New settlement on the Adelaide under Colonel Finniss.—Conditions of sale of lands.—Immediately bought up.—News of Colonel Finniss at Adam's Bay.—Hopes entertained from this settlement in the north-west.

FRESH EXPLORATIONS IN THE NORTH-EAST.—Dalrymple's tour in the district of the Burdekin.—Traces its course to the Rockingham Bay.—Exploration of its mouth by Governor Bowen.—Voyage of the Governor to Cape York to examine the site of a settlement.—His admiration of the scenery along the coast.—Advantages of the Great Barrier Reef.—Progress of steam navigation on the east course.—Sir Charles Nicholson recommends the exploration of New Guinea.—Importance of that island to Australia.—Mr. Scott traces the valley of the Burdekin from the Valley of Lagoons to the sea.—A new port and town contemplated at Rockingham Bay, and direct road to the Lagoons.—Amazing advance of settlement northwards.—Discoveries of other kinds than geographical.—Prospects of the great future.

In a work of this kind the success of the explorations of the Australian rivers by the means of steam vessels ought not to be omitted. By an article in the Geographical Journal, Vol. 31, p. 145, and by a note thereto appended, it would appear that Mr. W. R. Randall, in his small steamer the Mary Anne, " was the first, in 1853, to proceed up the Murray, and eventually reached Maiden's Punt." The same year, however, Captain Cadell proceeded in a steamer up the Murray to near Albury, about 1200 miles, with the greatest ease and success. The facility with which this was accomplished excited universal astonishment, and inaugurated a regular use of steam on that great river. This grand success was followed up by himself, Captains Johnson and Robertson, Mr. Randall, and others, on the Murrumbidgee, the Darling, and the Barwan, making accessible to the spread of squatting, trade, and population, an immense reach of country on those rivers, and on the Edwards.

In 1859 we find Captain Cadell and Mr. Randall almost at the same moment on the Darling. Lieutenant-Governor McDonnell reported that in February, 1859, he had undertaken an exploring voyage up the Darling with Captain Cadell, in the steamer Albany, and reached Mount Murchison, 600 miles by water, above the junction. Yet we have a letter to Governor McDonnell from Mr. W. R. Randall, dated Adelaide, April 16, 1859, informing him that he sailed in the steamer Gemini up the Darling, from the junction of the Darling and Murray, on February the 2nd of that same year. Still, it would appear that these voyagers did not see each other. How could this be? The Gemini, setting out from the junction on the 2nd of February, reached Fort Burke on the 20th, and Gunnewara, on the Barwan, on the 23rd. It was also a fortnight in returning down the Darling to the junction, thus occupying the whole of February, and more. Where were Governor McDonnell and Captain Cadell, who also sailed up the Darling in February? Probably their shorter voyage was made whilst Mr. Randall was farther up the Darling, and on the Barwan.

Mr. Randall followed the Darling and Barwan 1800 miles by water, though this was only 620 miles by land from the junction, such are the windings of these rivers. The whole distance of the voyage was, by the windings of the river, from the sea 2400 miles. He calculated that at Nonah, or, as it is called, the Black's Fishing-grounds, the highest point that he reached, to be in about 29° 25′ S. latitude, and 147° E. longitude, 120 miles above Fort Bourke, seventy miles below the junction of the Nammoy, and about 400 miles from the New South Wales seaboard. The existing state of the flood did not admit of his penetrating farther. Above Menindeche the river became much broader, straighter, freer from snags, than it is lower, so much so, that the Gemini pursued her course by moonlight as well as by day, without any difficulty whatever. At Nonah he was stopped by a fall, which, when the river is full, becomes a very swift rapid, the descent being eight feet in 200 or 300 yards, and the water boiling and foaming over rocks for that distance. Mr. Randall believes a passage might easily be cut through these rocks, which would open up another 100 miles of the Barwan, independent of the Nammoy, and other tributaries, which are doubtless navigable to small steamers. From Mount Murchison to Gunnewara, a distance of 280 miles by land, he found only one station occupied, though he was informed that every inch of it was taken up. Beyond the falls the country was completely occupied, chiefly by cattle, and heavily stocked, and the settlers said that they would put on sheep the moment there was a certainty of having steam to send their wool to Adelaide. The country above Mount Murchison Mr. Randall pronounced superior to any he had seen on the Murray or Murrumbidgee, and eminently suited to the vine and tropical fruits. The banks of the rivers, in many places, abounded with a variety of beautiful flowers and shrubs, as well as native oranges and melons eaten by the natives. The natives were numerous, but inoffensive. Mr. Randall thinks the navigation of the Darling capable of much improvement by damming-up the back-waters, by locks, etc., for which the character of the river is eminently suited.

But the impulse which the crossing of the Australian continent by Burke and Wills, combined with their tragic fate, gave to the spirit of discovery and the spread of population, has been little short of marvellous. The final success of Stuart soon after, a success enhanced in value by following on so many efforts, so many repulses; the prosperous and ably conducted journeys of McKinlay, Walker, Howitt, and Landsborough, created an entirely new epoch in Australian colonization. The terror of interior deserts vanished; the long pause, during which men cast longing glances towards the mysterious northern regions, yet remained hovering amid the pastures of the south was at an end : fresh travellers started for the yet unexplored latitudes, north, east, and west; and the possessors of flocks and herds, such as the ancient patriarchs never knew, began to move their bleating and lowing legions to "fresh woods and pastures new," undaunted by the certain prospect of hundreds and thousands of miles of unknown mountains, rivers, plains, and deserts before them. Two years have yet scarcely elapsed, and we hear of squatters having advanced far into the interior on the east by the routes of McKinlay, Gregory, Walker, and Landsborough, fast approaching the Gulf of Carpentaria; of their having actually entered York Peninsula in the farthest north-east, before thought even too inhospitable for the natives, and that the government of Queensland is preparing to build two towns on the peninsula. We hear of numerous flocks and herds spreading over the vast plains of the Barcoo, the Thomson, the Flinders, and the Gilbert, and amongst the mountains of the Belyando, the Burdekin, and the Lynd. In the central regions, other flocks and herds are fast hastening on the track of Burke and Wills, beyond the Darling and the Parroo, amongst the Barrier, the Grey, and the Stoke Ranges, on to Cooper's Creek. Howitt himself, before returning, saw traces of bucolic explorers on the very borders of the Stony Desert of Sturt, and found Hack, and Dean, and Stuckey with their trains and troops of live stock, far beyond the arid regions of the Torres, which had turned back as impracticable the undaunted Eyre, the man who braved the burning and waterless wastes of the great Australian Bight. He found them taking possession of the environs of Lake Hope, and advancing from that direction also to Cooper's Creek.

Mr. Stuart, before completing his journey across the continent, found squatting stations on the river Neale, about the 27th degree of latitude, and since then they have not only advanced much farther, but flocks and herds are said to be on their way, to travel to the farthest north by this route. Western Australia, at the same time, has been actively pushing her explorations farther into the interior from her position.

The discoveries of F. T. Gregory stimulated the spirit of not only Western Australia, but the squatting population of other Australian states, to explore and take up pasturage lands in that direction. Whilst these intentions of further explorations northwards both east and west were in activity, Captain Denham, also, of H.M.S. Herald, who had been stationed on the Australian coasts nine years, on his return homewards, on passing through Torres Strait, was enabled to clear away some of the reported dangers of that passage, and to fix the position of certain shoals. This was a great service, seeing that these straits must every year be more and more visited as northern settlement advances. Commander Yule completed the sailing directions for this track, thereby giving to the mariner the further security thus acquired.

In Western Australia Mr. F. T. Gregory was contemplating fresh explorations. In 1861, Messrs. C. E. and A. Dempster, B. Clarkson, C. Harper, and a native servant, made an excursion as far as Mount Kennedy, in which they observed an extensive chain of lakes, passing out of sight to the east, and heard from the natives that, long ago, three white men, with horses, had reached a large salt lake far to the east, and, after travelling about its shores, had turned back, and perished. Who could these be? Some have imagined that they might belong to Leichhardt's party.

The year 1863 was memorable for the spirited prosecution of enquiry into the regions opened up by Mr. F. T. Gregory, in the neighbourhood of the De Grey. Mr. Padbury followed up the steps of Mr. Gregory, and contributed, with Mr. Larnach and others, liberally towards an examination of the south-eastern part of the colony, setting out from Northam under Mr. Dempster, thence to Port Malcolm, and thence northwards into the interior. Such was the enthusiasm for exploration and pastoral settlement, that the most frightful deserts crossed by Mr. Eyre did not deter the adventurers, or dash their hopes of splendid *terræ incognitæ* lying beyond them. At the same time, Mr. Austin, in South Australia, was pursuing an examination of the mines of that colony.

Neither of the southern expeditions proved very satisfactory. Mr. Dempster, accompanied by William and Andrew Dempster, Messrs. Maxwell and Larnach, discovered nothing but barren, waterless country, and were driven back by these obstacles. Mr. Lefroy and his party penetrated eastward from York to longitude 122° 40′, and gave a more hopeful view of that part of the country, but the publication of his journal did not bear out to the intending settlers the promises he gave. The land, where it appeared tolerably good, had neither streams nor surface water: it was for the most part a waterless, treeless country, entirely destitute of animal life. In the contrary direction a company was formed to take up available lands, said to be seen by Delisser and Mackie, north of Fowler's Bay.

In the far north-west, more favourable results were obtained. Messrs. Brown and others found the mouth of the Glenelg in Doubtful Bay; in fact, that, as in Captain Grey's chart, there were two mouths. The best mouth of the Glenelg was found on the eastern side of George Water, in lat. 15° 47′ 30″ S., and long. 124° 40′ 50″ E. Twenty miles inland the two mouths united in a river eight miles wide, and from three to ten fathoms deep. Their vessel took them as far as the cascades seen by Captain Grey, and in addition to the fine land seen by him, they discovered large tracts besides, capable of taking all the stock and settlers which could be sent thither for the next twenty years. The explorers concluded that Camden Harbour, inside Brecknock Harbour, would be the site of the capital, as offering every advantage for communication with the Indian Archipelago. Accordingly numbers of farmers from about Mount Beckwith, and other districts near Talbot, Western Australia, were preparing to proceed thither, and locate the first township of Camden Harbour. Advantageous terms of rental of squatting stations and purchase of farms were offered by the government.

On the De Grey, Mr. F. Gregory's country, a party had landed from the Mystery and Tien-Tsin, consisting of Messrs. Hunt, Turner, Samson, Nairn, and Ridley, who found the country much as Gregory had described it, and professed to have discovered from 60,000 to 80,000 acres of good grazing country, not seen before. Much of the country seen by Gregory was, however, but indifferent, and the hilly parts full of loose stones, which made the travelling very trying for the horses. The spinifex grass, they had an idea might be exported for purposes similar to hemp.

In 1864 Mr. Turnbull, a Victorian colonist and his son applied for a lease of Dirk Hartog's Island, Shark Bay, on which it seems there are 200,000 acres of grazing country. Mr. Larnach also applied for the lease of Middle Island, in Recherche Archipelago, and 200,000 acres on the mainland, including the eastern shore of Israelite Bay, as far as the western extremity of Point Malcolm, where it was thought discovery might be extended into the southern interior, but the proposition was declined by the government. All these facts showed the immense desire for land, and that through this, exploration would be perpetually stimulated. Accordingly there were immediately proposals for an expedition to Camden Bay lying between the 15th and 16th degrees of latitude, and for founding a settlement between the rivers Glenelg and Prince Regent. Again, Mr. Panter and a large party, including the Messrs. Panter, Turner, Scott, Du Boulay, F. and H. Caporn, Gallop, Lawrence, Stokes, two natives, and Wilsman a convict, were preparing to start in March of the year 1864, with five pack-horses, to explore Dampier's Land, lying between the 17th and 18th degrees of latitude, whilst Mr. Nairn had been further examining the country of the De Grey. In September and October, 1863, he and one companion traced a good deal of country on the

Shaw, and near the junction of the De Grey and Ridley, but found it poor, sandy, and full of spinifex.

In the mean time, another attempt was being made to penetrate into the formidable regions of the Great Australian Bight. Mr. Thomas M'Farlane, towards the end of August, 1863, started from Streaky Bay, with a party of two men and six horses, whence he made his way to Fowler's Bay, through 200 miles of a country made famous for its dreary sterility by Eyre. There his men, having had quite enough of it, refused to go any further. In vain did he endeavour to procure others to supply their place; but undaunted, he set out alone on the 24th of November for the head of the Great Australian Bight, having three horses, and provisions for three months. He could not even induce a native to accompany him as guide. On this journey he was without water for his horses three and a half days, and for himself two and a half days. He saw there a few wretched natives, who subsisted on wallabies and snakes. He could discover no trace of a harbour between Fowler's Bay and the head of the Bight. It appears that he penetrated about fifty miles northwards, through a level country of some grass and salt bush, but of no water. Finding that he and his horses must perish of thirst if he proceeded, he retraced his steps, and again took the desperate journey from Fowler's to Streaky Bay, whence he made a detour to Gawler's Ranges, and back to Streaky Bay, whence he sailed for Adelaide. In this journey Mr. M'Farlane suffered all the hardships which Eyre had suffered before him, and which make it a desperate attempt to penetrate the southern interior from that coast.

But the crowning attempt of these various ones at extending the settlement of the coastal country of Southern, Western, and Northern Australia, has been that of South Australia, which in April, 1864, sent out a body of emigrants to occupy some site on the north-western extremity of the country, and thence to penetrate by degrees inland into the country opened up by Stuart and A. C. Gregory. The expedition consisted of about forty persons, exclusive of the crews of the ships. The settlers were to be conveyed to their destination in three vessels, the Henry Ellis, a vessel of 464 tons, commanded by Captain Phillips; the government schooner Yatala; and the survey ship Beatrice. These were to proceed by Cape Leeuwin, or Torres Straits, as best suited the sailing of the different vessels, and to rendezvous at Adam Bay in Clarence Straits, at the mouth of the Adelaide river. Colonel Finniss, one of the original founders of Adelaide, not yet thirty years ago, led forth this first swarm from the still young hive. They were well supplied with stores, arms, cattle, and horses; and were to build warehouses, and form a stockade in Adam Bay till they had had time to survey the situation, and the part of the coast best calculated for the site of the settlement. Half a million of acres were to be sold. These 500,000 acres were to be divided into two portions, one moiety to be offered in London, and the other in Adelaide, together with 1562 town lots of half an acre each. Of each of these portions, it was decided that one half, or 125,000 acres, should be sold in lots of 160 acres each with one town lot, at 7s. 6d. an acre if applied for before the 25th of March, 1864; the residue and remaining moiety to be offered at 12s. an acre. As soon as the first 500,000 acres were disposed of, the Crown Lands were to be sold in lots of not less than 160 acres each, at £1 per acre; the purchaser of one lot of 160 acres having a claim for one town lot. The first portion of 125,000 offered at Adelaide, 117,000 were sold previously to the 25th of March; the whole of the 125,000 offered in London were immediately taken up; and I hear that the whole 500,000 acres were speedily sold.

The instructions for determining the final site of the capital and port of this new colony, were evidently well considered. They were that, "a good and secure port, easily navigable, and conveniently situate for trading to and from Malay, Asia, and India. If the site be healthy and otherwise well situated for a capital, let port and capital be combined; but should it be desirable to form the port and capital on one and the same site, high table-land as near to the port as possible, but at the same time easily accessible from the interior, to be chosen. Under no circumstances are land-locked harbours, or swampy localities to be fixed upon. Should the Adelaide river not afford proper sites, Port Darwin, south of Adam Bay is next to be tried, and then Port Paterson, and the surrounding waters on to Victoria River. Should none of these places be proper as the site of a settlement, attention is then to be directed to the various inlets of Van Diemen's Gulf, including the North and South Alligator Rivers. If all these localities fail, the exploration is then to be turned eastward, if necessary, to the Gulf of Carpentaria, as far as the River Roper in Limmen Bight, but avoiding Port Essington and Raffle's Bay." Till such site be found, the party, stock, and stores were to remain at Adam Bay, where the depôt should be well guarded, while Colonel Finniss proceeded in the Yatala on the necessary search. Considerable discretionary power of deviation from the plan prescribed was left to the colonel.

The Messrs. Elder had already placed another ship on the berth for this northern settlement, to be despatched about the middle of May. Sheep were to be sent out in this vessel, and sheep and cattle were on the way overland.

By a recent mail, a despatch, dated August 13th, was received from Colonel Finniss, in Adelaide, announcing that the three vessels had all arrived safely in June last, at Adam Bay. The depôt had been made at Escape Cliffs, a few miles south of Cape Hotham, and that they were about to proceed with the survey of the country. They were unable yet to say where they should decide on the site for a town, but that the river Adelaide was navigable for sixty miles for vessels of any burthen, and that there was plenty of fine land on its banks, and timber at hand. Colonel Finniss felt persuaded that the country inland would answer well for wool-growing, and that cattle would thrive. He believed the soil would produce tropical vegetation generally, and, if the climate would permit, extra-tropical productions, especially such as succeed in South Australia. Commander Hutchinson had sent charts and sailing directions, direct to the Hydrographer's Office, Admiralty, London, but the early leaving of the mail prevented the sending of long accounts. They arrived without casualties, and landed the horses and the bullocks which they took out, safely.

It is calculated that abundant labour for the cultivation of these northern lands will be readily obtained in the shape of Malays, Chinese, and Coolies, who, it is said, will be ready to take employment in North Australia to any extent. That they will answer for all purposes except as stockmen, who must be obtained from the southern colonies of Australia, assisted by natives from the coast of Madras, who are said to be extremely fond of, and useful in shepherding, shearing, tailing out cattle, bullock-driving, and even horse-training, if well looked after by European overseers. These people have almost a monopoly of all employments connected with horses and cattle; and, moreover, are well adapted to field labour, and work well under the superintendence of Europeans. Mr. Earl has shown that they are fond of emigrating, and annually arrive in the Straits' settlements in large numbers, the voyage occupying only about six days. All necessary securities for their return home when they desire it, after their term of engagement, must be taken by the Imperial Government.

While these active measures for extending exploration and colonization on the west coasts of Australia proceeded, scarcely less have those been on the east, both alike taking a northern direction. In 1859, Mr. George Elphinstone Dalrymple undertook with five other Englishmen, an expedition of exploration in the districts of the Burdekin, Suttor, and Belyando, lying between the parallels 19° and 22° of south latitude.

In these regions they greatly extended the knowledge which Leichhardt, Mitchell, Kennedy, and Gregory had given us of them. They traced the Burdekin into the Pacific Ocean, at a point a short distance north of Cleveland Bay, and not near Cape Upstart, as Leichhardt had conjectured. They reported that the valley of the Burdekin would form an admirable route for the intended telegraphic line towards the Gulf of Carpentaria, and thus form a medium of quick communication with India and China. They felt assured from the abundance of water, and the richness of vast tracts of land, that this would become one of the finest and largest pastoral and agricultural regions of Australia. The rich, low country along the coast, and the alluvial flats of the Burdekin, they regarded as well adapted to tropical cultivation, and especially of cotton, sugar, tobacco, etc.

In consequence of this report, Sir George Bowen, the Governor of Queensland, sent out the Spitfire, under command of Mr. J. W. Smith, and conveying Mr. Dalrymple, Commissioner of Crown Lands, Mr. Stone, Surveyor, and Mr. Fitzallan, botanical collector, to examine the probable mouth of the Burdekin. They sailed in August, 1860. They found Port Molle closely shut in with mountains, unbroken, and covered with dense scrub, so as to cut off all communication with the interior. They then proceeded to Port Denison, and were gratified to find it a splendid little port, sheltered from all winds. Starting thence, the coast was carefully examined for the mouth of the Burdekin. This was eventually found in the inner western corner of Cape Cleveland. The entrances were discovered to form a delta exceeding sixty miles, and to present flood-marks at a height of twenty feet. These were all traced, and found to converge in one point close to Dalrymple's farthest in 1859. No doubt, therefore, remained that they were the outlets of the Burdekin, and at the same time that they were utterly useless for the purposes of navigation.

In 1862, the Governor, Sir George Bowen accompanied by Commodore Burnett, sailed in the Pioneer to Cape York, to determine the best site for a town. The situation chosen for the settlement was the bank immediately over the anchorage of Port Albany, the point before recommended by Lieutenant Chimmo, but the future town—destined perhaps, one day, to be the Singapore of Australia, would doubtless grow up on both sides of the narrow channel, separating Albany from the mainland. It was to be named Somerset, in acknowledgement of the aid given to the undertaking by the First Lord of the Admiralty. The governor gave a highly flattering account of the scenery of this part of the continent. He says:—"The general aspect of the coast along which the Pioneer sailed for nearly 2000 miles, resembled that of Southern Italy and Greece. The mountain ranges of Northern Queensland have much of the picturesque outline and rich colouring of the Appenines in Calabria, and of the hills of Eubœa, and of the Peloponessus, whilst the group of islands through which we threaded our way, often reminded us of the isles of the Ægean and Ionian Seas."

Plenty of fresh water was found at Albany; and Commodore Burnet thought the best site for the town would be on Seymour Point, Albany Island. Mr. Walter Hill, Director of the Botanic Gardens, at Brisbane, who accompanied the expedition, gives a very favourable description of the proposed place of settlement, as possessing fine water, rich valleys, and pleasant scenery: and Captain Robinson of the Pioneer, was struck with the safety offered to ships sailing towards the Straits by the Great Barrier Reef. That now it is known accurately, so far from an object of danger, it is, in fact, a great breakwater against the South Pacific Ocean, and offers within it, "one great and secure harbour," from the Percy Isles to Cape York. He states that H.M.S. Rattlesnake and two merchant ships reached Booby Islands in twelve days from Sydney, thus showing how speedy would be the communication by this route between Sydney and Singapore.

Sir Charles Nicholson, in a discussion on this route, in the Geographical Society, April 11th, 1864, whilst affirming the great beauty of the regions of the northeast, traversed by Leichhardt, and recently by Dalrymple, said, "That now we had steam all round along the south coast, and up as far as Port Dennison, the next point would be Rockingham Bay, and then Cape York; and then they would see what a short distance it was to Timor, with which the Dutch government had a fortnightly steam communication. The Dutch government had just made a contract with an English company for a line of steamers to traverse regularly the whole of the islands with which they have connection in the southern archipelago. As these steamers could come within a short distance of the coast of Australia, it would be an opprobrium to the English government, did they not take the opportunity of extending steam communication up to that point. He also hoped that Government might be induced to take some steps with a view to the exploration of New Guinea."

These facts present a prospect of rapid intercourse with the coasts of Northern Australia that is marvellous. The last hint of Sir Charles regarding New Guinea, introduces an idea which must have long rested on many minds. It is rather an act of Providence than of our own prudence, that this fine island, bounding the northern side of Torres Straits, and the Arafura Sea has not been seized by the French, and made an eternal nuisance to us. Let us imagine the permanent inconvenience of France commanding the north of Australia from the southern shore of New Guinea—a much finer possession than New Caledonia, and in such ominous proximity to us. England ought never to allow another nation to assume this position; yet a few days' sail only from New Caledonia lies between us and one of the most serious evils which could befall our great Australian empire.

Sir George Bowen and Commodore Burnett, on their return in the Pioneer from Cape York, examined Rockingham Bay, with a view to a settlement there. The Commodore was of opinion that there were two good anchorages in Rockingham Bay, at either of which a port might be opened; the question remaining whether a gap practicable for bullock-drays could be found through the mountains to the Valley of Lagoons, in the beautiful basaltic plateau discovered by Leichhardt, and now stocked with above 25,000 sheep and cattle by Mr. Scott and his partners. This fine district lies upwards of 200 miles from Port Denison, the then port of shipment, but only seventy miles from Rockingham Bay. A party was therefore sent out under Mr. Dalrymple and Mr. Scott, to endeavour to trace such an opening from the Valley of Lagoons to Rockingham Bay. Mr. Scott seems to have taken the active part in this exploration, and discovered a route lying along the course of one of the heads of the Burdekin to the sea in Rockingham Bay. At nine miles from the junction of the Great Anthill Creek with the Burdekin, he discovered a chain of lagoons, the southernmost of which, three miles in circumference, they named Lake Lucy. They observed also in the camps of the natives, drawings, as with a sharp stone, on the inside of box-bark, of men and women in the attitudes of the corrobborie. They also discovered a waterfall, which they heard twenty miles off. It was resolved to proceed to this valley, to open up a road to the settlements in this rich pastoral and romantic country, to meet the rapid demands of the onward rushing tide of life. In three years, the stations of the Queensland colonists having been pushed forward 500 miles towards the north, and a territory as large as the British Isles, during the last two years, more or less densely occupied by the flocks and herds of the squatter, in another year the advancing settlements would reach the shores of the Gulf of Carpentaria.

Here, then, with all these explorations, all these runnings to and fro, and settling down on all the coasts of Australia, east, west, and north, the day is evidently at hand, when the remaining portions of the interior, which lie now almost entirely westward, will be opened up. Every one of these coast settlements offers a new point of departure towards the interior, so that it will be approached by comparatively short journeys from a dozen directions. The velocity with which these movements have proceeded since the late passages across the continent is prodigious. The daring and irrepressible spirit with which the pastoral portion of the Australian population is advancing with its flocks and herds from all quarters, east, west, and midland towards the north, the marvellous growth and development of those flocks and herds, presents one of the most astonishing spectacles in history, and assures us that in a very little time the whole circuit of the vast coasts of Australia will be occupied by an Anglo-Saxon race, who will connect India, China, Japan, and the numerous islands of the Australasian seas by a new link with them, a new and middle link betwixt themselves and Europe, and presenting the nearest route for telegraphic intelligence. We therefore close this wonderful narrative of Australian discovery, still in a period of its most active operation, and with the certain and near prospect of its termination in the foundation of an Anglo-Austral nation, as august in its future as it has been unexampled in the rapidity of its creation.

In concluding this history of Australian discovery, whilst the reader bears it in mind that it is geographical discovery which is treated of, discovery in every other direction which can build up a great nation has been going on in almost every quarter of the Australian continent, and in the islands of Tasmania and New Zealand, with a rapidity of late years most astonishing. The great discovery of the amazing copper-mines of South Australia, and the equally amazing discovery of gold in New South Wales and Victoria, in 1851, were but the forerunnings of discoveries of copper, lead, silver, antimony, nickel, tin, coal, marble, granite, precious stones, pearl-oysters, and again of gold in Tasmania and New Zealand. There is a discovery besides, which is that of experience, that the vegetable productions bid fair, as they are more minutely and scientifically examined, to introduce yet vast and various articles of commerce, and that almost every fruit and fibre which add to the wealth and amenity of civilized life, will flourish pre-eminently in its soil in one quarter or other. The vine, the olive, the orange, lemon, and citron, the fig and banana, corn in all its varieties, cotton, silk, that half-vegetable, half-animal production, flax, hemp, the apple, the pear, the quince, the peach, nectarine, and apricot, all rejoice in emigration to these regions, and contend with the sheep and the alpaca, for a like abundant and auspicious growth. It is not, therefore, geographical, but universal discovery, which demand an antipodean history, and which is destined in its different departments to furnish long and grateful employment to the future literati and savans of the great new world of the South.

CHAPTER XXI.

INCIDENTS OF DISCOVERY AND SETTLEMENT IN NEW ZEALAND.

The survey of the coasts by Drury, D'Urville, and Stokes.—Early explorers, Brunner, Monro, Mitchell, Dashwood, Thomson, Lieutenant-Governor Eyre.—Discovery in the Northern Island—Earliest explorers, traders, Pakeha-Maories, missionaries.—Dr. Dieffenbach and Captain Symonds.—Dieffenbach visits the islands in Cook's Straits.—Examines the country north of Port Nicholson.—Settlement of Wellington.—Dieffenbach ascends Mount Egmont.—Lands in the Bay of Islands, accompanied by Captain Bernard.—Explores the north-east peninsula.—Natives, missionaries, etc.—Sets out, accompanied by Captain Symonds and Lieutenant Best, for the interior.—The Waipa river.—A stupendous rata tree.—The Chief Te-Whero-Whero.—The Waikato River.—A volcanic country.—Hot springs, sulphur jets, and boiling mud springs.—The great central lake, Taupo.—Forbidden to ascend the volcano Tongariro.—Former ascent of it by Mr. Bidwell.—The Warm Lake.—The Valley of the Thames.—Return to Auckland.—Explorations and death of Captain Symonds.—Explorations of Dr. Hochstetter, Messrs. Purchas and Heaphy.—Dana's visit to the Bay of Islands.—Hochstetter's journey to the Waipa, Waikato, and Tongariro, accompanied by Dr. Haast, Captain Drummond Hay, Bruno Hamel, and Herr Koch.—They go over the same ground as Dr. Dieffenbach.—The caves in the limestone district.—The Mora Cave.—Geologic results of this journey.—Gold discoveries.—German and French savans and naturalists, discoverers in New Zealand and Australia.—Progress of botanical knowledge in New Zealand.—Missionaries as openers-up of these islands.—Collectors of Maori knowledge and poetry.

THE comparative narrowness of the New Zealand Islands has prevented that scope of expeditionary discovery which has prevailed in Australia. Yet there are incidents attending the laying down of its coast lines, the settling and opening up of its islands, mountains, and forests, that possess a deep interest.

THE SURVEY OF THE COASTS.

The great work of surveying the coasts, which Cook commenced in 1769, was nearly completed by Drury in 1856. To D'Urville of the French marines, and Stokes and Drury of the Royal Navy, the world is indebted for a complete outline of the coast; and to Captain Richards, Royal Navy, and Mr. Evans, Royal Navy, for an excellent description of them. The New Zealand coast-line is, indeed, better laid down than that of almost any country save Great Britain. It is worthy of remark that all these officers bore testimony to the correctness of Captain Cook's early surveys, and were surprised that the great navigator could have obtained such accuracy with means so imperfect.

Every part of the North Island had now been visited by Europeans; but much of the interior of the Middle Island was yet unknown. Mr. Thomas Brunner received the Geographical Society's gold medal for a journey across it in 1846, (see Geographical Society's Transactions). Dr. Monro drove the first flock of sheep from Nelson to the Wairau; Captain Mitchell and Mr. Dashwood discovered a tract from Nelson to Canterbury; cattle were driven from Otago to Canterbury in 1853; and, in 1858, Mr. G. J. T. Thomson gave the first sketch of the province of Otago. Settlers had already ascended some of the highest mountains. Dr. Dieffenbach stood on the summit of Mount Egmont, Messrs. Bidwell and Dyson looked down the crater of Tongariro, and Lieutenant-Governor Eyre ascended the Kai Kora mountains in the Middle Island from the Wairau Valley, but returned without reaching the highest pinnacle, in consequence of a panic seizing most of his party on one of them, a native, falling over an immense precipice.—Vol. ii. p. 199, of Thomson's Story of New Zealand.

DISCOVERY IN THE NORTH ISLAND.

In speaking of the discovery of New Zealand in general, I have spoken of the discoveries on the coasts of the North Island. The interior, though bearing no proportion to that of Australia, is much more extended in breadth than that of the Middle Island, and this circumstance, as well as that of the much greater number of the native population, jealous of their lands and of their rights, have made the exploration of broad parts of the island more difficult. The missionaries, and the class of Europeans called by the natives

Pakeha-Maories, or Stranger-Maories, from their adopting the habits of the Maories, and marrying into their families, were the earliest explorers of the interior of the North Island. The Pakeha-Maories became the mediums of trade with the Europeans on the coasts, and found it a profitable business, till the Maories became familiar with them, and discovered that it was their interest to trade directly with the English and other nations who frequented their shores, and were making settlements on them.

The Missionaries, Church of England, Methodists, and Catholics gradually established their influence with the natives, and by degrees penetrated with their schools and chapels into the most central regions of the island.

Mr. Charles Darwin, the naturalist, who visited New Zealand in 1835 in his voyage with Captain Fitzroy in the Beagle, was one of the first to present us with some vivid glimpses of the Maories and the missionary settlements at that period in the Northern Island.

He says:—" I should think a more warlike race of inhabitants could not be found in any part of the world than the New Zealanders. Their conduct on first seeing a ship, as described by Captain Cook, strongly demonstrates this; the act of throwing volleys of stones at so great and novel an object, and their defiance of, 'Come on shore, and we will kill and eat you all,' shows uncommon boldness. This warlike spirit is evident in many of their customs, and even in their smallest actions. If a New Zealander is struck, although but in joke, the blow must be returned.

"At the present day, from the progress of civilization, there is much less warfare, except among some of the southern tribes. I heard a characteristic anecdote of what took place some time ago in the south. A missionary found a chief and his tribe in preparation for war; their muskets clean and bright, and their ammunition ready. He reasoned long on the inutility of the war, and the little provocation which had been given for it. The chief was much shaken in his resolution, and

seemed in doubt; but, at length, it occurred to him that a barrel of gunpowder was in a bad state, and that it would not keep much longer. This settled the matter."
—P. 419.

Mr. Darwin gives a striking illustration of the magical change produced in New Zealand by the introduction of European civilization:—" At length we reached Waimate. After having passed over so many miles of uninhabited useless country, the sudden appearance of an English farm-house and its well-dressed fields, placed there as by an enchanter's wand, was exceedingly pleasant.* * * * At Waimate there are three larger houses where the missionary gentlemen, Messrs. Williams, Davies, and Clarke, reside; and near them are the huts of the native labourers. On an adjoining slope fine crops of barley and wheat were standing in full ear, and, in another part, fields of potatoes and clover. But I cannot attempt to describe all I saw; there were large gardens, with every fruit and vegetable which England produces, and many belonging to warmer climates. I may instance asparagus, kidney-beans, cucumbers, rhubarb, apples, pears, figs, peaches, apricots, grapes, olives, gooseberries, currants, hops, gorse for fences, and English oaks; also many kinds of flowers. Around the farmyard there were stables, a thrashing barn, with its winnowing machine, a blacksmith's forge, and, on the ground, ploughshares and other tools; in the middle was that happy mixture of pigs and poultry, lying comfortably together, as in every English farm-yard. At the distance of a few hundred yards, where the water of a little rill had been dammed up into a pool, there was a large and substantial water-mill.

"This is very surprising when it is considered that five years ago nothing but the fern flourished here. Moreover, native workmanship, taught by the missionaries, has effected this change—the lesson of the missionary is the enchanter's wand. The house had been built, the windows framed, the fields ploughed, and even the trees grafted by the New Zealander. At the mill a

New Zealander was seen powdered white with flour, like his brother millers in England."—P. 425.

When Dr. Dieffenbach, in 1840 and 1841, visited, in company with Captain Symonds, the most interior regions of Auckland, along the rivers Waikato, Waipa, and the Thames, and amongst the volcanic hills and geysers of the central districts, he found the missionaries almost everywhere settled amongst the natives, and teaching them both from school and pulpit; yet Dieffenbach tells us that he "was the first to visit or describe Mount Egmont, many places in the northern parts of the island, and some of the picturesque and interesting lakes and thermal springs in the interior," and he was of opinion "that a further knowledge would be owing rather to the gradual spread of colonization than to a previous examination of the country." Dieffenbach's explorations were in the character of naturalist to the New Zealand Company. He arrived in the ship Tory from England in Queen Charlotte's Sound in August, 1839. After remaining some time in Ship Cove, he visited many places on the coasts, beginning first with excursions to the island of Motuara, Cannibals' Cove, named Tory Channel after the ship, and paid visits to Te-awa-iti, the settlement of the whalers in Cook's Strait, where they found the whalers all living with native wives, to the islands of Moioio and Arapaoa, Cloudy Bay, Port Underwood, and then crossed over to Port Nicholson in the Northern Island.

Here, at this time, the New Zealand Company purchased Port Nicholson, and commenced the foundation of the town of Wellington. From Port Nicholson, Dr. Dieffenbach made an excursion into the mountains to the north-east, called the Tararua Range. At that time there was no road connecting the town with the valley of the Hutt, or across the neck of land to the Pararua River opposite the island of Mana. Dieffenbach was desirous to cross the snowy mountains northward of Port Nicholson, and to enter the valley of the Manawatu, but as there were no roads through the thick scrub and dense forests, he was not able to accomplish it. The surveyors were just beginning to cut lines up the right bank of the Eritonga River. The settlers were just clearing the ground for the commencement of the town of Wellington. On the fourth day of their journey they came upon a party under Mr. Deans, who were cutting a track through the hills to the west. Mr. Deans and two men, making Dieffenbach's party eight, soon after joined them. It was in August, and the weather was very rainy, with occasional hail and snow. At about fifty miles from the sea, they came upon another stream running into the Eritonga, and saw numerous footprints of wild pigs, dogs, and cats. After ascending the Tararua Hills amid deep snow, and beholding a very wild prospect as far as Kapiti Island in Cook's Strait, and over regions all around exceedingly mountainous, and covered on the lower land with continuous woods, they returned to Port Nicholson, after an absence of sixteen days, without seeing a single native; but they convinced themselves that roads to Hawke's Bay north-eastward, and to the Manawatu north-westward, were quite practicable. At that time the natives in Port Nicholson district were estimated at 1500, but divided into several tribes, and living in the different coves of the harbour.

After again visiting different parts of the strait, they examined the Wanganui, Waimate, and other rivers, on the north of the strait to Cape Egmont. Whilst the company's agent was engaged in the purchase of the land from the natives, Dieffenbach set off with a small party to endeavour to ascend Mount Egmont, never yet ascended by any European. About Sugarloaf Point, where they landed from their boat, they found plenty of natives; the Taranaki tribe, however, were very much harassed by the powerful Waikatos, and glad to sell lands to the English to obtain their support against their too potent enemies.

The natives strove earnestly to dissuade Dieffenbach from ascending Mount Egmont, telling him that it was "tapu," or sacred, and that there were crocodiles and moas in its glens, and that he would assuredly be eaten. Spite of this, he persuaded an old priest and American man of colour to accompany him, and, on the 3rd of December, they started. On the way they came to concealed potato plantations, which the natives fled to in the woods, when their Waikato enemies came down. The cabbage-palm in the woods were the tallest Dieffenbach had ever seen. The heavy rains and the shortness of provisions, however, defeated their attempt, and they returned to the shore after an absence of fifteen days, but delighted with the beauty and fertility of the country as far as they could see it.

Having laid in a better store of provisions, and adding to their party a chief, E. Kake, and Mr. Heberley, a European, they again set out to ascend the mountain. This time they succeeded, but the natives would not go higher than the limits of perpetual snow, about 7204, the mountain itself being 8839 feet. The natives took out their books and began to pray, overpowered by the silent awe of the mountain heights, and their dread of the mysterious animals that they believe to exist there. Dieffenbach and Heberley found the mountain an old volcano, with its crater filled with snow, and a high piled cone of cinders and scoriaceous lava. The travellers descended, predicting that the picturesque valley of the Waiwakaio, Mount Egmont, and the smiling land at its base, would become as celebrated for their beauty as Vesuvius, and the Bay of Naples, and attract travellers from all parts of the globe.

From Taranaki Dr. Dieffenbach made an excursion to Mokau, but this was merely along the coast. He next made a voyage to the Chatham Islands, which lie to the S.E. of New Zealand, and found the surface of the largest island to contain 305,280 acres, of which 57,000 were occupied by lakes, and 100,000 were considered good for cultivation, the remainder for pasturage. Water and water-fowl in abundance, as well as fish, and materials for building not less so.

In October, 1840, Dr. Dieffenbach landed in the Bay of Islands, and proceeded with Captain Bernard, an adventurous Frenchman, to explore the northern long peninsular of the island. Commencing at Cape Maria Van Diemen, he traced the coast south-westward. He found on the peninsular missionary and squatting stations. A Mr. Southie was living on the Awaroa river, and employing 300 natives in clearing the land. There were natives busy fishing, and cultivating potatoes, kumeras, melons, pumpkins, and turnips, in neat enclosures. In the valley of the Awaroa, Dieffenbach calculated that there were 120,000 acres of arable land. A bridle road for fifty miles from Kaitaia had been cut through the forests by the natives, at the price of a blanket per mile. Dieffenbach and Captain Bernard extended their explorations into Lauriston Bay, the district round the harbour of Wangaroa, and the Pu-te-kaka river, amongst the forests of the mighty Kauri pines. They complained of the reckless destruction of the Kauri forests by the fire of the settlers, and the log-cutters, then going on; and of the equally wholesale destruction of the curious bird, the kiwi or apterix, which abound in those forests, by dogs and cats, and by the natives to make mats of their skins.

Crossing the peninsular, they visited the harbour of Wangaroa, celebrated for the massacre of the crew of the Boyd in 1809. Amongst the volcanic rocks and hills of this neighbourhood they found 2000 natives who had become christians, some protestants, some catholics, having missions of both creeds. Returning to the west coast they traced it down to Wangape and Hokianga, around which latter place were 200 Europeans, traders, and sawyers, and all the natives converted to catholicism or methodism. They visited in the interior the lake of Maupere, and the extinct volcanos, and the hot sulphurous springs about the Waimate, in the direction of the Bay of Islands. In the same manner crossing to and fro, they examined the Keri-Keri river, the Bay of Tauranga, the Bay of Islands, the Kaipara Harbour, and the

Wairoa river with its tributaries. Up these rivers they found Englishmen located as farmers and timber dealers, who claimed most of the land, some of the timber ships ascending the Wairoa to a distance of eighty-five miles from the sea. Thence they continued their examinations of the country to the Gulf of Hauraki, Coromandel Harbour, the Waiho or Thames, to Waitimata Harbour, and Auckland. At Kati-Kati they found the southern boundary of the Kauri forests on the east coast. On the different rivers they still found missions, most of which had possessed themselves of large tracts of country. The church mission catechist, Fairbairn, on the right bank of the Tamaki river claiming the country from thence to the Wairoa, ninety square miles.

From Waitemata, accompanied by Lieutenant Best, Dr. Dieffenbach proceeded to the Manukau, and thence, also accompanied by Captain William Cornwallis Symonds, directly southward into the interior as far as the great central lake Taupo. This was by far the most important exploration on the part of Dieffenbach and his English companions, of whom it is rather remarkable he says so little. We know that they went with him, and that is nearly all. The country from Waitemata to Manukau they found extremely interesting, as consisting of comparatively level land, with pleasant valleys, but with a number of extinct volcanos rising here and there out of the plains; the conical hills reaching 400 or 500 feet with still deep and well defined craters. The shores of the Manukau they represented as the last place on the western coast southward where the Kauri was found at all in any quantity.

Lieutenant Best accompanied some natives to the Awaroa, and thence proceeded to the Waikato, but Dr. Dieffenbach followed the coast southwards, accompanied by Captain Symonds. They found the mouth of the Waikato narrow and shallow, but the river within the heads capable of carrying large vessels for 100 miles. Near the embouchere of the river at the Church Missionary Station, Maraenui, they met with Lady Franklin,

Sir John Franklin at this time being engaged in an extensive examination of New Zealand. The party continued along the shore of Waingaroa harbour, which they found overlooked by limestone cliffs of seventy or eighty feet in height. At Waingaroa they found a tribe of 1200 natives, and a Wesleyan Mission. Thence they continued their coast journey to Aotea and Kawia, an extensive harbour, into which fall the Awaroa and Kauri rivers. On the northern shore of this harbour was formerly the head-quarters of the famous Rauparaha, who was driven from it by the Waikato, and settled at Entry Island. There were about 1500 of the Waikato living here, and they had all become Christians. From the size and capacity of this harbour, the depth of water, the rivers flowing into it, and the quality of the land, it appeared likely to become one of the most important ports of the western coast. There were already about forty Europeans settled on its northern shore, and the greatest part of the land in the vicinity of Kawia was claimed by them.

From this point they struck off into the interior, having engaged a numerous band of natives to carry their luggage, the payment for which service was a shirt or a gown to each. They crossed in a canoe to the small river Operau, and then ascended gentle hills towards the Waipa river. These hills were all of volcanic origin, covered with fern, and in many places with forests. In one place they saw a very ancient rata-tree, its stem fifty-four feet round, and having been hollowed out by fire, served for a convenient shelter to the natives. It was strictly "tapu," that is, no one was allowed to cut down or injure any portion of it. On reaching the summit of the hills overlooking the valley of the Waipa, they had a vast prospect. Seawards they saw Kawia and Aotea, to the N.E. Maunga-Tautari, a volcanic ridge in the interior; before them the broad valley of the Waipa, bounded to the east by distant hills, and to the south-west the hilly chain of Rangitoto, near Mokau. Only some small spots of the valley of the Waipa were wooded, and the burnt and blackened stems of old trees were the only signs of the intrusion of man into the dominions of nature.

Natives and missionaries welcomed them to the Valley of the Waipa, which was extensive, flat, and very fertile. At the Church Missionary station of Otawao, they found fine tobacco growing: most of the natives were Christians. Here they saw the old chief, Puata, the father of tha famous Te Whero-Whero, the head of the Waikato tribe. The Waipa there was fifty yards wide, and two fathoms deep. They directed their course eastward for the Valley of the Waikato, which joins the Waipa about a hundred miles below Otawao, passing the ranges of Maunga-Tautari, whence also flowed the rivers Piako and Waiho, or the Thames. The forests were chiefly of the Kahikatea pine. Here and there, in the level of the valley rose conical volcanic hills. As they approached the Waikato river, the woods changed to matai and totara pine; the one red and beautiful for furniture, the other most valuable for ship-building. They found the Waikato lying between steep banks, like an Australian river, about fifty yards broad, but showing that in floods it was frequently 150 yards wide. They saw in the far distance Horo-Horo, the mountain in which the Thames takes its rise. The Valley of the Waikato was very different to that of the Waipa. It was broken up into hillocks of cemented tufa and pumicestone, the hillocks not descending in regular slopes, but in steps or terraces, evidently formed by the fall of waters. The country was altogether volcanic, barren and stony. Numerous streams ran on all sides; the hills became even more rugged and broken, and the grand forest of totara, rimu, and matai pines, gave a solemn grandeur to the scene. They were now approaching the most extraordinary region of New Zealand, the land of volcanoes, boiling springs, steam and sulphur jets, and mud cauldrons, red as vermillion, and boiling and bubbling heavily. Still they found themselves amongst natives who were partly converted to Christianity.

Three miles from a pah of these natives at Ahirara,

they saw the masses of white vapour rising in jets from the hot springs. The scenes which now opened upon them were of the most extraordinary kind. The whole country appeared to be based upon a fire stratum, which was sending up through crevices and through gaping funnel-shaped chasms, boiling waters, spurting steams, and fumes of sulphur. The water which boiled up was not easily approached, and was of a milky, clayey appearance, apparently very much the colour of a glacial river. The water was above the boiling point, and in constant agitation. It had the appearance of a country existing over fire-regions, where a volcano might burst forth at any moment. The party visited similar regions on the opposite side of the hills. They found numbers of these boiling springs sending up their columns of steam in a rugged ravine, under deep and precipitous cliffs. The water in these was nearly clear, with a pleasant acidulous taste, smelling slightly of hydro-sulphurous gas, and throwing out incrustations of alum and sulphur.

One of the boiling mud-ponds lay at the base of a steep cliff, sixty feet high, white, oxidized, corroded, and undermined. The mud was continually boiling, with a white foam, throwing out jets of fluid ten feet high, with violence and noise. The pond was very deep. Many of these ponds threw up mud and sand, which hardened into truncated cones of about ten feet high, and stood up as many as eight in one pond. The whole scene was most impressive. It was a Tartarus above ground.

On reaching the great central lake, Taupo, they were struck with admiration at its extent, and at the scenery around it. Across it rose to the south-east, the still active volcano, Tongariro, and the mountains, Titiraupena, and Wakakahu. They found the rocks of which these hills consist, a leucitic lava of great fineness. On looking back at the Valley of the Waipa, which they had crossed, they gave the decided preference to it over that of the Waikato. "This valley," says Dieffenbach, " is bounded to the westward by a range of coast hills, to the eastward by the range of Maunga-Tautari. It has an average breadth of thirty miles, is even and flat in its lowest part, especially up to the point at which the river Waipa joins the Waikato. Higher up, the country is broken and undulating, covered with a vegetation of fern and coarse grass, alternating with groves of the Kahikatea pine. The lower part rivals in fertility the best districts of the island." He says it is not only very sheltered, but has the advantage of the river being navigable for sixty miles above its junction with the Waikato, while the Waikato in the middle of its course is impeded by rapids. The Valley of the Waipa has also easy communication with the harbour of Waingaroa, and has an almost uninterrupted water communication with Waitemata, or Auckland. They found a great demand for European commodities amongst the natives.

After crossing the lake, to ascend Tongariro, they found the chief Te-Heu-Heu was absent, and had laid a solemn "tapu" on the mysterious mountain.

Lake Taupo, which is thirty-six miles long and twenty-five broad, but very irregular in shape, is surrounded by a volcanic country all alive with boiling springs, solfataras, and stufas; and at its eastern end was an island, called Puhia-i-wakari, or White Island, still active as a volcano. On the western side, where the scenery was magnificent, they saw vapours bursting from hundreds of crevices, and heard a constant subterranean noise, like the working of a steam engine, or the blast of an iron-foundry. The natives cooked their food by laying it on fern over these crevices.

Tongariro had been tapued by Te-Heu-Heu, because Mr. Bidwell, an Englishman, had ascended it without leave; Dr. Dieffenbach could, therefore, only give us Mr. Bidwell's account of his ascent. It was on March 2nd, 1839, that he made his ascent. The natives whom he took with him would only ascend to a certain height, where they said they used to sit down and cover their heads, because it was "tapu" to look at the dreaded peak of the mountain, which they believed to be inhabited by powerful spirits. Two natives only would pass that spot, and they stopped short within a mile of the base of the cone. As Mr. Bidwell ascended, he heard a noise, and saw an eruption of black smoke. He found the cone composed of loose cinders, not to be climbed without intense labour. It was much higher than volcanic cones in general, and the crater was the most terrific abyss he ever looked into, or imagined. The rocks overhung it on all sides, it was continually discharging steam, and it appeared at least a quarter of a mile in diameter, and very deep. The stones he threw into it did not strike anything for seven or eight minutes, and many were heard no more. The mountains around stood up quite perpendicular, and most magnificent. They were all covered with snow. He had a vast prospect of lakes, rivers, and country clothed with wood. The natives said he ought to have seen Taranaki and the island of Kapiti, in Cook's Straits. Tongariro he calculated to be 6,200 feet above the level of the sea. It did not appear, from the accounts of the natives, that there had been any violent eruption for many years; but Tongariro must be regarded as the centre of the modern volcanic action of the northern island.

Dieffenbach calculated the natives around lake Taupo at 3200, including those about the Rotu-Aire and other hills and lakes of that region. He regarded them as the best specimen of the race he had met with in New Zealand, hospitable to strangers, industrious, cleanly, and disposed to Christianity.

From the Taupo the party continued their route down the banks of the Waikato, through a similar country of lakes, hills, hot springs, and sulphur springs, to the Rotu-Mahana, or Warm Lake. A lake of a blue colour, surrounded by verdant hills; in the lake several islets, in all of which steam issued from a hundred openings between the green foliage of the bushes, without impairing their verdure, and on the opposite side a flight of broad steps, of the colour of marble, of a rosy tint, and a cascade of boiling water falling over them into the lake. The steeps were firm, like porcelain, and had a tinge of carmine. They continued their journey to Tauranga by a number of other lakes, of which there are fifteen, extending at intervals from the Taranaki to the eastern coast. From Tauranga they travelled to the valley of the Thames, everywhere finding missionaries, and natives who had sold their land to Europeans, and were vainly trying to get some of it back again. From the valley of the Waiho, or Thames, they sailed up the gulf of Hauraki to Auckland. In this journey Dr. Dieffenbach made a valuable addition to the geology and natural history of New Zealand, the particulars of which will be found in his work.

Amongst the most active explorers of the Northern Island must be reckoned Captain William Cornwallis Symonds, one of Dieffenbach's companions in this journey. Captain Symonds was the son of Sir William Symonds, surveyor of the navy. He was himself deputy-surveyor of New Zealand, and besides this journey with Dieffenbach, made various explorations, especially to the sources of the Wanganui and Manematu rivers which fall into Cook's Straits. He had prepared a chart, and details of his observations, and had collected a vocabulary of 3000 native words, when he was cut short by the fate so common in New Zealand. He was upset in crossing the bay of Manukau, on a duty of friendly benevolence, and drowned in November of 1841.

At the close of December, 1858, the Novara, an Austrian frigate, out on a voyage of inquiry into the geology and natural history of various countries, especially of the southern hemisphere, entered the harbour of Auckland. On board of this frigate was Dr. Hochstetter, as the geologist of the expedition. At the Cape of Good Hope Sir George Grey, then governor there, had recommended Dr. Hochstetter to devote some time to a geological survey of the north island of New Zealand. On arriving he was readily engaged for this purpose by the Colonial Government. And the result of his visits to various parts of the coast, and into the interior, has resulted in two splendid works, one essentially geologic, the other uniting his scientific with his general observations, entitled simply, "Neu Seeland, von Dr. Ferdinand von Hochstetter," in quarto, Stuttgart, 1863.

The great object of Hochstetter's inquiries was the same volcanic district of the interior which Dieffenbach traversed, his aim being a more close and scientific survey of its geologic structure. Hochstetter informs us that Sir George Grey himself had traversed much of the interior of the North Island since Dieffenbach, and that the Rev. A. G. Purchas and Charles Heaphy had visited some particular districts of the North Island, and that James Dana, geologist of the American Exploring Expedition of 1849, had visited the Bay of Islands, and had scientifically examined the surrounding country. After some preparatory visits to places on the coasts, and a voyage across the straits to Nelson, Dr. Hochstetter prepared to set out for the interior. He was furnished with a strong party and plenty of provisions, and was accompanied by Julius Haast, a fellow German, and also a geologist, who had arrived at the same time on a professional tour in Auckland, and who has since become the government geologist of Canterbury. Captain Drummond Hay, an officer well acquainted both with the Maories and their language, was appointed manager of the expedition and interpreter. Mr. Bruno Hamel attended as photographer, and another German, Herr Koch.

Rich as was this journey in geologic and naturalistic acquisitions, it is unnecessary for us to follow the details of it, for it was chiefly over the ground traversed by Dieffenbach. Dr. Hochstetter describes the country and their reception by natives and missionaries, in terms of the highest enthusiasm. There is no new land that in his opinion can compare with New Zealand. It is a paradise of climate and scenery, and in the peculiarity of its natural productions. He luxuriates in its forests, its mountains, its wonderful volcanic regions, its friendly people, both native and European. "Indelible," he says, "remain in my memory those scenes, when after the labour and fatigue of the day, we encamped on the edge of the forest, near a rushing mountain stream. When the fire blazed up, and the natives sang their songs; and then all became silent till with the awakening day, the birds of the wood, the kokorimolo and the tui commenced their morning strains. I look back on such scenes, on our sailing on the rivers in the canoes of the natives, on our sojourn in their pahs, and on our wanderings through the dark old forests in the shade of trees which are unknown to every other land, with a joy which makes me truly feel how high the pleasures of nature stand above the pleasures of artificial life."

There are a few points which we may however notice. In the upper Waipa valley they explored one of the celebrated caves in the lime-stone hills, called the Moa Cave, the Spirit Cave, and the Dark Cave. The Moa Cave had been successfully examined in 1852, by Dr. A. Thomson, major Hume, and Captain Cooper, for the remains of moas. The Dark, examined by Hochstetter, he describes in one place as having a vault seventy feet high, and magnificent with stalactile formations. Scarcely a cave in these hills but formerly abounded in remains of the moa. They found the Tongariro volcano as strictly "tapu" as ever, but Mr. Dyson, in 1851, had ventured to ascend it unknown to the natives, and found it in much the same state as Mr. Bidwell in 1839. Dyson's account has been published in the Auckland "New Zealander." At Pukawa, on the Taupo Lake, they had an interview with the great chief Te-Heu-Heu, and at Tokanu saw some remarkable native carvings. Like Dieffenbach, Dr. Hochstetter and his party proceeded by the valley of the Thames and the Gulf of Hauraki to Auckland.

Besides the immediate results of this journey which greatly extended the knowledge of the geology of New Zealand, Dr. Hochstetter's work contained a great amount of information on the botany and zoology of the islands, on the discoveries of coal and gold, on the character, manners, poetry and romance of the Maories. The ground over which he went has been the great scene of the struggle in the late war, and he has given a lucid narrative of its origin and progress. Dr. Hochstetter gives a very lively narrative of the gold discoveries in New Zealand from the first formation of a "Reward Committee in Auckland, in 1852," and the discovery of this metal by Mr. Charles Ring, a settler on the peninsular of Cape Colville, near the Coromandel Harbour, of which Mr. Charles Heaphy was made commissioner, to the first faint discovery of gold in 1842 by Mr. M'Donald, one of a party sent out by Captain Wakefield, at Massacre Bay, then converted into Golden Bay, the more important discovery of the Aorere gold-field in the same quarter in 1857, and then the Takata Diggings, and finally, the great outburst of the gold-fever in Otago in 1861. Gold is said to have been found in Otago in 1857 and 1858, by Mr. Ligar, since Surveyor-General of Victoria in Australia: but the discovery of the prolific gold-field of Tuapeka by Mr. Gabriel Reed, in 1861, put the climax to the gold-fever of New Zealand, brought diggers by thousands from Australia, so that by the succeeding January 250,000 ounces of gold, worth one million sterling, were raised in the gold-fields of Otago. Well might the nurses be said to rock the children to sleep with the song—

"Gold! gold! gold! beautiful fine gold!
Wangapeka, Tuapeka—gold! gold! gold!"

Since then extensive gold-fields have been discovered on the western coast of Canterbury.

In quitting this notice of the explorations of the Northern Island I may remark how much German naturalists and scientific men have had to do with Australasian researches. Dr. Solander, who accompanied Sir Joseph Banks on Cook's first voyage to the South Seas, and Dr. Sparrmann, who added to the botanic knowledge of Dusky Bay, and of the south-west coast of the Middle Island, were Swedes; but the Forsters, father and son, who attended Cook on his second voyage, were Germans, as was Dr. Leichhardt, the first great explorer of Australia to the north coast, and Dr. Dieffenbach, and as are Doctors Haast and Hochstetter. It may not be altogether out of place in a work on Geographical Discovery to notice the distinguished men who have contributed to the botanic knowledge of New Zealand. Besides Captain Cook, Sir Joseph Banks, Doctors Solander and Sparrmann, and the Forsters, already mentioned, Dr. Menzies, who was the naturalist in Vancouver's voyage, collected, principally in Dusky Bay, many mosses and lichens, and added greatly to the collection of the cryptogamic plants of New Zealand. In 1824 and 1827 the French expeditions of Duperrey and D'Urville visited New Zealand, and Professor Richard published descriptions of 200 species of trees and plants there collected. After the establishment of the Sydney Botanic Garden, Charles Frazer, the Sydney botanist, visited New Zealand in 1825, and the brothers Allan and Richard Cunningham in 1826, 1833, and 1838, whilst, at the same time, zealous missionaries, as Dr. Logan and William Colenso, made extensive collections of specimens. Mr. Bidwell, who first climbed the volcano of Tongariro, in 1839, and Dr. Dieffenbach, the first European who ascended Mount Egmont, also in 1839, added very interesting contributions to the subalpine and alpine Flora of New Zealand. Then followed M. Raoul, the French savan, who accompanied the frigate L'Aubre from 1840 to 1841, and the frigate L'Allier, as naturalist, and described his botanic acquisitions in a splendid work. But it remained for Dr. J. D. Hooker, the son of Sir William Hooker, who attended the Antarctic Expedition under Captain James Ross, in 1839 to 1843, to put the crown to the botanic knowledge of New Zealand, in his magnificent and most scientific work, "The Flora of New Zealand." To this great work the collections of Dr. Lyall, who accompanied Captain Stokes in the Acheron, in 1847, of Dr. Menzies, rich in cryptogamias, of Captain Drury, Mr. Jolliffe, Lieutenant-Colonel Bolton, the Rev. — Taylor, Thomas H. Hulke, Dr. Andrew Sinclair, and Mr. Knight, of

Auckland, of Dr. Munro and Captain Rough, of Nelson. These enabled Dr. Hooker to complete the work down to 1853. The work contains nearly 1900 pages, to which Dr. Haast, Dr. Monro, W. T. L. Travers, Captain Rough and others, have since made additions, some of which have been described by Dr. Müller, of Melbourne, in the Edinburgh New Philosophical Journal, vol. xiv.

As the missionaries have been amongst the earliest and most extensive openers-up of New Zealand, it is due to them to remark that the first foundation of missions there originated with the venerable Samuel Marsden, the apostle of the South Sea. The Church Missionary Society established their mission in the Bay of Islands in 1814, the Wesleyans theirs on the Hokianga, in 1822, and the Catholics theirs in New Zealand, in 1838. The last act of cannibalism ceased under their teaching on the Katikati River, near Tauranga, in the Bay of Plenty, in 1843. New Zealand might be said to be a missionary dominion till the New Zealand Company, projected by Edward Gibbon Wakefield, landed their expedition, and founded their first settlement at Wellington, Port Nicholson, in 1839.

For a knowledge of the very interesting traditions, poems, and oratory of the Maories, we are indebted to the collections of Messrs. Polack, Backer, Shortland, and Dieffenbach, to Davis's "Maori Mementos," Taylor's "Te Ika a Maui," and Sir George Grey's "Poetry of the New Zealanders."

CHAPTER XXII.

DISCOVERY OF THE INSULARITY OF THE SOUTH ISLAND.

Discovery of the insularity of the South Island by Stewart, a sealer.—Settlement of the Middle Island in 1847.—The river Owerrie already explored in 1840 by the Pelorus.—Settlement of Otago by William Cargill.—Of Canterbury by a Company projected by Gibbon Wakefield, in 1850.—Failure of the project.—Surveys of Captain Stokes of the coasts of the Foveaux Strait.—Discovery of the ports and rivers of the southern extremity of the Middle Island.—Explores the New River.—Explorations of Mr. Hamilton and Mr. Spencer.—Journey from Jacob's River to Otago.—Account of the South Island by Captain Stokes.—Surveys of Mr. Tuckett.—Discoveries of Brown, Duppa, and Thomson.—Survey of M'Kerrow of the Lake District of Otago.

This island was discovered to be such by one Stewart, a sealer and whaler, a Scotchman, who found that what had been thought a bay, was in reality a strait, when in pursuit of his business as a sealer. The island is, therefore, now called Stewart Island, though the straits are called Foveaux Straits. Stewart died at Poverty Bay, and, unfortunately, in actual poverty, in 1851, at the age of eighty-five.

SETTLEMENT OF THE MIDDLE ISLAND.

The river Owerrie, in the Middle Island, was explored in 1840 by a party from the Pelorus, who gave it the name of that vessel; its waters are deep enough to serve as a port of refuge in Cook's Strait, though its entrance is not easily perceived. In November, 1847, the first ship of emigrants sailed from Greenock for Otago. This place, chosen for the settlement in place of Canterbury Plain, is near the southern extremity of the Middle Island, and on the east coast of it. The harbour is safe, but difficult of entrance; the land about Otago is hilly, but to the south of it there are large grassy plains, better adapted for pasturage than the land in any other part of New Zealand. There were few natives in this district, and all lived on a piece of ground which had been reserved for them. The leader of the colonists was Captain William Cargill, of the 74th regiment, an old soldier of the Peninsula, and a descendant of the celebrated Donald Cargill. Otago, in his hands, became Port Chalmers, the capital, Dunedin, and the settlers Pilgrim Fathers.

SETTLEMENT OF CANTERBURY.

As Otago was a settlement of the Scotch Church, so Canterbury was designed for a settlement of the English Church. It was a project of Edward Gibbon Wakefield's, and established on his land principles. Mr. John Robert Godley was his great coadjutor in the scheme. The association consisted of noblemen, archbishops, bishops, clergy, and gentlemen. Magnificent plans of palaces and colleges were exhibited at home, and as in the Adelaide Wakefield scheme, which had so egregiously failed, gentlemen were to purchase large estates, and labourers were to be brought over by the proceeds from the sale of lands, who were always to remain labourers. It was to be a bit of feudal Old England transported to the antipodes, and there stereotyped for ever. Land was to be sold at £3 an acre, 20s. of which were to be spent in churches and colleges, 20s. in emigration, 10s. in roads, and 10s. left as profits on the land sales to the company.

The first settlers arrived on the 16th of December, 1850, but as God and nature were opposed to any such schemes of aristocrats and helots, the whole went to the wall like the experiment at Adelaide, and government had to step in, advance money as at Adelaide, and then break up the so-much vaunted Canterbury Association, because it could not discharge its engagements to the New Zealand Company for the land. The charter was cancelled in 1852, after a trial of only two years. "In the mean time," says Dr. Thomson, in his "Story of New Zealand," "discontentment and disappointment had spread amongst the upper classes. The bishop designate returned home, and his place was not supplied until 1856; the lord fled to Sydney, and thence to England; several priests emigrated to other settlements, and Mr. Godley, the leader of the pilgrims, returned to England in 1853."

The church and Wakefield's plans being broken up, the settlement at once began to prosper.

We have briefly alluded to the coast surveys of New Zealand. In those made by Captain Lort Stokes in 1850, he examined and laid down the seaboard of the Middle Island from Otago to Preservation Harbour on the south-east coast, a distance of 220 miles, and he gives some interesting particulars of that part of the island in a report to the Admiralty, dated Wellington, September 1st, 1850.

In this stretch of coast, Captain Stokes found only four roadsteads and one port; and of the twenty-three rivers in this extent of coast line, four only were available for small vessels, and only two, the Waikawa and Orete or Eurete, the New River, for ships of from 300 to 400 tons. The latter he considered of the most importance, since it led to a fertile district, and is separated nearly by a half-mile pasturage from the head-waters of Bluff Harbour, which had an available block of land within the eastern entrance of Foveaux Strait and distant 130 miles from Otago. This prairie land is bounded by a range of rugged, snow-clad mountains, the highest at a distance of eighty miles, rising to an elevation of 6700 feet. Three openings in the northern hills show the course of the Aparima or Jacob River, winding along the western edge of the plain, that of the New River traversing its central part, with the Mataura running on its eastern side.

They ascended the New River in a whale-boat for nearly thirty miles in a north half east direction. In that distance, the land rose gradually 200 feet by three steps, occasioning somewhat dangerous rapids. The depth of water varied from two to eight feet, the width from 50 to 500 yards. The banks on either side were rich in soil, and varied by verdant meadows or woods. The Mataura and Jacob Rivers were partially examined by Mr. Hamilton and Mr. Spencer of the Acheron, the surveying vessel, whilst she was occupied on the shores of Stewart Island. They explored the intermediate country, and reached Otago in sixteen days, each carrying 30lbs. weight of baggage, which from unexpected accidents, was frequently increased to 70lbs., they being the first Europeans who had accomplished that journey. They regarded the country westward of the Clutha as far as Jacob's River, as well calculated for settlement, the plains stretching eastward of the Jacob to a distance of forty miles, including 600,000 acres of rich soil. Eastward of this plain, a chain of densely wooded hills, extend as far as the Molyneux district, having an elevation towards the sea of 2000 feet. Inland they are lower and more free from wood. This tract of land, broadest towards the south, has an area of from 700,000 to 800,000 acres of good land. There were indications of peat or turf suitable for fuel, and at Tuturau the richness of the soil was shown by a solitary Maori family having raised potatoes, which exceeded those brought by Bishop Selwyn from the Chatham Isles, nine inches each way, which were considered the most remarkable specimens of this root grown in the southern hemisphere. The natives offered to sell all the land from Otago to the western coast, making certain reserves.

Captain Stokes gives a few particulars regarding Stewart Island. He found its coasts, except the south end, which had been surveyed by Cook, extremely inaccurately laid down. The eastern and northern sides have good harbours, Paterson Inlet having no superior in New Zealand. It has many convenient heaving-down coves, and was generally surrounded by fine timber, such as rimu, rata, pine, totara, etc. This inlet appeared very eligible for a small, pastoral settlement. He found on a narrow tongue of land twelve out of the 107 European inhabitants of Foveaux Strait, who had a few cattle. The other white men lived scattered over the north and south shores. Some had passed twenty-two years in that solitude, and were generally married to Maori women, and their daughters were the wives of Europeans also. Their small clearings exhibited a fertile but shallow soil. Of the Maori population, amounting to 280 individuals, 105 resided on Ruapuki Island, and though they had sold some portions to Europeans, appeared desirous to retain the rest. A few plants common to the Auckland Islands, were found in Foveaux Strait, and a bird, a snipe, excited their surprise, being the first of the species seen in New Zealand. They heard rumours of beaver in the great lakes on the Middle Island, but could find no native who had seen them, and, therefore, deemed them fabulous. They were told of a large lizard which inspired feelings of awe and fear. They saw 200 head of cattle in fine condition on the New River, and observed lignite on the river, and an inferior coal on the Mataura.

Captain Stokes and Mr. Hamilton had explored a portion of the interior near Bank's Peninsula, and were preparing to proceed to New Plymouth, and afterwards to the west coast of the Middle Island, and expected to complete the survey of these coasts during the summer.

Mr. Tuckett, who had been employed in surveying for the New Zealand Company, had also discovered coal in Foveaux Strait, but did not think so favourably of the climate of that part of the island as Captain Stokes, Mr. Hamilton, and their friends.

DISCOVERIES IN THE MIDDLE ISLAND CONTINUED.

In 1856, Mr. G. H. Brown and Mr. George Duppa succeeded in riding through, from Nelson to Canterbury, by Mr. Weld's track, who first explored it, namely, by the Wairau gorge and Lake Tennyson. In a letter published in the *Nelson Examiner*, they reported the route unattended by any difficulty or danger, excepting at one ford in the Wairau gorge, which could be easily avoided by a side cutting less than a hundred yards in length.

In the beginning of 1857, Mr. J. Turnbull Thomson, chief surveyor of Otago, explored, in successive trips, the southern extremity of New Zealand on foot, carrying his theodolite and "swag" of clothes over 1500 miles of difficult country, and driving pack-horses laden with flour. It is now curious to see his estimate of the characteristics of the different parts of the country and its population betwixt the Waiau and Mataura Rivers and the Umbrella, Eyre, and Takitimo Mountains.

	Square Miles.		Population.
Forest land	570		
Moss and swamp	108		
Agricultural	400	Europeans	253
Pastoral	2150	Half Castes	70
Barren Mountains	500	Maories	119
Total	3728	Total	442

On the 6th of January, they left Dunedin, and sailed to the mouth of the Oreti, or New River, in Foveaux's Strait. They ascended this river to some distance, and visited some stations amongst the tropical-looking forests on its banks. In this route they were in the early mornings delighted by the songs of birds, which so much charmed Captain Cook. They were aroused by the familiarity of the robin, which was close to them as they sate by their fire, and by the tui, or parson bird, which, of a jet black, seems to be imitating the gestures and exclamations of a preacher in a pulpit. Returning down the New River, he and his companions Drummond and Lindsay went to Invercargill, and hired a pack-horse to carry their provisions into the interior. On their way up the country they came upon various Maori ovens, such as they used till they adopted the camp-oven of the white man. Mr. Thomson made the remains of these ovens indications of the former population of the country. They were holes in the ground, four or five feet in diameter, and of the same depth, lined with stones, which they heated in the same manner as the natives of Polynesia. As these were placed near the forest for the convenience of fuel, when now found far from forest, he regarded that as a proof that the forest had receded, having been destroyed by fires.

Their progress was now to the Hokunnui Hills, of which the Ship Cone was 2000 feet high. These hills were timbered half-way up their southern sides. Thence they proceeded to the foot of the Dome Mountain, complaining much in their progress of *Spaniards*, that is, cacti with sharp-pointed blades, and *Wild Irishmen*, scrub full of prickles, and difficult to penetrate. They ascended the Dome and Cupola, the first 4505 feet above the level of the sea, the second 4045 feet. The heads of the Mataura River were seen to come out of the Eyre Mountains, issuing by a deep gorge into the Waimea Plains. On these mountains they gathered the New Zealand strawberry. To the N.N.E. they saw an opening in the hills, through which no high land was visible, and conjectured it to be the pass into the central district, then entirely unknown to the European, and but vaguely described by the Maori. The panorama of the Dome Mountain was extremely fine, presenting to view the snow-clad and serrated outline of the Eyre Mountains, the extensive plains of Waiopai, Mataura, Waiau, Clutha, and Waimea, Molyneux Bay, Tewaiwais Bay, Solander Island, and the boundless Southern Ocean. They then crossed the Oreti; they held down the Aparima, and proceeded to Jacob's River Settlement. This was an old whaling station. Formerly the Maories of that district amounted to 3000 or 4000; many were driven over to Codfish and Centre Island by more powerful northern tribes, and many have perished by the white men's vices, drink, and diseases. At Mr. Thomson's visit, they were estimated at about 400. The settlers, descendants of the old whalers and sealers, struck Mr. Thomson in their secluded and independent life, with their simple hospitality and country manners, as much resembling the Shetlanders, as described by Sir Walter Scott. They frequented the rainy west coast of Middle Island in pursuit of whaling and sealing, and this coast, at that time, was almost exclusively left to their visits. The Maories of the settlement had adopted European houses and costume. Their houses, however, contained only one room, abounded with fleas, and they still squatted on the floor instead of using chairs.

Mr. Thomson gives a vivid idea of the perils of the life of these sealers of Jacob River Settlement, and says:—"In these remote regions how many have been the cries of agony and despair emitted in vain! Even the few hardy Europeans of Codfish Island, when occupied in their adventurous enterprises, how often were their experiences of hardships from shipwreck and starvation aggravated by the cannibal tribes which surrounded them! Of these times the 'old hands' have many a heart-rending tale to relate, but they relate them without deigning to expect your sympathy—hard lives and rough usage, surfeits in plenty, and starvation in poverty, have blunted or effaced all relics of what civilization calls 'feelings.'"

On the 26th of February they proceeded with their pack-horses across the Waiau Plains, ascended Twinlaw, and saw the Waiau, the great river of the west, coming from the Takitimo mountains. They forded the Orawia, and saw the great forests extending from the Waiau to the sea, and upwards to the regions of snow. In washing the sands of the Waiau they found a speck of gold. The recent remains of the gigantic moa, led them to believe that this Titan of birds might yet possibly exist amid the deep forests and mountain gorges of this wild region. On the 11th of March they ascended Centre Hill, and traced the Oreti and Waiau to the gorges of the snowy mountains, fifty and seventy miles distant. Mr. Howell, an enterprising settler, informed them of a native track between Milford Sound and the head of the Waiau, the same referred to by Dr. Hector. The area of Mount Hamilton to the south, extending over the valleys of the upper Waiau and Oreti, he calculated at 600 square miles, containing much good pasturage.

They now directed their course eastward to the upper

Mataura, passing the gorges of the Dome, and reaching and ascending the Slate Range, 2000 feet above the valley, which divides the waters of the Clutha from those of the Mataura, and found a comparatively low and undulating region, stretching as far as the Canterbury province, thus ascertaining an extensive available country in the interior. They saw no lakes, but three Maories told them that the great lake Wakatip was not more than five miles higher up the Mataura. The scenery from the top of the Slate Range was truly magnificent, for they had the bold, precipitous, and peaked Eyre mountains opposite to them; while at their feet in the blue distance meandered the silver Mataura, which they could trace from its source in Eyre's Peak, till it lost itself in the deep gorge beneath the Dome. The prospect was quite Alpine, imitating in wildness the valleys of Savoy, but without the cultivated fields and green pastures of the interval. Thence they returned by the Taringtura Downs, and thence to Jacob River Settlement. In this tour Mr. Thomson surveyed extensive tracts of country, indeed he estimated that he had travelled over 1500 miles of difficult country, chiefly on foot, and surveyed by reconnoisance nearly 2,500,000 acres.

About this time Mr. M'Kerrow, District Surveyor, made a survey of the lake districts of the province of Otago.

CHAPTER XXIII.

DISCOVERIES IN THE MIDDLE ISLAND CONTINUED.

Mr. Dobson's discovery of a route over the Canterbury Mountains to the west coast.—Discoveries of Mr. Torlesse.—Harper's expedition to the west coast.—Mr. Dobson's attempt to find a way through the mountains to Nelson.—Surveys of Mr. Rochfort in the mountains westward.—Discoveries of Mr. Mackay. DR. HAAST'S EXPLORATIONS OF THE MOUNTAINS AND RIVERS OF THE MIDDLE ISLAND.—Report of Dr. Haast's explorations in 1860.—Proceeds from Nelson with a party to discover a route to the Buller on the west coast.—Wairau valley.—Lake Howard.—Passes discovered by Brunner, Heaphy, and Fox.—Junction of the Tutaki and Buller.—Ascend Mount Murchison.—Cross the Buller, and various rivers to the Grey.—Ascend the Grey.—Vast view from Mount Deception.—Lakes Brunner and Hochstetter.—Beds of coal on the Grey.—Follow the coast north.—Mounts Rochfort, William, and Frederick.—Follow the coast to Cape Farewell, and sail to Nelson.—Explorations of the Canterbury mountains in 1861.—Death by drowning of his companion, Dr. Sinclair.—Continues these explorations in 1862.—Sources of the Kowai.—Ascends Mount Torlesse.—Lakes Tekapo and Pukaki.—The Great Tasman glacier and Moorhouse Range.—Poetic beauty of the Southern Alps.—In 1863 Dr. Haast pursues his explorations into the mountains of Otago.—Dr. Drake reports good country between the rivers Grey and Hokitika.—Further explorations of Dr. Haast.—Dr. Hector in 1863 discovered the river Kaduku, the lake Kakapo, and a track to the central lake, Wakatipua.—A direct highway across the island.—Part of these discoveries made previously by Messrs. Caple, Alabaster, and others.—Passes discovered by Mr. Rochfort and Mr. Clarke.—These explorations small in extent, but arduous from the obstacles of high mountains, glaciers, and impetuous rivers.—Mr. Rochfort's surveys.—M. A. Dobson.

MR. DOBSON'S DISCOVERY OF A ROUTE OVER THE MOUNTAINS TO THE WEST COAST OF THE MIDDLE ISLAND OF NEW ZEALAND.

IN the *Lyttleton Times* of October 14, 1857, appeared a report of an expedition by Mr. Dobson, the Provincial Engineer, along the river Hurunui, and over a low saddle to where the waters began to run westward. It appears that a Maori path had been always known from the east to the west coast by the gorge of the Hurunui, at what is called Mount Noble, near Mr. Mason's station, Waitu, and from accounts of Maories, the existence of some level land in the interior had long been understood. A certain precipitous gulley in the gorge above mentioned, which the Maories crossed with flax ropes and ladders, has always been the obstacle to exploring expeditions in this direction. Mr. Dobson endeavoured to find a passable road for horses along this route, and with Mr. Mason, Mr. Taylor of the Wairau, Mr. Dampier, a shepherd of Mr. Mason's, and I believe another man, attacked the precipitous gulley in question with spades and pick-axes. In four days a track was cut by which horses could be led from one side to the other, and the party pursued their way up the gorge, keeping a little above the river bank on the south side.

In a very short time they came upon flat land. This was the half-expected country, superior to their anticipations in many respects. Dry, though well watered, open, grassy country, with clumps of wood standing upon it, and with corners of the forest running down to it from the mountain spurs, enclosed in hills, but containing more or less 60,000 acres of pasture land. A good deal of limestone and quartz prevailed in the neighbourhood. The timber trees were the ordinary varieties of pine and totara, with some white birch. The general level was about the same as the great plain, perhaps at the highest 600 feet above the water level. The main branch of the Hurunui flowed slowly along the northern edge of the basin, forming the boundary of the province. On the southern side of the basin another stream of the river flowed and formed an island, which again was divided down the middle by a third water-course.

On all the streams were lakes, six in number, to which the discoverers gave names; one of them, named Lake Sumner, is of considerable dimensions. "The valley is picturesque, having low, grassy hills, and separating streams, with insulated mounds, diversified by woods, and offsets of the mountains. Following this pleasant valley, the head waters of the Hurunui were reached, a low saddle was passed, and the party found themselves upon a tolerable stream running westward. They had thus passed the dividing range, and could have reached the sea without difficulty, but continuous bad weather stopped them. The stream running westward was the Brunner, only about thirty miles from the west coast, and the highest point of the line was found to be only about 1,000 feet above the sea level. A few miles down the Hurunui, there was a branch valley also passing over a low saddle to the river Grey, said by Brunner to run through a valley sixty miles long, and full of lakes.

Mr. Dobson's report and sketches of this newly discovered country brought instant applications for the land, and all that was available was at once taken up as sheep runs. Quartz, indicating gold, abounded on the western slopes of the mountains. It was decided that a road should be laid out through this route to the west.

This successful expedition soon produced others. Mr. Torlesse reported a tour, and brought down a map of the country discovered by him in the upper valley of the Ashley, and a district lying between Harewood Forest and the snowy range, dividing the basin of the Upper Ashley from the valley of the Hurunui. He stated that from the ranges dividing the Ashley from the Waimakiriri, he had a good view of the country watered by the Waimakiriri, and estimated the available land at 500,000 acres.

Soon after, Mr. Leonard Harper, with a party, made an expedition to the western coast. They started on the 4th of November, 1857, from Mr. Mason's out-station in the Waitohi valley, and passed through the Maori gulley along the south bank of the Hurunui. They then followed the south branch of the Hurunui to Loch Katrine, a small lake connected with Lake Sumner. Arrived at the north western extremity of Lake Sumner, they thence ascended the eastern Teramakau, up to the saddle, which was then covered with melting snow. They then made their way down the north side to the western Teramakau, and followed the bed of the stream to the junction of the Otira, a south branch of the Hurunui. The natives informed them that out of the Otira ran the river Waimakiriri, and not from a lake, as was supposed. They next reached the Cross Range, and a lake, out of which the natives told them a stream ran into the Grey, navigable for canoes. Embarking on a raft on the Teramakau, which they soon after reached, they were whirled amongst trees and bushes torn away by the torrent, to the western coast. Owing to delays, occasioned by bad weather, snow, and want of food, the journey from Mr. Mason's to the coast lasted twenty-three days, but they made the return journey in fourteen days, of which only eight were spent in travelling. The natives assured them that there was an easy way up the valley of the Waitanga to the east coast, through an open country, but which does not yet seem to have been discovered. They found many wild dogs in the bush, which the natives tamed, and used for catching birds. These natives all professed Christianity, and had no pigs or wheat, but lived on potatoes, Maori cabbage, and fern, with eels and other fish.

ROCHFORT'S SURVEYS.

Mr. Rochfort gives some account of two excursions made during the surveys, in the Geographical Journal, vol. xxxii. These took place in 1858. The first excursion was from Port Cooper up the Hurunui to the Taramakau, across Lake Brunner, and down the Arnold, or Kotukuwakaho river to the Grey, on the west coast, now a very familiar track, across the island. In his survey of the Arnold, which runs out at the N.W. end of the lake Brunner, he and his men suffered great hardships. The Arnold at its source is a wide river, taking the overflow of Lake Brunner, and for two miles passes through a dense forest of pine and birch, but has little current, and no fall; but when joined by two streams from the north, falls follow each other in rapid succession: the current increases with such velocity that it becomes a race, and the snags are so plentiful as to leave no available channel whatever. In attempting to sail down this river in a canoe, they were, as might have been expected, soon stuck fast, and were compelled to carry their instruments, papers, and small stock of flour, and march on through the bush amid almost continual and drenching rain—the common account which travellers have to give on the west side of Middle Island. For weeks they had been living on starvation rations. "We suffered," says Mr. Rochford, "other inconveniences than those of wet and cold, for our larder boasted no greater delicacy than thin paste, made of a tablespoonful of flour boiled in a quart of water. This we had twice a day while the flour lasted. In our exhausted condition we were enabled to accomplish but a short distance each day, and our small stock of flour soon vanished. One day we would have nothing to eat; another day, only a small robin between three of us and the dog; and a chance pigeon or two on another day, until at length we reached the Maori pah. Here every civility and kindness awaited us, and though only potatoes were procurable, they were sufficient not merely to support life, but to stimulate appetites, which, for six long months, had submitted to worse than English paupers' fare.

With these Maories, Mr. Rochford says he learned the existence of a wild tribe of natives—the Ngationamoi—or wild men of the bush. A woman of this tribe had been captured by the Maories two years before, but soon eluded them, and escaped into the bush.

Mr. Rochfort's second campaign of survey was on the west coast, commencing from the mouth of the River Buller. He pursued the coast southward some distance, crossing the Okari, the Waitakeri, and the Waitohi, on the latter rivers finding seams of coal. But his most thorough survey was that of the River Buller and the country adjoining it, as far as the nine feet fall, where they lost their canoe and instruments, which were all carried down the rapids, and whirled away from them, as they were endeavouring to haul the canoe up the rocks of the fall. The great incident, during this survey, was the discovery of gold, as described in the following entry of the journal:—"November the 8th, While I was chaining, I was surprised and no less gratified by one of the hands—F. Millington—announcing the discovery of gold, an event as unexpected as propitious, and one which must have a powerful influence on the future prospects of this long-neglected west land. The royal mineral was lying on the edge of the river, glittering in the sun, and in such quantity as induced rather a mutinous spirit, my hands having a greater preference for the golden prospects before them than for the sterner duties of surveying."

In 1858 Mr. Dobson made an adventurous attempt to force a way through the mountains from the Hurunui towards Nelson, in the hope of establishing an inland route to that colony.

In the province of Nelson Mr. Rochfort, the government surveyor, has been for some years engaged in tracing and mapping out the hitherto little known parts of the country, especially on the west coast. In these openings up of the mountains of the Middle Island and its west coast, the indefatigable explorations and discoveries of coal by Mr. J. Mackay also require a prominent mention.

DR. HAAST'S EXPLORATIONS OF THE MOUNTAINOUS REGIONS AND THE RIVERS OF THE MIDDLE ISLAND OF NEW ZEALAND.

In 1860 Dr. Julius Haast, the geologist of the province, set out to make an examination of the mountainous regions of Nelson; and the report of this exploratory tour was published by the provincial government in 1861. From this report we learn that Dr. Haast set out on the 8th of January, 1860, from Nelson, the capital of the province, accompanied by Mr. James Burnett, a surveyor, and by three other Europeans, two Maories, and pack-horses carrying their provisions. One of their principal objects was to find a practicable route from Nelson to the Rivers Buller and Grey on the west coast, where coal and gold fields had been discovered. They ascended into the mountains from the Motueka Valley, and directed their course through the hills to the Lake Roto-iti. They were greatly struck with the magnificent scenery near this lake, the hills there being nearly 5000 feet high, and giving grand views into the celebrated Wairau Valley. Thence they proceeded through the mountains to Lake Howard, naming a lofty range on the way Mount Franklin, after Sir John Franklin. From the Howard, or Rotoroa, they directed their course over mountains and through passes formerly penetrated by Messrs. Brunner, Heaphy, and Fox, towards the Tiraumea Plains, and through scenery which they pronounced equal to that of Switzerland. On this route they named Mounts McLean and Murchison. On the 31st of January, they arrived at the junction of the Tutaki and Buller. After ascending Mount Murchison, and enjoying a wide view over the surrounding country, and perceiving that a route to the southward was practicable from Nelson, they descended the Buller some distance, and then struck southward for the Grey. On this coast they named a rocky range westward Mount Lyell. Crossing the Tutaki, the Mataki-taki, the Matiri, and the Buller, and other rivers, they struck the Grey, and crossed it and its tributaries repeatedly, amid continual rains, which all travellers alike find plentifully towards the west, or, as some of the party preferred to call it, the wet coast; and, on the 21st of March, they embarked in a canoe, and reached the mouth of the Grey. Going down the river, they passed the camp of Mr. John Rochfort, the surveyor. Thus they had proved the practicability of a track from Nelson to the Grey on the west coast.

Obtaining fresh supplies here, they then ascended the Grey, still through pouring rains, towards its sources, and from the summit of a mountain, which they named Mount Deception, supposing it to have a neighbouring height called Black Hill, they enjoyed immense views of the southern Alps, Mount Cook being conspicuous amid his snows. They had full view of Lake Brunner and another water, which they named Lake Hochstetter. The whole of the route of the Grey lay below them. On returning to the mouth of the river, Dr. Haast observed valuable beds of coal. Thence they set out, and traced the coast to the Buller, which they reached on the 13th of June. From this point, still continuing their way north-east along the coast, crossing numerous streams, and enduring much hardship from wet and cold, they named three hills Mounts Rochfort, William, and Frederick. After ascending Mounts Rochfort and William, and taking observations of the country from their summits, they returned to the Buller, and thence followed the wild and precipitous coast all the way to Cape Farewell, whence they sailed to Nelson. The results of this journey were an elaborate topographical map of the south-west portion of the province and a mass of information in the report on its physical geography, geology, zoology, and botany.

Since then Dr. Haast has been laboriously pursuing his labours amongst the mountains of Canterbury. In 1861 he gave a lecture in Canterbury, detailing his journey up the River Rangitata and its tributaries the Havelock and the Clyde. His descriptions of the scenery amongst these mountains represent it as sublime in the highest degree, mountain peaks piercing the blue sky at from 5000 to 12,000 feet above the level of the sea, glaciers shining like molten silver, waterfalls descending over their sides to a depth sometimes of 1700 feet; huge pyramids rising sublimely from the midst of torrents which swept around them, and vast chains and ridges covered with eternal snows, from whose ice caverns the waters of the Waimakariri, Rakaia, Ashburton, Rangitata, Waitaki, and Waitanga rush. It was in this journey that his companion, Dr. Sinclair, lost his life in attempting to cross a river.

In the following year, Dr. Haast was exploring the sources of the Kowai amongst the mountains of that name, 3000 feet above the plains of Christchurch. His object was to visit the coal beds lying in the heart of these mountains, and in his continued examinations of which he discovered extensive beds of iron ore; he ascended also the highest peak of the Mount Torlesse Range, whence he could gaze, as it were, over a great part of the province, and saw the Southern Alps in all their majesty bound the horizon, amongst which Mount Cook, 13,200 feet high, with its tent-shaped form, rose conspicuously over other ranges, whilst, more in the foreground, Mount Arrowsmith, Mount Ashburton, and the Moorhouse Glaciers, through the clear New Zealand atmosphere, seem almost close at hand. From the Big Ben, the highest summit of the Thirteen Mile Bush Range, the picturesque Rakaia, from its icy sources to its mouth, was wholly visible, and the blue waters of Lake Coleridge, lying at the base of this latter range, gave a striking charm to the noble panorama.

From these mountains, Dr. Haast, in his indefatigable explorations, pursued his way through the valleys and passes to Lake Tekapo, and on to Lake Pukaki, the Great Tasman Glacier, and the Moorhouse Range. It is not often that we hear a sober geologist breaking out into raptures at the scenes around him, his mind being generally attracted by the peculiar substance and tissue of the rocks, but we find Dr. Haast thus exclaiming at the sights around him:—"Oh! that I were a poet to sing the beauty of the Southern Alps. The time will surely come when pilgrims from all parts of the southern hemisphere will hasten to visit these mountains, and then the good folks of Canterbury will be inundated with poetical effusions, and 'My Rambles to the Southern Alps,' or 'Impressions of a Journey to Mount Cook,' with splendid engravings, will be on the drawing-room tables of future generations." This journey was continued to the Ohou, and, in the researches for gold, as well as in his own proper geological pursuits, Dr. Haast bids fair to make the complete tour and survey of the mountains and rivers of the Middle Island.

This idea is confirmed by our last news of Dr. Haast, who, in the early months of 1863, was penetrating into the mountains of Otago, whilst Mr. Drake was pursuing researches in the field he had left, and reported having crossed the Canterbury Mountains to the mouth of the River Taramakau, and reported a large tract of level country, though thickly timbered, between the Grey and the Hokitika.

Dr. Haast, meanwhile, had proceeded from the Ahuriri River to Mount Hawea, on the frontiers of Otago, and thence to Lake Oanaka, or Wanaka. Thence they ascended the Makarora, and, from Wilkin's Station, proceeded through dense forests; they returned to Lake Hawea, and back to the Ahuriri. Dr. Haast and his party reached Christchurch on the 12th of May, and reported the country they had explored another Switzerland.

In these latter researches Dr. Haast had entered a field then undergoing examination by Dr. Hector, the government geologist of Otago. In February Dr. Hector left Dunedin to ascend the mountain range of Matukituki, where he encountered tumultuously rushing rivers, eternal snows, and glaciers with awful crevasses and traces of devastating avalanches. The principal glacier he named Haast's Glacier, in honour of the enterprising geologist of Canterbury. Intensely wet weather and shortness of provisions prevented them reaching the west coast in this direction. His companion, Mr. Sullivan, editor of the *Otago Times*, has given a very vivid description of the scenes and dangers of his journey, which were by no means trivial, especially on the lofty icefields of Mount Aspiring.

In May of the same year Dr. Hector left Port Chalmers in a small schooner of 20 tons, to examine the numerous inlets and sounds of the west coast of Otago. At Preservation Inlet he noticed immense quantities of splendid granite, capable of being easily quarried and shipped; at Paterson's Point strata of very good coal. But his greatest discovery was that of a considerable river between Martin's Bay and the Awarua river, which was named the Kaduku. Tracing this up, it led him to a lake called by him Kakapo Lake, ten miles in length, by four or five miles in width, whence he followed a valley to the central Lake Wakatipua, near the Greenstone River. Dr. Hector was only forty-six hours from leaving the schooner to reaching Queen's Town, and it could have been done in much less time. As these regions lie very near the great Clutha river, this route opens up a direct highway across the island; but Dr. Hector was of opinion that a still better and more direct route to these lakes could be found from Milford Sound, whence there is an old Maori pass. This, on further examination, was found cut off by a large precipice. On Dr. Hector's publication of his discovery, it was soon notified that part of this route had been opened up at an earlier date by a Mr. Charles Cameron, who had in consequence asked for the lease of a squatting station as a reward, as well as by Messrs. Caple, Alabaster and others. Dr. Hector freely admitted these prior claims on their being made known to him, which chiefly consisted of the discovery of the river Kaduku, and the Lake Kakapo.

About the same time Mr. Rochfort announced the discovery of an easy pass connecting the Wangapeka with the Karamea and the Lyell, or some other river running into the Buller on the west coast of Nelson, and another by Mr. David Clarke from the Motupika to the Buller.

The newspapers of Canterbury of Oct. 13, 1863, stated that Mr. A. Dobson, and a surveying party had gone to the west coast of that province *viâ* Nelson in a small schooner, which had been wrecked at the entrance of the Grey river, but that Mr. Dobson and his companions escaped and were making their examination of that coast.

Many of these expeditions of exploration are but small compared with the great journeys across the Australian continent, but, though less in extent, they are not the less arduous, as far as they go, from the nature of the country. The steepness, ruggedness, and intricacy of the mountains which run like a huge back-bone from end to end of these islands, from the wild impetus of the mountain rivers, the density of the forest, and the snow, cataracts, and ice-bergs, which are encountered in the Alpine regions. These expeditions show a spirit of research and adventure which have well nigh laid open the whole of New Zealand to the feet and the knowledge of its population.

CHAPTER XXIV.

OPENING COMMUNICATION WITH THE WEST COAST.

Opening the way to the West Coast.—Arduous nature of the undertaking.—The fatalities of 1863.—The story of the loss of Mr. Whitcombe.—Loss of Mr. Charlton Howitt and Party.—Life and Character of Mr. Charlton Howitt. Sojourn in Australia.—Employed in Canterbury to seek for gold.—Engaged in making a bridle-road over the mountains to the West Coast.—Reputation for zeal and energy.—Progress of the work.—Wetness of the West Coast.—Mode of subsistence in the mountains.—Bird-catching.—Mr. Sherrins' account of crossing the mountains.—The grandeur of the mountain scenery.—The charms of the forests of New Zealand.—Enormous and curious trees.—Mr. Howitt and two men drowned in Lake Brunner.—The sufferings of James Hammett the survivor.—Unavailing researches for the remains of the drowned.—Subsequent drowning of Mr. Townsend in the Grey.—Remarks on the climate of the West Coast.—Concluding remarks.—Probable extinction of the native race.—Remarkable exemplification of native rights by a native.—Persuasion of the Maories of their own fate.—Appeal to our countrymen in New Zealand on their behalf.

COMPARATIVELY small as is the breadth of the islands of New Zealand, yet the height and extent of its mountains, the impetuous rapidity of its rivers, descending from the steep declivities of ranges from 10,000 to 12,000 feet in height, and the denseness of its woods, thick grown with supplejacks and knit together with vines, have made it arduous work for those who have attempted to open up its savage hills and intricate defiles to the passage of civilization. In the Middle Island Mr. Brunner explored at great risk, and amid much hardship, its mountain heights; Dr. Haast, the government geologist, has made these tracks more known, and pointed out fresh saddles and ways of access. Others, equally adventurous but less fortunate, have laid down their lives in these patriotic enterprises. Perhaps in no country are the casualties of drowning so numerous in proportion to the population. The rivers descend with such momentum and velocity from the precipitous hills that persons even passing known fords are continually swept away irresistibly. So that drowning has been said to be a natural death in these islands.

The year 1863 was prolific of such fatalities amongst

gentlemen in the public service, whose employments led them into the mountains, and required them to cross lakes and rivers. Amongst these was Mr. Whitcombe the civil engineer, a young man of great spirit and power of endurance. He was sent out to endeavour to discover a passage through the range of mountains which separate the east and west sides of the Middle Island. The discovery of extensive fields of gold and coal on the western slopes of the mountains, made such a passage of the highest importance.

The voyage round the island was circuitous and frequently dangerous; a tolerably direct road by land was most desirable. Mr. Whitcombe set out from Christchurch on the 13th of April, 1863, with an ample supply of men, horses, and provisions, but after crossing the Rakaia, on entering the mountains, he soon found that these were useless, for the most part. The horses could not clamber where it was necessary to go; the men carrying their own provisions would consume them without adding to the speed or success of the expedition. He, therefore, sent men and horses back, retaining only Mr. Louper, a Swiss, accustomed to mountain climbing, and as much provision as they could carry on their backs.

They came upon a deep fissure in the mountains, and Mr. Whitcombe thinking this would prove the pass they sought, calculated that they could find their way to the saddle of the Teramakau, in ten days. If their provisions fell short, they could, he said, fall back on Mr. Howitt's tent on Lake Brunner. In the passes of the mountains, they were soon enveloped in blinding snow, and cut off from all apparent progress by gigantic walls of ice. The snowing soon changed to raining, and all at once they found themselves stopped by a perpendicular fall of the river into the pass, descending from rock to rock, into a roaring whirlpool below. They could not now return, as the pass behind them was snowed up; and to all but a Swiss mountaineer, to cross this cataract and gulf would have been impossible, but by letting himself down from rock to rock by the rope, Louper managed to get across, and by fastening the rope to the rocks on the other side, got over their swags, and finally Mr. Whitcombe, Louper having, however, to descend himself up to the neck in the boiling abyss.

Thus, repeatedly crossing torrents and scrambling over rocks, their food getting short, their covering insufficient for the severe nights, they at length came out on the other side of the mountains. They found that the river they were upon was the Hokatika, and on its banks they discovered traces of gold. On reaching the sea-shore they followed the beach to the River Brunner. From the time they left the Rakaia to their reaching the sea was thirteen days. They were now in the extremities of famine, for their provisions husbanded with the utmost care, had been totally exhausted for several days. To their consternation and despair, they found the huts of the Maories, where they had confidently expected relief, totally deserted, and destitute of all provisions. In one of the gardens they found a little cabbage and a handful of very small potatoes, which they cooked and eat. They then walked on in this exhausted state, waded up to their chests across the Brunner, and pursued the coast to the Teramakau, but again found no one there. The next morning they could see the Maori Pah on the other side, but, as no smoke issued from it, they feared that that side of the river was deserted too. Mr. Whitcombe was bent on crossing the river where they were, and thought it might be done on two logs of wood tied together. Louper declared it to be impossible, saying that he had crossed there twice in a canoe with five men and a Maori, but it was all they could do to row over from the force of the stream. He advised that they should ascend the river for some distance, and endeavour to catch some wood-hens for food, and cross where it was practicable.

Mr. Whitcombe, who dreaded in their enfeebled state to encounter the woods again, especially as they found that all the wood-hens in the tracts they had lately passed, had been killed by the wild dogs, would not listen to this; and finding two old native canoes, he commenced lashing them together by tying two poles across them with flax. Louper helped, and also prepared two oars and two steering poles from young trees, and, though Louper had no hope, they began to cross. In vain had Louper assured Mr. Whitcombe, that they might reach an island which appeared in the middle of the stream, but there they would be swamped, or swept out to sea by the violence of the current. Mr. Whitcombe was deaf to remonstrance, for he saw no chance of escaping death by starvation, except by getting over the river. They entered the boat, reached the island, but the moment they shot beyond it, the boat was swept down the current and began to sink under them. Mr. Whitcombe then seeing the full and awful truth of Louper's assertions, exclaimed,—" We are lost! it is all my fault!"—and pulling off his coat, plunged into the water, to attempt to swim to land. Louper who remained in the boat, was carried away with arrow speed, and was soon whirled over and over in the surf, and finally hurled out upon the sand. When he began to recover his senses and composure, he saw himself standing alone on the desert sands, saved from the water, but with every prospect of perishing by famine on land. His first care, however, was to seek for his companion, and he soon found his dead body flung on the beach, and his head plunged into the sands. After burying his remains as well as he could, having no instrument but his hands to do it with, and in a state of fearful exhaustion from previous famine, and immediate violence of the surf, he managed to make his way to a Maori hut, where he obtained a few potatoes, and by help of these he reached the party under Mr. Charlton Howitt, who were making the horse track over the mountains, and were camped near Lake Brunner. There he arrived a most pitiable spectacle, famished, drenched with wet, perishing with cold, his clothes being saturated with water and sand, and his body, as it were, bedded in it. He was speedily furnished with food and warm tea; his clothes were stripped off, his body washed, and he was put to bed. By the hospitable care, of this party, in a few days he was sufficiently recovered to be able to proceed on his journey to Christchurch to convey to the government and to his wife and friends the melancholy news of the fate of poor Whitcombe. As Mr. Howitt was wishing to send his horses for the winter down to Mr. Taylor's station, which was on Louper's way, he was mounted on one of these, and furnished with provisions, so that he could lead the other. The poor fellow took his leave of his entertainers, who had no doubt been the savers of his life, with deep emotion. "I came here," he said, "like a beggar, perishing from cold and hunger, and sinking with fatigue, and now I go away refreshed, clothed, strengthened, and on horseback like a gentleman!"

Little did he think that the head of that party, who had given him such timely help, and two of his men were soon themselves to disappear from amongst men without possibility of mortal aid.

LOSS OF MR. CHARLTON HOWITT AND PARTY.

I now come to a narrative which nearly concerns myself. It has been my fortune to have my only two sons engaged in the work of opening-up the wilderness of the antipodes. The share taken in the exploration of Australia by my eldest son, the discoverer of the lost expedition of Burke and Wills, is well known, and is narrated in these volumes. That of my second son, in aiding the accessibility of the interior of New Zealand, I shall now state in as succinct a form as I can. This story is one that may serve as a stimulus to young men in a life of simple and unswerving devotion to the cause of virtue and of progress.

Herbert Charlton Howitt, born at Esher in the year 1838, was remarkable from his infancy for his intense love of nature, and especially for all her forms of animal life. It was his intensest pleasure as a little boy to

watch all the proceedings of animals, birds, and insects.
He soon became as familiar with them as if he had been
admitted by them to all their tenements, and their most
secret practices. This disposition grew up with him.
For town and conventional life he had not the smallest
taste. The warm friendship of a few congenial people,
and the enjoyment of the country and its objects, made
the constant happiness of his life. Of all the knowledge
connected with these things and this life, he had a ready
power of acquisition, for the classical and many other
departments of knowledge in which so many years of
youthful existence are usually spent laboriously, only to
be insensibly dropped on the after highways of the
world, he had no desire. Work, in gardening, farming,
or in constructing the implements and apparatus for
these fields of labour, was a sort of passion with him,
and it is a singular fact, that scarcely any one who knew
him can recollect him ever saying that he was weary.
The vigour of his frame, created by this simple, healthy,
and active mode of life, was, as it seemed, inexhaustible.
For a series of years he walked to the City of London
every day, Sundays excepted, a distance of five miles,
and back again, thus ten miles a day, walked generally
most days some miles about town on business, and both
in the morning before going to town, and in the evening
after his return, worked in a large garden, in which, as
with an avarice of labour, he scarcely allowed any other
person to do anything, even of the more laborious kinds
of exertion. Sometimes he varied this routine by setting
off, after his ten miles' walk to and from Town, including
the day's business, to visit some of his most intimate
friends, five miles off, and again frequently returning the
same evening. Two years in which he lived with myself and his brother in the Australian bush, were, perhaps, his *beau ideal* of life's perfection. There, travelling on from day to day through the forests, or camping
on the banks of some pleasant stream, his mind was
constantly engaged in observing the new forms of nature
and animal life around him. Trees, flowers, the infinite

variety of birds and insects, the flying-fox and squirrel, the climbing opossum, the bounding kangaroo, the glittering shapes, and quaint cries of emus, pelicans, native-companions, the gliding serpent, and the soaring eagle, were a perpetual delight to him, yet little more than a boy. With his train of dogs, he would set out to seek the horses which had strayed during the night in the forests, and amid these various tenants of the woods and the waters whole days would glide over him as a dream. No place was too solitary, no wilderness too vast for him; amid nature and her numerous and ever-varied family, he was everywhere at home.

New Zealand became the country of his choice, and though he passed through several disappointments and hardships there, he grew most affectionately attached to it. Perhaps no person of his age, but five-and-twenty at his death, was ever more qualified for the life of an explorer or pioneer of civilization. From the time when he reluctantly returned with me from Australia, to that of his going out to New Zealand, he never, if he could avoid it, slept in a bed. Rolled up in his blanket, or his opossum rug, with a pillow under his head, on the floor, and his window set invariably open, summer and winter, thus he slept, and sometimes awoke in the morning with a pile of drifted snow on his head, but never took cold, except when the housemaid had closed his chamber-window by mistake, and he had slept without observing it!

In the Canterbury settlement, his rare qualifications for an explorer, and the general energy and uprightness of his character, soon attracted the attention of the Government. He was first employed in an expedition for the discovery of a gold-field, and during the last six months of his life in cutting a horse-track over the mountains between Christchurch and the western coast, where extensive gold and coal-fields had been found. I may quote from the Canterbury journals, and from official reports, the circumstances connected with this undertaking. The following is from the *Lyttleton Times* of September 12th, 1863:—

"Last week will long be memorable as having brought us the intelligence of the death of one of the most active and intelligent explorers who has ever responded to the call which has so often to be made in a new and partially-explored country by those whose duty it is to open-up the waste, by forcing roads through what has hitherto been impenetrable mountains and forests. It is now just nine months since Mr. Wylde, as acting head of the public works department, was instructed by the Government to endeavour to cut a track from the Hurunui Plains to the mouth of the Grey or Teramakau, on the West Coast. In pursuance of these instructions, he engaged the services of Mr. Charlton Howitt, who had been previously engaged in exploring for gold in that locality. This gentleman started on the first of January last, accompanied by five men, taking with him two pack-horses, and the necessary outfit, with instructions to track out a line of road on a route indicated by Mr. Wylde, and, if possible, to open it for pack-horse traffic from Lake Taylor to the coast. No one could have been chosen more fitted for this work than Mr. Howitt, a young, active man, somewhat below the ordinary stature, but possessed of immense energy and endurance. No amount of danger or fatigue seemed able to daunt him, and in the prosecution of his work he has been known to carry on his back for twenty miles at a stretch, and over mountains, and through rivers, which would have turned back most men, loads of flour and other necessaries for the use of his companions, which would generally have been considered sufficient for a pack-horse. Out of the five men who accompanied Howitt, two were soon sent back by him as unable to endure the hardships incidental to the work; but with the other three he succeeded in marking out, and cutting, where necessary, a track for a length of about forty miles, over the great dividing range, and down the Teramakau, until he encountered what was before known to be the great difficulty to be overcome. This difficulty occurs at a part of the river where it is shut in by rugged, perpendicular rocks for many miles, covered on their summits by dense, impenetrable bush. The only way of passing down the river from this point was by the aid of Mokis (rafts made of flax sticks), which, on being launched on the river, are swept down between the rocks with fearful rapidity.

"As it was useless to attempt to carry the road further in this direction, and the provisions being nearly exhausted, Mr. Howitt returned to Christchurch for instructions. As the winter was then approaching, and it was known that the pass over the mountains would probably be blocked up with snow for some months, it became a grave question whether the prosecution of the work should not be suspended until the spring; but at the urgent request of Mr. Howitt, and his representation that he could support himself and party in a great measure through the winter on the natural productions of the country—such as eels and wild-fowl—Mr. Wylde consented to fit him out again with a fresh supply of provisions, etc., and he again started with instructions to endeavour to carry on the track, by leaving the Teramakau, and striking across the country for Lake Brunner, following the shore of the lake, and then back to the river beyond the point of difficulty.

"The plan of operations embraced the packing over the hills of flour, etc. sufficient for the winter months, and then sending the horses back to Mr. Taylor's station, there not being sufficient food to keep them during the winter on the other side. The packing occupied about six weeks, and then Jacob Louper, the companion of the unfortunate Mr. Whitcombe, having made his way to Mr. Howitt's camp, and having been most kindly treated by him, the horses were given to him to help him over the Teramakau saddle to Mr. Taylor's station. How little could Mr. Howitt have supposed, when succouring Louper, that himself and two out of his three companions were so soon to share the fate of the lamented Mr. Whitcombe."

I may here interrupt the narrative to remark that Charlton with his love of work, partook of all the labours and hardships of his men. He never asked them to do a thing which he would not assist in doing himself. As to "roughing it," he persuaded his men to continue at their labour under circumstances that perhaps no other man could. The climate of New Zealand in the lowlands on the east coast is deemed delicious, but in the mountains and on the west coast, the rains are something extraordinary for strength and continuance. From Charlton's private diary, for months together they seem to have scarcely had a fair day. The journal of Mr. R. A. A. Sherrin, in a journey to the west coast, published in the *Christchurch Press*, January, 1864, confirms this view of the climate in those parts. The journal of the unfortunate Hammett does the same. This is especially so in the winter months. Mr. Sherrin's journey over the mountains, and westward, commenced on the 21st of June, and lasted six months. This was, of course, during part of the winter, and through the spring to midsummer, and this is his concluding entry regarding the weather—" Whatever may be the cause, there is no doubt that a more considerable quantity of rain falls on the western than on the eastern side of the province. *I remember only three fine weeks during the six months we were on the coast.*" He adds, " I have, however, reason to believe that the cold there is not so excessive, as on this side of the island. In rainy weather the mercury is scarcely ever below 50°. Notwithstanding the quantity of heavy fogs and mists continually arising, the place may be considered eminently healthy. None of us had even a cold during the whole of the winter, and from ailments of every kind we were singularly free. The natives appear to live to a good old age unless cut off by accident." Of course, the cold in the lofty mountain ranges is very much greater. There are glaciers, and avalanches as in the European Alps. Mr. Sherrin gives some little idea of the weather in the spring month of August, in the very region where my son and his party were at work during the winter, and where they lost their lives. "From the solicitations of Mr. Townsend, I consented to go with him, and form a party for the purpose of searching Lake Brunner, to endeavour to discover the bodies of Mr. Howitt and his men. On the 11th of August we left the Grey with the intention of searching the lake thoroughly, and making a canoe there. It was not until the 25th of the month that we reached the lake. Oh! the unutterable misery of that journey! Rain every day; directed wrongly by the natives; having to cut a line through three or four miles of bad bush, this trip, as a whole, is the worst and hardest that I remember in the whole course of my life. Wet through all the time; scarcely ever dry at night; freshes every hour; a mist heavy and dense, covering everything, the journey was worse than description can paint it. Gone astray; two men knocked up, no chance of retracing our steps, the trip was one that will long be remembered. While travelling the bush, how vividly Humboldt's description of South America are remembered. 'The density of the vegetation; the rottenness of the soil, the wonderful amount of rain and water; the thousands of decomposed and decomposing trees; the being hemmed in on every side by keikei, supplejack, and tatarama; the network of roots to crawl leisurely over; the canons and rivers to cross and recross with a heavy swag, will only give an idea of travelling in constant rain."

Such was the place, the scene, the weather, and obstacles, against which my son and his party were laboriously forcing their way through the winter months, but which his enthusiasm in performing a public and most necessary work, made him write in his diary, after an encounter of months of such fight with the elements, the savage forest, and the rocks,—"And yet I like it!" It may be wondered how he expected to find food in such a region? Sometimes they were compelled to descend to the west coast for flour, tea, sugar, etc., and to carry them up through these dripping woods and hills; but they had abundance of fish, and especially eels, in the waters, and the mode of catching birds there is something curious to our European notions.

The Maories have a mode of calling the birds in the country around them, by making a peculiar noise with a leaf in their mouths. I saw this experiment tried by the New Zealand natives lately, in London, in a party in some suburban pleasure grounds, to which they had been invited, and they were much surprised to see our birds, instead of being attracted by the call, fly away. In New Zealand, my son had learned this call, and could, on any occasion in the forest assemble around him an audience of numerous and various birds, like another St. Francis, about to preach to them. Amongst the New Zealand birds is one of such extreme simplicity, called the Wood Hen, that he used, at any time, where these birds abounded, to procure as many as were wanted for a meal, by going out with two long rods. At the end of one was hung a bit of red rag; at the end of the other was a noose. Having made the call, on the wood-hens running on all sides out of the thickets, he shook the red rag, and they ran forward to examine it; and whilst they were thus engaged, he slipped the noose, at the end of the other rod, over their heads, one after another, and captured what he wanted.

Of the sort of climate in which the work of my son's party was carried on, we may take another description from Mr. Sherrin's journal:—"It continued to rain steadily from June till November 22nd, and, as a necessary consequence, all the rivers were very high. Of the many dangers encountered and privations endured in a residence for six months on the coast, continually shifting about in constant rain, a better idea can be formed than any description could give. No child's play will be found in travelling by others who will follow in our footsteps, as the fearful loss of life in the neighbourhood will testify. No pecuniary inducement would tempt me to travel over the same ground again, in the winter months. You may rise in the morning with the conviction on your mind, that the dangers of the day may possibly be more than you can overcome. In fact, it is a country where no man's life is safe who has constantly to travel, however much experience he may possess, while the constant deaths on the coast from disaster, tend to unnerve your energies, and make you ridiculously cautious. The natives at the Grey were thoroughly persuaded that we were dead, 'like poor Howitt,' having been so impressed by visions of the night, that were corroborated by the constant rain, and almost appeared incredulous to see us safely return. Fifty times have they howled the consolation in my ear, that by-and-by I should be like poor Howitt."

And yet those mountain regions are very magnificent. "Any person," says Mr. Sherrin, "however insensible to the beauties of nature, cannot help gazing on this magnificent tier of peaks whenever the mist clears away. Only with a south-east wind will this occur, when every pinnacle, rugged outline, and snow-field will be distinctly seen. At every place along the beach, wherever the hills are visible, one's pleasure is increased by observing how the difference of position creates a different grouping, how the rugged becomes softened by distance, and that which appeared unbroken and smooth, on closer inspection is found to be broken and confused. The residents of Christchurch will never have any idea of the beauty of the west coast, until some enterprising Albert Smith brings a panorama to their Town Hall, to be appreciated by lamp-light."

The forest scenery is described by Mr. Thomson, with equal admiration :—

"Indescribable is the charm of New Zealand forests for the lovers of nature. There generations of noble trees are seen decaying, and fresh generations rising up around the moss-covered trunks of fallen patriarchs. The profound silence which reigns in these regions produces a pleasing gloom on the mind, and the scene displays, better than the most classic architecture, the grandeur of repose. No sound is heard, save the falling of trees, or the parrot's shrill screech, as birds which enliven the outskirts of forests are mute in their interior. Around the graves of past generations of trees the air is hushed into stillness, while the tops of the living generation are agitated with gales and breezes. At Christmas the pohutukaua (metro-sideros) is covered with scarlet flowers, and is then the most gaudy of forest trees; and the rimu (dacrydium cupressimum) possesses a melancholy beauty, and an indescribable grandeur. Few of the pines recall to the settler's eyes the same trees in England, and, singular to relate, unlike their congeners, the majority of them grow intermixed with other trees. The celebrated and beautiful kauri (dammara australis), is the only pine bearing a cone, and the male and female cones are found on the same tree."

Of the size of these trees Mr. Darwin gives us a good idea. "I measured," he says, "one of the famous kauri pines, and found it thirty-one feet in circumference above the roots. I heard of one no less than forty feet. They are remarkable for their smooth, cylindrical boles, which run up to a height of sixty, and even ninety feet, with a nearly equal diameter, and without a single branch."

Still more wonderful is the pohutukaua, or rata tree of New Zealand, mentioned above (metrosideros robusta). The stranger in the forest sees a slender, creeping plant on the ground, more resembling a running moss, or weed, than anything. It is the infant rata, seeking a tree up which to climb. Still it creeps onwards, till, finding a tree, up it goes. It runs rapidly up it. It encloses it on all sides. Still ascending, it at length reaches the loftiest summit. It throws out a head, which smothers the native head of the tree, and the once wiry threads, swelling into thick stems, all unite together, destroy the original usurped bole, and becomes a tree. It assumes a massive trunk, solid as teak, and admirable for ship-building, whilst its magnificent head, towering over the forest, catches the eye everywhere with its blaze of scarlet flowers.

Amid this superb, but dangerous and inclement scenery, Charlton Howitt and his three men had for six months been forcing their way, following the courses of the rivers Hurunui and Teramakau for the most part, examining these rivers for fords, and planting flags to mark them to the traveller. They had arrived at the Brunner, a lake of some ten miles long, and five wide, and were cutting the road along its margin. As the thickness of the bush yet uncut prevented them getting their stores from the west coast to their hut, these were deposited on the other side of the lake in a wooden hut raised on poles, called a watti, or whata. To cross to this, they constructed a canoe, after the fashion of those of the natives, of green pine, and Charlton, in his letters, describes the pleasure with which they launched this canoe from a cliff, and saw it plunge deep under water, and then rise and swim buoyantly on the surface. In this canoe they had crossed the lake repeatedly, to fetch stores from the watti. Once more Charlton set out with two of the men, Robert Little, and Henry Muller, on Saturday, June 27th, to fetch some flour from the watti, and to fish for eels in the river Arnold, which runs out of the head of the lake. They left James Belgrave Hammett alone in the hut. The next day, the wind rose, and it rained heavily. On Monday it was fine, but still blowing. Tuesday and Wednesday passing without their return, Hammett in great alarm set off to walk, or, rather, wade, round the lake, through deep bogs and water, often up to his chest, to seek his missing companions. Finding he could not get further along the swampy shore, Hammett made a raft, and coasted the lake, camping on shore on Thursday night; and on Friday and Saturday he makes these notices in his diary, which include all the discoveries that have ever been made of the fate of the missing party.

"Friday, July 3. Started again. On going round a bend of the lake, near the mouth of the Hohono, I saw something lying on the beach which, to my dismay, on reaching it, proved to be Mr. Howitt's swag rolled up in the little calico tent which he used for travelling with. This, by preventing the blanket becoming soaked with water, had been blown on shore. I searched all around, but I could see nothing else. I have, therefore, every reason for supposing that the canoe sank with them during the strong wind that has been blowing. The canoe was but of green wood, and floated scarcely three inches out of the water in smooth weather. I took the swag along with me to my watti, made a fire to dry the papers, and camped there. It rained heavily.

"Saturday, July 4. Still raining heavily. Started round the lake again towards the Arnold. Saw no sign of smoke in any direction, no portion of the canoe, nothing which indicated that Mr. Howitt and my mates were alive. I made fast the raft at the mouth of the river, and went down along its bank. I saw that they had been there, because their bobs and lines were there. I made myself a bit of a hut of some flax, and camped till morning. Still raining very heavily, and the lake still rising. I saw no other sign save what I have stated, that Mr. Howitt had been here."

And that is the whole which has transpired of the fate of Charlton Howitt and his two men. Poor Hammett, after getting back to the hut, in the faint hope that they might have reached it by some other way, and finding all as he had left it, set out once more to examine every portion of the lake shores for traces of his lost companions. In this research he persevered in a state of starvation and drenched with continual rains, making raft after raft, and going round and round and round the lake but without any the slightest further discovery. His state of mind was bordering on madness. In his entry of July 7th, he says :—" Rain pouring as hard as ever, I feel lonely, miserable, and cold indeed. No fire, nothing to eat, nothing of any kind, but a little fire and cold water. To tell all the imaginings which are continually passing through my mind could do no good. Frequently, during the last few days, while sitting in this down-pouring rain, and while perfectly awake, have I fancied that I could see Mr. Howitt and the others walking towards me, first in one direction and then in another. By an effort, I have shook off this depressing dulness, and have then spoken with my faithful dog as though he was a Christian. Again I wonder whether I shall be able to recover the bodies, that I may give them a burial in a place which I may be able to point out to their surviving friends. No human being can conceive my almost maddening thoughts. If it should please God that I become insane, what will become of me?"

Driven by famine and his ever haunting thoughts, after being twenty-three days on the lake without seeing a sign of any living person, he made one more visit to the hut at their camp, and finding all as he had left it, he started for the Buller diggings, quite certain that his companions had perished. He carried with him Mr. Howitt's tin of maps and papers, and only reached the Teramakau diggings to find them deserted. In a state of the extremest exhaustion, his feet swollen with the rough ground he had had to pass, he reached the beach near the mouth of the Teramakau, where he was kindly received by Mr. Sherrin. This gentleman, in company with Mr. Townsend, the government officer at the Grey, set off to the Lake Brunner, and made a five days' search for the remains of the lost party. In vain: not a trace was discoverable. Afterwards Mr. Sherrin traced the sea-shore for a hundred miles, to see whether the canoe or the oars had been washed to sea, and then thrown on land again, as whatever is carried down those rivers from the lake Brunner is thus cast up again. Not a trace of boat or oar could be found. They were no doubt all at the bottom of that very deep lake with the bodies.

Poor Hammett continued his journey in his worn-out condition to the Buller contrary to the entreaties of Mr. Sherrin and Mr. Townsend, who believed it would cost him his life: but the faithful fellow could not be turned from endeavouring to reach Canterbury by going round by sea to Nelson, the mountain road being, of course, stopped by snow, and conveying to the government and their friends the earliest news of the fate of Mr. Howitt and the two men. He said he had a duty to perform, and he would do it. He accomplished his object, but has since died, probably from the consequences of his sufferings, both of body and mind, on this melancholy occasion. Many a less devoted and heroic soul than that of this poor fellow has been stamped with the highest honours of fame: but the faithful Hammett has this simple record!

Melancholy as is this story of the opening up of a wild country, it cannot be closed without another catastrophe. Mr. Townsend, whose letter first announced to us the loss of our son, and who so generously volunteered to accompany Mr. Sherrin to Lake Brunner to search for the remains of him and his men, soon after perished himself by drowning. This accident occurred near the mouth of the river Grey, when a boat was swamped in a great swell, and Messrs. Townsend and Sherrin, with one white man and two Maories, Simon and Solomon, well known there to the settlers. Mr. Townsend, the man, Peter Michelmore, and Solomon the Maori were drowned, and Mr. Sherrin nearly suffered the same fate in endeavouring to rescue his companions.

Yet let no one imagine that the life of our son in New Zealand was by any means a sad one. On the contrary, I am persuaded that it was one of the highest enjoyment. It was that of all others which he *did* choose, and would have chosen whatever else had been offered to him. He had lived in, and highly enjoyed the forest life of Australia; but when his brother wished him to return from New Zealand, and join in his fortunes there, though the temptation of being with his brother was great, he could not bring himself to quit New Zealand, saying that its scenery and the friends he had found there were become very dear to him. I am persuaded that the storms and rains during the winter in the mountains would scarcely make an impression on his mind, except as they added to the wild solemnity of the scene. He loved to battle with the elements; and it was a source of exquisite delight to him to be able ever and anon to rescue some traveller from the rapid torrent, and to receive weary and famishing wanderers to his mountain hut—to revive them, and furnish them with provisions for their further journey, for which he never would receive compensation. Throughout all his private letters he expressed his deep satisfaction with the country of his adoption, and his chosen track of life. The stormy season in the mountains was but a contrast to the delicious summer days passed on Banks's Peninsula, amid trees, flowers, and creatures all new to him, and in themselves beautiful. With what pleasure he spoke of the tameness of the birds, which, as he cultivated his garden or his fields, came and settled on his spade, and even eat from his hands. Then the wild forests, and the snow-peaked mountains, such as Mr. William Strut has so beautifully painted from intimate acquaintance, were objects of his constant love and admiration. In one of his communications he said to us—" Read all the descriptions of New Zealand scenery that you can find, and then you will understand how happy I am in being in a country so beautiful." As to the moisture of the West Coast, he always asserted that it would greatly diminish as the woods were cut down in the progress of settlement, just as the climates of England, France, Germany, Italy, and, indeed, every part of Europe have become drier and milder since the time when their dense woods were opened up by the Romans. Compare the climate of Italy now with what it is represented in Virgil and Horace. Compare those of England, France, and Germany, with their character in Cæsar and Agricola. The dense woods being removed, he believed that the mountain regions would be no wetter than those of Switzerland. As to the general climate of New Zealand, he thought it perfection. " The clear atmosphere, and the lovely scenery," he said, " I consider as a most happy combination, and as the country lies in a temperate latitude, you are able to travel or labour without any drawback to your own sense of beauty, and your plans of utility. Take the climate and the scenery together, and it would be impossible to find any more beautiful."

Besides his love of the country, he had a great interest in the natives. Regarding them as a remarkable race, scarcely risen out of cannibalism, yet aspiring to the highest reaches of civilization and Christianity, he felt for them as a people pushed by the white man out of their heritage of ages, and showed them on all occasions the most friendly attention. Add to this, that the transparency, the pure principles, and the indomitable energy of his character, had won for him the public esteem in no ordinary degree, and the deep attachment of friends, which he warmly reciprocated, and there is nothing in such a life, not even its shortness in this stage of being, to a Christian mind, but what is bright, beautiful, and complete.

And now, in putting the last page to this wonderful history of discovery, this wonderful history of the inexhaustible energies of the English race, it is with a deep sense of the magnificent home which they are creating for a numerous branch of that race in New Zealand. In reflecting on its happily located group of islands, its numerous and accessible bays, its noble mountains, and impetuous rivers descending from them, its fertile plains and sheltered valleys, its mineral wealth, its grand forests, and peculiar vegetation, its freedom from poisonous plants, and venomous and destructive animals, all crowned by its mild and genial climate, it is impossible not to admit its claim to entitle itself the Britain of the South. Here, as in Australia, we have but one regret, namely, that the splendour of the future too probably includes the extinction of its native race. Yet, amongst all the aboriginal races none appear so capable of accepting civilization. Stern, but at heart kindly, they have less of the aversion to labour and to agriculture than the aboriginal Australian. They have a lively sense of property, and have shown great aptness to trade. Christianity they have widely accepted, and have shown themselves highly capable of civil organization, and of military defence. Unfortunately, in these latter qualities lie the sources of their greatest danger. They stem the onward, inevitable march of European expansion, and thus it is too clear that, whether strong or weak, the aboriginal tribes of earth in general are destined to disappear in the on-rolling tide of Anglo-Saxon civilization.

The sense of this has forced a very severe exclamation from one of the English friends of the Maories, which, I believe, will be found in an Auckland Blue Book:—" I have long since come to the conclusion that the Modern Englishman is as cruel and unprincipled a scoundrel as the world has ever seen. In simple truth, we pay the Maori large sums for his land because he is an acute and powerful savage ; we swindle the Australian out of his birth-right, because he is simple and helpless."

Severe as this censure is, every one must concede that as a general feature of English, as well as American advance against the aboriginal races, there is too much truth in it. Yet in no country has the Maori found more noble, more disinterested, more ardent friends— men who have boldly borne the character of genuine Christians in the face of political aggression. But the independent character of the Maories creates difficulties for their friends and the advocates of their just rights. No people feel more acutely the right and wrong of human actions than the Maories. When pressed to sell their lands against their inclinations, and told that God has given it not to lie waste, but that the Bible says, "Thou shalt *till* the land, that it may bring forth a hundred-fold," they reply—" Yes, but it is nowhere written that we shall sell it for a shilling an acre."

The New Zealand journals record the following striking case. An old Chief in Katiabo, on the Upper Wanganui, when discussing the propriety of joining Werimu Kingi, took three sticks of the edible fern, one long, and two short ones. The long one, he said, represented God, and he planted it upright in the earth before him: the two short ones represented the Maori and the Pakeha, or stranger. "Before the Pakeha came," he said, "we thought ourselves the nearest to God, and standing nearly equal with him," and he planted the Maori stick close to the one representing the Godhead. "But when the Pakehas came, we thought that they stood higher than us—that they stood next to the Godhead," and he now struck down the Pakeha stick near the Godhead, and removed the Maori stick farther off, and struck it deeper into the earth. "But now," added he, "we have learned that the Maori and the Pakeha issue from one and the same source—from God; that they have both good and evil qualities, and are alike before Him." Then he took up the two sticks representing Maori and Pakeha, and planted them near each other before the tall and single stem representing God. "Pakeha and Maori," he said, "are equal; they have equal rights, and it is perfectly natural that the Maories should have their king as the Pakehas have."

Yet with all their spirit of resistance, they have a melancholy internal conviction that they are a doomed race. One of them has said:—"As the clover destroys the fern, and the European dog the Maori dog; as the Maori rat has been annihilated by the Pakeha rat, even so will our people be pushed back and exterminated by the Europeans."

Let us hope for a brighter reality. Let us hope that the bravery and the military skill displayed by the Maori race, in their late struggle to defend their hereditary land; that the tact, and power, and intellectual aptitude of this race, so lately sunk in savagery and cannibalism; the evidences of poetic, oratoric, and literary power, shown amply by various English collections of their productions to be inherent in them; their capacity for civilized life and civilized arts; and, finally, their ready adoption of our Christian faith, may raise them friends, counsellors, and protectors, who may avert from them the common fate of aboriginal tribes. That, especially, the missionaries, who have laboured so lovingly and successfully amongst them, and the clergy, with the noble-minded and able Bishop Selwyn at their head, may so influence the colonial and imperial spirit towards them, that a greater than any simply geographical discovery may yet be made---namely, how a noble native race may be preserved amid the triumphs of European civilization, or by gradual amalgamation may add new forces of character, and new features of intellect to the already vigorous and aspiring race of the New Britain of the South.

THE END.

www.ingramcontent.com/pod-product-compliance
Lightning Source LLC
Chambersburg PA
CBHW020836020526
44114CB00040B/800